OXFORD CLASSICAL MONOGRAPHS

Published under the supervisio
Faculty of Literae Humaniores in

OXFORD CLASSICAL MONOGRAPHS

The aim of the Oxford Classical Monographs series (which replaces the Oxford Classical and Philosophical Monographs) is to publish outstanding theses on Greek and Latin literature, ancient history, and ancient philosophy examined by the faculty board of Literae Humaniores.

INVENTING THE BARBARIAN

Greek Self-Definition through Tragedy

EDITH HALL

CLARENDON PRESS · OXFORD

Oxford University Press, Walton Street, Oxford OX2 6DP

Oxford New York Toronto
Delhi Bombay Calcutta Madras Karachi
Petaling Jaya Singapore Hong Kong Tokyo
Nairobi Dar es Salaam Cape Town
Melbourne Auckland

and associated companies in
Berlin Ibadan

Oxford is a trade mark of Oxford University Press

Published in the United States by
Oxford University Press, New York

British Library Cataloguing in Publication Data

Hall, Edith
Inventing the barbarian: Greek self-definition through tragedy.
1. Drama in Greek Tragedies, to ca. 400 BC. Special
themes. Barbarians. Critical studies
I. Title   II. Series
882'.01' 09358

ISBN 0-19-814895-X
0-19-814780-5 (pbk)

Library of Congress Cataloging in Publication Data

Hall, Edith.
Inventing the barbarian: Greek self-definition through tragedy/
Includes index. Bibliography
1. Greek drama (Tragedy)—History and criticism.   2. Aliens in literature.
3. Primitivism in literature.   4. Ethnocentrism in literature.
5. Ethnic groups in literature.   6. National characteristics in literature.
I. Title.   II. Series. PA3136.H35   1989   882'.0109352—dc20   89-3369
ISBN 0-19-814895-X
0-19-814780-5 (pbk)

Printed in Great Britain by
Bookcraft (Bath) Ltd
Midsomer Norton, Avon

To Ares Axiotis

Acknowledgements

THIS book began as a doctoral thesis written at St Hugh's College, Oxford, between 1984 and 1987. It was completed at New Hall, Cambridge, in 1988. Thanks must go to the presidents and fellows of both colleges. But my warmest thanks go to my supervisors. Hugh Lloyd-Jones's vast knowledge and unfailing enthusiasm for the subject helped to shape the thesis more than he realizes; he also made many helpful suggestions when it came to turning it into a book. Jasper Griffin, who was my supervisor for two terms, provided much shrewd advice and gentle criticism. Many of the improvements made to the text in the transition from thesis to book are the result of the detailed and enlightening observations made by my examiners, Martin West and John Gould, and by Paul Cartledge; any errors are of course my own responsibility. My first term of research was supervised by Tom Stinton, who had also been my undergraduate tutor at Wadham College; it saddens me greatly that his early death prevented him from seeing the work completed. Laetitia Edwards and Nigel Wilson both read and commented upon portions of the text, but they also helped me in other ways, for which I am extremely grateful. Many people have taken the time to discuss aspects of my work, or to answer queries; I am especially grateful to Sir Harold Bailey, Jan Bažant, Myles Burnyeat, Anna Butler, Richard Buxton, Peter Collett, Jerzy Danielewicz, John Davies, Pat Easterling, Lin Foxhall, Elvira Gangutia, Timothy Long, M. M. Mackenzie, Ruth Padel, Robert Parker, Zsigmond Ritook, Ian Rutherford, Richard Rutherford, Rudolf Schottländer, Nigel Spivey, Oliver Taplin, the late George Thomson, Jürgen Werner, and David Whitehead. Heartfelt thanks also go to my parents, my aunt, and Lavinia Kennett for all kinds of support academic and otherwise; my mother, Brenda Hall, expertly typed earlier drafts, and is responsible for the excellent index. But the book would never have been written without the constant encouragement of Ares Axiotis, to whom it is gratefully dedicated.

Preface

EVERY era finds in the study of the ancient world a context in which to express its own preoccupations. One of the imperatives of the late twentieth century is the destruction of the barriers of misperception which perpetuate conflict between different nations, peoples, and ethnic groups. This book is confined to the examination of one ancient people's view of others, but it has been written in the conviction that ethnic stereotypes, ancient and modern, though revealing almost nothing about the groups they are intended to define, say a great deal about the community which produces them. The title might therefore almost as well have been *Inventing the Hellene* as *Inventing the Barbarian*.

Two points need to be made about terminology. First, the language used in defining the Greeks' perception of other peoples is that of 'invention', 'innovation', and 'creativity'. This is not because the ideas under discussion are being admired or condoned, but because it is important to stress that the conceptual boundaries which estrange different peoples, as they divided Greeks from non-Greeks, are socially produced rather than inherent in nature. Secondly, although the oppressive behaviour which resulted from the Greeks' sense of their own superiority took similar forms to the racial discrimination of modern times, the terms 'racism' and 'racist' have been avoided as anachronistic. The idea of biologically determined ethnic inequality, though occasionally apparent, was not central to the ancient Greco-Roman world-view.[1] It was not until the mid-nineteenth century that the theory of a handful of distinct and permanent human 'races' or 'racial types' was developed; it was not until the 1930s that the word 'racism' was introduced into the English language in order to attack the dogmas of inequality stemming from this theory.[2] It has been preferred, therefore, to characterize the ancient Greek world-view by such terms as 'xenophobia', 'ethnocentrism', and 'chauvinism' in its authentic sense, as a doctrine declaring the superiority of a particular *culture*, and legitimizing its oppression of others.

The context chosen for this analysis of ancient Greek ethnocentrism is Athenian tragedy. Expressions of the ideological polarization of

[1] See Benedict 1942, ch. VII; Snowden 1983.

[2] Banton 1977, pp. 5, 156–7.

Hellene and barbarian pervade ancient art and literature from the fifth
century onwards, but drama is a source for the Greeks' conceptualization of the non-Greek world, and therefore of themselves, which rivals
Herodotus' *Histories*.[3] It is not until the turn of the fourth century that
oratory's vituperative xenophobia, and philosophy's theoretical justi-
fications of the pre-eminence of Greek culture, supersede drama as
sources for the idea of the barbarian. Comedy, of course, reveals the
Athenians' sense of their own superiority. Outrageous ethnic stereotypes and chauvinist jokes abound in both Aristophanes and the fragments of the other poets of Old Comedy. But tragedy is a more
important source than comedy for statements on the barbarians. First,
it provides evidence for the near half-century between the production
of *Persae* in 472 BC and the earliest of Aristophanes' surviving
comedies, *Acharnenses*, a period during which Athens was at her most
powerful and self-confident. But tragedy also produces a much more
complex presentation of the antinomies by which the Greeks demarcated their world from barbarism, in this respect reflecting developments in contemporary thought and society. Characters in tragedy
raise arguments informed by political philosophy, the theory of
cultural relativism, slavery, and the xenophobia institutionalized in
Athenian law. It is therefore astonishing how little scholarly attention
the relation of Hellene to barbarian, at least in this genre, has attracted.
Considerable work has been done by historians and archaeologists on
the realities of Greek/non-Greek cultural, commercial, and political
interchange.[4] Recent publications have appeared on barbarians in
Greek comedy,[5] Greek art,[6] thought,[7] and historiography,[8] and also in
Roman literature.[9] Studies have also been made of the role played by
individual barbarian peoples in ancient thought and literature.[10] But
the earliest extant formulations of the theory of Hellenic superiority
are in tragedy, and these have been largely ignored.

[3] There has been some exciting work published on Herodotus' portrayal of barbarians,
especially Rosellini and Said 1978; Laurot 1981; Hartog 1988.

[4] See e.g. Lewis 1977; Boardman 1980; Hind 1983–4; Baslez 1984; Lordkipanidze 1985;
Rankin 1987; Cunliffe 1988.

[5] Long 1986, reviewed by Hall 1987a.

[6] Raeck 1981.   [7] R. Müller 1980; Nikolaidis 1986.

[8] Hirsch 1985.   [9] Balsdon 1979; Dauge 1981; Wiedemann 1986.

[10] See e.g. the collection of essays in *Ktema*, vi (1981), and the forthcoming *Die Antike
und Europa: Zentrum und Peripherie in der antiken Welt* (Proceedings of the 17th International
Eirene Conference, held at Berlin in 1986).

The history of works devoted to this topic is slight. The first publication of any significance is Hecht's dissertation of 1892, *Die Darstellung fremder Nationalitäten im Drama der Griechen*, which though brief and simplistic laid the foundations for later scholarship on both tragedy and comedy. Jüthner's *Hellenen und Barbaren* of 1923 remains an important account of the development of the Greeks' ethnic self-consciousness in all genres, and contains some important insights into tragedy. But it was Kranz's pathbreaking book *Stasimon*, published in 1933, which first provided a stimulating approach to the barbarians in tragedy; the third chapter, 'Das Nichthellenische in der hellenischen Tragödie', was devoted largely to Aeschylus' *Persae* and *Supplices*, and although Kranz tended to overstate the poet's knowledge of and references to foreign customs and literature, he had an unsurpassed capacity for judging the less obvious implications of a passage, and demonstrating the subtle exoticism often missed by crude ethnography-spotters. The only other significant contribution to the field was made by the publication in 1961 of Bacon's *Barbarians in Greek Tragedy*.[11] Bacon made an honest attempt to gather in one book all the important passages in Aeschylus, Sophocles, and Euripides where barbarians are discussed, and to catalogue each poet's references to foreign languages, customs, geography, and so on, but the book suffers from an almost complete absence of historical and philosophical perspective. Bacon was concerned to differentiate between Aeschylus, Sophocles, and Euripides: this book concentrates on tragedy as a producer and product of contemporary ideology and therefore frequently discusses the works of Phrynichus or Ion of Chios, or anonymous fragments, alongside the three major poets. It is not concerned with such problems as the authorship of *PV* or *Rhesus* or the extent to which *IA* or *Phoenissae* is actually Euripidean, for in all these texts are found manifestations of the Athenian way of perceiving the world—however mediated through poetic form and mythical content—in the fifth or early fourth centuries BC.

When Finley reviewed an *Entretiens Hardt* volume discussing Greeks and barbarians[12] he criticized it on several grounds, but a particular charge was that it had little new to offer. On the issue of Greeks and barbarians in literature he caustically asked, 'Is it really

[11] For a review see Winnington-Ingram 1963. Other works touching on barbarians in this genre are cited as they arise.
[12] *Grecs et barbares*, 1962.

necessary that we be told once again . . . that the tragedians were much exercised by the question?"[13] This book does not aim to repeat Bacon's work, but to ask two important questions which have not been asked before: *why* were the tragedians so interested in barbarians, and how was their interpretation of myth affected by this preoccupation? I hope that the exercise will prove to have been worthwhile.

[13] M. I. Finley 1965.

Contents

Editions and Abbreviations

Editions

1. Unless otherwise stated, references to the extant plays of the tragedians are to the following OCT editions:

Aeschylus: D. L. Page (1972).
Sophocles: A. C. Pearson (1924).
Euripides i and ii: J. Diggle (1984 and 1981).
Euripides iii: Gilbert Murray (1913²).

2. Tragic fragments except those of Euripides are cited from *Tragicorum Graecorum Fragmenta*. Volumes iii (Aeschylus, 1985) and iv (Sophocles, 1977) are edited by Stefan Radt; volumes i² (the minor tragedians, 1986) and ii (the fragments of unknown authorship, 1981) by Bruno Snell and Richard Kannicht.

3. Fragments of Euripides' *Archelaus*, *Erechtheus*, *Cresphontes*, *Cretes*, *Oedipus*, and *Telephus* are cited from Colin Austin's *Nova Fragmenta Euripidea in Papyris Reperta* (Berlin, 1968). For Euripides' other fragments the text referred to (unless otherwise stated) is A. Nauck's *Tragicorum Graecorum Fragmenta*², reprinted with supplement by Bruno Snell (Hildesheim, 1964).

4. Fragments of other authors are cited from the following editions:

Hesiod: R. Merkelbach and M. L. West (eds.), *Fragmenta Hesiodea* (Oxford, 1967).
Menander: A. Körte and A. Thierfelder (eds.), *Menandri Reliquiae* ii² (Leipzig, 1959).
Pindar: Bruno Snell and H. Maehler (eds.), *Pindarus* ii (Leipzig, 1975).

Abbreviations

The abbreviations of the names of ancient authors and works normally follow those of the *Oxford Classical Dictionary*² (Oxford, 1970). Other abbreviations are as follows:

AJA   *American Journal of Archaeology*
AJP   *American Journal of Philology*
AK   *Antike Kunst*

*ARV*²	J. D. Beazley, *Attic Red-figure Vase-painters*² (Oxford, 1963)
BCH	*Bulletin de correspondance hellénique*
BICS	*Bulletin of the Institute of Classical Studies*
Boisacq	E. Boisacq, *Dictionnaire étymologique de la langue grecque*⁴ (Heidelberg, 1950)
Bond	G. W. Bond (ed.), *Euripides' Hypsipyle* (Oxford, 1963)
Chantraine	P. Chantraine, *Dictionnaire étymologique de la langue grecque*⁴ (Paris, 1968)
Chron. d'Ég.	*Chronique d'Égypte*
CP	*Classical Philology*
CQ	*Classical Quarterly*
CR	*Classical Review*
Davies	Malcolm Davies (ed.), *Epicorum Graecorum Fragmenta* (Göttingen, 1988)
Diggle	James Diggle (ed.), *Euripides' Phaethon* (Cambridge, 1970)
DK	Hermann Diels and Walther Kranz (eds.), *Die Fragmente der Vorsokratiker*⁶ (Dublin/Zürich, 1951–2)
Ent. Hardt	*Entretiens sur l'antiquité classique* (Fondation Hardt pour l'étude de l'antiquité classique)
FgrH	Felix Jacoby (ed.), *Die Fragmente der griechischen Historiker* (Berlin/Leiden, 1923–58)
Frisk	H. Frisk, *Griechisches etymologisches Wörterbuch* (Heidelberg 1960–70)
GB	*Grazer Beiträge*
G&R	*Greece and Rome*
GRBS	*Greek, Roman, and Byzantine Studies*
ICS	*Illinois Classical Studies*
IEG	M. L. West (ed.), *Iambi et Elegi Graeci ante Alexandrum Cantati* (Oxford, 1971–2)
Iran. Ant.	*Iranica Antiqua*
JHS	*Journal of Hellenic Studies*
K	Gottfried Kinkel (ed.), *Epicorum Graecorum Fragmenta* (Leipzig, 1877)
KA	R. Kassel and C. Austin (eds.), *Poetae Comici Graeci* (Berlin/New York, 1983–)
Kock	T. Kock (ed.), *Comicorum Atticorum Fragmenta* (Leipzig, 1880–8)
l'Ant. Class.	*l'Antiquité Classique*
Mnem.	*Mnemosyne*
Mus. Helv.	*Museum Helveticum*
Pap. Oxy.	*Oxyrhynchus Papyri*
PCPS	*Proceedings of the Cambridge Philological Society*

PLF	Edgar Lobel and Denys Page (eds.), *Poetarum Lesbiorum Fragmenta* (Oxford, 1955)
PMG	Denys Page (ed.), *Poetae Melici Graeci* (Oxford, 1962)
RE	A. Pauly, G. Wissowa, and W. Kroll (eds.), *Real-Encyclopädie der classischen Altertumswissenschaft* (Stuttgart, 1894–1980)
REA	*Revue des études anciennes*
Rh. Mus.	*Rheinisches Museum für Philologie*
SBE	F. Max Müller (ed.), *Sacred Books of the East* (Oxford, 1879–1910)
SLG	Denys Page (ed.), *Supplementum Lyricis Graecis* (Oxford, 1974)
Stud. Ital.	*Studi Italiana di filologia classica*
TAPA	*Transactions and Proceedings of the American Philological Association*
WS	*Wiener Studien*
YCS	*Yale Classical Studies*
ZPE	*Zeitschrift für Papyrologie und Epigraphik*

I

Setting the Stage

I INTRODUCTION

THE Athenian theatre of the fifth century BC saw the production of at least a thousand tragedies. Something is known about just under three hundred of them, whether from a complete text, fragments, a title, or from passages which have turned up on papyrus.[1] Nearly half of these portrayed barbarian characters, or were set in a non-Greek land, or both:[2] almost all the extant plays at least refer to barbarian customs or inferiority. These strikingly high proportions are usually explained by pointing to the popularity of themes from the tale of the Trojan war, but this can account neither for the great difference between the portrayal of the Trojans of epic and those of tragedy, nor for the frequent introduction of invented barbarian characters and choruses into plays where Greeks could have satisfied the demands of the plot. There was no requirement, for example, for the slave who reports the assault on Helen in *Orestes* to be Phrygian, nor for the libation-bearers in *Choephoroe* to be Asiatic. The visual and musical possibilities created by introducing foreigners into plays no doubt contributed to their popularity, but this leaves unexplained the pervasiveness of the rhetorical polarization of Greek and barbarian in plays with an exclusively Greek cast. Supernumerary foreign characters or choruses, and the ubiquity of allusions to the other, inferior, world beyond Hellas, therefore provide evidence that barbarians were a particular preoccupation of the Greek tragedians. This book sets out to explain why.

It argues that Greek writing about barbarians is usually an exercise in self-definition, for the barbarian is often portrayed as the opposite of the ideal Greek. It suggests that the polarization of Hellene and barbarian was invented in specific historical circumstances during the early years of the fifth century BC, partly as a result of the combined Greek

---

[1] See Knox 1979, p. 8.
[2] See Bacon 1961, pp. 7–9 and n. 5.

military efforts against the Persians. The notions of Panhellenism and its corollary, all non-Greeks as a collective genus, were however more particularly elements of the Athenian ideology which buttressed first the Delian league, the alliance against the Persians formed in the years immediately after the wars, and subsequently the Athenian empire. The image of an enemy extraneous to Hellas helped to foster a sense of community between the allied states. The Athenian empire was built on two pillars. First, itself based on a democratic constitution, it encouraged and sometimes violently imposed democratic systems on its allies or dependencies. The most important distinction Athenian writers draw between themselves and barbarians is therefore political. Greeks are democratic and egalitarian; the barbarians are tyrannical and hierarchical. But the economic basis of the Athenian empire was slavery, and most of the large number of slaves in fifth-century Athens were not Greek. This class division along ethnic lines provided further stimulus for the generation of arguments which supported the belief that barbarians were generically inferior, even slavish by nature.

The book also argues that it was one function of the tragic performances at Athens, which took place at the City Dionysia, to provide cultural authorization for the democracy and the inter-state alliances: the enormous interest in the barbarian manifested in the tragic texts can therefore partly be explained in terms of the Athenian and Panhellenic ideology which the poets both produced and reflected. Chapters 2 and 3 show how the poets created a whole new 'discourse of barbarism', as a component of this ideology, a complex system of signifiers denoting the ethnically, psychologically, and politically 'other': terms, themes, actions, and images. Many of these were to be of lasting influence on western views of foreign cultures, especially the portrait of Asiatic peoples as effeminate, despotic, and cruel. But the new dimension which the *idea* of the barbarian had introduced to the theatre assumed an autonomy of its own, affecting the poets' remodelling of myth, their evocation of the mythical world of the 'then and there' from which they sought to bring meaning to contemporary reality, and enriching their repertoire of theatrical effects. Chapter 4 discusses the rhetorical treatment of the antithesis of Hellene and barbarian; chapter 5 shows how the antithesis could be questioned and deconstructed.

Chapter 1, however, sets the stage for the entrance of the barbarian of tragedy. Although this book tries to show that the idea of 'the barbarians' as fully fledged anti-Greeks was an invention of the early years of the fifth century BC, it did not spring from a cultural vacuum. All new inventions, ideological or technological, are produced from the interaction of innovation on well-tried materials. The writers and artists of fifth-century Athens had at their disposal a melting-pot of traditional materials, of mythical definitions of civilization, of divine, supernatural, and heroic agents of order and chaos, of earlier poetry in a variety of metres and with a variety of purposes and tonal effects. The invention of the barbarian marked a new phase in the Greeks' conception both of themselves and of the outside world, but not a complete break with the cultural tradition. There are instances of phenomena in archaic poetry and art which anticipate the fifth-century portrait of the barbarian. There are others which have been misunderstood as doing so. Indeed, the whole area of the Greeks' view of the non-Greek world in the archaic period is highly controversial. If the nature and degree of the tragic poets' contribution to the polarization in Greek thought of Hellene and barbarian are to be accurately assessed, it is essential to sift through the remains of archaic Greek poetry in order to discover the precursors of the barbarian of fifth-century tragedy, to attempt to distinguish the old from the new, and thereby to show how radical was the ideological turn taken early in the Athenian democratic era.

2 GREEK ETHNIC SELF-CONSCIOUSNESS

Definitions of ethnicity fall into two categories; the subjective and the objective. The subjective definition treats ethnicity as a process by which tribes, 'races', or nation-states identify themselves, other groups, and the boundaries between them; the objective definition relies on such 'real' criteria as physical characteristics resulting from a shared gene-pool. This discussion has nothing at all to say about whether the Greeks formed an objective biological unit, but is concerned exclusively with their own subjective definitions of their ethnicity, that is, with their ideology.[3]

In fifth-century tragedy the Greeks are insistently demarcated from the rest of the world by the conceptual polarity of which all other

[3] For a discussion of the various definitions of ethnicity, and the subjective/objective distinction, see Isajiw 1974.

distinctions in culture or psychology are corollaries, the polarity labelled as the gulf between Hellene and barbarian. This terminology finds analogues in the conceptual schemes of other ancient cultures, but no exact equivalent even among the xenophobic ancient Mesopotamians, Chinese, and Egyptians, none of whom invented a term which precisely and exclusively embraced *all* who did not share their ethnicity.[4] The Greek term *barbaros*, by the fifth century used both as a noun and an adjective, was ironically oriental in origin, and formed by reduplicative onomatopoeia. Originally it was simply an adjective representing the sound of incomprehensible speech.[5]

The criteria in determining ethnic self-consciousness vary widely from one ethnic group to another; social scientists most frequently cite physiological similarity,[6] and shared geographical origin, ancestors, culture, mode of production, religion, values, political institutions, or language.[7] Different ethnic groups privilege one or more of these above the others: some may be absent. The Egyptians of the Old Kingdom, for example, felt themselves entirely separate from the rest of the world, but 'the rest of the world' included Nubians, whose physical appearance and costumes were portrayed identically in Egyptian art, and Libyans who spoke the same language;[8] the exclusive criterion of Egyptian ethnicity was participation in the organized system of the imperial cities.[9] But the word the Greeks used to denote non-Greeks evolved from a word meaning 'heterophone'. The priority of the linguistic criterion in the Greeks' self-determination of their ethnicity is not surprising when one considers their geographical dispersal over numerous coasts and countless islands, and the enor-

[4] On the Sumerian terms for 'foreigner' see Limet 1972. From earliest times the Chinese ideogram for 'simplicity' or 'naturalness' (*chih*) is found in descriptions of non-Chinese, in opposition to the 'culture' (*wen*) of the Chinese (Bauer 1980, p. 9), but no generic label developed equivalent to the Greek *barbaroi* (Owen Lattimore 1962, p. 455). The Egyptians called every foreign land, as part of Chaos, *hsj*, but the term was not restricted to foreigners (Helck 1964, pp. 104–9).

[5] See Weidner 1913; Specht 1939, p. 11; Limet 1972, p. 124. There are similar words in several early oriental languages, especially the Babylonian-Sumerian *barbaru*, 'foreigner'. Pokorny 1959, pp. 91–2, connects the term with numerous Indo-European words designating the meaningless or inarticulate, including the Latin *balbutio*, and the English *baby*.

[6] See Reynolds, Falger, and Vine 1987.

[7] Isajiw 1974, p. 117; Isaacs 1975, pp. 32–4.

[8] On communities where language is not emblematic of ethnic difference see Keyes 1981b, p. 7.

[9] See ch. 2, n. 14.

mous variety in way of life, political allegiance, cult, and tradition amongst the different communities, whether Ionian, Dorian, or Aeolian.[10] Had the Greek-speakers walled themselves into cities on a single mainland, like the ancient Chinese, many of whose words for 'barbarian' were connected with lifestyle and habitat ('nomads', 'shepherds', 'jungle people'),[11] the original criterion of Hellenic ethnicity might *not* have been their language.[12] It has been suggested that the closest parallel in the ancient world to the Greeks' self-image was that of the Hebrews; both travelled widely and settled everywhere, but their language was in both cases remarkably resilient and inextricably bound up with their sense of 'peopleness'.[13] But religion was central to the difference felt by the Hebrews between themselves and Gentiles, as it was to the Hindus' distinction between themselves and the non-Hindus, *mlechhas*;[14] Greek polytheism, on the other hand, was remarkably flexible and able to assimilate foreign gods and cults. No other ancient people privileged language to such an extent in defining its own ethnicity.

This book argues that it was the fifth century which invented the notion of the barbarian as the universal anti-Greek against whom Hellenic—especially Athenian—culture was defined, and that tragedy's contribution to the theory of the barbarian has been underestimated. It is therefore necessary to address the problem of the date at which the concept of the barbarian emerged. Thucydides astutely pointed out that the collective term *barbaroi* presupposed a collective ethnic name shared by all Hellenic people (1. 3), for the barbarian assumes the

[10] On the importance of their language to the Greeks' collective identity see Bologna 1978, pp. 305-17. For a social anthropologist's discussion of the role of language in determining ethnic identity see Haarmann 1986.

[11] *Hu, chiang*, and *ching* (Owen Lattimore 1962, pp. 451, 455). The same principle applies to the Sumerians' pejorative terms designating the barbarians of the steppe and highlands, 'nomads' and 'mountain-dwellers', for their criterion of civilized existence was the sedentary urban lifestyle of the plain (Limet 1972, p. 124). Wilson 1956, p. 112, quotes an Egyptian text from towards the end of the Old Kingdom which gives the urban Egyptian's contemptuous view of the mobile Asiatic barbarian: 'it goes ill with the place where he is, afflicted with water, difficult from many trees, the ways thereof painful because of the mountains. He does not dwell in a single place, [but] his legs are made to go astray.'

[12] In Herodotus the Athenians define the four main criteria of Hellenic ethnicity as shared blood, language, religion, and culture (8. 144): see below, ch. 4.

[13] See the section 'Classical Hebreo-Greek social theory' in Fishman 1983, pp. 130-2.

[14] See Diamond 1974, p. 125. On religion as a determinant of ethnic identity see Keyes 1981b, pp. 7-8.

Hellene; a discussion of the date of the invention of the barbarian
cannot proceed, therefore, without assessing the problem of the
development of the Greeks' ethnic self-consciousness, a problem
which has elicited the most heated controversy. There are four main
hypotheses. (1) The notions of 'Hellene' and 'barbarian' and their
polarization were elements in archaic ideology well before the
substantial completion of the *Iliad*.[15] (2) The two notions emerged
simultaneously at some point between the eighth and the late sixth
centuries.[16] (3) It was the Persian wars which first produced a sense of
collective Panhellenic identity and the notion of the barbarians as the
universal 'other'.[17] (4) Although a sense of shared ethnicity between all
Hellenes existed in the archaic period, it was the Persian wars which
engendered the polarization of Greek and barbarian.[18] The first three
views all assume that Hellenic self-consciousness could not exist
without the fully developed idea of the barbarian, and so the notions
'Hellene' and 'barbarian' must have emerged simultaneously. But
although the barbarian presupposes the Greek, the Greek does not
necessarily presuppose the barbarian. A clear sense of ethnicity does
not necessitate the uniform sense of hostility towards all outsiders
implied by the concept *barbarian*. Such hostility waxes and wanes
according to historical circumstances. This section therefore supports
the fourth proposition; while it is self-evident that one Greek-speaker
could distinguish another from a speaker of a non-Greek language in
the archaic period, and clear that developments in the eighth to sixth
centuries created a new Hellenic consciousness, the Greeks' sense of
the importance of an ethnicity which went beyond individual city-
states nevertheless increased enormously around the beginning of the
fifth century BC, a change which precipitated the invention of the
barbarian.

An important factor usually ignored in discussions of Hellenic
ethnic self-consciousness is the complex plurality of groups to which
individuals simultaneously belong. In the modern world any person is
a member of numerous distinct though overlapping groups—
immediate family, extended family, work community, religious

[15] Gilbert Murray 1934, pp. 144–5; Weiler 1968.
[16] See e.g. Stier 1970, p. 21; Snell 1952, pp. 7–8.
[17] Schwabl 1962.
[18] See Jüthner 1923, p. 3; Ehrenberg 1935, pp. 44–62, 127–39; Bengtson 1954, pp. 27–8;
Oliver 1960, p. 142; H. Diller 1962; Baslez 1984, p. 89.

community, club or team, town or city, ethnic minority or majority in mixed societies, nation-state, and international military or political alliance.[19] He or she will in certain circumstances define themselves as a child of Mr and Mrs X, but in others as a member of the extended X family, a teacher, a Christian, a member of a particular sports team, a citizen of Glasgow, a Scot, a Briton, a European, or even as an ally of the USA. Different historical eventualities, especially oppression of one group by another, war, 'unification' of states, and the redrawing of boundaries, bring the identities attached to ethnicity and nationality into far greater prominence than normal. In the ancient world the nature of the groups may have been different, but the picture is just as complex. A Greek even in the fifth century would at times have identified himself by his patronymic, but in some circumstances (in Athens at least) by his deme, tribe, phratry, or *genos*,[20] in others as a citizen of a particular polis, or as an Ionian, Dorian, or Aeolian. Only in special circumstances—Panhellenic festivals in particular—did Greek-ness supersede the other criteria of self-description. The 'development' of Greek ethnic self-consciousness is therefore best viewed not as a process by which 'Greekness' came to *replace* an identity attached to the individual polis, but by which its relative importance increased or diminished according to historical circumstances.

One Greek-speaker could always distinguish another from those who spoke a different language, but there was almost certainly a time when the Greeks did not collectively describe themselves as 'Hellenes', but by a variety of tribal names. In the *Iliad*'s picture of a past era different ethnic groups are called 'Aetolians' or 'Cretans' or 'Boeotians'; collectively they are described as 'Achaeans' (occasionally 'Pana-chaeans'), 'Argives', and 'Danaans'. The Hellenes are still the in-habitants of the original 'Hellas', one district in Thessaly (just as 'Asia' still means a small area on the eastern Aegean seaboard, 2. 461). Achilles comes from 'Hellas and Phthia' (9. 395). The word 'Panhel-lenes', which occurs only once, may only refer to the population of north-west Greece as opposed to the Peloponnese (2. 530).[21] Even the

[19] See Light 1981, pp. 70–3.
[20] On the complexities of group identity in Attica, especially after Cleisthenes' reforms, see Kearns 1985.
[21] Werner 1986, p. 4, argues that the word does not refer to all the Greeks. Aristarchus assumed that it did, and therefore atheticized the line as an interpolation; Bengtson, who thinks that attempts were made to turn the Catalogues into documents of Panhellenism (1954, pp. 29–30), considers that he was right to do so (see below, n. 30).

Odyssey's phrase 'throughout Hellas and Argos' (e.g. 1. 344) may only mean 'throughout north-west Greece and the Peloponnese'. But in Hesiod 'Hellas' refers to the whole of mainland Greece, and Archilochus knew the term 'Panhellenes' (*Op*. 653; fr. 102 *IEG*);[22] the concept of an extended 'Hellas' therefore must have existed at least by the beginning of the seventh century, and possibly earlier. Other evidence supports the view that the eighth to sixth centuries saw an upsurge in Hellenic self-consciousness, to which several factors contributed: the sending out of colonies which retained ties to the mother city, diffusion of the alphabet and of the epic poems themselves, and the foundation of Panhellenic institutions and cult centres.[23] Although the games at Olympia may originally have been an exclusively Peloponnesian affair,[24] by the sixth century competitors were coming from Greek cities as far afield as Ionia and Sicily,[25] and the judges were called the *Hellanodikai*.[26] The sixth-century shrine for nine Greek cities founded at Naucratis was called the *Hellēnion* (Hdt. 2. 178).

Although in the archaic period there was a growing trend of Panhellenism, it was, however, far less important than it was to become during the Persian wars. Identity attached to the city-state remained by far the most important group to which any individual or family belonged. Epic terminology reveals a system of social relations between communities of all languages where ethnic identity remains tied to each individual's kingdom. A Homeric character's home is his *patrē*, a word which refers to the town or district of provenance. Strangers are asked who their parents are, and what their town; they answer by naming their town and father and famous ancestors. Both Achaeans and Trojans, when abroad, are 'far from their *patrē*', or in a 'strange *dēmos*' or '*gaia*' (*Il*. 1. 30; *Od*. 9. 36). This terminology seems to reflect the primacy of the polis in the archaic period as the unit to which

[22] See Strabo 8. 6. 6, who also attributes the word 'Panhellenes' to 'Hesiod' (fr. 130).

[23] Rostovtzeff 1930, pp. 229–35; Snodgrass 1971, p. 421; Nagy 1979, pp. 7–8, 119–20, etc., and 1983, p. 189.

[24] Before the seventh century it seems that the competitors came from the Peloponnese and Megara (Moretti 1957, pp. 59–62). Jüthner 1939, pp. 258–61, discusses the significance of the original choice of Pelops as the mythical founder of the games.

[25] See Moretti 1957, pp. 63–80; Oliver 1960, pp. 124–30. Renfrew 1988, p. 23, emphasizes 'the fundamental role of the Panhellenic games in the development of Greek ethnicity'.

[26] See A. Diller 1937 p. 21 n. 23; Jüthner 1939, p. 241; the term *Ellanozikai* appears on an inscription from Olympia which dates from before 580 BC: see Buck 1955, pp. 259–60.

ethnic identity was attached: being Greek was of far less importance than being Athenian or Spartan or Theban. The full significance of belonging to a wider Greek family was not to become apparent until most of the Greek-speaking communities came under threat from Persia; even then some were slower than others to accept that they had any responsibility towards other Greeks, and quicker to abandon Panhellenism after the Persian wars. It is perhaps useful to invoke a modern parallel in order to illustrate the situation when the Greeks needed to replace the archaic ethnic identity, tied to the individual city-state, with the broader sense of a shared Panhellenic responsibility. Anthropological work on the constituents of ethnic identity has shown that in India, a country only recently unified in any geopolitical or macroeconomic sense, it is proving difficult to override individual groups' names, and to establish a sense of collective nationality, even where different regional groups are homophone.[27]

The idea of the barbarian as the generic opponent to Greek civilization was a result of this heightening in Hellenic self-consciousness caused by the rise of Persia. This is reasonably clear from the historical development of the word *barbaros* itself. Before the fifth century its reference remains tied to language, and it is never used in the plural as a noun to denote the entire non-Greek world. The Greeks' preoccupation with the linguistic difference they felt between themselves and other peoples is occasionally reflected in archaic literature (see below, sections 4 and 5a), and there is one sign in the Homeric poems of the term *barbaros*, in a compound adjective *barbarophōnos*, 'of foreign speech', used of the Carians in the Trojan Catalogue (*Il.* 2. 867).[28] The epithet may assume the prior existence of the adjective *barbaros*, referring simply to language;[29] even so it could be a late entrant into the language of epic, perhaps even later than Thucydides, who did not believe that Homer knew the term *barbarian* (1. 3).[30] Late in the sixth

[27] Isaacs 1975, p. 49.

[28] This line has elicited heated controversy. Page 1959, p. 139, used it to 'prove' that the Catalogues originated in Mycenaean times, by arguing that barbarophone Carians had been driven out of Miletus by an early date. Kirk 1985, p. 262, claims, on the other hand, that the reference must represent deliberate archaizing.

[29] Although see Dörrie 1972, pp. 147–8. He suggests that the word *barbaros* was formed by shortening the original *barbarophōnos*, familiar from the *Iliad*.

[30] Bengston 1954, pp. 29–30, believes that the Catalogues may have been doctored in order to heighten their Panhellenic appeal (see n. 21). It is of course plausible that the word entered the tradition at a fairly late date, replacing a metrical equivalent (T interestingly

century, however, two eastern Greeks were certainly familiar with the adjectival use of the word. Anacreon of Teos deployed it pejoratively, but its reference is still confined to language (fr. 313b *SLG*). Heraclitus of Ephesus observes that the eyes and ears of men 'with barbarian souls' bear bad witness (22 B 107 *DK*): this fragment is notoriously difficult to interpret, but whatever the philosopher means, he is 'hardly advancing the chauvinist thesis that non-Greek speakers cannot attain knowledge'.[31] His use of the word seems to be metaphorical: the sense-perceptions of those 'who do not understand' are unreliable. This instance certainly does not imply the generic sense designating all non-Greeks which the word was to possess in the fifth century.

With regard to mainland Greek literature, the lines referring to the Persian threat attributed to the Megarian Theognis speak only of 'Medes' (764, 775 *IEG*).[32] The word *barbaros* was not used by the closed society of Sparta even after the battle of Salamis, 'for they called the barbarians *xeinoi*' (Hdt. 9. 11. 2, see also 9. 55. 2), and the Theban Pindar uses it only adjectivally, and then in an ode performed after the 490 invasion (*Isthm*. 6. 24). It is significant that the epigrams attributed to Simonides which have some claim to authenticity all call the Persians either 'Medes' or 'Persians' but never use the word *barbaros*, even though some of its inflections (*barbaros*, *barbara*) would fit the metre.[33] There is indeed little evidence for the category 'the barbarians', encompassing the entire genus of non-Greeks, until Aeschylus' *Persae* of 472 BC.[34] It looks, therefore, as though the term *barbaros*,

gives a variant reading *barbarophōnōn* for *karterothumōn*, 'stout-hearted', of the Mysians at 14. 512).

[31] Barnes 1982, p. 148. See also Kahn 1979, pp. 35, 107, whose translation does justice to the metaphor: 'Eyes and ears are poor witnesses for men if their souls do not understand the language.'

[32] The prayers for protection against the Mede in the Theognidea are 'intrusive', in that much of the corpus must antedate the Persian threat: see Podlecki 1984, p. 144.

[33] See Page 1975, V. 1, VI. 1 (Medes), and XV. 3 (Persians). In only one possibly authentic poem is the adjective *barbarikos* found, in reference to the enemy's hand (XIXa. 3–4).

[34] The oracle for Battus concerning the foundation of Cyrene which calls the Libyans 'barbarian men', reported by Diodorus Siculus (8. 29), is almost certainly apocryphal. Strabo's paraphrase of Hecataeus' discussion of the original inhabitants of the Peloponnese uses the term 'barbarians', (Strabo 7. 7. 1 = 1 *FgrH* F 119), but Strabo probably means 'Pelasgians'. See Weiler 1968, p. 25; below, ch. 4. 2. All the other pre-Herodotean ethnographic fragments apparently avoid the term, using the proper names 'Lydians' and 'Persians', etc., but as an eastern Greek in the late sixth century it is possible that Hecataeus used it elsewhere.

meaning 'not speaking Greek', filtered across from the eastern Aegean to the Greek mainland during the Persian wars,[35] the first occasion in Greek history when a large number of states from all over the Greek-speaking world were involved in a united military campaign.[36] Its reference was at first primarily to the Persians, but because their empire covered so many of the foreign peoples with whom the Greeks had contact—Egyptians, Phoenicians, Phrygians, Thracians—it was soon to acquire the generic sense denoting all non-Greeks which was to reflect and bolster the Greeks' sense of their own superiority to a varying degree until the fall of Constantinople. In fifth-century literature the label *the Hellenes* is customarily used to designate the whole Greek-speaking world from Sicily to the Black Sea, including the islands and free eastern cities: it was then and only then that *the barbarians* could come to mean the entire remainder of the human race.

The polarization of barbarian and Hellene became a popular rhetorical topos in tragedy. It has already been seen that the term *barbarian* is not present in archaic poetry. But at a highly abstract level much hexameter poetry is ethnocentric (see below, section 6), and the ubiquity of the antithesis between Hellene and barbarian in Greek thought from the repulse of Xerxes to the Turkocracy has led to the belief that it must have affected archaic poets singing in a language prescribed by tradition about a heroic age. Some have argued that it was already familiar in the archaic era, and that the poets were consciously archaizing by omitting the term *barbarian*.[37] It is just possible that they are right. The materials an epic poet used—an artificial dialect, formulae, stock situations and action-patterns—were relatively independent of ephemeral influence, relatively free from assimilation of contemporary diction and ideas. Just because epic does not use a particular concept or item of vocabulary, it cannot be taken as

[35] Papyrus finds may one day illuminate the history of the word during the crucial period from the mid-sixth century until Aeschylus. A line in a papyrus scrap of undated literary Doric (*Pap. Oxy.* 3696. 8) has recently been supplemented to read *bar]barik[* (Haslam 1986, pp. 8–9); a fragment of Corinna, whose date is controversial, uses the word *barbaros* (655 fr. 4. 4 *PMG*).

[36] Walbank 1951, p. 53, argues that an important contribution to Hellenic collective orientation was made by inter-state military alliances and common conventions of warfare. See the decision to send envoys to Crete, Corcyra, and the western Greeks when it was learned that Xerxes had reached Sardis (Hdt. 7. 145).

[37] Gilbert Murray 1934, pp. 144–5. Numerous scholars misleadingly call the *Iliad*'s Trojans 'barbarians'; see below, section 5b.

incontrovertible proof that the idea or word did not exist by a certain date, particularly if the relevant terms do not sit happily in the dactylic hexameter. But here one must tread a fragile tightrope between a simplistic lexical positivism on the one hand, and on the other a subjectivism which asserts the absolute primacy of a poet's aesthetic motives and the unimportance of the actual society in which he worked to the discourse he produced. This middle road is a difficult one to tread: Homeric detail cannot be tied down to any one period in pre-classical Greek thought, but the poets' overall world-view must basically have been determined by the general aims and conceptions of the milieu in which they lived and worked. If it were the case that the idea of the generic barbarian was an element of archaic ideology, it would be likely that it would be found at an implicit level, and it is extremely hard to find any sign of a homogeneous category 'non-Greek' before the fifth century.

Numerous factors besides language may contribute to ethnic identity, such as political allegiance, economic interdependence, cultural similarity, and geographical proximity; subjective ethnicity is connected with social conditions such as co-operation and conflict, and changes when such conditions alter.[38] In the archaic period many Greek families and communities had relations of ritualized friendship with non-Greek dynasties, and Greek city-states often looked on 'foreign' cultures neighbouring them as partners, equals, and cultural leaders. The Spartan and Mytilenean attitudes to Lydia are important examples.[39] Thus the *Odyssey*'s term 'of another tongue' (*allothroos*, 1. 183) does not put all Greek-speakers and all *allothrooi* on different sides of a conceptual or cultural fence. Even the formulaic question asked about the inhabitants of a country, for example by Odysseus in the land of the Cyclopes, when he ponders whether they are 'arrogant, wild and lawless, or hospitable and god-fearing' (9. 175–6), does not use language as a criterion for assessing the community:[40] there is no suggestion that the lands of 'arrogant and lawless' men are coterminous with those of men who do not speak Greek, nor that the

[38] On the speed at which ethnic orientation can alter as a result of social, political, or economic changes, see Banton 1981; Keyes 1981b, pp. 14–28.

[39] On the guest-friendship between Sparta and Croesus see Hdt. 1. 69 and M. I. Finley 1979, p. 100. For the Mytileneans' complex attitude to Lydia see Radet 1893, p. 304; Rostovtzeff 1930, pp. 249–51; Page 1955, pp. 228–33; Podlecki 1984, pp. 77, 82–3.

[40] On this formula see Schwabl 1962, pp. 6–7.

'hospitable and godfearing' are confined to Greece. One has only to think of the kind treatment Menelaus received in Egypt on his travels among 'men who speak another tongue' (4. 124-30; 3. 302), or of the overweening suitors, Odysseus' own compatriots. In the Homeric epics there is a variety of words used to describe a person not from the same town, *xeinos*, *allos*, *allodapos*, *allotrios phōs*, but these are used of strangers both on the same side and in the opposite camp. Sarpedon is an *allodapos* at Troy (*Il.* 16. 550), northern Greeks are *allodapoi* in the Peloponnese. Enemies whatever their ethnicity are *andres dēïoi*. The remains of the cyclic epics show that they perpetuated this traditional terminology. In genealogical poetry, again, the world is homogeneous and undivided by any polarity between Greek and non-Greek; there is no sign of an eponymous ancestor *Barbaros* standing in opposition to the genealogists' *Hellēn*, father of the eponymous tribal ancestors Dorus and Aeolus, and grandfather of Ion and Achaeus (Hesiod, fr. 9). On the contrary, the genealogists sought to trace numerous foreign peoples back to Greek ancestors (see below, section 5b).

3 THE MISSING LINK

By far the most important area in which Greek and barbarian are polarized in classical Greek rhetoric is political. In the works of the tragedians, historians, and orators, the democratic Athenian ideal is insistently defined and applauded by comparison with the tyranny thought to characterize most barbarian societies. Now although at the time of the epic poets' work democracy itself had not been invented, it is of the greatest significance that there is little adumbration of the polarity between 'free' Greeks and 'enslaved' foreigners in the archaic texts. Even the Cyclopes, who hold no assemblies, do not represent despotism but primitivism, and the utopian images of the archaic thought world have not yet acquired a distinct political dimension.[41] During the seventh and sixth centuries there were numerous tyrants in Greek city-states, and archaic poetry in metres other than the hexameter illustrates the fear of tyranny, but there is no question as yet that the tyrant has become exclusively identified with the non-Greek. Archilochus may decline the wealth of an Asiatic tyranny (fr. 19 *IEG*), but Solon is concerned about the effects of a tyranny at Athens (frr.

---

[41] Vidal-Naquet 1986, p. 29.

32. 2, 34. 7), and Alcaeus inveighs against his local tyrant from the standpoint of a displaced aristocrat.[42]

The central institution of the Homeric poems is the polis; both epics are about threats posed to a civic community, Troy or Ithaca. It is Aeneas' account of the founding of Troy which most clearly defines man's separation as a city-dweller from the chaos of the natural world (*Il.* 20. 215–18).[43] The Homeric polis is of course an artistic portrayal of the imagined social relations of the heroic age, and therefore does not correspond exactly either to the centralized monarchies of the Mycenaean period, or to the emergent Ionian city-states of the eighth/ seventh centuries which completed the poems. The Homeric king may live in a gorgeous palace like the rulers of Mycenae, but he also lives in a city, complete with civic amenities (docks, market-place, temples), a picture which Snodgrass believes cannot derive from earlier than the eighth century.[44] But however imaginative an amalgam of different historical strata, the social system of the Homeric poems reveals a pattern of power relations and organization shared by Greeks and non-Greeks alike.

The world of the Homeric poems is divided by a great gulf, but it separates not groups of different ethnicity or language, but the aristocrats and the common people. In the *Iliad* the Achaean *aristoi*, the heroes, are all kings, *basilēes* (2. 86), but so are the leaders among the Trojans' allies, Rhesus (10. 435), and Glaucus and Sarpedon (12. 319). Each king rules over his own district and household.[45] The relation of each king to his people is based on reciprocal obligation, for in return for honour and gifts the *basileus* provides protection and leadership in battle:[46] the most formal codification of this relationship is placed in the mouth of a non-Greek, Lycian Sarpedon (12. 310–21). There is an alternative word for 'king', *anax*, but both *anax* and *basileus* are used interchangeably of kings in both Trojan and Achaean camps. Even the relations between Agamemnon and the other Greek kings, and Priam and Hector and their allies, seem to be approximately the same: they are first among equals, pre-eminent by virtue of their superior strength

---

[42] The tyranny deplored by Xenophanes (21 B 3 *DK*) may have been a reaction *against* the Lydizing tendencies of the aristocrats of Colophon (Podlecki 1984, p. 166).

[43] See Scully 1981, pp. 2–6.

[44] Snodgrass 1971, p. 435.

[45] M. I. Finley 1979, p. 83.

[46] Ibid., p. 97.

and the size of the forces they can muster. Two passages in the Catalogues define the nature of their authority. Agamemnon was 'pre-eminent among all the warriors, because he was the noblest, and the people he led was far the largest in number' (2. 579–80). Hector (to whom the military responsibility for the defence of Troy has been delegated, though the supreme command still lies with Priam, 2. 802; 20. 179–82) correspondingly led on the Trojan side 'by far the greatest forces and the best' (2. 817–18). Achilles may accuse Aeneas of wishing to overthrow Priam (20. 179–82), but this is not an early indication of the kind of intrigue Greek writers later impute to eastern imperial households; in epic kings must rule by might, *iphi anassein*, or risk being replaced. Laertes was too old and weak to maintain authority in Ithaca, and the shade of Achilles asks Odysseus if Peleus still retains his kingship, or has been replaced because of his advancing years (*Od.* 11. 494–503).[47]

Nor is there any difference between the constraints imposed upon Agamemnon and Priam or Hector by the institutions of civic debate. The leaders on each side attend advisory councils of elders, Agamemnon by Nestor's ship (2. 53–4), Priam on the wall at the Scaean gates (3. 146–53). Both sides also hold general assemblies, the Achaeans at their ships (1. 305), and the Trojans at Priam's doors (2. 788); at one point Achaeans and Trojans both adjourn to hold parallel assemblies (7. 325–44, 345–79).[48] Each king's authority is also controlled by his family's participation in the intricate web of obligations and alliances created by intermarriage between aristocratic households and guest-friendship,[49] and in the Homeric world such relations by no means connect only Hellenic heroes: Diomedes and Glaucus, Greek and Lycian, agree not to fight because they are bound by an ancestral guest-friendship (6. 226–31): this powerful bond transcends the particular hostilities of the war.[50] Menelaus has guest-friendships in Egypt and with the king of Sidon in Phoenicia (*Od.* 4. 124–30, 617–19). One of Odysseus' fictional narratives describes an incident of outstanding hospitality he experienced in Egypt (14. 278–86).[51]

[47] Ibid., p. 83–6.
[48] See Andrewes 1956, p. 10.
[49] M. I. Finley 1979, pp. 98–104.
[50] See Davies 1984, p. 101.
[51] Historically, of course, *xenia* relations did frequently exist between Greeks and non-Greeks (Herman 1987, p. 12). On the *Odyssey*'s fascination with Egypt and Egyptian hospitality, see Stephanie West 1988, pp. 192, 201–3, 206–7.

If the corner-stone of the conceptual polarization of Greek and barbarian was political, and if there was no foreshadowing of a political distinction between Greeks and non-Greeks in the archaic thought world, then it must have been more than the simple fact of the collective Greek repulse of Darius and Xerxes which forced the new ideology into flower. The subtle comparison of Greek and barbarian in *Persae*, later to develop into a full-scale rhetoric which emanates from the tragic stage, places overwhelming emphasis on the respective political ideals of Greek and non-Greek.[52] This must be directly referred to the new *Athenian* vision of the polis. The opposite of barbarian despotism is not a vague model of the generalized Greek city-state, but quite specifically democracy, and rhetoric in praise of democracy was an Athenian invention.[53] This is the source of the tension between Panhellenic and Athenian propaganda in Athenian discourse of the fifth century, for representations of the barbarian in art and literature were inseparable from the cultural authorization of democracy. After the Peisistratids had been deposed, being against the democracy was equivalent to being in collusion with Persia. When the Persians had been repelled and the Delian League established, the battle against the Persians for hegemony in the Aegean became synonymous with the battle to instate or protect democracies (see below, chapter 2. 1). So the polarization of Greek and barbarian around the notion of political difference must be seen not merely as a reflection of pride in the collective military action of the thirty-one Greek states who could inscribe their names on the victory monument at Delphi, but as a legitimization of the Athenian leadership of the Delian league, which fostered a new sense of collective identity amongst the allied states. The members of the league, by the middle of the century redefined as the Athenian empire, were encouraged to think of themselves not just as inhabitants of a particular island or state, but as Hellenes, as democrats, and supporters of Athens, the school of Hellas; their duty was to roll back the tide of Persian influence. The invention of the barbarian in the early years of the fifth century was a response to the need for an alliance against Persian expansionism and the imposition of pro-Persian tyrants: but the

[52] Schwabl 1962, p. 23, concludes his essay with the suggestion that the tyranny/freedom polarity was the catalyst in the invention of the barbarian, but does not expand the thesis. See also Oliver 1960, pp. 142–5; Momigliano 1979.

[53] See Loraux 1986, *passim*.

tenacity of the polarizing ideology after the wars can only be fully understood in the context of the whole conceptual system which underpinned Athenian supremacy.[54]

4 THE HERE AND NOW

The Athenian tragedians of the fifth century did not only invent a rhetoric around the antithesis of Greek and barbarian, democrat and despot, but distinguished their barbarian characters from their Greeks in various areas, parallel to the different meanings of the term *barbaros* in this period. They were barbarians in the primary, linguistic sense of the term, in that they were not Greek-speakers, and the tragic poets used a variety of techniques to suggest this, including cacophony, other acoustic effects, and the use of scattered items of foreign vocabulary in their speeches. Barbarians are also made to behave in ways which fell short of the standards of Hellenic virtue: they are emotional, stupid, cruel, subservient, or cowardly. Culturally their ways are barbarian; ethnographic material is used to distinguish their customs from those of Greeks. Some of these aspects of the tragedians' characterization of foreigners are foreshadowed in archaic poetry, but not in the poetry of the mythical plane, the 'there and then' which forms the landscape of epic, distant in time, inhabited by heroes, with its own immutable conventions and values. It is in the lyric, elegiac, and iambic poetry of the seventh and sixth centuries with subject-matter drawn from the 'here and now', the contemporary plane, reflecting at a much more immediate level the experiences and aspirations of the 'real' world.

These songs of the eastern and Aegean Greeks are products of an age of continually widening horizons, and they refer to people and places as far north as Scythia, as far east as Babylon, as far south as Egypt. To Archilochus, for example, the Carians are not the Carians of the *Iliad*, allies of Troy, but modern mercenaries (fr. 216 *IEG*). Anthropologists view language imitation as an important stimulus in ethnic humour and the maintenance of subjective ethnicity;[55] poetic exploitation of

---

[54] On the tension between Athenian and Panhellenic propaganda see Dunkel 1937, pp. 54-8, and Perlman 1976, p. 5: 'during the classical period, the *Panhellenic* ideal served as a tool of propaganda for the hegemonial or imperial rule of a *polis*; it served to justify the hegemony and the mastery of one *polis* over other states by proposing a common aim, war against the barbarians'. Herodotus' *Histories* also reveal a 'double vision' of Athenian supremacy and Panhellenic unity.

[55] See Apte 1985, pp. 119–20.

foreign languages appears in a fragment of Hipponax, the iambic poet of the second half of the sixth century, who lived in the cosmopolitan atmosphere of Asia Minor, on the fringes of the Persian empire. It portrays a woman uttering an incantation, supposedly in Lydian (*ludizousa*, fr. 92. 1 *IEG*) but in what is actually Greek with a few Lydian and Phrygian words. This woman almost certainly belongs to Hipponax's 'here and now' rather than the world of myth, but the poetic imitation of direct speech in a foreign language shows how far the possibilities for the literary presentation of non-Greeks were opening up by the period which saw the founding of dramatic competitions at Athens; the woman in this fragment is the direct literary ancestor of Pseudartabas in Aristophanes' *Acharnenses*, the Triballian god in *Aves*, the Scythian archer in *Thesmophoriazusae*, and the demagogue's mother in Plato Comicus' *Cleophon*, who appeared as a Thracian, *barbarizousa* (Plato fr. 60 Kock = Σ Ar. *Ran*. 681). But the same technique was applied to some of the barbarians of tragedy, for example in Aeschylus' *Persae* and *Supplices*.

Pre-tragic poetry in metres other than the hexameter also reveals behavioural and ethnographic contrasts between Greeks and non-Greeks when the context is the 'here and now'. Archilochus records the struggles of the Parian colonists on Thasos against the Saians, a Thracian tribe, one of whom came to possess the shield he left behind (fr. 5 *IEG*). An inscription found on Paros quoting some of his poems where he referred to negotiations with the Thracians demonstrates a capacity for abuse on ethnic lines, if the reading 'Thracian dogs' (*kusi Threïxin*) is correct (fr. 93a. 6 *IEG*). He also invokes the drinking habits of the Thracians and Phrygians to illustrate an obscenity (42 *IEG*). The Lesbian poets testify to the close relations between Mytilene and the nearest power to Lesbos, the influential Mermnad dynasty rising in Lydia, which was for the Greeks of the time accepted as an equal and hardly dissimilar state.[56] Sappho's girlfriends wear Lydian fashions and consort with Lydian high society (39. 2–3; 98a. 10–11 *PLF*); Alcaeus is interested in the political possibilities of relations with the Lydians, for his faction received financial support from the mainland (fr. 69 *PLF*). Anacreon's poetry eroticizes Thracian adolescents (417. 1, 422 *PMG*), and characterizes the symposiastic habits of Scythia as uncouth (356b. 1–4 *PMG*). Hipponax vividly evokes the

---

[56] See above, n. 39.

cosmopolitan atmosphere of the Ionians' cities. So Archilochus' poems provide the earliest examples of poetic expressions of the Greeks' views of their foreign neighbours, whether in ethnographic observation, exotic detail, or in abuse along ethnic lines. But ethnography, exoticism, and chauvinist rhetoric were to be taken to new levels in the fifth century's representations of the barbarian world.

5 THE WORLD OF HEROES

(a) *Language*

Pre-tragic poetry on non-mythical themes reflects the archaic Greeks' apprehension of other peoples, in ethnographic and exotic detail and sometimes in abusive tone. But were the heroes of myth ever portrayed like the foreigners of the poetry of the 'here and now'? This section examines the evidence for linguistic, behavioural, and cultural differentiation between Greeks and non-Greeks in archaic heroic literature in order to see how far, if at all, the barbarian world of the tragic stage was adumbrated in poetry with mythical subject-matter. For even though the growing sense of alliance between the various Greek city-states is an element lying beneath the surface of the epic texts (especially reflected in the pantheon of Olympian gods who have come to replace the discrete cults and deities of the independent communities),[57] there is as yet no sign of the all-embracing genus of anti-Greek, later to be called the barbarian. The heroic world remains homogeneous, its inhabitants of more or less uniformly heroic status.

The archaic literary world of heroes remained largely untouched by interest even in foreign languages. Besides the 'barbarophone' Carians, the *Iliad* mentions twice the languages of the Trojans' allies, incorporating into its poetic landscape, in isolated touches of realism penetrating the stylized literary milieu, the awareness that the allies cannot have been Greek-speakers (2. 804, 4. 437-8). The *Odyssey* knows two terms approximately equivalent to *barbarophōnos*: *allothroos* ('of another tongue'), and *agriophōnos* ('of wild speech'). The Homeric *Hymn to Aphrodite*, which may be very early,[58] portrays Aphrodite disguised as a Phrygian talking to Anchises, and remarks on their

---

[57] See Nagy 1979, pp. 7-8, 115-17, 119-20, etc.; 1983, p. 189.
[58] Janko 1982, p. 180.

Phrygian and Trojan tongues (113–17). But otherwise there is little
interest in archaic literature even in foreigners' different languages,[59]
and with one possible exception no evidence for cacophony or the
inclusion of foreign vocabulary.

The exception may be the use in epic of names with foreign
elements, especially for the allies of Troy. A study by von Kamptz
examines the roots of all the Homeric proper names. He divides those
which are foreign or contain foreign elements into two categories,
'north Balkan' (i.e. Illyrian, Thracian, or Phrygian), and names which
he thinks are pre-Greek or stem from Asia Minor.[60] Some of the
Trojans and their allies have names which may have sounded 'north
Balkan' to the poem's audience, despite their adaptation to the inflections of Greek (e.g. Priam, Assaracus, Dares, Paris, Rhesus, Sarpedon). A
'north Balkan' origin, however, is not confined to the names on the
Trojan side (e.g. Alcestis). A very few names of individuals on the
Trojan side have clearly Asiatic elements (e.g. *Cas*sandra), but a high
proportion of the pre-Greek or Asiatic names belong to Greeks
(Achilles, Zethus, Theseus), and the *Iliad* gives many of its Trojans
typically Greek names, such as Andromache and Alexander.[61] It is
therefore a possibility that foreign colouring was lent to the *Iliad* by
the appropriation of Balkan and Asiatic names for some of the Trojans
and their allies: perhaps clearly Asiatic names (especially when they
appear in concentration, for example those of the Lycians Atymnius,

---

[59] Ardent defenders of the theory of Homeric chauvinism have claimed that references
to the different language of the *gods* imply the superiority of the Greek tongue (van der
Valk 1953, pp. 21–2). The argument runs that in each case the divine name is more easily
traceable to a Greek root than is its mortal counterpart, and so the Greeks must have looked
on their own language as divine, and on other languages as those of mere mortals. But an
examination of the six references to the gods' language (*Il.* 1. 403; 2. 814; 14. 291; 20. 74;
Od. 10. 305; 12. 61) reveals that only one instance (*Il.* 14. 291) fits what is anyway a far-
fetched theory; Ramsay 1927, p. 144, therefore concluded that the language of the gods is
related to Old Anatolian as *opposed* to Greek. But the distinction between the two languages
has nothing to do with ethnicity; it is concerned with the secret words used in mystery religions, and as such is paralleled in the literature of other Indo-European cultures, such as the
Rig Veda and the Old Norse *Edda* (Watkins 1970). See also Socrates' discussion of this
Homeric phenomenon in Plato's *Cratylus*, 391d–392b.

[60] von Kamptz 1982, pp. 45–52, 335–67.

[61] 'Alexander' has been thought to be a Hellenization of a Hittite representation of the
Wilusian name 'Alakšanduš', but the female name 'Alexandra' has been found in
Mycenaean Greek (Chadwick 1976, pp. 61, 66–7). It is possible that Paris' alternative name
was borrowed from his sister Alexandra/Cassandra; the cult of Agamemnon and Alexandra
at Amyclae in Sparta may be of great antiquity (Hooker 1980, pp. 66–9).

Maris, and Amisodarus described at 16. 317–29) conceal historically authentic figures, while the Trojan figures with Greek names were invented for the purposes of the epic.[62]

(b) Behaviour

Euripides recognizes the homogeneity of the antique world of hexameter poetry, the immunity of its inhabitants from the harshly polarized categories of his own day, when he makes Antigone invent a third class of human being alongside the familiar Hellene and barbarian: 'what Greek or barbarian *or ancient hero*', she asks, 'suffered what we suffer today?' (*Phoen.* 1509–13). Many critics, however, have viewed the Trojans of archaic poetry, especially of the *Iliad*, as barbarians scarcely distinguishable from those of Aeschylus or Herodotus. This is clearly wrong. But the problem of the presentation of the Trojans in the *Iliad* deserves much more comprehensive treatment than is possible here, and so the argument will concentrate on a few illuminating issues rather than attempting a detailed discussion of every controversial passage.

The authors of the Hellenistic and Byzantine commentaries and scholia on the poem, up to and including Eustathius, were unanimous in their condemnation of the barbarism of the Trojans and their praise of the nobility of the Achaeans. But, as we shall see, there are reasons for disregarding their interpretation. The eighteenth century turned its attention towards the behaviour of Achilles, which was rightly seen to exceed in savagery any barbarisms committed by the Trojans.[63] Classicists in the nineteenth century returned to the view that regarded the Trojans as disorderly and untrustworthy barbarians who needed to be taught a lesson; but this might say more about the ideology of the era of European imperialism than about the thought-world of archaic Ionia. In the present century the published views on the poem's depiction of the Trojans range from demonstrations of its all-pervasive chauvinism to defences of its humanistic impartiality.[64] Others,

---

[62] See Kirk 1985, p. 257.

[63] See Rubel 1978, pp. 94–5.

[64] Works asserting or assuming a 'pro-Greek bias', 'chauvinism', 'nationalism', or 'patriotism' include Bethe 1914, pp. 59, 335–7, etc.; Dornseiff 1935; Howald 1937, p. 18; van der Valk 1953 and 1966, pp. 30–2; Thomas 1962; Willcock 1976, pp. 80, 151, etc.; Pinsent 1984. Those who have argued for an absence of bias in the poem include Jüthner 1923, ch. 1;

concerned by the pathos with which the sufferings of the Trojans and
their allies are invested, have adopted more moderate positions. Bowra,
for example, wrote of Homer, 'Of national or racial boundaries he
takes little heed. It does not matter that Hector is a barbarian provided
he behaves as a true soldier.'[65] He therefore believes that the Trojans
fall into that anachronistic category of 'barbarians', but that valour can
excuse their ethnicity. Another theory is that although the allies are
barbarians, Trojans and Dardanians are somehow honorary Greeks,
sharing a status and even a language with the Achaeans.[66] On the other
hand, it has been suggested that the poem's favourites on the Trojan
side are the Lycians.[67] The radical divergence of the views suggests that
this issue is unusually problematic.

First, there is the problem of the circumstances of the poem's
composition. It is constituted by hexameters in a language with roots
certainly in Mycenaean times, perhaps even in proto-Indo-European
poetry, transmitted through the so-called Dark Ages to about the
eighth or early seventh century BC, not given any kind of recension
until the age of Peisistratus, and vulnerable to editing and interpolation even beyond the sixth century. It is not tied exactly to any specific
ideology because it took centuries to compose and the accumulated
layers are so densely woven as to be ultimately inseparable. The best
informed attempts at dating specific customs or artefacts to any one
century have come up with meagre results.[68] It may be that the view of
the Trojans evolved over several centuries and is inherently contradictory, being informed by the disparate aims and ideologies of
different periods. Perhaps a traditional epic standpoint, sympathetic
towards the defenders of a beleaguered citadel (probably the moral
predicate of the cyclic *Thebais*),[69] was diluted by sequences resulting
from a growing sense of Greek collectivity and superiority. This would
be the likely result of a poem originally telling the story of a war

Ehrenberg 1935, ch. III; Weil 1957, pp. 45, 51; Kakridis 1956; Reinhardt 1960, p. 9 and 1961,
pp. 248–50; Schwabl 1962, pp. 3–23.

    [65] Bowra 1930, p. 241.
    [66] Kirk 1985, p. 261, says that Euphorbus 'was not a barbarian in any sense' since he is a
Dardanian, 'and that means a real Trojan'; von Scheliha 1943, p. 366, thinks that the true
Trojans are represented as speaking the same language as the Achaeans. (In reality, the
original Trojans are now thought to have been some kind of Luwians.)
    [67] See Bowra 1930, p. 209.
    [68] Kirk 1964.
    [69] Reinhardt 1960, pp. 14–15.

between two Greek communities (Hector seems originally to have been a Theban hero),[70] later transferred to the Hellespont, and altered here and there to fit the new ethnicity of the defending team. Secondly, the critic must be wary of basing judgements on unprovable assumptions about the ethical values of the society which produced the poem. No external frame of reference exists by which to illuminate the values of either archaic Ionia, or the Iron Age through which the core of the poem must have passed, or the contemporaries of Troy vııa, let alone the mysterious synthesis of the three, enhanced by poetic hyperbole and imagination, which is misleadingly known as 'Homeric Society'. There is no philosophy from these periods, no prose narrative, no handbook of Archaic Popular Morality. Homer should only be elucidated by Homer. But this has never stopped the critics from judging phenomena in the *Iliad* anachronistically according to much later criteria, and 'proving' that it clearly anticipated Periclean or Hellenistic Greek chauvinism.

Most of the confusion which has arisen in discussions of the Trojans in the *Iliad* stems ultimately from the scholia. These contain subjective responses to early literature of more use to the student of the Hellenistic or Byzantine world-view than to the Homeric critic. But this has not prevented repeated appeals being made in modern times to the Hellenocentric interpretations which flowed from ancient scholars. The most extreme proponent of Homeric 'nationalism', van der Valk, opened the article in which he set out his theory by referring to numerous ancient comments, from Aristarchus to Eustathius, on the inferiority of the Trojans,[71] despite their authors' failure to see that their own concept *barbarian* (integral to both the Hellenistic and the Byzantine world-views) was inapplicable to the *Iliad*. An indication of the way in which the poem was made to conform to the preoccupations of later Greeks is that when a scholion compares speeches delivered by Menelaus and Hector to their respective troops, it juxtaposes neither style nor content, but the Greek and the barbarian character (*parabalōmen . . . Hellēnikōi barbaron ēthos, Σ bT* 17. 220–32). When by a unique simile Hector's attack on the Achaeans at the battle at the ships is likened to the inexorable rolling of a boulder downhill, it is diagnosed as a 'barbaric and irrational assault' (*ΣAbT* 13. 137). There

---

[70] Hector was worshipped in Thebes, and the graves, cults, and myths of those he kills cluster around Boeotia. See Gilbert Murray 1934, pp. 225–6; M. I. Finley 1979, p. 44.

[71] van der Valk 1953.

is a plethora of such criticisms of the Trojans, as a glance in the index to
the scholia under *barbaros* and its cognates will show; forms of
behaviour such as threatening, boasting, retreating, and resistance to
persuasion (most of them inherent in the 'fixed action-patterns' of the
epic tradition and by no means confined to the Trojan side)[72] are said
to illustrate the barbarian personality. Most of these comments derive
from the *bT* scholia, *b* often elaborating them further than *T*.[73] Van
der Valk himself elsewhere said that *b*, the re-edition of an earlier
Byzantine redaction of the *bT* scholia, aimed 'to offer a new edition . . .
adapted to the taste and understanding of a Byzantine public';[74] a
public who had always been obsessed, like their counterparts in the
western empire, with the 'barbarian peril'. Comments which are the
result of ancient scholars' subjective and anachronistic readings
impede elucidation of the poem's presentation of the Trojans. There
are one or two exceptions, however: it is true that only Trojans beg for
their lives when staring into an enemy's spear-tip, and there is a
demonstrable difference in the way in which the two sides express
pain: some verbs are used only of the Trojans.[75] But many of the claims
of those who perceive a bias cannot be substantiated.

The argument that the Trojans are depicted as vainglorious boasters
originated in the scholia. It is not valid to claim that in early epic
boasting is an indication of anything but the heroic temper, a ritual
prelude to battle performed by Achaeans and Trojans alike. But it has
been argued that *all* the epithets applied to the Trojans are 'approximately synonymous in meaning' and depict them 'as a proud, arrogant
people'.[76] This is vastly to overstate the case, for most of them are either
line-fillers or ambiguous in implication. By far the most common
(twenty-three occurrences) is 'horse-taming'. 'Fighting with the spear'
is hardly implicitly critical, nor is 'having breastplates'. The second
most common epithet, 'great-hearted' (*megathumoi*), is also used of the
Achaeans, as is 'lovers of war' (*philoptolemoisi*). Others, though not used
of the Achaeans, may simply reflect heroic values, such as 'great-
hearted' and 'proud' (*megalētores*, *agauoi*). There is a single, con-

[72] See Fenik 1968.
[73] See e.g. Σ *b* 7. 90: 'Hector is always characterized as self-aggrandizing, boastful, and
barbarian in personality'. See also Σ *bT* 10. 277.
[74] van der Valk 1963, p. 134.
[75] *asthmainō*, *bebruche*, *ēruge*. See Snell 1952, p. 7. (*Not ōimōxe*: see 3.364.)
[76] Blegen 1963, p. 17; see also Pinsent 1984, pp. 147-8. Page 1959, pp. 251-2, seems to be
the source of this view.

spicuous, *hubristēisi* ('doers of hubris', 13. 633), in the exceptionally bitter speech on the seizure of Helen made by Menelaus over Peisander's corpse. There are also a few epithets occurring on very rare occasions which are difficult to assess because their *huper-* prefix could indicate either an excess of pride or spirit or a laudable courage (*huperphialos* and *huperēnoreontes*, once only). 'Great-spirited' (*huperthumos*), on the other hand, is relatively frequent (seven occurrences) but is not confined to the Trojan side, and anyway seems to be approximately synonymous with *megathumos* though metrically diverse, thereby finding its way into different formulaic structures. A critic who believes that the Trojans' epithets portray them as significantly more arrogant than the Achaeans therefore betrays his or her own pro-Achaean bias, not the poem's: the rare occurrences of debatably pejorative epithets and the single *hubristēisi* on an objective reading must pale into complete insignificance besides the fifty or so occasions on which the Trojans are simply tamers of horses, great-hearted, breastplated, or fond of war.[77]

Epic portrays various forms of behaviour later regarded as primitive or barbaric by the Greeks. The critical response to these, ancient and modern, has been informed by a remarkable double standard. In the case of the Achaeans, these forms of behaviour are excused as acceptable under the 'heroic code', but when the perpetrators are Trojan, they are adduced as tangible proof of the poem's chauvinism. This kind of loose thinking can only be rectified by closely comparing the conduct of each party, and judging their actions only by the immanent criteria of epic.

First, it must be conceded that it is the Trojan Paris who has broken the covenant of Zeus Xeinios in abducting Helen in the first place, and it is a Lycian, Pandarus, who offends Zeus Horkios by breaking the truce. Neither of these actions finds exact parallels on the Achaean side: the Greeks later defined the barbarian character as one which was impervious to the 'common laws' of Hellas (see chapter 4. 4). But beyond these it is hard to discover any distinction between the conduct of the heroes on either side. Mutilation of corpses, for example, was thought in classical Greece to be 'a practice more suited to barbarians than Hellenes', as Herodotus' Pausanias insists (9. 79). But this distinction finds no adumbration in epic, where the actual or threatened

[77] On the epithets for the city of Troy itself see Bowra 1960.

mutilation of a corpse by warriors on both sides is relatively frequent. The Achaeans Agamemnon, Ajax son of Oileus, and Peneleos all behead corpses of their victims (11. 261; 13. 202–3; 14. 496–8): the Trojans Euphorbus and Hector only threaten or intend to do so (17. 39–40, 126). Iris of course alleges that Hector wants to stick Patroclus' head on the stakes of the palisade (18. 176–7), an act which has provoked censorious reactions from the critics, for example the claim that it 'would be as shocking to Greek taste as it is to us'.[78] This is certainly true of later periods (see chapter 3. 8). But in the light of the unparalleled indignities to which Achilles actually does subject Hector's corpse, it is strange to use an intention only imputed to Hector as evidence that the hero is modelled on cruel eastern potentates. Literature of the fifth century leaves no doubt that the right to a decent burial was upheld by the 'common laws of Hellas', and there are passages in the *Iliad* where respect for the enemy's dead is a marker of civilization. But it is the Trojan Hector who suggests before his duel with Achilles that they each pledge to honour the other's rights to a decent funeral (22. 256–9), and it is Achilles who rejects the proposal with derision. Generally, however, it is standard procedure for warriors on *both* sides to intimidate their opponents by threatening to leave their bodies unburied to be eaten by dogs and birds of prey. The vicious struggle over the corpse of Patroclus is mirrored by that over Sarpedon. The desecration of corpses is by no means the prerogative of non-Greeks in the poem.

Nowhere does the *Iliad* tell of the mutilation of a *living* being, human or divine, quite parallel to the reported threat of Laomedon, an earlier king of Troy, to cut off the ears of the gods Poseidon and Apollo (21. 455); later Greeks regarded the removal of ears, eyes, noses, and tongues as 'barbaric' (see chapter 3. 8). But there are two passages in the *Odyssey* which show that such mutilations were not reserved in epic discourse for performance by non-Greeks. Antinous threatens to send Irus off to King Echetus 'on the mainland', who will cut off his nose and ears (18. 85–7); later Melanthius incurs just such a punishment at the hands of Telemachus and Odysseus' servants (22. 475–7). In just one passage Hector threatens that if any of his *own* men refuse to follow him into battle he will kill them (15. 347–51). But so does

---

[78] Willcock 1976, p. 205. Segal 1971, pp. 19–25, sees this passage as the culmination of a gradual deterioration in Hector's attitudes towards the dead.

Agamemnon (2. 391–3), and in practice the Trojan heroes of the *Iliad* kill no one but the enemy in the honourable circumstances of battle. It is the Achaeans who slaughter the sleeping Rhesus in his bed and it is Achilles who sacrifices twelve high-born Trojan youths on Patroclus' pyre. Achilles twice expresses his intention (18. 336–7; 23. 22–3), is seen selecting his victims (21. 26–7), and finally does the deed (23. 175–6). Given the weight attached in the fifth century and beyond to human sacrifice as a mark of barbarism, it is certain that had it been Hector who slaughtered twelve Achaean youths, scholars ancient and modern would have adduced this as incontrovertible proof of an anti-Trojan bias. As it is, Achilles' atrocity is excused as 'not culpable in the "shame-culture" heroic code of the *Iliad*'.[79] Another savage practice later attributed almost exclusively to barbarian peoples was cannibalism. In the *Odyssey* it is reserved for those monstrous beings who exist outside the poem's boundaries of civilized behaviour, the Cyclopes and Laestrygonians (see below, section 7). It is therefore at first sight intriguing to find Hecuba announcing that she would devour Achilles' liver if she could (24. 212–13). But this is a rhetorical figure not restricted to speeches delivered by Trojan figures; Zeus suggests in a spirit of sarcastic hyperbole that the pro-Achaean Hera should glut her fury against Troy by devouring Priam and his sons (4. 35), and Achilles envisages the possibility of eating Hector raw (22. 346–8).[80]

A central concern of the poem is the wrath of Achilles, and it is Achilles who is responsible for many of the atrocities committed by the Achaeans; a more sophisticated version of the argument for the poem's pro-Greek bias might suggest that it defines Hellenic values by showing Achilles rejecting them and descending into the barbarism unfit for his compatriots. But for such an argument to stand up the Trojans would have to outrage corpses in the way that Achilles desecrates Hector's corpse, and perform human sacrifice, neither of which they do. His behaviour, savage in the extreme, finds no parallels among the heroes of Troy. He has alienated himself not just from his

---

[79] Willcock 1976, p. 207.

[80] Combellack's attempt to show that Achilles is using raw-eating as an example of an impossible act is unconvincing (1981, p. 117). A better assessment of the impact of his words is given by Nagy 1979, p. 136: he is brought 'to the verge of a bestial deed'. See also *Il.* 24. 207 (where Hecuba calls him *ōmēstēs*, 'raw-meat-eating', the only time this word is used of a Homeric hero); Redfield 1975, pp. 197–9. I am grateful to Simon Goldhill for pointing this out to me.

own Achaean community but from humanity at large; his eventual
return to civilization is marked by his acceptance of a Trojan, Priam, as
suppliant. It may well be that Murray was correct when he suggested
that the 'master hand' tried to expunge formulaic atrocities from the
oral tradition out of which the *Iliad* was developed, and that the
occasional incidents of blood-curdling savagery are remnants from a
much less civilized mythical tradition of earlier times.[81] It is another
question whether the formulaic atrocities originally entered the
tradition as memories of the Greeks' own prehistoric savagery, or as a
reflection of the macabre punishments and indignities which we know
were customary in Assyria.[82] But whatever the age and origin of the
Iliad's atrocities, it is impossible to show that they are the prerogative
of the Trojans rather than the Achaeans.

Those who perceive a difference between the success of the
Achaeans and the Trojans on the battlefield are on firmer ground, but
have grossly exaggerated the poem's preoccupation with extolling the
Achaeans.[83] First, it must be remembered that the division of the poem
into twenty-four books was an Alexandrian contribution. In many
cases it looks as though the choice of place for division partly resulted
from a desire to emphasize Achaean victories and Trojan defeats. Some
books, of course, form self-contained units, but others break at
apparently arbitrary points in the middle of continuous narrative,
often resulting in books of greatly unequal length. In such cases the
point of division was determined by the Hellenistic scholars' own
criteria. It is revealing, therefore, that several books end in the
temporary embarrassment of the Trojans, when they have the upper
hand tens of lines previously, and/or shortly into the next book. Book
6, for example, ends with Hector berating Paris for giving up too easily
in battle, whereas shortly into 7 Paris, Hector, and Glaucus are shown
killing three Achaean heroes. Again, 11 narrates numerous Trojan
successes, but ends with the recovery of the Greek Eurypylus from his
wound. Book 14 ends on an optimistic note for the Achaeans, who are

[81] Gilbert Murray 1934, pp. 126-45. He thinks that the sacrifices of Iphigeneia and
Polyxena were deliberately suppressed (p. 134).

[82] See Luckenbill 1926, pp. 145, 156, 168, etc.

[83] Howald 1937, p. 18, asserts that the poet's chauvinism meant that he found the
vicissitudes of the war 'embarrassing', and led him to conceal the Achaeans' defeats by any
possible means; van der Valk's theory of Homeric 'nationalism' also rested largely on the
construction of the battle narratives (1953). For a detailed refutation of these arguments see
Kakridis 1971.

to be vanquished in 15; had 14 had 700 lines, rather than under 500, it would have ended with Apollo and Hector spreading terror among the Achaean forces. There are other examples. Care must therefore be taken when reading the poem in the units determined by later antiquity that the effect of the carefully chosen divisions does not distort assessment of the treatment of the Trojans.

A good illustration of the poets' refusal to direct their audience to take sides is produced by a comparison with the *Odyssey*: there, an invitation is extended for the audience to support Athena and her protégé against the machinations of Poseidon, a piece of authorial guidance quite unlike anything in the *Iliad*. It is helpful to identify what the poets' intentions were *not*: their conception of the Trojan war is completely alien to the later idea of a Hellenic 'crusade' against eastern effeminacy, complacency, materialism, or tyranny.[84] Still less was it their neglect of heaven which led to the Trojans' annihilation; the people of 'sacred Ilium', and Priam 'of the good ashen spear', were loved by Zeus above all others, for they always tended his altar well (4. 44-9). The Trojan side sports so many priests and seers that it is almost possible to argue that their tendance of heaven is superior to that of the Achaeans. Hector was particularly attentive to the gods (24. 425-8). Even the motive of revenge for the theft of Helen is subordinated to the necessity for individual warriors to prove themselves in the conflict at hand. The introduction of the episode of Achilles' wrath into the traditional story of the siege of Troy produced the period occupying much of the poem during which the Achaeans suffered calamitous reverses.[85] But the whole story of the war from the judgement of Paris to the fall of Troy is telescoped into the poem's narrative; the successes of the Achaeans in the earlier parts of the poem therefore prove not that the epic poets were jingoists, but that they were recapitulating the Achaean victories in the first nine years of the conflict. The poem clearly could not kill those Achaeans whom the tradition required to outlive Hector, so it goes out of its way to wound them instead.[86] In order to enhance Hector's reputation as a warrior,

---

[84] See F. E. Harrison 1960, p. 13, and Hainsworth 1969, p. 38: 'Struggle is a fact for Homer . . . it has no metaphysics . . . Consequently war is not a crusade, nor an Alamo, nor an Independence Struggle, nor any other Purpose . . . Homer is strikingly fair to the Trojans.'

[85] See Kakridis 1971, pp. 59-62.

[86] Ibid., pp. 66-7.

the narrative includes 'long lists of warriors who fall before the Trojan hero; the mere accumulation of names gives the desired effect'.[87] See, for example, 5. 705-10 and 11. 299-309.

There are a few indications, however, that at some stage in the poem's composition a tendency began to portray the Trojans as inferior in the military sphere. There is the simile at the opening of the hostilities, where the silence with which the Achaeans entered battle is contrasted with the clamour of the Trojans, which is likened to the screaming of cranes (3. 2-9, see also 4. 436-8). This can be read as suggesting that the Achaeans are more disciplined and resolved.[88] But even this is not conclusive evidence of the poem's bias, for when it is the Trojans' turn to march implacably against the Achaeans, in the battle at the ships, it is they who proceed 'silently and without a cry' (*abromoi auïachoi*, 13. 41).[89] More significant is the single occasion on which the Achaeans are described as losing far fewer men because they concentrated on bringing help to one another in battle (17. 364-5). But this is the exception that almost proves the rule; such authorial comment on the antagonists' different deportment and success on the battlefield is conspicuous precisely because it is unique. The only fact which carries considerable weight in this regard is that one hundred and eighty-nine named Trojans and only fifty-three named Achaeans are killed in battle in the poem.[90] This disparity can only be partially explained by reference to the substitution of wounding in the case of the Achaeans who must outlive Hector, and by the fact that the tradition required Troy's ultimate fall, which meant that a large number of Achaean deaths had to be invented in order to even things up. It seems, then, that the balance is tilted in favour of the Achaeans on the battlefield. But the poem's involvement in the personal and civic lives of the Trojans, its emphasis on the *pathos* of Hector's family, tips the balance off the battlefield down on the other side.

[87] Richmond Lattimore 1943, p. 88 n. 14. The names or patronymics of Achilles and Hector are used on about the same number of occasions (around 450 times each), and far more often than those of any other hero, Achaean or Trojan (Bassett 1933, p. 41 n. 1). Hector also speaks at much greater length than any other character except Achilles.

[88] Lucretius certainly interpreted this passage to the detriment of the Trojans (*De Rer. Nat.* 4. 176-82). More recently see e.g. Kirk 1985, p. 265.

[89] Aristarchus took the initial alphas to be intensive rather than negative (*anti tou agan bromountes kai agan iachountes*), but he was influenced by the opening of book 3. Had these adjectives been applied to the Achaeans, their negative force would of course never have been doubted.   [90] Bethe 1914, p. 59.

This is the one fundamental difference in the portrayal of the two sides. The Trojans are shown in their home environment, in domestic scenes, and on the walls of their well-built town. The listener or reader meets old Trojan men, young Trojan women, a Trojan baby, Trojan priests and priestesses, a bereaved Trojan father and mother and widow.[91] The Achaeans, with the exception of Helen, are almost exclusively warriors; even the women in their camp are foreigners won by the spear.[92] So although Paris' abduction of Helen was the catalyst which long ago set in motion the whole tragic train of events, the poem's protagonists, Achilles and Hector, do battle for different reasons. One fights to avenge the death of his friend, the other to defend his homeland (12. 243). The Trojans and their allies are united in their goal: it is the Achaeans whose success is jeopardized by a divisive argument.[93] It is impossible to ascertain at what period in the poem's composition it first came to concentrate to such an extent on the charming community which exists within the walls of Troy. A very few passages perhaps anticipate the later stereotype of the eastern barbarian in suggesting that the Trojans, especially Paris, preferred the pleasures of love and dancing to making war (see 3. 54; 24. 261), although Paris' performance as a warrior is usually underestimated, for he kills or wounds a number of Achaeans.[94] It is certain, however, that the glimpses into the Trojans' former peacetime activities and their domestic lives heighten immeasurably the pathos of their forthcoming destruction, for example the mention of Phereclus, the Trojan carpenter loved by Athena above all men (5. 59–61), the nostalgic picture of the wives and daughters of the Trojans, who used to wash their glossy clothes by the springs of Scamander, before the Achaeans came (22. 154–6), and Andromache at work on her loom when she receives the news of Hector's death (22. 440–6).

The Doloneia represents an exception in this as in other respects. Dolon's behaviour is clearly contrasted with that of Diomedes and

[91] Even van der Valk 1953, pp. 5–6, concedes that considerable pathos informs the portrayal of the Trojans' domestic lives. On the importance of Priam as the type of the bereaved father see Griffin 1976, p. 168 n. 29.

[92] The degree to which the poem focuses on the Trojans' women and domestic lives even led Gilbert Murray 1934, pp. 133–4, to conjecture that the Achaeans, in contrast, are adhering to a warrior-society's ritual abstinence from sex during warfare.

[93] Strasburger 1954, p. 24, sees a deliberate contrast between the unified Trojans and the Achaeans who compete and quarrel with one another.

[94] For a defence of Paris see Bowra 1930, p. 210.

Odysseus, in particular his recklessness and cowardice.[95] Here a foreigner is outwitted and humiliated by two Greeks, a pattern which was to become popular in the tragedians, and although book 10 may well represent a later stage of the epic tradition than much of the rest of the *Iliad*,[96] it is impossible to push it further forward than the sixth century. But besides this overall structure, there is no more expression of the antithesis of Hellene and barbarian in terms of language, ethnography, or rhetoric than elsewhere in epic. Apart from the presentation of Dolon himself there is no denigration of the Trojans; indeed, at the beginning of the book Agamemnon delivers an usually flattering eulogy of Hector's prowess (10. 47–52). Rhesus is of little importance; he is certainly not given the opportunity to develop into the vaunting barbarian monarch of the *Rhesus* attributed to Euripides. And the important feature of Dolon is not that he is foreign but that, like Thersites, he is not a hero. The overall effect of the Doloneia is not a contrast between the different levels of valour of the Trojans and their allies and the Achaeans, but between cowards and heroes, just as Thersites' episode points out the distinction between common people and aristocrats. Dolon and Thersites, as non-heroes, are two of a kind regardless of ethnicity.

The majority of the tragic poets' plots were drawn not from the two Homeric poems but from later epics, long since lost.[97] Already in the plays and fragments of Aeschylus material is represented from every one of the Trojan cyclic epics (except perhaps the *Iliu Persis*), a fact which has led one scholar to infer that Aeschylus 'set out systematically to rival or replace the entire corpus of cyclic epic'.[98] Sophocles and Euripides found a rich source in the *Iliu Persis*,[99] and also took themes from the *Cypria* and *Nosti*.[100] Many of these tragedies were concerned

[95] Klingner 1940, pp. 354–6.

[96] It has numerous *hapax legomena* and stylistic quirks which distinguish its language from that of the other books, and ancient scholars believed that it was interpolated by Peisistratus. Even those critics who have rightly objected to the excesses of the Homeric 'analysts' have regarded it as later than most of the rest of the poem (see e.g. Reinhardt 1960, p. 9 and 1961, pp. 248–50).

[97] Dating the lost epics presents serious problems, but it is probable that they were composed in the seventh or early sixth century, fitting around the two major poems. For a summary of the arguments see Kullmann 1960, pp. 18–28.

[98] Herington 1985, p. 135. The *Iliu Persis* may lie behind some passages of *Agamemnon*.

[99] From the *Iliu Persis* Sophocles drew his *Laocoon*, *Sinon*, and *Aias Lokros*; Euripides his *Troades* and parts of *Hecuba*. On the tragedians' use of the *Aethiopis* see Martin 1975.

[100] See Jouan 1966, pp. 6–7.

with Trojan characters, often portrayed in the fifth century like barbarian Phrygians or Persians. Another group dealt with the important allies who came to fight and die before Troy whose stories derived from the cyclic poems: Cycnus from the *Cypria*, Ethiopian Memnon from the *Aethiopis*, and the Mysian Eurypylus from the *Ilias Parva*. It is therefore of crucial importance to attempt to ascertain whether the world of the cyclic poems was as homogeneous as that of the *Iliad*, or whether those critics are right who assume that the antithesis of Greek and barbarian became prominent in the later epics.[101] It must be borne in mind that our knowledge of the cyclic poems is confined to about 120 original lines, and some information about their contents, notably Proclus' epitome. It is possible to make conjectures about them from the derivative tragedies, but there is always the danger of underestimating the tragedians' capacity for innovation. To extend such guesswork to the presentation of non-Greeks in cyclic epic is extremely hazardous. All the other evidence suggests that it was the tragic poets who 'barbarized' the non-Greek figures of myth.

Certain differences can however be established between the tone of the *Iliad* and that of the cyclic poems. They abounded in prophecies, oracles, and fabulous, romantic, or bizarre elements alien to the *Iliad*.[102] But there is no evidence at all that they were any more Hellenocentric than the Homeric epics; the numerous vases illustrating scenes from them do not show any signs of the Trojans and their allies (except the Amazon Penthesilea) being differentiated from Greek heroes or orientalized until the fifth century,[103] by which time the inspiration could well have come from tragedy. The fragments of the cycle throw little light on this problem, and Photius' text of Proclus' epitome is hardly more helpful. Often its emphases may be misleading. A famous episode in the *Cypria*, for example, was the death of the Trojan Troilus, treated on numerous archaic vases;[104] the epitome,

---

[101] Snell 1952, pp. 7-8. But *contra* see Nagy 1979, p. 7, par. 14 n. 4, who argues that the cyclic poems differed from the Homeric epics precisely because they were *local* in orientation and diffusion.   [102] See Kullmann 1960, pp. 221-2; Griffin 1977.

[103] See Jüthner 1923, pp. 2-3. Hector, Euphorbus, Aeneas, and even Paris are all portrayed as 'Ionic' hoplites. On vases illustrating scenes from the *Iliu Persis*, especially the death of Priam, see Wiencke 1954; for the *Aethiopis*, Schadewaldt 1952, figs. 1-2. The Scythian archers who serve both Achaeans and Trojans on sixth-century Attic vases have nothing to do with this question: see Vos 1963, pp. 34-9.

[104] See Bethe 1966, p. 96.

however, mentions it only in passing (p. 32, Davies). The *Cypria* concluded with a catalogue of the Trojan allies, which may have been impressive: in the *Iliad* Agamemnon says that it is the allies who are making Troy invincible (2. 123–33). Cycnus was killed by Achilles in the poem, but the victory was counterbalanced by the death of Protesilaus at Hector's hands. In the *Aethiopis* Penthesilea and Memnon were killed by Achilles, showing that the Cycle brought the Amazons and Ethiopians—peoples who were marginal and fabulous in the *Iliad*—into a more central role. Penthesilea's story did not apparently attract the three great tragedians, but Memnon appeared in plays by both Aeschylus and Sophocles. In the epic poem (which was of considerable length)[105] his characterization was calculated to mirror that of Achilles. He too was the son of a goddess, Eos, who delivered a lament for her son as Thetis did for Achilles in the same poem. His arms were almost as famous as those of Achilles, and before his death he was awarded an *aristeia*; his soul was weighed by Zeus against that of Achilles as Hector's had been. The evidence suggests that Achilles and Memnon were portrayed as virtual equivalents.[106]

In the *Ilias Parva* the last of the great allies, Eurypylus the Mysian, was killed by Neoptolemus. Eurypylus is mentioned in the *Odyssey* as the leader of the Kēteioi (11. 520–1), who may conceal a shadowy reminiscence of the Hittites.[107] The epitome tells us that he was granted his own display of prowess (p. 52, Davies). Through its flat prose there perhaps glimmers a tone similar to that of the Doloneia after the account of Eurypylus' death. Odysseus visits Troy in secret and conspires with Helen; then, 'after killing some of the Trojans' he returns to the ships. The epitome concludes that the Trojans took the wooden horse into the city and 'feasted as though they had conquered the Hellenes'; perhaps the poem stressed that their festivities were precipitate. The *Iliu Persis* saw Troy finally fall. Glorification of Hellenic valour might be expected here. But the summary, on the contrary, sounds like a catalogue of Achaean crimes (p. 62, Davies):

Neoptolemus kills Priam, who has fled to the altar of Zeus Herkeios . . . Ajax the son of Ileus, in trying to drag Cassandra off by force, tears away with her the image of Athena . . . The Greeks, after burning the city, sacrifice Polyxena at the tomb of Achilles; Odysseus murders Astyanax . . .

---

[105] See Schadewaldt 1952, pp. 25–6.
[106] On this laborious symmetry see Reinhardt 1960, p. 15.
[107] See Huxley 1960, p. 40.

The terrible story of the destruction of Troy, the city which became the eternal emblem of the community ravaged by war, later provided the plots for a large number of tragedies. Already in archaic art the sufferings of the Trojan women at Greek hands were informed with pathos, especially the rape of Cassandra and the sacrifice of Polyxena; but the violent and sacrilegious Achaeans were fast earning the hatred of the gods.

The *Nosti* and *Telegonia* were more concerned with Greeks than with foreigners, though it would be interesting to know what the cyclic Menelaus did in Egypt, and Odysseus in Thrace. There were also barbarians in tragedies whose mythical complexes were less closely connected with the Trojan saga, for example the Colchian Medea. But she was originally not even foreign. She probably began as the Peloponnesian Agamede of the *Iliad*, who was also a granddaughter of the sun and knew 'all the drugs . . . which the wide earth nourishes' (11. 741).[108] Eumelus, the Corinthian poet whose name is associated with the earliest known Argonautic epic, made a conscious attempt to link the story of the Argo with Corinthian cult.[109] In doing so he turned Aeetes, father of Medea, into a Corinthian hero who emigrated to the Black Sea; later in the poem Medea was recalled to Hellas to rule the Corinthians (Paus. 2. 3. 10). Her pharmaceutical skills were an old element in the story, but her conversion into a barbarian was almost certainly an invention of tragedy, probably of Euripides himself.[110]

Other mythical figures portrayed by the tragedians as barbarians had however already been brought into association with non-Greek

---

[108] Will 1955, p. 122; Huxley 1969, p. 61.

[109] Barron and Easterling 1985, p. 108. Will 1955, pp. 85–129, discusses in detail the process by which Medea became involved in the Argonautic myth. Drews 1976, pp. 19, 24–9, argues that Eumelus was manipulating myth in order to justify Corinthian claims to Black Sea territory in the eighth century.

[110] The Colchians are first mentioned in an Assyrian inscription of the twelfth/eleventh centuries BC (Lordkipanidze 1985, p. 11), but the evidence for Greek influence does not begin until the seventh century, after the foundation of the Milesian colony at Phasis. It is just possible that the similarity of Medea's name with that of the Medes, and her father's mother's name *Persē* (*Od*. 10. 138–9), brought her into connection with the *Persians* once they had achieved international importance in the mid-sixth century. But although she had appeared in several tragedies previously, she was never portrayed on vases in oriental costume until after the production of Euripides' *Medea* in 431, which strongly implies that it was this tragedian who first turned her into a barbarian. See Page 1938, p. lxii n. 1. This was at a time when *Athenian* interest in and commerce with Colchis had recently become extremely vigorous (Lordkipanidze 1985, p. 38).

peoples as their founders and progenitors in the genealogical *Ehoiai* attributed to Hesiod, but probably composed in the mid-sixth century after Greek colonies had been sent to all corners of the Mediterranean.[111] The widening horizons of the Greeks are reflected in the assimilation to Hellenic stemmata not only of oriental gods (Adonis becomes a son of Phoenix, fr. 139), but of numerous foreign peoples. The catalogue traced most of its Greeks, including their eponymous ancestor Hellen, back to the *Urvater* Deucalion, but in its second and third books it concentrated on the descendants of Inachus, and it was from one of them, Io, the Argive princess now diverted to Egypt,[112] that the largest group of foreign peoples was thought to have sprung. Argos became the centre of a huge international genealogy, and Io's family the ancestors and founders of the Egyptians, Arabs, Phoenicians, and Libyans.[113] Belus (a Hellenization of the oriental divinity Ba'al) heads the family of Aegyptus and Danaus, and Agenor's descendants include numerous other figures known or thought to have been envisaged by the tragedians as barbarians: Phineus, Cadmus, Cepheus, Sarpedon. Phineus' flight from the Harpies gave the poet a chance to review other real and fantastic peoples on the margins of the known world (frr. 150–3). These genealogies were on an abstract plane profoundly ethnocentric, in that they sought to trace all the peoples of the world back to their own Greek gods and heroes,[114] providing mythical prefiguration and legitimization of Greek residence in foreign parts (see below, section 6). But how far were these mythical figures envisaged as 'foreign' at this stage? The primary task of the genealogists was to systematize the mass of traditional figures into intelligible stemmata, and their world is homogeneously heroic. There is no evidence that the mythical forefathers of foreign peoples became rationalized in the manner of tragedy as recognizably different from 'Greek' mythical figures. Danaus, for example, becomes associated

---

[111] M. L. West 1985, p. 136.

[112] She had previously given birth to Epaphus not at the mouth of the Nile but in Euboea (*Aegimius* fr. 3 *K* = 'Hesiod' fr. 296). Her connection with Egypt was probably a result of her identification as horned maiden with Isis, the Egyptians' bovine goddess, after Psamthek (Herodotus' 'Psammetichus') had opened up his country to outside contact in the first half of the seventh century BC.

[113] See Merkelbach 1968, pp. 136–9; M. L. West 1985, pp. 76–91, 144–54.

[114] Bickerman 1952, p. 70, sees the genealogists' rationalizing interpretation of the descent of all peoples, Greeks and barbarians, as an attempt to provide the Greeks with 'a scientific prehistory which no other people of the ancient world possessed'.

with Egypt, but given the nature of catalogue poetry it is highly unlikely that he and his daughters in the *Ehoiai* (or for that matter in the sixth-century epic *Danais*) were graphically barbarized as they were in Aeschylus' *Supplices*.

The archaic poets who composed in metres other than the hexameter often talked about the foreign peoples with whom they had contact and the foreign places of which they had heard; ethnography and abuse along ethnic lines sometimes creep into a text when its context is the poet's own contemporary world (see above, section 4). But although the lyric, elegiac, and iambic poets did not confine themselves to heroic narrative or catalogues, the exploits of the heroes and the epic themes pervade even their invective, love poetry, drinking songs, hymns, and festal choruses. Whether in brief allusion, mythical paradigm, episodic narrative, or colourful simile, the mythical time of the 'then and there', the world of the heroes, exists parallel to and constantly illuminates the discourse of the 'here and now'. But despite the juxtaposition of the heroic and the modern planes, the mingling of the mythical and the personal or political, the heroic world remains homogeneous, the ethnicity of its inhabitants of as little importance as in epic. Archilochus, for example, treated the stories of Eurypylus the Trojan ally (304 *IEG*), and of Lynceus and Danaus (305), but there is no evidence that his mythical foreigners were in any sense differentiated from his mythical Greeks.

So little is left of the mythical narrative in lyric metre from this period that a search for evidence of xenophobia becomes almost redundant. Hardly a section of continuous mythical narrative before Pindar and Bacchylides has survived which might permit observation of the way in which foreigners were portrayed. The loss of most of Stesichorus' work is frustrating in this regard, since a papyrus commentary on the lyric poets appears to state that he was one of the most important sources for the tragic poets (*Pap. Oxy.* 2506 fr. 26 col. ii. 2–7 = fr. 217. 2–7 *PMG*). It cites as examples Electra's recognition of Orestes by his lock of hair in *Choephoroe* (7–12), Apollo's gift to Orestes of the bow in *Orestes*, and the deception of Iphigeneia in *IA* (14–27). The commentator was therefore more interested in Stesichorus' ingenious plots than in trying to assess the 'tone' of his poems or whether his adaptation of epic material to a less sombre metre might have paved the way for the quite different milieu of tragedy, into which contemporary interests such as ethnography and political science were to intrude. The ancient verdict was that this 'most Homeric' of poets ([Longinus] *Subl*. 13. 3) sang of great wars and famous generals, and gave his characters the 'appropriate dignity' in their speech and actions (Quint. 10. 1. 62), which indicates that he stuck fairly closely to the heroic conventions and language of Homeric epic. Such fragments as survive of the poems which certainly dealt with non-Greek characters, the *Iliu Persis* (frr. 88–132 *SLG*) and the *Nosti* (209 *PMG*), indicate that he perpetuated the epic terminology for 'Trojans' and 'foreigners';[115] the pathos of his treatment of the monster in the *Geryoneis* does not suggest that elsewhere his Greeks' enemies were treated in a crudely xenophobic light.[116] The long papyrus fragment of an encomium by Ibycus dealing with the Trojan war abounds in formulaic epithets, and seems to be just as 'Homeric', and as little interested in the ethnicity of the Trojans, as the poems of Stesichorus (fr. 282 *PMG*).

It has sometimes been thought that Alcaeus made an important step towards the orientalization of Troy, for a supplement by Wilamowitz to a poem about Helen and Thetis names the Trojans 'Phrygians' (fr. 42. 15 *PLF*). This new name for the Trojans combines literary and heroic credentials (the Phrygians were already *allies* of Troy in the *Iliad*) with an intelligible contemporary reference: eastern Greeks especially had views on their Phrygian neighbours.[117] The use of this alternative label for the legendary inhabitants of Troy thus marks an important point in the process of their barbarization, for once Priam or Hector or Paris was identified as a Phrygian, all the *contemporary* resonances of that term, such as high luxury, began to affect the way in which he was portrayed. It is just possible that Alcaeus was responsible for this influential innovation, but given (*a*) that nowhere else does he or any of the other archaic poets deviate from the standard epic terminology for the Trojans,[118] and (*b*) that it

---

[115] See e.g. fr. 209 ii. 3 *PMG*; 88 fr. 1 col. ii. 7; 89. 11; 105b. 14, 16; 118. 6 *SLG*.

[116] See Geryon's scene with his mother (13. 1–5 *SLG*), and the heroic pathos with which his death was invested (11. 16–26; 15. ii. 14–17 *SLG*).

[117] Archilochus 42. 2 *IEG*; Sappho 92. 12 *PLF*; Alcaeus 280. 22 *SLG* (where a papyrus commentary on lyric poetry mentions his reference to a Phrygian people); Hipponax 27. 2 *IEG*.

[118] Although see 477 col. i. 4 *SLG*. The context of the word *Ph]rugios*, *if* that is the correct reading, is mythical. But the poem is undated; the handwriting dates the papyrus to the second century BC. There is no indication that the 'Phrygian song' in Alcman fr. 126 *PMG* has anything to do with mythical Troy.

is certainly possible to find an alternative supplement which removes the Phrygians from this poem,[119] it seems much more likely that it was the fifth century which first saw the Phrygianization of Troy: there is evidence that Aeschylus himself was responsible.[120] The remnants of archaic lyric treatment of heroic subject matter do not suggest, therefore, that this genre in any way developed the behavioural differentiation of mythical foreigners: the argument that too much of this poetry has been lost to allow such a firm conclusion to be drawn can perhaps be countered by the fact that in Pindar and Bacchylides, the heirs to lyric mythical narrative, mythical foreigners are never portrayed as barbarians, but as inhabitants of the homogeneous world of heroes.

Indeed, this heroic landscape, the mythical plane, exerted such a magnetic force over the archaic poets' interpretation of experience that 'modern' foreigners, along with the poets' Greek contemporaries, are sometimes turned into epic warriors. Strabo writes that Callinus, for example, composed an elegiac poem about the sack of Sardis by the Cimmerians (14. 1. 40), the northern tribe who in the seventh century were pushed by the Scythians out of the Crimea into Asia, and sacked Sardis in 652 BC. In a fragment probably from this poem[121] Callinus urges his townsmen to battle in vocabulary outstanding for its dependence on Homer (1 *IEG*). The present struggle of the Asiatic cities against the Cimmerians is honoured by elevation to the heroic plane. Callinus' successor in elegy, Mimnermus, shows the same propensity. In his *Smyrneis* he described 'the battle of the Smyrnaeans against Gyges and the Lydians' (Paus. 9. 29. 4), in which the generation before him had fought. His language could scarcely be more Homeric,[122] but the subject of the poem is recent history. It ennobles the harsh facts of historical experience by perceiving them through a softening mythopoeic filter. This process is the exact opposite of the tragedians' treatment of foreigners: they turned heroes into barbarians, while Callinus and Mimnermus (and later, to an outstanding degree, Pindar), by the

[119] See Hall 1988.

[120] See Σ A on *Il.* 2. 862 = Aesch. fr. 446: '*Phrygians*: Because the later [poets] called Troy and Phrygia the same thing, whereas Homer did not. Aeschylus confused the two.'

[121] Podlecki 1984, p. 56, gives reasons for assigning this fragment to the poem dealing with the Cimmerians.

[122] See e.g. fr. 14. 3, where the 'historical' Lydians are *hippomachoi* like the Phrygians in the *Iliad* (10. 431).

reverse process, recreated their conflicts against foreign peoples on the heroic plane.[123]

(c) *Ethnography*

Exotica and comments on foreigners are found in archaic poetry when the temporal context is 'the here and now'. Ethnography itself was not an invention of tragedy, for the prose writers of late sixth-century Ionia began to develop a systematic science for comparing and contrasting the different ways of life among the various peoples of the world (see below, chapter 2. 3). But this section will argue that its importation into the world of heroes did not happen on any significant scale until the fifth century, and that the perception of myth through a filter informed by ethnographic discoveries was to be the domain of the tragedians.

The epic poems have been a happy hunting-ground for those who wish to establish disparities in the portrayal of Greek and non-Greek culture. Troy has been thought to embody an archaic Greek impression of ancient Anatolian civilizations.[124] But most of the examples do not stand up to examination. Homeric narrative, for example, has no place for lengthy physical description: a man is defined by his actions, not his looks, and women are more or less uniformly beautiful. There is no apparent physiological difference between the Achaeans and the Trojans.[125] The Homeric warrior, whatever his race, would like to be able to say with Achilles (*Il*. 21. 108), 'Do you not see that I too am big and beautiful?' Achilles and Priam take pleasure in regarding each other's beauty (24. 629–32), and Chryseis is in no way inferior to Clytaemnestra, either in looks or brains (1. 115). Ugliness in anti-

---

[123] On the process by which history turns into myth see below, ch. 2. 2. Pindar equates the sailors who saved Greece at Salamis with the Salaminians who fought at Troy under Ajax (*Isthm*. 5. 48–50). His description of the defeats of the Carthaginians and Persians reads like an episode out of the Trojan war (*Pyth*. 1. 71–80).

[124] See e.g. Dornseiff 1935, p. 244.

[125] See Treu 1968, p. 84. But it is just possible that Hector's black hair (*chaitai/kuaneai*, *Il*. 22. 401–2), which streams around his head as his corpse is dragged around Troy, distinguishes him from the Achaean heroes, who are generally *xanthos*, 'fair' (Achilles, 1. 197; Menelaus, 3. 284). Irwin's study of the implications of *kuaneos* (1974, pp. 91, 107) does not, however, discuss any possible ethnic significance. Hades, like Boreas and Poseidon, is *kuanochaitēs* in archaic poetry; I suspect that the colour of Hector's hair in this immensely important passage has more to do with his death than with his ethnicity, though Irwin denies that the term *kuaneos* has any 'unearthly' or 'hieratic' connotations.

heroes is confined to neither side (Thersites 2. 216, Dolon 10. 316). All Homer's characters seem to have worn the same costumes and armour. Paris' leopardskin (3. 17) is not 'a foreign touch':[126] Agamemnon and Menelaus elsewhere don a lionskin and a leopardskin respectively (10. 23, 29). Paris wore his hair in a particular style (11. 385), but there is no reason to think that this was peculiarly Trojan. The unique case of the golden brooches in Euphorbus' hair (17. 52) may, however, signify a male vanity more suited in Greek eyes to the Orient than Achaea, although Kirk has denied this, and sees it simply as a sign that this hero is to be defeated.[127]

Although the individual Greeks are not distinguishable from the Trojans by their dress, there are a few signs of ethnological interest in the epithets applied to different groups. It was noticed in antiquity that the epithet *bathukolpos*, 'deep-bosomed', is only used of Greek women (Σ *A Il*. 2. 484). Lycian Sarpedon addresses his *amitrochitōnas* ('beltless') companions (16. 419); the Thracians allied with the Trojans are 'top-knotted' (*akrokomoi*, 4. 533); the Abantes of Euboea kept their hair long only at the back (*opithen komoōntes*, 2. 542), whereas the Achaeans kept their hair long all over (*karē komoōntas*, 2. 11). This last phrase could reflect a Peloponnesian custom of dressing the hair as a rite in preparation for battle, which Herodotus observes in the Spartans (7. 208).[128] In a small number of epithets attached to certain ethnic groups, then, it looks as though the seed of later systematic ethnological science was germinating, though the clothing and appearance of non-Greeks are not prominent concerns in heroic poetry.

The argument that pipes (*auloi*) are played only by the Trojans (10. 13) is unimpressive.[129] In the town at peace hammered on to Achilles' shield by Hephaestus they are played at a wedding feast: there is no reason to suppose that the god or the poet did not have a Greek wedding in mind (18. 495). The scarcity of pipes in the *Iliad* is at least in part to be explained by their special association with Dionysus, of whom this epic has little to say. Another distinction has been perceived between the Greeks' skill in naval matters and the supposedly land-bound Trojans. In Aeschylus' *Persae* and other later texts barbarians are often presented as in possession of expert infantry and cavalry, but

---

[126] Thomas 1962, p. 300.
[127] Kirk 1985, p. 261.
[128] See Whallon 1961, p. 117.
[129] Dornseiff 1935, p. 244; von Scheliha 1943, pp. 126, 367.

vulnerable to the Greeks' skill as mariners; this polarity crystallized after Salamis (see below, chapter 2. 4c). It might therefore be justifiable to see in the *Iliad* an emphasis on the Trojans' deficiency as sailors, if it were true that they 'remarkably . . . are never mentioned as having any ships'.[130] But this view is simply incorrect: when the Trojans need ships the poet provides them (3. 443–4, 5. 62–4).

It has also been asserted that archery is a more predominant mode of warfare among the Trojans than among the Greeks.[131] Since in classical times archery was despised and considered suitable only for Cretans and Scythians, this has been taken to imply the cowardice and inferiority of the Trojans. The only cogent evidence for this view is a single line in which Diomedes insults Paris, calling him, amongst other things, 'archer' (*toxota*, 11. 385). The word itself is a Homeric *hapax*, which may indicate that it is a late entrant into the language of epic, and what we seem to be dealing with here is two different and historically discrete views of the status of the archer, for elsewhere, of course, the poem does not support Diomedes' opinion. Two of the most conspicuous archers in the poem, Teucer and Meriones, are Greeks. Philoctetes, 'well-skilled in archery', who was to become so important at the end of war, merits a place in the Catalogue despite his absence (2. 718). The archery contest at Patroclus' funeral games is emphasized by its position at their culmination (23. 850–83). Nor should it be forgotten how essential the hero's bowmanship is to the *Odyssey*: the archery contest for the hand of a woman may even be an Indo-European theme dating back to pre-Greek days.[132] A study of the epithets used of bows in the Homeric epics has shown that the bows were composite rather than single-stave like those of the classical period, suggesting the very early influence of Ugaritic or Egyptian culture.[133] The bows of the Homeric heroes had almost certainly become embedded in the formulaic language of epic in Mycenaean times, when archery among the Greeks was at its acme.

There may, however, be one difference between the Achaean and Trojan communities. The Achaeans make a distinction between wives

---

[130] Pinsent (discussion contribution) in Foxhall and Davies 1984, p. 175.

[131] Thomas 1962, p. 300.

[132] There are close parallels in the *Mahābhārata* and *Rāmāyana* (Germain 1954, pp. 14–26; Page 1973, pp. 106–8).

[133] *Palintonos, ankulos, kampulos*. See McLeod 1966.

and mistresses,[134] and normally consort at any one time with only one mistress. Later Greeks believed, probably wrongly, that Anatolian monarchs actually *married* more than one woman (see below, chapter 5. 1), and certain passages in the *Iliad* imply that Priam is an oriental polygamist, or keeps a large number of women for his own use in his palace.[135] At 24. 495-7 he states that he had once had fifty sons, nineteen by one woman (presumably Hecuba), and the others by *gunaikes* ('women' or 'wives') in his palace. The problem is the ambiguity of the word *gunaikes*. Hecuba, as mother of Hector, clearly enjoys some kind of superior rank, but the poem is reticent about the other women and their exact status. There is a brief mention of one Castianeira from Thrace, the mother by Priam of a son, Gorgythion (8. 302-5). When another youth, Lycaon, begs for his life, he says that his mother Laothoe was the 'daughter of old Altes . . . Priam "had" his daughter, along with many˙other *gunaikes*' (21. 87-8). It is not clear whether such sons were bastards or not; the ambiguity is probably deliberate. Priam's numerous consorts may have been a traditional feature of the Trojan royal house, reflecting for once clear cultural differentiation; the poem, however, plays down its implications and leaves the situation vague. It is highly unlikely that the poets of the *Iliad* invented Priam's polygamy or harem: it is much more likely that they invented the monogamy of his sons.[136]

Achaeans and Trojans of course share the same religious beliefs. Far too much has been made of 3. 103-4, where Menelaus proposes that the Trojans bring sheep to sacrifice to Earth and Sun, while the Achaeans will bring one for Zeus. This does not indicate that the Trojans were not worthy to sacrifice to Zeus,[137] for elsewhere they are of course his favourite people, who always keep his altars fully replenished (for example, 4. 44-9). The forces arrayed on either side at the ceremony give up exactly the same prayer; that their beliefs are identical is stressed by a formulaic line (3. 297). At 21. 132 Achilles says that the Trojans sacrifice live horses in addition to bulls to the river Scamander, and some scholars have adduced here Herodotus' report

---

[134] On Achilles' relationship with Briseis see A. Diller 1937, pp. 74-7.

[135] See Buchholz 1883, pp. 8-9.

[136] See Redfield 1975, p. 243 n. 12; von Scheliha 1943, p. 126. Except perhaps for Euripides at *Andr.* 168-80, the tragedians do not seem to have regarded Priam as polygamous. Was even this minor cultural difference suppressed in the cyclic poems from which most tragic plots were drawn?

[137] Thomas 1962, pp. 300-1.

that horse-sacrifice was a Medo–Persian custom (7. 113). But as so often the alleged difference between Achaean and Trojan culture provides to be no difference at all (see 23. 171–2).

Later Greek discourse presents extremes of mourning, especially self-mutilation and the use of professional wailers, as practices fit only for barbarians. Among Solon's alleged legislative reforms at Athens was the outlawing of certain rites, 'for he made the Athenians decorous and careful in their religious services, and milder in their rites of mourning . . . by taking away the harsh and barbaric practices (*to sklēron aphelōn kai to barbarikon*) in which their women had usually indulged up to that time' (Plut. *Sol.* 12. 8).[138] Plutarch goes on to specify laceration of the flesh. When in the *Iliad* Briseis saw the corpse of Patroclus, she screamed and 'tore with her hands her breast and tender neck and lovely face' (19. 284–5); Leaf thought that this was 'meant for a "barbarian" custom'.[139] But after the Greek Protesilaus' death his wife was left at home 'with both cheeks lacerated' (2. 700; see also 11. 393). Slightly more impressive are the singers, *aoidoi*, brought in to mourn Hector (24. 720). It is possible that they conceal an allusion to the professional mourners of the east, like Menander's Carian wailing woman in his *Karinē*.[140] But there is no way of telling whether such singers would not have made an appearance had any of the Achaeans' slaughtered heroes been mourned in their palaces.

Certain members of the divine syndicate of course favour one side above the other, and the routing of pro-Trojan gods tends to presage or emphasize a parallel defeat of their protégés, but there is no question of the Trojans' gods being identifiably 'foreign'. Perhaps Aphrodite retained in the eighth century an oriental significance, though the legendary motif of the judgement of Paris is very early.[141] Ares' home in the poem may be Thrace, but this divinity is clearly named in Mycenaean Greek.[142] All the gods, whatever their historical proven-

---

[138] See also Dem. 43. 62–3, for the Athenian law limiting the number of female mourners allowed at funerals. For other testimony to Solon's legislation on mourning rites see Ruschenbusch 1966, pp. 95–7. Herodotus compares the *Spartans'* extravagant royal funeral rites, on the other hand, with those of the Asiatic barbarians (6. 58). Plutarch had a theory that the barbarians had exerted a bad influence on all aspects of Greek culture; see Nikolaidis 1986, and below, ch. 2. 4e.

[139] Leaf 1902, p. 338.   [140] See Willcock 1976, p. 274.

[141] Burkert 1985a, p. 153. On Aphrodite's 'oriental significance' see Reinhardt 1960, p. 21; on the process by which she may have entered the epic tradition, see Boedeker 1974.

[142] See below ch. 3. 7 with n. 159.

ance, have in epic been thoroughly Hellenized, become completely Greek through assimilation, and are honoured by both sides. An interpretation of the poem which sees the Trojans as particularly beloved of Aphrodite and Ares might argue that they 'symbolize' passion and violence, barbarian characteristics in later Greek thought,[143] but this may be anachronistically allegorical. In any case, those who favour this view have to deal with the support of Troy by Apollo, the grim companion who leads Hector into his most victorious battles, holding the aegis before him: Stesichorus' version even turned Hector into the son of Apollo (fr. 224 *PMG*). This god was of course the quintessentially 'Hellenic' personification of reason and order, who stands in opposition to the Persians on the 'Darius vase',[144] and is commonly found in antithesis to the frenzy and chaos of the 'foreign' Dionysus.[145] The pro-Achaean gods have much more in common with the pro-Trojan inhabitants of Olympus than with the Achaeans. They scheme and squabble, but distance themselves from human suffering, and therefore their role finds no parallel in myths which clearly legitimize the ascendancy of one culture over another, like the Egyptian tale of Horus' expulsion of Seth and his followers to Asia, or the *Rāmāyana*'s validation of the spread of Aryan culture through its mythical agent, Rāma, to Dravidian southern India.[146]

Even in non-hexameter poetry there are few signs of ethnography penetrating the world of heroes. In the 'Louvre Partheneion' Alcman passes effortlessly from heroic narrative (1. 1–35 *PMG*) to the 'here and now' in which the Spartan maidens heckle one another, and make exotic references to foreign breeds of horses (50–1, 59) and Lydian attire (67–8). But the two worlds remain distinct. Two fragmentary poems by Sappho in particular use material from the Trojan nexus of myths. Fragment 16 *PLF* could have provided the impulse for her at

---

[143] Griffin's interpretation of the poem rests partly on his view that Paris, as the darling of Aphrodite, represents the 'archetypal Trojan' (1980, p. 5).

[144] Oliver 1960, p. 119. On the 'Darius vase' see below, ch. 2 nn. 5 and 27. Parke's explanation of Apollo's support of Troy and Hector by reference to the god's ambiguous connections with Lycia is not really adequate (1967, p. 29).

[145] Ultimately the reason for Apollo's protection of Hector may lie in his role as ritual antagonist to Achilles. See Nagy 1979, pp. 62, 118–50.

[146] On the Horus/Seth myth see Anthes 1961, p. 76; on the *Rāmāyana*, W. Norman Brown 1961, p. 291. Fittipaldi's discussion of the roles attributed to the various gods in the *Iliad* shows how little prominence is actually given to their motives for wishing to save or destroy Troy (1979, pp. 7–19).

least to compare Trojans with contemporary Asiatics. After implying
that it was for love that Helen went off to Troy (16. 9–12), she says that
Helen has reminded her of her own Anactoria, whom she would rather
behold than 'the chariots and armed infantry of the Lydians' 19–20);
but ancient Troy and modern Lydia remain unassociated except by the
suggestiveness of textual proximity. The substantial fragment which
recounts the marriage of Hector and Andromache (fr. 44 *PLF*)
however represents a significant step forward in the narration of a
heroic sequence. It is much closer to Homeric dialect and vocabulary
than Sappho's other work, a common phenomenon when poets who
normally compose in their own vernacular select metres with dactylic
elements. But there are several items of vocabulary which are distinctly
un-Homeric, the *satinai* (mule-driven sedan chairs), the castanets
(*krotala*), and the 'myrrh, cassia, and frankincense' (13, 25, 30). Page
concludes: 'The σατίναι, carriages for women, might be seen in the
streets, and the myrrh, cassia and frankincense on the altars, of modern
Mytilene: they have no place in Homeric Troy . . . The old and the new
are fused and transmuted into a new element.'[147]

Satinai, always plural, is a rare word used for a women's carriage.[148]
Frisk and Chantraine agree that it is probably a Phrygian word, though
it may be Thracian.[149] Another fragment of Sappho shows that it was
not only Lydia which exerted an eastern cultural influence on
Mytilene, for the word 'Phrygian' or a cognate appears in a context
describing luxurious clothing (92. 12 *PLF*). But it is not clear whether
the Phrygian carriages in fr. 44 had become 'Greek' by assimilation, or
whether Sappho is tinting her Trojans with an eastern hue by using a
word which retained the flavour of its provenance. *Libanos* ('frankincense') and *murra* are semitic loan words: *kasia* is Assyrian. Herodotus
said that these substances could only be grown in Arabia (3. 107). It is
therefore possible that in enumerating them Sappho was aiming at an
oriental effect. *Krotalon* is a Greek word. Castanets make their first
appearance in Greek literature in this fragment, unless the Homeric
Hymn to the Mother of the Gods is earlier, which is unlikely. In it the
Mother is pleased by the 'sound of castanets and tympani and the voice
of pipes' (3).[150] Castanets were always associated with the Mother

[147] Page 1955, p. 71.
[148] It is found elsewhere only in *Hymn. hom. Ven.* 13; Anac. 388. 10 *PMG*; Eur. *Hel*. 1311.
See Page 1955, p. 71 n. 2.
[149] Schmitt 1966, p. 151.   [150] On this goddess see below, ch. 3. 7.

(Pindar fr. 70b. 10). Euripides was also to mention *satinai* and castanets in the ode to Demeter-Cybele in his *Helen*; when the goddess with Phrygian affinities searches for her missing daughter, the castanets sound and beasts are yoked to her *satinai* (1308-11). The first evidence for the Adonis cult among the Greeks is in Sappho (frr. 140. 1; 211b iii *PLF*); perhaps in fr. 44 she is borrowing details from Asiatic ritual and transferring them to her Trojan narrative. If it were possible to be certain that had she had been describing a Greek wedding these details would have been omitted, the suspicion would be confirmed that the earliest evidence for *mythical* foreigners donning an identifiably non-Greek mantle would be in the poetry of Sappho.

There is hardly any other evidence in archaic poetry for the merging of the heroic and contemporary planes except in Hipponax. Besides some scraps of an account of the labours of Heracles (fr. 102 *IEG*) there are few signs of mythical subject-matter, but one papyrus fragment applies a foreign title to a Homeric warrior. The Thracian Rhesus is referred to as a *palmus* (72. 7 *IEG*), a Lydian term meaning 'king', which Hipponax elsewhere applies comically also to Zeus and Hermes (frr. 3; 38. 1 *IEG*); this word turns up in a fragment of Aeschylus (fr. 437). Hipponax's work probably has greater relevance to comic foreigners given the similarity between invective and comedy (though some have thought that tragic dialogue adopted certain elements of the Ionic iambus),[151] but it is significant that the same half-century which saw the establishment of serious drama at Athens produced in the semi-oriental milieu of the eastern Greeks a poet who for the first time in extant Greek literature indisputably jumbled his heroic and contemporary worlds—epic subject-matter and a 'modern' tone of voice.

6 THE DISCOURSE OF COLONIZATION

The archaic poetry of which the temporal context is the world of the 'here and now' foreshadowed some of the techniques used by the tragedians in characterizing their barbarians. Section 5 of this chapter has, however, shown that these techniques are almost completely lacking from the archaic poetic representations of the foreigners of the

---

[151] See Fraenkel 1950, ii, p. 251.

world of myth, the 'then and there' of the heroic plane, the chronologically prior. One of the tragedians' great innovations was therefore
the importation of the exoticism and ethnography of the discourse of
the present into the mythical past, a process which formed part of their
central project, the refraction of heroic myth through the prism of
fifth-century polis ideology. But even though epic poetry shows little
interest in drawing linguistic, behavioural, or cultural distinctions
between Greek and non-Greek, on one plane it is profoundly ethnocentric.[152] At a non-literal level the poets of the *Iliad* were producing a
discourse which tamed and subordinated in the Greek imagination the
land mass which came to be known as Asia, by creating Troy,
representing the words and deeds and defeats of the Trojans and their
allies. Asia was thus familiarized and defused by assimilation into
hexameter poetry, the common property of the Greek-speakers'
archaic intellectual world. The celebration of Greek victory over the
inhabitants of Asia Minor must legitimize the actions of the colonizers
and express the spirit of the age when Greek cities were beginning to
expand self-confidently all over the Mediterranean and the Black Sea.
A similar dynamic informs the literature of the age which discovered
America; all the danger of penetrating unknown territory, of conflict
with indigenous tribes, is manifested in the colonialist discourse of
Elizabethan and early Stuart England, especially in Shakespeare's vile
Caliban of *The Tempest*.[153] But the *Iliad*'s relation to Greek colonization is much less transparent and easy to define. The myth it narrates
presents no simple *aition* for the colonization of Asia, as the Cyrene
myth in Pindar's ninth Pythian ode authorizes the colonization of
north Africa, or the story of the sun goddess's victory over Susanowo,
'the impetuous one', in Japanese mythology represents a simple
cultural *aition* for the victory of the Imperial Ancestors over the
barbarians.[154] Nor does it provide genealogies legitimizing Greek
expansion abroad in the way that some of the stemmata descending
from Io in the sixth-century Hesiodic *Ehoiai* bind the colonies by
mythically conceived ties to the mainland.[155] The *Iliad* avoids

[152] The important concept of ethnocentrism, the collective orientation of each ethnic
group, and the process by which it organizes its perceptions of others, was first formulated
and discussed by Sumner 1906.

[153] On Europe's first images of the New World see Chiapelli, Allen, and Benson 1976.
For a discussion of *The Tempest* as colonialist discourse see Paul Brown 1985.

[154] On this Japanese colonization myth see Saunders 1961, pp. 421-2.

[155] See M. L. West 1985, pp. 149-50; Drews 1973, pp. 7-9.

references to future events,[156] and its genealogies go backwards rather than forwards into historic time; it does not provide a usable paradigm of the Greek/barbarian geopolitical boundary, whatever use was later made of it to justify or explain Greek actions and experiences;[157] despite the presence of Greek-speakers at Miletus from at least as early as the fourteenth century BC, there are no Asiatic Hellenes in the Homeric world.

The aspirations and experiences of the Greek colonizers are more clearly reproduced by the *Odyssey*. The world conjured up by the poem is much concerned with the danger and excitement of traversing unknown seas to distant lands, and is peopled with figures drawn from the milieu of trade and travel. The text introduces Athena disguised as a merchant, and Phoenician traders and slave-dealers.[158] Passages in the episodes of the Phaeacians and the Cyclopes seem to express the invitation of new-found land and the experiences of Greek settlers.[159] But the poem's validation of the colonists' subjection of indigenous tribes on hostile shores takes a highly sophisticated form,[160] for although Odysseus' adventures owe much to the more concrete and traceable itinerary of the Argo,[161] on a superficial level they have little to do with history, geography, or even ethnography.[162] Odysseus is no Hanno nor Scylax, his voyage no *periplous* of the Mediterranean. The resistance Greek colonizers must have encountered in foreign lands informs the poem, but is highly mediated by the vocabulary of myth: it is embodied in supernatural creatures, monstrous Cyclopes or gigantic Laestrygonians.

[156] Snodgrass 1971, p. 3.

[157] See Davies 1984, pp. 95–6. He questions Burkert's view (1979, p. 24) that the *Iliad* narrates 'a myth through which the self-consciousness of Greeks versus barbarians first asserts itself', by arguing that the horizons of the time of the poem's composition must not be confused with those of the use later made of it.

[158] See 13. 272–3; 14. 288–97 (the Phoenician merchant who in Odysseus' fictional narrative tried to sell him into slavery, perhaps the first real barbarian in Greek literature, as his ethnicity is central to his characterization as a scoundrel); 15. 415–81. The stereotype of the mercenary Phoenician was to inform a fragment of Sophocles (909). It is usually thought that the Phoenicians entered the epic tradition during the period of their great westward expansion between the ninth and seventh centuries, but it is possible that they stem from much earlier. See Muhly 1970, pp. 19–22.

[159] 5. 279–80; 6. 10; 9. 130–5. See J. H. Finley 1978, p. 61; Vidal-Naquet 1986, pp. 21, 26.

[160] See also Schwabl 1962, pp. 14–15.

[161] Meuli 1921.

[162] See Fränkel 1975, p. 49.

Colonization myths expressing conflict with the ethnically other often conceptualize the enemy as subhuman, bestial, or monstrous. The Chinese 'civilizer' hero Yü visits the lands of the black-teethed people and the winged people,[163] and in the *Rāmāyana* the inhabitants of Sri Lanka resisting Aryan conquest are portrayed as demons, monkeys, and bears.[164] Archaic Greek poets envisaged numerous semi-monstrous beings, besides the Cyclopes and Laestrygonians, living beyond the boundary-stones of civilization. Aristeas of Proconnesus' *Arimaspeia* told of griffins and one-eyed Arimaspians living in the far north,[165] Alcman mentioned Sciapods and Steganopods (fr. 148 *PMG*), and in the *Ehoiai* Phineus was pursued by the harpies all over the world, giving the poet an opportunity to survey the outlandish Sirens, griffins, half-hounds, and longheads (frr. 150. 33; 152-3). These monstrous races of the world's margins were catalogued by Ctesias, Megasthenes, and Pliny,[166] resuscitated in the Middle Ages,[167] and reports of their existence in the West Indies were recorded by Christopher Columbus;[168] indeed the species *homo monstrosus*, thought to inhabit distant imperial territories, did not die out as a scientific concept until the last great era of European colonization in the nineteenth century.[169] But already in the Hesiodic fragments the fantastic coexists with the concrete and credible; the half-hounds and longheads rub shoulders with Ethiopians, Libyans, and Scythians (fr. 150. 15). Here are early signs of the process by which the 'real' foreigner, the fifth-century barbarian, was to be assimilated to the mythical archetype of the supernatural agent of disorder.

---

[163] Bodde 1961, pp. 400-3.

[164] W. Norman Brown 1961, pp. 291, 296.

[165] This poem was probably composed in the seventh century: see Bolton 1962, p. 7. Phillips 1955, pp. 171-7, argues that some of Aristeas' strange beings were known to the Greeks from the art and folklore of central Asia and southern Siberia. The influence of the poem is apparent in the ethnography of the far north throughout antiquity; in the fifth century its most notable debtors are the author of *PV* (803-6, see Griffith 1983, pp. 214, 230-1), and Herodotus (4. 13-27).

[166] Friedman 1981, pp. 5-25.

[167] Ibid., pp. 26-36; Chew 1937, p. 12.

[168] See the rumoured 'men with one eye, and others with dogs' noses who ate men' in Columbus' journal, translated in Jane 1960, p. 52.

[169] See Arens 1979, p. 33.

7 SUPERNATURAL BARBARIANS

The non-Greeks of archaic literature did not perform the central function of the barbarians in the fifth century and beyond, that of anti-Greeks against whom Hellenic culture and character were defined. But this does not mean that the myths of the early period were not concerned with most of the oppositions later assimilated to the cardinal antagonism of Greek versus barbarian—civilization against primitivism, order against chaos, observance of law and taboo against transgression. These oppositions, on the contrary, lie at the heart of the archaic thought-world, for the struggle to conceptualize the nature of civilization is as old as civilization itself. From the texts surviving from the archaic city-states of Mesopotamia[170] to the academic discipline of anthropology in modern universities, 'civilized' societies have sought to define their own nature and achievements by comparison with their former selves.[171] The idea of movement, of an evolutionary journey towards new levels of culture and technology, an idea generic to civilization, holds implicit within it the notion of a lost way of life, a past, a chaos from which society arose (or, paradoxically, of a utopia from which it fell),[172] and the search for this past becomes an essential component of a culture's quest for an identity.

Civilization often finds its former self in primitive tribes contemporary with it, but in archaic Greek thought the abstractions later to be conceptualized as ethnically other, as Not Greek, are embodied in the monstrous or supernatural, the Not Human. In cosmogonic myth it is the Titans, incarnations of primordial violence, who are subdued by Zeus and the comely Olympian gods, imposers of decorum on the divine plane (Hes. *Theog.* 700-35). In the myths of the Greeks' great

[170] Kramer 1963, pp. 282-6; Oppenheim 1977, p. 261.

[171] See Diamond 1974, pp. 120-1, 207, 211.

[172] It is one of the paradoxes of mythical thought that man's evolution can be conceptualized almost simultaneously as a perpetual fall and a permanent rise; on the complexities of Hesiod's myth of the cycle of generations see Vernant 1983, pp. 3-72. Greek myths define both 'disorderly' tribes and utopian societies as chronologically anterior (the golden age) or spatially marginal (Homeric Ethiopians, Abii, and Phaeacians; the Hyperboreans). But although utopianism informs some portrayals of barbarians in the fifth century and beyond, tragedy's role as a celebration of civic values meant that it generally defined human evolution as progress rather than decline (although see below, ch. 3. 7). On this kind of anti-primitivism in Greek thought generally see Lovejoy and Boas 1935, pp. 192-221.

civilizer, Heracles, it is the giants and monsters he grappled with and subdued, clearing the earth of the disorderly and bestial to make way for the ordered life of the community; epic briefly tells of other famous heroes who fought with monstrous incarnations of violence—Perseus and the Gorgon, Bellerophon and the Chimaera.[173] In the *Iliad* it is not the Trojans but the fabulous communities of savage Centaurs and matriarchal Amazons, who live on the spatial margins of the world and are put down by the heroic Lapiths and Phrygians respectively, in parallel anecdotes recorded by the Greek Nestor and the Trojan Priam (1. 266–72; 3. 184–9). But it is primarily the *Odyssey* which contrasts the 'real' world of Ithaca, Pylos, and Sparta with the fabulous world of Odysseus' wanderings, and through the contrast defines both what it is to be human, and the nature of civilized existence.[174]

Odysseus' humanity itself is jeopardized on his travels. Humankind exists on a plane between the beasts and the gods: Calypso wants to make him immortal, Circe to turn him into an animal. None of the inhabitants of the imaginary world of the wanderings are like ordinary mortals. Their environmental conditions may be unnatural—the Cimmerians live shrouded in eternal night (11. 14–15). They may be divine or semi-divine, like Calypso, Circe, and the Phaeacians. Or they may be physiologically inhuman—Scylla, the Sirens, the one-eyed Cyclopes, and gigantic Laestrygonians.

The various beings Odysseus encounters either lack certain social practices integral to the 'real' world, or they completely reverse them. A mark of civilization is defined as the consumption of bread, meat, and wine: the Cyclopes eat dairy products, and the Lotus-eaters fruit (9. 219–23, 84). In the real world men fight with bronze weapons: on the imaginary plane Polyphemus throws paleolithic boulders, and the Laestrygonians spear men like fish (9. 537; 10. 124). Civilization depends on agricultural labour: the Cyclopes neither sow nor plough, and on Scherie everything grows in abundance all year round (9. 108; 7. 114–26). Trade requires seafaring: the Cyclopes have no ships (9. 126–9). Community life demands laws and decision-making bodies: the Cyclopes know no communal rules or assemblies (9. 112). The real world is dominated by men: Odysseus meets goddesses who

---

[173] These stories of individual monster-slaying were generally imported from the non-Greek east to enjoy popularity in the poetry and art of the seventh and early sixth centuries: see Dunbabin 1957, pp. 55–6; Burkert 1987.

[174] The following remarks owe much to Vidal-Naquet 1986, pp. 18–30.

threaten his patriarchal status. The most distinctive signs of civilized life are however the imperatives and taboos it constructs for itself. The performance of sacrifice is in epic poetry one of the central concerns of the real world, and it is conspicuously absent from several of the inhuman communities Odysseus visits. Civilization respects guests and looks kindly on suppliants, whereas Odysseus' men are maltreated by most of the beings they encounter. Incest and cannibalism—the two signifiers of the pre-civilized state to be found in the myth-systems of virtually every culture[175]—are the most extreme of the taboos underscored by the poem. Human communities are defined as exogamous, and Aeolus' sons marry his daughters (10. 5–7). A civilized man must not devour another, for this is the way of beasts (Hes. *Op.* 276–80): Polyphemus and the king of the Laestrygonians both eat members of Odysseus' crew.[176]

Later chapters will show how the new Panhellenic ideology of the fifth century assimilates the historical enemies of Greece to these mythical archetypes. Battles against the Persians are now represented as reiterations of the gods' and heroes' wars on the Titans, Giants, Amazons, and Centaurs. Lawlessness, incest, cannibalism, and other deviations from the socially authorized way of life are 'discovered' by Greek ethnographers not amongst mythical tribes but in known barbarian communities. Alongside the matriarchal Amazons of myth appear the concrete, rationalized, matriarchal Lycians. This process is just beginning in the archaic period with the mingling on the margins of civilization of supernatural tribes with 'real', distant communities; the edges of the world support Amazons, Cyclopes, and griffins, but they are also inhabited by Mysians and Ethiopians (*Il.* 13. 5; 1. 423). It was not until the fifth century, however, that the archaic world's ranks of divine, supernatural, and inhuman antagonists of civilization were to be joined forever by the barbarian.

---

[175] Neither incest nor anthropophagy are anything like as pervasive in primitive culture as a literal handling of myth would suggest. Arens 1979 denies that cannibalism, except *in extremis*, has ever been practised at all, and shows how false charges of both man-eating and incest have been levelled against primitive or oppressed peoples throughout history. In the case of mythical patterns involving incest and cannibalism a psychoanalytical approach is much more fruitful (see Bremmer 1987b); dreams about them are attested in all cultures (see e.g. the dreams of native Australasians analysed by Róheim 1947), and as early as Assurbanipal, whose library included a dream book listing apotropaic rituals against the evil consequences of nightmares about such crimes (Oppenheim 1977, p. 222).

[176] On cannibalism see below, ch. 3. 5.

8 CONCLUSION

The view of the non-Greek world in archaic literature has been found to be extremely complex. The Greeks' sense of collective identity was an element underlying even the earliest epic, but is still in competition with and overshadowed by the group identity attached to individual city-states. The all-embracing genus of anti-Greeks later to be termed 'the barbarians' does not appear until the fifth century. There is an important distinction between the presentation of non-Greeks in poetry which deals with the mythical past and that whose temporal context is the 'here and now', the contemporary world of merchants and mercenaries, travel and trade. Ethnography, exoticism, and a chauvinist tone are sometimes to be found in the poetry evoking the present, but they hardly ever infect the world of heroes where status is assessed by lineage and valour, never by ethnicity. The difference between the presentation of the foreigners of myth in archaic poetry and in tragedy comes down to area of focus and emphasis. To an archaic Greek Priam was a king, Hector a hero, Memnon the son of the Dawn, and Medea a sorceress; to the fifth-century theatre-goer an essential aspect of such figures' identities was that they were bar-barians.

Though at the deepest level the *Iliad*, some passages of the *Odyssey*, and the Hesiodic *Ehoiai* legitimized colonization by providing mythical and genealogical precedents for the Greeks' activities over-seas, there are no signs of the collective genus of anti-Greek or the polarizing rhetoric which characterized the tragedians' treatment of the non-Greek world. When archaic poetry defines the Greeks' way of life—their adherence to laws, their rituals and sacrifices and strictly defined taboos, their patriarchal social structure—it is not in contrast with the discrepant mores of non-Greek heroes, but with the anarchy and violence, sacrilege and gynaecocracy of the 'supernatural bar-barians', the Giants, Centaurs, Cyclopes, and Amazons. Most impor-tantly of all, poetry neither on mythical nor contemporary themes is ever concerned with the most important distinction fifth-century literature draws between Greeks and barbarians, the polarity between democracy and despotism. It can hardly be an accident that the emergence of the barbarian and the tragedians' reinterpretation of myth from a radically ethnocentric viewpoint coincide not only with the combined Greek efforts against the Persian empire but also with the consolidation of Athenian democracy and Athenian hegemony in the Aegean.

Inventing Persia

I ENTER THE BARBARIAN

THE story of the invention of the barbarian is the story of the Greeks'
conflict with the Persians, a people who had risen suddenly in the
middle of the sixth century to international prominence. In central
Asia the Babylonians and the Medes had fought for possession of the
ancient Assyrian empire, and had divided it between them by the
beginning of the century. But in 550/49 the power of Media was itself
crushed by Persis, or 'Persia', one of its own dependencies, whose
leader was the ambitious Cyrus. The Persian and Median cultures
fused; the Greeks used the two names interchangeably. In western Asia
the Lydians had been expanding their power base; their conquests
included the Greek cities of Ionia. Persia and Lydia now inevitably
came into conflict, and Persia won. Cyrus took Lydia in 547/6, and
with it became master of the Ionian Greeks. Eight years later he
completed his conquest of Asia by taking Babylon. Thus in a few years
a vassal kingdom had established sovereignty over an area stretching
from the borders of India to the Hellespont.

Cyrus' son Cambyses added Egypt to the empire, but the greatest of
all the Persian kings was Darius I, who took power in 522 after a
mysterious coup,[1] and embarked on a programme of imperial
reorganization and expansion. With the help of Athens and Eretria the
Greek cities of Ionia revolted against him in 499, and sacked Sardis.
The revolt continued until 494, when, after a disastrous sea battle

---

[1] Darius headed a conspiracy which succeeded in killing the incumbent of the Persian
throne. Both Darius himself and Herodotus report that the rightful heir, the true brother of
Cambyses, had died, and an impostor taken his place. This impostor was named 'Gaumāta',
by Darius, 'Smerdis' by Herodotus (3. 61). Whether or not *Persae* line 778 is interpolated,
Aeschylus' version of the events preceding Darius' accession (774-9) is unique in that there
is no suggestion that the man killed by the conspirators, whom the poet calls 'Mardos', was
an impostor; it is important evidence that the 'impostor' theory was invented by Darius to
legitimize his coup. See Dandamaev 1976, part 2, ch. II, especially pp. 108-63, which discuss
Aeschylus' version of the events.

against the Phoenician fleets at Darius' disposal, the great city of Miletus was destroyed. Darius now extended Persian power to Macedonia and demanded submission from Greece.[2] The Persians reached the plain of Marathon in 490 BC, where they were decisively defeated. But ten years later they returned under Xerxes, Darius' son and successor, and managed to subjugate much of Greece, and raze Athens, before being defeated at sea off Salamis and on land at Plataea.

Aeschylus' *Persae*, which celebrates the victories over Persia, is the earliest testimony to the absolute polarization in Greek thought of Hellene and barbarian,[3] which had emerged at some point in response to the increasing threat posed to the Greek-speaking world by the immense Persian empire. Rhetorical examination of the abstract opposition of Hellenism and barbarism of the kind particularly common in Euripides is not to be found in *Persae*:[4] philosophical treatments of the antithesis develop later under the influence of the sophists. But the term *barbaros* itself, never found in extant mainland Greek literature before the Persian wars, is found no fewer than ten times, and the contrast of Hellas with Persia or Greeks with barbarians underlies the rhesis, dialogue, and lyrics. The Ionian geographer Hecataeus had conceived the world as divided into two vast continents, Europe and Asia (the titles of the two books of his *Periegesis*), and the division of human civilization ever after to be symbolized by the Persian wars is established on a geographical plane already in the opening two lines of the play: the *Persians* have gone away to the land of *Hellas* (1–2), a contrast reified by the account of Xerxes' bridging of the two continents (130–2), which are contrasted again at 270–1 and 798–9. The contrast is also personified in the two beautiful women in the queen's dream, one struggling free from Xerxes' bridle, the other

[2] For a discussion of the reasons behind the Persian invasions see Will 1980, pp. 89–94.

[3] Although the Greeks did use the terms *ho barbaros* and *hoi barbaroi* to designate the Persians alone (e.g. Thuc. 1. 82. 1), *barbaros* can refer to the 'whole non-Greek world' already in *Persae* (e.g. 434).

[4] It is this circumstance which has led some scholars, most recently Walser 1984, p. 7, to claim that the term *barbaros* had no pejorative implication until the *middle* of the fifth century: he identifies the *agōn* between Teucer and Agamemnon in *Ajax* as furnishing the earliest example of the word bearing such a connotation (see below, ch. 4. 3). But the contrast of the Hellenic and barbarian character to the detriment of the latter is, as will be shown, already unmistakable in *Persae*. See also Paduano's chapter 'Voce Greca e mondo Persiano' (1978, pp. 15–29).

submissive to it, 'one having obtained as her portion the land of Hellas, the other the land of the barbarians' (186–7).[5]

The conceptualization of the conflict with Persia as a struggle of united and disciplined Greeks against alien violence was one impetus behind the invention of the barbarian. But simultaneous with the appearance of the Persians as a threat looming in the east had been the turn in Athens to democracy. Tyrannies had been widespread in Greek cities during the seventh and sixth centuries; in many cases the tyrants had come to power by supporting the common people in their struggles against the old aristocratic families. But the Lydians and subsequently the Persians had ruled the Asiatic Greek cities through tyrants, a practice which lasted until the fourth century.[6] Tyrants in other Greek cities maintained friendly relations with the Persians, in whose interests it was to oppose the establishment of democracies. And so the tyrants came to be associated with support of Persia. Athens was ruled by a tyrant, Peisistratus, from the middle of the sixth century until his death in 528/7 BC. But under his son Hippias the conflict between tyrant and *dēmos* became acute. Hippias' brother Hipparchus was killed in 514 BC, and Sparta, along with the Alcmaeonid family, who were to introduce democratic reforms, finally deposed Hippias in 510. The new Athenian democracy created a 'myth' around the figures of Harmodius and Aristogeiton, the assassins of Hipparchus, Hippias' brother.[7] Even though Hippias had not actually been deposed until four years after this event, the assassination, commemorated in a famous statue-group by Antenor, came to symbolize the liberation of the *dēmos* from tyranny; Theseus was now adopted as the mythical founder and patron of Athenian democracy, the prototype of the tyrannicides.[8]

The production of such ideas in support of the democracy was not,

---

[5] Some scholars have regarded the two sisters as personifications of the mainland and Asiatic *Greeks* respectively. In order to refute this view, however, there is no need to follow the obscure—and possibly much later—genealogy quoted in the scholion *ad loc*. Keiper 1877, p. 11, is surely right in drawing attention to the 'Darius vase' on which Hellas and Persia are personified by two young women (see below, n. 27). That Aeschylus calls them 'sisters of one race' can be explained by his familiarity with the genealogy also mentioned in Herodotus (7. 61), which makes the Persians descendants of the Greek hero Perseus. See below, section 4b.

[6] See Andrewes 1956, pp. 123–4; de Ste. Croix 1972, pp. 37–40.

[7] See Taylor 1981.

[8] Ibid., pp. 78–134.

however, in itself sufficient to neutralize the threat still posed by Persia. Hippias had stayed in contact with the Persian court, hoping to be reinstated; the Persians brought him to Marathon in 490 BC with precisely this aim in mind. The result in the 480s was that many members of the old Athenian aristocratic families were suspected of harbouring tyrannical aspirations, and therefore accused of colluding with Persia and plotting to overthrow the democracy. Ostraca from this period graphically illustrate the fusion of the concepts 'pro-tyrant' and 'pro-Persian'; Callias son of Cratias, a leading candidate for ostracism in this period, is nicknamed 'the Mede', and on one ostracon is actually caricatured in Persian clothes.[9] And so the defeat of the Persians in 480–79 was conceptualized at Athens not only as a triumphant affirmation of Greek culture and collectivity over alien invaders, but over the demon of tyranny. The 'barbarian' in the most complete sense, the despotic adversary of free Hellenes everywhere, had well and truly been invented.

The further development of the polarization of Greek and barbarian in Athenian art and thought throughout the fifth century, however, needs explanation. The answer lies in the ideology which bound together with ties of collective loyalty the members of the Delian league, the alliance of Ionian, Hellespontine, and island states under Athenian leadership formed in 478/7 against the Persians. Their aim was to push the Persians ever further eastwards and to compensate themselves for the losses they had incurred (Thuc. 1. 96). The 'Persian wars', in effect, lasted for another two decades. But the league under Athenian leadership soon began to look more like an Athenian empire,[10] and when Naxos tried to secede from the alliance in 468 she was violently crushed by Athens and lost her independence (Thuc. 1. 98). In the next decade the league's treasury, into which the allies and dependencies had to pay tribute, was moved to Athens. The Athenians also sought to encourage democracies in the allied or subjugated states;[11] a typical example is the case of Erythrae, which under the

---

[9] Daux 1968, p. 732; Thomsen 1972, pp. 97–8.

[10] There is great controversy both about the Athenians' view of their role in the league from its inception, and about the process of transition from 'alliance' to 'empire'; for a summary of the arguments see Powell 1988, pp. 1–95.

[11] De Ste. Croix 1972, pp. 37–40; 1981, p. 288. There is, however, debate as to whether the Athenians' undoubted preference for democracies in the allied states took the form of *systematic* imposition: for bibliography see Loraux 1986, p. 420 n. 161.

influence of Medizers attempted to secede from the league and install a tyrant sympathetic to Persia; Athens intervened and imposed or reimposed a democratic constitution.[12] This political and economic centralization of numerous previously autonomous Greek states is connected with the upsurge in discourses supporting the ideal not only of democracy but of Panhellenism; the officials appointed to be responsible for the collection of tribute from the league were called the *Hellēnotamiai*, the 'treasurers of the *Greeks*' (Thuc. 1. 96). And the invariable corollary of Panhellenism in Greek thought from this time onwards is the maintenance of the image of an enemy common to all Hellenes, the ethnically other, the anti-Greek, the barbarian.

The notion of the barbarian in his developed form as the 'other', the generically hostile outsider just beyond the gates, appears at a similar stage in the history of other ancient cultures.[13] In Egypt it was certainly the experience of founding an empire which created the sense of a unified Egyptian identity, and its corollary, the barbarians of the periphery.[14] In ancient China the process is even clearer. During the Chou dynasty, which reigned over part of what was to become China for much of the first millennium BC, there was no clear-cut antithesis between Chinese and non-Chinese. There was already a sense that Chou territory was the middle of the universe, but many of the peoples later to be unified into 'China' were regarded as foreign, and alliances were made arbitrarily with Chinese and non-Chinese peoples.[15] The Chou and their neighbours were constantly at war with one another, and had developed no collective identity. But in 221 BC, at a time when the threat presented by barbarians to the north was becoming acute, the Chou dynasty was overthrown by the Ch'in emperor Shih Huang-ti, who then unified all the 'warring states'. The Hsiung-nu, the most powerful of the northern tribes, organized a confederacy against the new empire;[16] Shih Huang-ti's response was to clarify the boundaries

---

[12] Ehrenberg 1973, pp. 229–30; Meiggs 1973, pp. 112–15.

[13] See Diamond 1974, p. 211.

[14] Helck 1964, p. 104. For the Egyptians of the Old Kingdom it was acknowledgement of the ideal of the imperial state's regulated lifestyle, with its unalterable laws and allotment of discrete function to each class, which was thought to bestow not only Egyptian identity but humanity, for they reserved the title 'the people' strictly for themselves. See also Wilson 1956, pp. 110–12.

[15] See Owen Lattimore 1962, p. 337; Bauer 1980, p. 9; Claudius C. Müller 1980, pp. 43, 49, 56–7.

[16] See Rodzinski 1979, p. 48; Loewe 1986, p. 16.

of China and to order the building of the great wall.[17] Radical changes
were undertaken to draw the previously autonomous feudal states into
a huge centralized network; a culture was fostered to bind together the
separate Chinese regions which had been in conflict with one another
for centuries.[18] An absolute distinction now appeared between the
'inner' Chinese agriculturalists and the 'outer' barbarians, nomadic and
pastoral peoples.[19] In the Chou period the word for 'people' (*min*) had
been used for both Chinese and non-Chinese tribes, but now it came
to refer exclusively to the privileged Chinese 'hundred clans'. The distinction between the Chinese and the non-Chinese had acquired for
the first time a political dimension.[20]

The Han dynasty who came to power a few years later developed a
complex administrative machinery which assumed this absolute
distinction between Chinese and non-Chinese. There was a special
bureau for dealing with the barbarians, and maps were drawn showing
which border regions were most at risk from barbarian incursions;[21] an
imperial offensive was launched against the Hsiung-nu. It was at the
court of emperor Wu, who brought the Han empire to its peak at the
beginning of the second century, that the grand historian Ssu-Ma
Ch'ien wrote his *Shih chi*, a monumental history of the Chinese people
(a documentation of the pan-Chinese achievement from earliest times
down to the lifetime of the historian), which bears extraordinary
similarities to Herodotus' history of the Greco-Persian conflict. It
records the conflicts of barbarian peoples with China, and authorizes
their subjection. It also consistently seeks to celebrate Chinese unity
and to define the Chinese character and civilization by contrast with
the mores of the barbarians of the periphery, especially the Hsiung-nu.
In chapter 110 their customs and character are transparently conceived
as the reverse of Han ideals, just as Herodotus' barbarian peoples are
often portrayed as the exact opposite of Greeks.[22] The Chinese prided
themselves on their building skills and their well-run farms; the
Hsiung-nu are therefore nomads who know nothing of walled cities
and agriculture. The Chinese had an almost obsessive reverence for old

---

[17] Rodzinski 1979, p. 48; Bauer 1980, p. 29.
[18] Ibid., p. 29; Bodde 1986, pp. 54–60.
[19] Claudius C. Müller 1980, p. 44.
[20] Ibid., pp. 46, 49.
[21] Bielenstein 1980, pp. 48, 100, 123.
[22] See the translation of ch. 110 of the *Shih chi* in Watson 1961, ii, pp. 155–192,
especially 155–7.

age; the barbarians honour their young and despise their old people. The Chinese were highly literate: the Hsiung-nu cannot write. The Chinese promoted strict conventions of warfare and an ideal of bravery; the barbarians are therefore cowards in battle and indulge in plundering expeditions, for 'this seems to be their inborn nature'. Their only concern is self-advantage, and 'they know nothing of propriety or righteousness'. Just as Herodotus presents Xerxes' invasion of Greece as an act of hubris, the Hsiung-nu's aggression against the Chinese is a symptom of their arrogance, and their defeat a divinely sanctioned triumph of Chinese discipline.[23] A radically new ethnocentrism colours the literature of this period.[24]

The Athenian empire was by no means as unified a system as the pyramidal Chinese bureaucracy, but similar circumstances precipitated the invention of the barbarian as the generically hostile 'other' in Greece and in China. In both cases ethnic self-consciousness and xenophobia were radically heightened as a result both of a particular conflict with an outside people, and of internal political centralization. Although it was the collective action of numerous Greek city-states in the Persian wars which produced the concept of the barbarian, it was the Panhellenic ideology of the Delian league and latterly of the Athenian empire which ensured its preservation.

2 HISTORY INTO MYTH

The form of tragedy is inherently 'Panhellenic', in that its constituent parts were drawn from other poetic genres indigenous to different and widespread Greek communities. Indeed, chapter 1's discussion of the antecedents of the literary barbarian never arrived at Athens, though ranging over much of the archaic Greek-speaking world, for there is no evidence that this city produced any poet of distinction before Solon, and between Solon and Thespis, the traditional founder of tragedy, no poetry emerges that can be recognized as Attic either in dialect or metre. The literary invention and glory of Athens was

[23] The importance attached to beating the Hsiung-nu is shown by the fact that Ssu-ma Ch'ien was himself castrated for defending a general who had surrendered to them! (Watson 1961, ii, p. 4).

[24] For a discussion of barbarians in Chinese historiography and ethnography, including the *Shih chi*, see Claudius C. Müller 1980, pp. 66–75.

tragedy, though no single poetic genre which went into its creation was Attic. The Athenians prided themselves on their openness to external influence (Thuc. 2. 39), and this cosmopolitanism, in conjunction with their sensitivity to the visual arts, facilitated the emergence of the mimetic *enactment* of myth by actors and dancer-singers in a variety of non-Attic metres juxtaposed in a new and unique way. The sixth-century Athenians took Doric choral lyric and Aeolian monody, ritual iambi, trochees, and anapaestic marching songs; by adding to them the subject-matter of heroic and catalogue poetry in hexameters, and the vital element of spectacle, they produced their first truly indigenous literary genre.[25]

This is not the place to confront the problem of the origins of tragic drama; it is important simply to note that by 472 BC, the date of the production of the earliest extant example, Aeschylus' *Persae*, tragedies had been produced at Athenian competitions for at least half a century, and the formal elements (separation of actor and chorus, distinct parodos, episode, stasimon, and kommos, with the deployment of appropriate metrical forms in each) are clearly established. So are the less tangible qualities which mark tragedy off from comedy and satyr-drama, namely a theological frame of reference, elevated tone, and avoidance of the obscene. In form and solemnity *Persae* is a typical tragedy: in content however it is unusual, and raises the question of the nature of the subject-matter deemed appropriate to the genre in the earlier phase. Amongst fifth-century tragedies it forms in conjunction with two lost plays by Phrynichus a group treating not only recent historical events, but specifically events of the wars against Persia, rather than the mythical past (which as tragedy further stabilized became its almost exclusive subject-matter).[26] The Athenians had been involved in the Ionian uprising which had culminated in the catastrophic destruction by the Persians of the great city of Miletus; the execution and enslavement of its inhabitants were commemorated in the first 'historical' tragedy to which there is testimony, and possibly the first ever composed, Phrynichus' *Sack of Miletus*. But the mainland Greeks succeeded in repelling the Persians, and it was their victories

[25] On tragedy's complex fusion of earlier poetic forms see Herington 1985.

[26] It is not until after the fifth century that there is certain testimony again to tragedies on 'historical' events: in the fourth century Theodectas wrote a *Mausolus*, and in the third Moschion is credited with a *Themistocles*. But by this time Themistocles' story must have been approaching the status of myth: see below.

which inspired both Phrynichus' *Phoenissae* (produced probably in 476 with Themistocles himself as choregus)[27] and Aeschylus' *Persae* of 472, which was to an unknown degree imitative of the earlier play (hypoth. Aesch. *Pers*. 1–7). Our knowledge of Phrynichus' two 'historical' tragedies is slight, and it is not clear whether Darius or his commanders actually appeared in *Sack of Miletus*, but either way there must have been considerable reference to the Persians and their Phoenician fleets. After 480 it is even possible that besides an annual commemoration of the repulse of Xerxes at the Eleutheria,[28] there was for a time a regular *dramatic* celebration of the Persian wars at the City Dionysia,[29] of which the only known examples are *Phoenissae* and *Persae*.[30]

The distinction assumed here between 'mythical' and 'historical' subject-matter has not been accepted by all scholars.[31] It is often said that the Greeks recognized no such distinction; the evidence most frequently invoked in support of this claim is the rationalist historian Thucydides' belief in the historicity of the Trojan wars and of Agamemnon's generalship (Thuc. 1. 9).[32] When it comes to the view of historical figures from well beyond living memory the distinction

[27] It has normally been accepted since Bentley that *Phoenissae* formed part of Phrynichus' victorious trilogy of 476, for which Themistocles acted as choregus (Plut. *Them*. 5. 4). The Suda records that there was a play by Phrynichus variously known as *Persae*, *Dikaioi*, or *Sunthōkoi* (Phrynichus fr. 4a); Lloyd-Jones 1966, pp. 23–5, suggests that this play was in the same trilogy as *Phoenissae*. It is possible, however, that the three titles were alternatives for *Phoenissae*, which could have had two choruses, one of Phoenician women, and one of Persian counsellors. See Groeneboom 1960, p. 8 n. 7. For a discussion of whether the 'Darius vase' (Naples 3253; Trendall and Webster 1971, p. 112, no. III. 5, 6) illustrates Phrynichus' *Persae*, see Anti 1952.

[28] On the evidence for this festival see Raubitschek 1960, p. 180.

[29] Gilbert Murray 1940, p. 115. Podlecki 1966, p. 14, goes so far as to approve the suggestion that *Phoenissae* was produced in a ceremony solemnizing Themistocles' restoration of the theatre (see O'Neill 1942).

[30] Another play possibly celebrating at a fairly explicit level the victory over the Persians was Aeschylus' *Oreithyia*, in which Boreas' friendship with Athens was explained by his relationship with the Athenian princess Oreithyia. During the post-war years there is a sudden efflorescence of both literary and artistic testimony to this story: see also Simonides' *Naumachia* (frr. 532–5 *PMG*). Simon 1967, pp. 107–21, argues that *Oreithyia* had some connection with the shrine established for Boreas in gratitude for the storm which helped the Greeks to beat the Persians at Artemisium (Hdt. 7. 189); on the evidence for an annual Athenian ceremony to give thanks to Boreas see Hampe 1967, pp. 11–12. For treatments of the Persian wars in somewhat later poetry see Timotheus' dithyramb *Persae*, Choerilus' epic on the wars, and tr. fr. adesp. 685.

[31] See e.g. Snell 1928, p. 66.

[32] On the Greeks' belief in the historicity of the Trojan war see Gomme 1954, p. 6.

between history and myth indeed becomes invalid.[33] The immolation of Croesus, for example, historically the last king of Lydia in the first half of the sixth century, already took the place of a myth in an ode by Bacchylides and on a famous vase by Myson,[34] 'a rare illustration of a recent historical figure already becoming myth'.[35] Fragments of a hydria by the Leningrad painter suggest that Croesus was also the subject of a *tragedy* in the second quarter of the fifth century, for the scene portrays both a Greek *aulos*-player and a figure which is almost certainly the Lydian king on his pyre, attended by barbarians.[36] But this is not 'historical drama', for his story was for the Athenians of the mid-fifth century indistinguishable from myth; the same goes for the post-fifth century 'Gyges' tragedy a portion of which has been recovered on a papyrus.[37]

The Thucydidean passage, on the other hand, proves nothing as to the nature of the Athenians' memories of the recent struggle during the decades immediately after the Persian wars. Survivors of Marathon

---

[33] The period required for oral history to become 'myth' is usually estimated at two centuries at the very most. See Oswyn Murray 1980, pp. 29–30. On the process by which individual events and historical figures are assimilated to mythical archetypes see Eliade 1955, pp. 37–48.

[34] Bacchylides 3. The Myson vase: ARV^2, p. 238, no. 1.

[35] Boardman 1975, p. 112.

[36] Corinth T 1144 = ARV^2, p. 571, no. 74. When Beazley first published these fragments (Beazley 1955), he suggested that they might be evidence for a 'Croesus' tragedy during the first quarter of the fifth century. The Oriental on what looks like a pyre is portrayed with both a Greek *aulos*-player in attendance, and with other Orientals; one has a clearly shocked or distressed expression. Myson, like Bacchylides, had not presented Croesus as an Oriental, which suggests that if a play does lie behind the hydria fragments, it was the tragedian who 'barbarized' Croesus. Hammond and Moon 1978, pp. 373–4, claim, however, that the picture represents not Croesus but Darius in *Persae* emerging from his tomb. There are two reasons for rejecting this view. (*a*) There are clearly flames emerging from the pyre. (*b*) The delineation of the logs reproduces that in Myson's version of the Croesus story. The Leningrad painter was an early mannerist who could well have been influenced by Myson's work: Beazley regarded Myson as the father of the mannerists.

[37] *Pap. Oxy.* 2382 = tr. fr. adesp. 664. Lobel 1949, in the first edition of the papyrus, argued that the play was early. Page 1951, pp. 27–8, suggested that it formed part of a fifth-century trilogy portraying the history of the Lydian royal family from Gyges to Croesus, or to the fall of Sardis. Later he believed that this theory was confirmed by the fragments of the Croesus vase (Page 1962). Argument raged over the date of the 'Gyges' play, however: was it early or Hellenistic? The picture was even further complicated by the possibility that a tragedy lies behind the Atys episode in Hdt. 1. 35–45, a view more recently attacked by Lesky 1977, p. 228. For further bibliography on this debate see Holzberg 1973, but his conclusion leaves the problem open. Latte's objections to an early date for the Gyges fragment still hold, especially the metrical arguments (1950, p. 138).

may well have 'believed in' the existence of a historical king Agamemnon in the distant past, but this does not mean that the nature of such a belief was indistinguishable from the nature of their memories of the war which occurred in their own lifetime. An Athenian war veteran cannot simply be assumed to have regarded his recollections of the battles with Persia as exact equivalents of the collective 'national' memories of Eliade's *illud tempus*, the primeval time enshrined in the flexible corpus of myth from which the 'here and now' acquired meaning and explanation,[38] and there is no reason why the ability to differentiate between them should be denied to him, even though the criterion of differentiation was not, as the Thucydides passage shows, a question of historical *veracity*, but of recentness, concreteness, autopsy, and, hitherto, appropriateness for artistic representation.

Greek visual arts, like the epics from which most tragic plots were to be drawn, had previously confined themselves almost exclusively to the deeds of gods and legendary heroes, which is proof in itself that the Greeks could distinguish myth from immediate recent history: a yardstick had existed which told them that statues and vases and epic poems were unsuitable vehicles for the celebration of yesterday's local triumphs. But the victory over tyranny—indigenous or alien—for the first time provided subject-matter which was exempt from the usual exclusion, not only for the sculptors and vase painters but also for the tragedians.[39] The suggestion that it was simply because the fate of Persia exemplified the law of hubris/*atē* that it was admitted into the tragic theatre does not constitute an adequate explanation;[40] rather, it was tragedy which lent the story this theological shape. No more convincing is Else's proposal that historical subject-matter would have been used elsewhere by the tragic poets, but that nothing 'pathetic' enough ever happened again.[41] A more plausible view is that during the decade after Salamis there developed a political struggle between Cimon and Themistocles which was expressed in a propaganda battle, the former seeking to emphasize the importance of Marathon (of which his father Miltiades had been the hero) and the latter of Salamis. It has been suggested that each side 'enlisted the help not only of poets, but also of

[38] On myth as 'archaic ontology' see Eliade 1955, p. 35.

[39] Although in the case of all three attested historical tragedies of the period the effect of the physical remoteness of their settings is at least analogous to the effect in other plays of a mythical ambience.   [40] Lembke and Herington 1981, pp. 10–11.

[41] Else 1965, p. 88. This is to push much too far his theory that tragedy originated in the enactment of an heroic *pathos*.

painters and sculptors', in a bid to publicize their own reading of recent events.[42] This view could deal with *Phoenissae* and *Persae*, interpreting both as showpieces designed to rehabilitate Themistocles, whose popularity was waning.[43] But unless propagandist overtones are also to be detected in *Sack of Miletus*,[44] it does not explain why perhaps even before the 490 invasion Phrynichus was free to select as his subject very recent history, a circumstance which points rather to the experimental nature of tragedy in its earlier phase,[45] for even the dismally slight evidence for the tragedies produced before the 470s suggests that the epic cycle, at least, had not yet been canonized as the exclusive appropriate source of the tragedians' subject-matter.[46] It must also be borne in mind that at least two pre-tragic poetic genres, the epinician ode and elegiac poetry such as that of Callinus and Mimnermus, could be used as vehicles for the commemoration of recent military events.

Most illuminating of all, however, are the analogues in the visual arts to Phrynichus' and Aeschylus' exceptional use of historical subject-matter in tragedy. The visual representations of the tyrannicides and of battles against the Persians are similar to the tragedies written commemorating the wars in that they represent exceptions to artistic conventions made permissible precisely because of the importance of the cultural messages being disseminated: order over irrationality, democracy over tyranny, Hellas over barbarism. The tyrant-slayers were commemorated in a famous statue-group by Antenor which was stolen by Xerxes (an action which seemed to symbolize his intention to deprive Athens of her liberty and helped to foster a connection between the tyrannicides and the heroes of Marathon and Salamis);[47] thereafter a replacement group was made

---

[42] Podlecki 1966, p. 13, who recapitulates the view of Amandry 1960, pp. 6–8.

[43] Those who hold this view must assume that Themistocles was choregus for *Phoenissae* (see above, n. 27): the same function was performed for *Persae* by Pericles.

[44] Phrynichus was fined after the production of the play (Hdt. 6. 21): it is unlikely that the anodyne reason Herodotus supplies—that the poet had upset his audience by reminding them of the catastrophe—reveals the whole truth. See Burn 1984, p. 224; Roisman 1988, pp. 19–21.

[45] See Knox 1979, pp. 7–8. *Sack of Miletus* is not firmly dated, but it could have been performed in the late 490s.

[46] Although at least two of Thespis' titles, *Pentheus*, and *The Funeral Games of Pelias*, certainly suggest epic sources. See Lloyd-Jones 1966, p. 13.

[47] Taylor 1981, p. 45, points out that in Herodotus 6. 109 a reason Miltiades gives to Callimachus for fighting at Marathon is that it will present an opportunity to outshine even the tyrannicides.

and placed conspicuously in the agora, the only such sculpture to receive this honour during the fifth century (Dem. 20. 70).[48] The productive dialectic between the images of the 'historical' heroes, Harmodius and Aristogeiton, and their mythical archetype, Theseus, is shown by the way in which his figure appeared on vases in a stance consciously designed to mirror the famous statue.[49] A similar interaction between history and myth is shown in the form taken by the battles against the Persians which now became a popular theme in friezes and on vases, modelled on and parallel to the familiar Amazonomachies, Centauromachies, and Gigantomachies. For the idea of a struggle with a being or beings essentially 'other' was of course not new. It was foreshadowed in archaic poetry and art not by the story of the Trojan war, but by the myths of conflict with the 'supernatural barbarians' of the archaic thought-world, the disorderly tribes on the spatial margins of the heroic world, or individual embodiments of the monstrous or inhuman. The substitution after the Persian wars of foreigners for mythical Amazons and monsters in the antagonistic role in this conceptual framework is materially demonstrated by the simple overlay in the visual arts of Persian details on to the traditional type of the Amazonomachy scene; this process produced a fusion, possessing profound symbolic force, of familiar motif and contemporary observation. The old and familiar mythical conflict was adapted for patriotic ends, thus contributing to the ease with which the new ethnocentric ideology was assimilated.[50]

The story of the Trojan war could now be interpreted as a precursor of recent history, a previous defeat of Asia by Hellas. The drawing of parallels between the conquest of Amazons or Trojans and the recent struggle validated the latter, bestowing upon it the heroic splendour of myth.[51] This process is exemplified by Polygnotus' mural in the Stoa

[48] On both statue-groups see Taylor 1981, pp. 33–50.

[49] Ibid., pp. 78–134. On one extraordinary black-figure amphora of about 500 BC (Bonn, Akademisches Museum 39), the portrayal of the death of Priam is also apparently modelled on the earlier of the two tyrannicide groups. For the first time the king of Troy has turned into a tyrant, and Neoptolemus into Aristogeiton; the Trojan myth is beginning to serve the interests of the new democracy. See Wiencke 1954, p. 298 with plate 58, fig. 17.

[50] Bovon 1963, pp. 597–8.

[51] The Amazonomachy was perhaps first used as a mythical analogue for the Greek victory over Persia on a metope of the Athenian treasury at Delphi, which may have been dedicated after Marathon. On the other hand Boardman 1982, pp. 12–13, suggests that the treasury commemorated the Athenians' 499 expedition in support of the Ionian uprising.

Poikile, painted a few years later, in which the victory at Marathon was portrayed alongside the victories of Theseus and Heracles over the Trojans and Amazons (Paus. 1. 15. 3); the frieze of the temple of Athena Nike on the acropolis was later to portray neither Amazono-machy nor Centauromachy but the battle of Plataea. It is with artistic parallels in mind that the 'historical' tragedies should be approached. Their subject-matter was indeed qualitatively different, but rather than being glaring anomalies in their genre, they formed part of the mythopoeic process by which the Persian wars were commemorated, their story repeatedly recounted and gradually canonized, and the antagonists assimilated to existing mythical types of adversary, heroes against Amazons or Centaurs or Cyclopes, transmuted into Hellenes against Persians together with their subject races, or to use the new generic terminology which had arrived from the east, Hellenes against *barbarians*.

It is simultaneously true, therefore, that the war veteran could distinguish what he had lived through himself from the old stories he had heard recounted, and that the battles of the Persian wars were accepted almost immediately into the visual and tragic artistic media. The 'anomalous' nature of historical tragedy is, however, of much less importance than the dialectical process by which such epoch-making events as the expulsion of the tyrants and the defence of the democracy against Persia acquired stature and theological meaning by being moulded along familiar mythopoeic lines,[52] and by which inter-pretations of the traditional stories—especially of the Trojan war—were in turn profoundly affected by the new *logos* in the Athenian repertoire which told of Marathon and Salamis. An important feature of the latter process was the tragic 'barbarization' of mythical foreigners, which chapters 3 and 4 of this book aim to illustrate, but for the present it is the former on which the discussion must concentrate.

3 HISTORY INTO TRAGEDY

The mythologizing of the Persian wars relied heavily on the moral shape with which Aeschylus invested them and which Herodotus

[52] Eitrem 1928, pp. 14–16, suggests that Aeschylus' interpretation of Xerxes' story was affected by his own *Heliades*, in which Phaethon, the son of Helios, drove his father's chariot from the golden east to the west; his hubris was punished by a fatal crash to earth.

developed: a moral shape based on the fundamental Greek law of human existence, which prescribed that excessive prosperity and satiety lead first to hubris and then to destruction.[53] This ancient theme, made explicit in the archaic Athenian poetry of Solon (frr. 6 and 13. 9–25 *IEG*), is a corner-stone of Aeschylus' theology, especially in *Persae*; the defeat of the Persian imperial army is presented as a historical paradigm of the moral truth that gods cut down the great.[54] The decorous prosperity of Darius' empire, moderated by *sōphrosunē* and wisely governed (see especially 852–903), was not, in Aeschylus' interpretation, guilty of excess or transgression, but against it 'the egregious quality of Xerxes' mad career' stands in stark contrast.[55] It is implied, and was perhaps believed, that in defeat at Salamis not only Xerxes' rule but the entire history of the Persian state had reached its final chapter, for all the world as if the Persians' failure to annex a single people (however influential) to their west could bring the whole vast edifice of their empire crashing down.[56] The impression left by the play is that the wealth of the empire, embodied in the gorgeous robes with which the queen and Darius' ghost had been adorned, has been destroyed as surely as Xerxes' clothes are torn and besmirched with filth.[57] This moral lesson—destruction attends upon hubris—informs the whole play, but is formulated most explicitly in Darius' scene, where he gives the theological explanation for the disaster in terms so distinctively Greek (739–52, 821–31) that it is easy for modern critics to forget that this play is the earliest fully fledged testimony to one of the most important of the Greeks' ideological inventions and one of the most influential in western thought, the culturally other, the anti-Greek, the *barbarian*.

It is universally accepted that the illustration of the moral truth described above is an essential element in *Persae*, but beyond this there is wide dissent regarding the poet's intentions. Critical opinion is

[53] In *Persae* Xerxes' catastrophe is anticipated particularly by the emphasis on the size (*plēthos*) of the Persian empire, Persian wealth, etc., and the theme reappears in Herodotus 7. 49. See Michelini 1982, pp. 86–98.

[54] An idea which reaches its most famous formulation in the mouth of Herodotus' Artabanus (7. 10. 5). Patzer 1962, p. 159, argues that the idea of the gods assisting the self-destruction of transgressors was the *Leitidee* of all early tragedy.

[55] Conacher 1974, p. 163.

[56] For the Greeks' exaggeration of the harm they had inflicted on the Persians see Olmstead 1948, p. 271.

[57] See Thalmann 1980.

divided into two main camps. The first view, commonly held in the nineteenth century and still finding advocates today, holds that the play was primarily designed as a patriotic eulogy, and that it is written from an unashamedly Greek perspective:[58] some critics have even regarded it as failing to be 'truly tragic', on the ground that the genre was an inappropriate vehicle for concentrated praise of the fatherland.[59] Those who agree that the 'patriotic' element is foremost are themselves divided on the primary focus of Aeschylus' encomium: is it the Hellenic character and ideals of freedom, discipline, and moderation,[60] the Athenians' role in the war as opposed to that of the Spartans or other Greek states,[61] or the individual contribution of Themistocles, implying the elevation of Salamis over Marathon?[62] All these variant views are, however, united in recognizing the distinctions drawn between Greek and Persian mores and regarding the theme of hubris and its punishment as inseparable from the evocation of barbarism. In this play at least, the argument runs, Aeschylus implies not that all men are subject to the same human laws, but that the barbarian character, *in contrast* with the free and disciplined Hellene, is luxuriant and materialistic, emotional, impulsive, and despotic, and therefore especially liable to excess and its consequences.

The view held by the majority of recent scholars, however, reinstates the play as a 'true tragedy', sees the inherently Greek theological and moral infrastructure as its key, and regards the portrayal of the Persians as notably sympathetic. This approach may emphasize the contrast between the wise reign of Darius and the irresponsibility of Xerxes,[63] or may determine that the chorus, in representing the unfortunate Persian people, is a collective tragic 'hero' and the centre of attention.[64] Critics who take this line seek to play

[58] See the following commentaries: Blomfield 1818; Prickard 1879, pp. xxviii–xxix; Sidgwick 1903. More recently see Clifton 1963.

[59] Blomfield 1818, p. xii; Gilbert Murray 1939, p. 8.

[60] Kranz 1933, pp. 77–8, writes of Aeschylus: 'Grundgedanke seiner Seele ist und bleibt vielmehr, dass das Hellenische das Freie, zugleich aber auch das Zucht- und Massvolle, das Formende und Begrenzende ist, das Ausserhellenische dagegen das Sklavische, aber zugleich das Masslose, Formen Sprengende . . . die weiche, unterwürfige Art des persischen Volkes und Königs zerbricht an der Härte hellenischer Form und Kraft.'

[61] Richmond Lattimore 1943. See also Goldhill 1988.

[62] Podlecki 1966, ch. II.

[63] Broadhead 1960, pp. xxviii–xxix. See S. Said 1981, pp. 31–6, who emphasizes the extent to which Aeschylus played down Darius' own aggressive policy towards Greece.

[64] Perrotta 1931, p. 55.

down the antithesis between Greek and barbarian, for they agree that
the lesson to be drawn by the drama, even by the contemporary
audience, was primarily a universal one, concerned with all humankind's relations with the gods.[65] Thus the contrast of, for example,
Greek freedom with despotism, is seen only as one of a mere handful of
'incidental motifs' which do not imply any real distinction between the
two peoples;[66] more sophisticated versions of this view may allow
touches of clear oriental colour, but claim that they are either
'transcended by [sc. Aeschylus'] sense of human unity',[67] or even that
they demand the audience's denial of ethnic boundaries dividing
mankind: 'By discouraging provincialism, they would have prompted
the reflection that all men are subject to the same human laws.'[68] One
critic goes a step further, and argues that the spectator must have
associated Persian expansionism with the imperial successes scored by
the Athenians during the 470s, and interprets the play as the poet's
didactic warning to his fellow citizens against breaking the moral law
so disastrously transgressed by Persia.[69]

Scholarly discussions of *Persae* have therefore tended to concentrate
on its theology, or purpose in the contemporary social and political
climate; in such discussions the 'barbarian' element has been mini-
mized or emphasized according to the overall interpretation favoured.
A result has been that even works devoted to the ethnography in the
play[70] have failed to assess the extraordinarily powerful and original
nature of the techniques deployed in the evocation of the foreign
setting and characters.[71] The early tragic poets were breaking new
ground in utilizing every aspect of their medium—spectacle, song,
language, thought, and characterization—in their (pejorative) depiction of the contemporary non-Greek world, but their inventiveness
has been overlooked. This is perhaps understandable. In an era which

[65] See e.g. Vogt 1972, p. 132; de Romilly 1974, p. 16.

[66] Perrotta 1931, p. 54.

[67] This was the conclusion of Moss's Ph.D. dissertation 'Persian Ethnography in
Aeschylus' (1979), quoted from *Dissertation Abstracts*.

[68] Thalmann 1980, pp. 281-2.   [69] Melchinger 1979, p. 36.

[70] Besides Kranz's discussion of *Persae* (1933, pp. 77-98), the most important contribu-
tions on the ethnography of the play have been Keiper 1877, and Gow 1928. Two
unpublished American dissertations which the authors do not wish to be seen may contain
relevant research: Moss 1979, and Georges 1981.

[71] Some scholars (e.g. Vogt 1972) have even argued that the interesting aspect of *Persae* is
the extent to which the Persians are 'Hellenized', rather than orientalized, as if there were
extensive literary precedent for 'barbarian' effects in Greek literature.

must see the fight against racism and nationalism as crucial to the survival of mankind, there may have been a reluctance to spend time on this artistic expression of one of the most unattractive aspects of classical Greek ideology, its arrogant and insistent chauvinism. But the Greek mind will never be understood unless its faults are accepted alongside its virtues, and the remainder of this chapter therefore aims to illustrate the invention of the fifth-century literary barbarian.

First, a word of caution. Aeschylus' *Persae*, from which this inventiveness must be illustrated, was not the first tragedy to experiment with Orientalism. It is known from the hypothesis to *Persae* (4–6) that the prologue of Phrynichus' *Phoenissae* was delivered by a eunuch, who was preparing the seats for a royal council, a 'realistic' touch which would immediately have translated the audience in their imaginations to the east. It is possible that besides *Sack of Miletus* other 'historical' tragedies were produced during this period, which treated the struggle with Persia. It is also conceivable that the means by which mythical foreigners were differentiated from Greeks in tragedy developed before those used by Phrynichus in his historical plays, for he composed tragedies representing mythical Egyptians, Libyans, and possibly Lydians[72] for whom, it might be argued, he first evolved these techniques, only subsequently applying them to his historical Persians and Phoenicians. But two arguments powerfully suggest the contrary. First, unlike the Trojans, Thracians, or Egyptians, the Medes and Persians had no real literary ancestry,[73] and almost certainly no antecedents in heroic hexameter poetry whose portrayal, by supplying the tragedians with the homogeneous milieu and vocabulary of epic, might have prevented them from exploring all the possibilities for ethnography and exoticism born of observation and hearsay; plays about the Persians were automatically receptive to ethnological colour. There is, on the other hand, no reason to suppose that the tragedians, any more than Stesichorus or Pindar or the vase-painters, should independently have abandoned the conventions of epic when it came to the portrayal of non-Greeks culled from that genre. Secondly, no mythical barbarians in tragedy except perhaps Euripides' Phrygian in

[72] In his *Aiguptioi*, *Antaeus*, and *Tantalus*.

[73] It may well have been Cyrus' defeat of Croesus in 547/6 BC which first drew the Greeks' attention to the Medes and the Persians. The *Mēdeios* of Hesiod *Theog.* 1011 seems to be the genealogists' archetypal Mede, and was most likely invented in the latter half of the sixth century. See M. L. West 1966, p. 430. Thereafter there are a few scattered allusions in Greek literature; Ibycus fr. 320 *PMG*, for example, apparently refers to Cyrus.

Orestes are ever so lavishly invested with foreign detail as Aeschylus'
Persians, which implies that the impetus behind the invention of the
stage barbarian was the experience of war against Persia, and therefore
that the techniques of differentiation were created for historical drama
and transferred (in diluted form) by an imaginative leap to the non-
Greek figures of myth, the effectively raceless foreigners of epic, trans-
forming them into barbarians.

Before turning to the text of *Persae* itself, a word must be said about
Aeschylus' sources of information on Persia. There was of course
literary precedent in Phrynichus' historical tragedies for Aeschylus'
Persians, but the younger poet was himself a veteran of the wars, had
seen for himself the enemy forces, and therefore the Persian colour in
the play must owe something to the logographers' principle of autopsy.
For over twenty years the Athenians had been preoccupied with
Persian imperialism, and traditions surrounding the Persians must
have been carried to the Greek mainland by those who had first-hand
information; contact between the two peoples, and availability of
linguistic expertise in Greek cities, are now thought to have been much
more extensive than hitherto.[74] Perhaps Greek deserters and Persian
prisoners-of-war in particular contributed to Aeschylus' knowledge:[75]
Greeks who had actually been to Susa or Persepolis would have had
much to report about the monumental architectural achievements of
the Persian kings.[76] Spoils from the victories were displayed at Athens
as material proof of Greek supremacy over barbarism, and Phoenician
triremes were dedicated at the Isthmus, Sounion, and Salamis (Hdt.
8. 121);[77] it is even possible that timbers from the enemy's fleet were
used in the restoration of the theatre itself early in the 470s.[78]

[74] Lewis (1977 and 1985) has laid to rest once and for all the 'iron curtain' theory. On the
evidence for interpreters and translators in Greek cities during this period (most of them
barbarians with an expertise in Greek rather than the other way round) see Mosley 1971.

[75] Kranz 1933, p. 92.

[76] Indeed, 'Ionian' workmen and nursing mothers have now been identified at
Persepolis (see Cameron 1948, p. 110, no. 15. 6; Hallock 1969, no. 1224), and are known to
have participated in the building of Susa and Pasargadae (Nylander 1970, pp. 14-15, 69-
149). It is highly likely that Persepolis exerted a strong influence on the architecture and art
of the Athenian acropolis: see Lawrence 1951; Root 1985.

[77] On the Persian spoils at Athens and the importance attached to them see Dorothy
Burr Thompson 1956; Hall (forthcoming).

[78] See O'Neill 1942. It has also been speculated that the tent which Xerxes left to
Mardonius (Hdt. 9. 82) was taken to Athens and served as the scenic background for
'historical' tragedies (Broneer 1944).

The source of inspiration and information which may have been the most influential of all is also the most controversial, namely Ionian prose-writing. Comparative ethnography was an interest of the early Ionian philosopher-scientists (see chapter 4. 4), but the two identifiable figures whose works may have been important in forming the Athenians' vision of the Persian empire are the Milesians Hecataeus and Dionysius. The testimony about the latter is so obscure and so frequently confuses him with later historians of the same name that nothing certain can be deduced. Of Hecataeus' geographical *Periegesis* no fragment can incontrovertibly be shown to contain data reduplicated in *Persae*: it is presumably this circumstance which has led certain scholars to overlook such a possibly important source.[79] But it is simply an accident of transmission that the sections of the *Periegesis* dealing with Asia's western coast (1 *FgrH* F 217–68) and the provinces of the Asiatic interior (F 269–99) are so poorly represented; there are, furthermore, certain geographical items mentioned in the Hecataean fragments which do appear in the play.[80] The *Periegesis* was probably composed before the Ionian revolt,[81] allowing at least twenty-five years for knowledge of its contents to penetrate to Athens, and elsewhere in Aeschylus there are several examples of Hecataean influence, admitted even by the more circumspect of scholars.[82] Further indirect evidence that if in this play Aeschylus was not simply converting prose catalogues into poetry[83] he was at least dependent upon them may be drawn from Herodotus 5. 36 where Hecataeus is described in a meeting at Miletus before the Ionian revolt, 'enumerating all the tribes under Darius and showing how great that king's power was . . .':[84] it is difficult not to be reminded of the catalogues of the Persian forces in the parodos of *Persae*. Most scholars therefore assume that Hecataean catalogues of peoples and places lie behind not only the 'map' of Pelasgia in *Supplices*, the beacon-relay in *Agamemnon*,

[79] e.g. Gow 1928; Broadhead 1960; Bernand's discussion of Aeschylus' geography of Asia Minor and Persia does not mention Hecataeus (1985, pp. 55–68).

[80] Mariandynians: *Pers*. 938/Hecataeus 1 *FgrH* F 198. Cissia: *Pers*. 17, 120, etc./F 284. Arabians: *Pers*. 317 (reading *Magos* as the proper name; see Schmitt 1978, pp. 38–9)/F 271.

[81] Lionel Pearson 1939, pp. 26–7.

[82] Jacoby 1912, coll. 2680–1.

[83] Kranz's claim (1933, p. 80).

[84] See Armayor 1978a. He argues that the exotic costumes and weaponry in Herodotus account of the Persian army in bk. 7 can only be drawn from earlier literature (rather than, for example, from the Persepolis reliefs), and that Hecataeus is the likeliest candidate.

and the travelogues of the *Prometheus* plays[85] and of Sophocles' early *Triptolemus* (see frr. 598, 602, 604), but also behind the geography of *Persae*. But can it be argued that Hecataeus' work also influenced the play's portrayal of Persian customs and history?

Such claims rest on unprovable assertions about the nature of Hecataeus' work. The periegesis was a simple literary form, developed out of the handbooks of mariners, which described peoples and places in the order a traveller would arrive at them; the fragments of Hecataeus do not suggest that he attached comments any more extensive or profound than brief aetiological or ethnographic tags. Besides two fragments mentioning clothing (F 284, 287), there is nothing to indicate that Aeschylus' knowledge of Persian customs and administration could have derived from the *Periegesis*.[86] Kranz even believed that many of the proper names of the high-ranking Persians, and the history of the Medo-Persian kings (765–79) also derived from Hecataeus,[87] but his assertion depended on the now discredited belief that the latter's work included a history of eastern peoples, of the Median kings, and of Cyrus.[88] Even more suspect is one scholar's attempt to refer the amplitude of the messenger speech and the view of Persian destiny in the play to the influence of Ionian historical methodology.[89] Nothing can therefore be ascertained other than that Aeschylus perhaps derived some specific place-names from Hecataeus,[90] and was influenced throughout the play by the cataloguing techniques of Ionian logography (themselves the legacy of hexameter poetry).

4 PERSIANS IN THE THEATRE

(a) *Language*

In terms of linguistic differentiation *Persae* marks a milestone in extant Greek literature, for the methods are as varied and the impression as deep as a poet writing about a foreign culture in his own language

---

[85] Bacon's discussion of Aeschylean geography (1961, pp. 45–59) is one of the more successful features of her book.

[86] *Contra*: Lionel Pearson 1939, p. 79.

[87] Kranz 1933, pp. 94–5.

[88] A theory propounded earlier this century. See e.g. Prašek 1904.

[89] Deichgräber 1974, pp. 37–40.

[90] See Drews 1973, p. 14.

could hope to achieve. Aeschylus calls attention to the different sounds made by Greeks and barbarians during the messenger's description of the battle of Salamis, in the paean sung by the Hellenes (393) and their stirring battle-shout, 'sons of the Greeks, liberate your children, women, and fatherland' (402–5), juxtaposed with the confused clamour (*rhothos*) in the Persian tongue which answered it (406). He also describes the Persians' utterances as 'barbarian' in the primary, linguistic sense of the word (e.g. 635). But he predominantly used implicit suggestion and aural effect to create within Greek diction the impression of barbarian speech, especially in the long catalogues of proper names of barbarian places and leaders in the parodos, the messenger's speech, and the kommos (see especially 958–61, 966–72, 993–9), sometimes listed consecutively with no interspersed Greek words to dilute the result. The names of the commanders for the most part do not accord with those in Herodotus, and both their historical authenticity and their etymological possibility in the Iranian language are controversial. Keiper, an Orientalist, concluded that about 75 per cent of them were recognizably Iranian.[91] Kranz thought that beneath all the names lay a historically authentic figure, but that most of them had been disguised in form or considerably Hellenized.[92] Lattimore, on the other hand, while regarding the prosopography of the barbarian leaders as largely fictitious, believed that the majority of Aeschylus' 'invented' warriors bore genuine Iranian proper names.[93] Schmitt's more recent study concludes that the poet had only a small repertoire of Iranian names to hand, and that the names in the parodos (21–51) are much more plausible than those in the *thrēnos* (958–99).[94] There is no doubt that several of the elements in the names of leaders about whom nothing else is known indicate—if they are invented—a sensitivity to the sound of the Iranian language: -*aspes* in Astaspes (22), for example, derives from the Iranian for 'horse', and *Art-* ('the Right') in Artabes the Bactrian at 317 is a Hellenization of a root common in attested Iranian names.[95] The problem of the veracity of Aeschylus' account of the barbarian leaders will, however, probably never be solved, but this need not preclude an appreciation of the extraordinary aural impact

[91] Keiper 1877, pp. 53–114.
[92] Kranz 1933, pp. 90–3.
[93] Richmond Lattimore 1943, pp. 86–7.
[94] Schmitt 1978, pp. 70–1.
[95] Benveniste 1966, pp. 83–5, 97, 101–2, 107, 117.

his cacophonous catalogues must have made on his audience, who were of course neither historians nor comparative philologists; the lists imply both the strangeness of the Persians' language and their superiority in numerical terms.

Section 4e will discuss Aeschylus' translation into Greek poetic diction certain Persian terms, especially 'king of kings' and *chiliarchos*, but he also attempts to imitate specific items of foreign vocabulary without translating them.[96] Darius is twice in one line addressed as *balēn* (658); this is probably a Phrygian word equivalent to *basileus*.[97] He is also named *Dariana* (accusative, 651) and *Darian* (vocative, 672), both of which approximate more nearly to the native Iranian *Dārayava^h uš* than the normal Hellenized 'Dareios' and therefore seem calculated to lend an authentic flavour.[98] The word *baris* occurs at 554 and 1076: at Herodotus 2. 96 this refers to an Egyptian cargo-boat, and so it has been suggested that in describing a Persian or Phoenician trireme it may be pejorative.[99] But the word may just as well have been applicable to any boat which came from a foreign country, for at *IA* 297 the *barides* are Trojan. Perhaps most striking of all is the repeated use in Persian mouths of the term 'Ionians' to denote *all* Greeks (178, 563, 949, 950, 1011, 1025): the evidence of a scholion on Ar. *Ach*. 104, which says that all the Greeks were known [sc. by barbarians] as 'Ionians' has been supported by the appearance in the Persepolis tablets of high-ranking Greek aides known by the ethnic *Yaunā*.[100]

Aeschylus therefore made a concerted effort to suggest the formal language of the Persian court not only by elaborate style of expression but by scattered items of Persian vocabulary. Passionate repetition of words and anaphora are probably also designed to suggest barbarian

---

[96] This section is largely dependent on the studies of foreign vocabulary in *Persae* by Keiper 1877, Kranz 1933, and Schmitt 1978.

[97] Hesychius s.v. *balēn*. On the other hand, it may be connected with the Phoenician Ba'al.

[98] Kranz 1933, p. 86, also points out that Aeschylus' spelling 'Agbatana' (16, 535, 961) corresponds more nearly to the authentic Persian *Ha^m gmatāna* than the usual Hellenization 'Ekbatana'.

[99] Broadhead 1960, p. 147. See also Aesch. *Supp*. 874, where the word occurs in an Egyptian context; for a description of the Egyptian cargo-boats used on the Nile see Lionel Casson 1971, p. 335.

[100] Hallock 1969, nos. 1800. 21–2; 1810. 18–19: see also above n. 76. The term is known to have been used by the Assyrians under Sargon II as early as the eighth century (Bengtson 1954, p. 30). Genesis 10: 2 makes 'Javan' a grandson of Noah.

diction, as are the numerous cries and interjections.[101] Equally remarkable is the high proportion of Ionicisms (eg. 13, 61, 556, 761). These must have lent an eastern atmosphere to the language,[102] even if it is that of eastern *Greek*, 'for Persian authorities, when they had occasion to use Greek for official purposes, employed that dialect which lay nearest to them'.[103] The use of specifically epic words, such as *hippiocharmēs*, *bathuzōnos*, and *toi d'* (29, 155, 424)[104] create the foreign effect by slightly different means: obsolete diction is in this play a substitute for the ethnically alien, and the use of epic language to connote the barbarian *ēthos* consciously associates it with the arrogant boasting behaviour of all epic warriors, for example in the use of the rare form *steuntai* for the vaunting Mysians (49).[105]

(b) *Behaviour*

Although there are no Greek characters in *Persae* there are certain aspects of the Persians' conduct and attitudes which Aeschylus clearly intends to relate to their ethnicity; as the genre developed they were to be canonized as features of barbarian psychology (see below, chapter 3. 5). Examples from the messenger's speech are the cruelty in Xerxes' threat to behead every one of his sea captains (371),[106] the craven fear which gripped all the barbarians on hearing the Greeks singing their

---

[101] Discussed by Scott 1984, p. 153. See especially *ēē*, oi (without *moi* or *egō*), and the recurrent exclamation *oa*, said by Σ *Pers*. 117 to be a 'Persian lament'. This aspect of *Persae* seems to have been particularly distinctive and memorable, for Aristophanes chose to recall the cries made by the chorus at *Ran*. 1028–9. He remembered the lament *iauoi* which the chorus of *Persae* do not utter in the transmitted text, but they do say *iōa* (1070–1). Stanford 1983, p. 163, suggests that Aristophanes 'has deliberately distorted this cry to give a barbaric effect'. The chorus of *Persae* also did some memorable hand-clapping: see *Ran*. 1029.

[102] This point was first fully appreciated by Headlam 1898, pp. 189–90.

[103] Rose 1957–8, i, p. 13.

[104] On the Homericisms in *Persae* see Sideras 1971, pp. 198–200, 212–15. The word *bathuzōnos* is used of the queen (155), and was taken by Gow, following a scholion on *Od*. 3. 154, to be especially appropriate for barbarians (Gow 1928, p. 137 n. 15). If it means 'with deeply receding girdle', implying a generous quantity of fabric, it might be more suitable for describing the voluminous Ionic chiton, in which Persian women are sometimes portrayed, than for the simpler Doric version. But it is used of goddesses in epic, the Homeric hymns, Hesiod, and Pindar, and at Aesch. *Cho*. 169 of any female.

[105] See Michelini 1982, pp. 77–8, 105.

[106] Cook 1985, p. 290 n. 3, expresses reservations about the Greek view that Persians were significantly crueller than themselves; the stories of court intrigues and vicious punishments in Ctesias are highly unreliable.

paean (391),[107] the vulnerability of barbarian might to Greek cunning intelligence, epitomized by the success of the ruse of the false message (355–68), and the barbarians' chaotic flight, contrasted with the Greeks' discipline (374, 422).[108] But the three main flaws in the barbarian psychology selected for repeated emphasis are its hierarchicalism, its immoderate luxuriousness, and its unrestrained emotionalism: all three find correlative virtues, however briefly implied, in the idealization of the egalitarian, austere, and self-disciplined Greek character, and therefore contain more truth about the Greeks' view of themselves than about the Persian temperament. The fawning attitude of the chorus towards the queen, implicitly contrasted with the Athenian ideal of equality and free speech (see 592–3), is suggested by both diction and sentiment in their ornamental and high-flown addresses; they express unequivocal obedience to her and compare her appearance to the light streaming from the eyes of gods (173–4; 150–8). They also bestow an extravagant accumulation of titles on Darius (for example, 556–7), and perform prostration (see below, section 4e).[109]

The high luxury enjoyed by the Persian ruling class which was to become a central tenet of Greek belief about the Asiatic way of life is suggested by the use of certain symbols, items of vocabulary, and even possibly metrical forms, which were to become its standard poetic 'signifiers'.[110] Their fabulous wealth, *ploutos* (see especially 842), rather than the decorous prosperity implied by *olbos*, is established in the opening sentence: the palace is 'rich and golden' (3). Gold is mentioned no fewer than three further times in the parodos alone (9, 45, 53). Even their race is 'born from gold' (79–80),[111] as Aeschylus renders symbolically relevant the genealogy recorded by Herodotus (7. 150), that the Persians were descended from Perseus, who was conceived in a shower of gold. Later the queen leaves her 'golden-doored' palace' (159): when

[107] The contrast of the triumphant paean and *ololugē* with the dismal *thrēnos* is in *Persae* associated with the Greeks and barbarians respectively. Similar contrasts appear in *Septem* and the *Oresteia*: see Haldane 1965, pp. 35–6, and below, ch. 3. 5.

[108] Throughout the messenger's speech the imagery is designed to throw the Greeks' valorous achievements into relief. See Kakridis 1975.

[109] See also Darius' elaborate address to the queen at 704. A wide range of titles and honorifics was conferred on Asiatic kings from earliest times. See Hallo 1957.

[110] The vase-painters used analogous visual symbols to suggest the luxury of the Persian court. See Raeck 1981, p. 152.

[111] Reading *chrusogonou* (see the schol. ad loc.) which fits the interpretation of the queen's dream accepted above.

briefly mentioned, the treasure to be found near Athens, on the other hand, is the *silver* from the mines of Laureion (240). The plentiful supply of precious metals, and the skill in working them characteristic of the peoples under Xerxes' sway, produce repeated references to their military hardware (the Lydians' chariots, the spears of the men of Tmolus and Mysia, the bows of Babylon, the short swords worn by the hordes of Asia, and Xerxes' own Syrian chariot[112] (46–8, 49–52, 55, 56–7, 84)) which create an impression of the clangour of arms, of brilliance and hardness, almost at odds with the cushioned softness of the palace life believed to be enjoyed by the Persian royal family and imperial staff.[113]

Various terms used in *Persae* to evoke the luxury of the Persian court were to become closely associated with the barbarian *ēthos*, especially *chlidē*, 'luxury', 'pomp' (608, see also 544), and the concept of *habrosunē* or *habrotēs*, an untranslatable term combining the senses of 'softness', 'delicacy', and 'lack of restraint'. Although not a Homeric word, the epithet *habros* is found in a Hesiodic fragment in reference to the delicacy of a young woman (fr. 339), and in the archaic period it is parti- cularly common in the Lesbian poets. In respect of women, goddesses, and even eastern gods it is neutral or even complimentary (Sappho frr. 44. 7, 128, 140. 1 *PLF* of Andromache, the Graces, and Adonis respectively), but in connection with men and cities it is from early times pejorative. In *Persae* the number of compound adjectives with *habro-* in the evocation of the Asiatic milieu is quite remarkable, and may have been an important factor in the welding of the concepts of easternness and *habrosunē* (see especially Hdt. 1. 71. 4 and Antiphanes fr. 91 Kock):[114] the Lydians are 'soft' in their lifestyle, the Persian women in their grief and in their laments, and, significantly close to the end of the play, Xerxes addresses the chorus, 'weep, *habrobatai*', describ- ing them as soft or refined in their gait or tread (41, 135, 541, 1073).[115]

---

[112] Probably visualized as *Assyrian* in design. See Broadhead 1960, p. 52.

[113] In reality the Persians were extremely tough and highly trained in the manly arts. Their luxuriousness was undoubtedly exaggerated by the Greeks. See Burn 1984, p. 64, and n. 133 below.

[114] Verdenius 1962 discusses the unusual use of *habrōs* of the *Athenians'* tread at Eur. *Med.* 829–30; see also Bacchylides 18. 1–2. His interpretation rests, however, on the etymological connection of the word with *hēbē* (youth, freshness), which Chantraine (s.v. *habros*) considers improbable.

[115] Bayfield 1904, pp. 162–3, argued that in the last three cases the *habro-* element implies, rather than softness or abandonment, recognizably Asiatic postures and gestures of mourning. On Asiatic dance movements in tragedy see below, ch. 3. 5.

There is a theory in the fourth-century writers Plato and Aristotle, and especially in the *Elements of Harmony* by Aristoxenus, by which different musical modes are credited with distinct ethical qualities: the Dorian was conducive to the Greek virtues of masculinity, *megaloprepeia*, and self-discipline, while the Ionian mode was smooth, soft, and suitable for symposia.[116] The theory was undoubtedly older than Plato, but the loss of the music accompanying tragedy means that it can only be speculated that in *Persae* it reinforced the voluptuous atmosphere created by the language and visual effects, though tragedy was certainly said to be an amazing aural and visual experience (*thaumaston akroama kai theama*, Plut. *de glor. Athen.* 348c).[117] There are, however, clear indications that *metre* and sense were coordinated. The connection of subject-matter and rhythm in Greek poetry is a highly controversial area, but it is just possible that the frequency of the evocation of eastern luxury and abandonment in Ionics *a minore* (vv − −) is no coincidence.[118] This metre is not only used in an eastern context in *Persae*, but in association with the oriental Dionysus of *Bac-*

---

[116] See Plato *Resp.* 3. 398e–400e; Arist. *Pol.* 8. 1342a 32–b 17; Lucian *Harmon.* 1. The best edition of Aristoxenus is still da Rios 1954. On the *ēthos* of the various modes see Michaelides 1978, under 'Aristoxenus', 'Ethos of Harmoniai', and 'Harmoniai', with bibliographies.

[117] It would be pleasant to be able to believe Plutarch's story that Euripides rebuked a chorus member for laughing while the poet was singing in the plaintive Mixolydian mode (*de Audiendo* 46b). The fragments of Damon, a fifth-century figure known to have discussed the educative value of music (on which he is cited by Plato's Socrates), unfortunately yield little information concerning his views on the modes' ethical properties (37 B 1–10 *DK*). But an oration on music preserved on *Hibeh Papyri* 13 (ed. Grenfell and Hunt 1906, pp. 45–8), composed either in the fifth century (perhaps by Hippias), or the early fourth (see Mountford 1929, p. 182), polemicized against Damon or others who held similar views; its discussion of the tragedians' use of the enharmonic scale, allegedly conducive to bravery (col. ii), indicates that tragedy figured large in contemporary debate about music. Pickard-Cambridge 1968, pp. 258–60, assembles other evidence about the music in tragedy. On the papyrus fragment preserving the music for *Orestes* 338–44 see Feaver 1960, and M. L. West 1987, pp. 203–4. For a discussion of what the 'barbarian songs' sometimes referred to in tragedy (e.g. *IT* 180) might have entailed, see Moutsopoulos 1984.

[118] Metrical experts, though rightly sceptical in general about metre/theme correlations, are inclined to accept this one. See Dale 1968, pp. 120–6; Korzeniewski 1968, pp. 116–18. M. L. West 1982, p. 124, points out that some of the cults in which Ionic songs were sung were of Asiatic provenance. Besides Ionics and related Anacreontics there is no tragic metre which can be shown to have any such connotation; dochmiacs, for example, are associated with excitement in both Greek and barbarian contexts. But see the remarks of Lloyd-Jones 1966, pp. 31–2, on the possible significance of the Lesbian greater Asclepiad found in the fragments of Phrynichus but not elsewhere in tragedy.

chae and Aristophanes' *Ranae*.[119] If its connection with the themes of *habrosunē*, refinement, abandonment, or easternness were accepted, then the predominant Ionic rhythm in the parodos of *Persae*, which resurfaces throughout the play, could be thought to work almost subliminally in conjunction with significant words and images to set the eastern atmosphere.[120]

The unrestrained emotionalism of these dramatic Persians is a component of their *habrosunē*, and the great dirge which concludes the tragedy is usually advanced as the primary evidence that Aeschylus presents abandonment to grief as an oriental characteristic.[121] The *thrēnos* has been anticipated by the pictures of Asia's lamentation conjured up by the chorus: the citadel of Cissia, they sing, will echo to the cries of women, tearing their robes (120–5, see also 537–83). The audience has been allowed a photographic glimpse into Xerxes' grief, in the messenger's report that as he witnessed the disaster at Salamis the king ripped his clothes and shrilly screamed (468), but it is his delayed entrance at 908 which marks the beginning of unrelieved lamentation in the form of an extended kommos. Anapaests (909–30) give way to strophic responses shared between Xerxes and the chorus (931–1001), which in turn finally fragment in a climax of despair into single-line antiphony continuing from 1002 to the end of the play. In this section the words come to resemble a wailing *goos*, as recollections of the disaster are superseded by almost undiluted groans, accompanied by weeping, breast-beating, and beard-plucking (1046, 1054, 1056), and culminating in the closing epode distinguished by its unprecedentedly high proportion of metrically integrated cries, *oioi*, *iō*, *iōa*, and *ēē*, producing an effect of near-hysteria.[122] But the formal antiphonal dirge, though eastern in origin,[123] is performed not only by Trojans but also by goddesses in Homer, and in several tragedies by

---

[119] Eur. *Bacch.* 113–14 = 128–9, 144–53; Ar. *Ran.* 324–36 = 340–53. See also Sappho fr. 140 *PLF*. Headlam 1900, p. 108, was the first to see that the subject-matter of these passages might be linked to the metre; Tichelmann's dissertation on Ionics *a minore* (1884) did not discuss their possible thematic associations.

[120] See especially 650–5; 694–6 = 700–2. See Scott 1984, p. 155, who stresses, however, that the predominant metre of the overtly threnodic sections is the iambic.

[121] See e.g. Else 1977, p. 78.

[122] Scott 1984, pp. 156–8.

[123] A fragment from Assurbanipal's library portrays a royal funeral; Jeremias 1900, pp. 9–10, translates the words inscribed upon it, 'Es wehklagten die Gattinen, es antworteten die Freunde.' Nilsson 1911, p. 620 n. 2, deduced that the oriental dirge was the precursor of the Greek antiphonal lament.

Greeks and non-Greeks alike.[124] In tragedy scenes of lamentation mark either the faraway (Persia) or the long ago (the world of heroes), which in many ways overlap.[125] But in *Persae* the dirge, unusually, is performed by men, and is of inordinate length and emotional abandonment; *excessive* mourning practices were considered 'barbaric' and discouraged at Athens (see chapter 1. 5c). It is these features, along with the references to Mariandynian and Mysian styles of mourning (937, 1054),[126] which ensure that the atmosphere created is distinctively 'un-Greek'.

(c) *Ethnography*

The costumes of characters and chorus were probably designed to represent Persian garments.[127] The robes which the chorus describe the Cissian women as tearing (125) are made of *bussos*, a fine linen to whose use by the Persians Herodotus attests (7. 181), and which Pollux claims actually came from India (7. 75). Darius will appear, sing the chorus, in yellow-dyed Persian slippers (*eumarides*) and a tiara, the distinctive turban of the Persian court (660-2). It was made of flexible material and the shape was altered according to the wearer's status. Only kings might wear it upright (Photius s.v. *kurbasia*): 'revealing the crest of your tiara' (661-2) alludes to this. Xerxes' clothes, though tattered and begrimed, were once *poikila esthēmata*, richly patterned or embroidered robes (836): Conacher thinks that the importance attached to fine clothing, and the queen's shame at Xerxes' undignified apparel, are portrayed as Persian characteristics.[128]

[124] See Alexiou 1974, pp. 11-12; Broadhead 1960, appendix 4.

[125] See Hartog 1988, pp. 142-3.

[126] On the famous Mariandynian lament, attested as late as the first century BC, see Alexiou 1974, pp. 58-9 and n. 14.

[127] Throughout this book it is assumed that characters and choruses of barbarian provenance were wearing ethnically differentiated clothing, at least when a tragedian makes explicit reference to it. There is just enough evidence on vases to give an idea of what such barbarian costumes must have looked like. The hydria fragments discussed in n. 36 above, which seem to have portrayed a 'Croesus' tragedy from the earlier part of the fifth century, clearly show Orientals in flapped headgear, heavily patterned tunics and trousers, and beards. Other vases for which a tragic context is probable depict 'mythical' barbarians in distinctive foreign dress, for example Orpheus in a Thracian cloak (*ARV*², p. 574, no. 6), and Laomedon and Hesione in tiaras on the 'Pronomos vase' (*ARV*², p. 1336, no. 1). See Pickard-Cambridge 1968, pp. 182-3, 186-7, 199, with figs. 36, 48, 49. Other vases with barbarians *possibly* closely mirroring scenes from tragedies are discussed as they arise.

[128] Conacher 1974, p. 165 n. 36.

An important cultural distinction in the play is drawn between barbarian and Greek modes of warfare. The Persians are seen as suited by nature to waging war on land, but the Greeks are the pre-eminent sailors, and already in the parodos it is implied that by venturing on to the sea the Persians have tempted fate.[129] Accordingly the picture painted early in the play of Xerxes at the head of a proud army mowing down cities in his path (21–58, 101–5) yields to the evocation of the destruction of his fleet, of barbarians struggling and drowning in the alien element where Greek supremacy had proved invincible.[130] A more emphatic contrast develops between the Persian bow and the Greek spear. In the parodos the chorus anticipates that their king will bring down destruction with the bow on the spear-bearing Hellenes (85), and concludes by pondering whether it was the bow or the spear (i.e. Persia or Hellas) which had emerged victorious from the war (147–9). The contrast is driven home in the dialogue about Athens between the queen and the chorus (237–8), fused with the land/sea polarity (278–9), and underlies the title *toxarchos* later bestowed on Darius (556). Aeschylus may have heard of one of the Persian sculptures (notably that at Behistun) where Darius is portrayed as an archer, and he may actually have seen one of the golden darics introduced by and named after the king, on which his figure is distinguished by a conspicuous bow; the hypothesis that these coins had circulated to Athens is likely, since they were used mainly in the western empire among the Greek communities.[131]

Aeschylus' bow/spear antithesis has been regarded as too simplistic, for of course neither weapon was historically confined to either side.[132] It is true that kings in Persian art are regularly attended by both a spear-carrier and a quiver-bearer, and Darius himself seems to have regarded his spearmanship to be as important as his skills in archery.[133]

---

[129] This interpretation holds regardless of whether the popular transposition of lines 93–100/101–14 is accepted: see 550–3.

[130] And yet at this time the Phoenicians were considerably more skilled in naval warfare than the Greeks, who won at Salamis simply by luring the enemy into the narrow straits. Melchinger 1979, p. 35 and n. 44, proposes that the theme of the sea provided a link with the other plays in the tetralogy, *Phineus*, *Glaucus*, and a satyric *Prometheus*.

[131] Cook 1985, pp. 221–2 and plate 12. 3.

[132] Gow 1928, pp. 156–7.

[133] See the words inscribed on Darius' tomb, in the translation by Kent 1953, p. 140, par. 8h: 'Trained am I both with hands and with feet . . . As a bowman I am a good bowman both afoot and on horseback. As a spearman I am a good spearman both afoot and on horseback.'

In fact the poet did mention in passing the participation in the war of both barbarian spearmen and Greek archers (320, 460). But it is more important to remember that Aeschylus is creating a poetic discourse by which to define the difference between barbarian and Greek, and in the victory of the spear over the bow he is using a conceptual shorthand which enables him to reduce history to accessible symbolic form; this reaches a climax in the attention he draws in the closing scene to Xerxes' quiver, which serves simultaneously as a remnant of his barbarian royal insignia, and as a reminder of his squandered greatness (1017–23).[134]

(d) *Religion*

Olmstead unequivocally stated that the alien Persian religion familiar from Herodotus had previously been portrayed by Aeschylus.[135] Orientalists have continually debated the nature of Persian religion during this period, a synthesis of the old Indo-Iranian Ahuric beliefs of the Median and Persian tribesmen, and the revolutionary dualistic doctrines propounded in the second millennium by the prophet Zarathustra (Hellenized as Zoroaster) which had gradually filtered through from eastern Iran.[136] Most are now agreed, however, that this process of assimilation was largely completed by the sixth century BC, and that the religion of the Achaemenid dynasty from Cyrus onwards was at least predominantly Zoroastrian. But however much the earlier Greek philosophers in Asia Minor may have been influenced by Zoroastrian concepts,[137] the mainland Greeks, at least, understood little about them. Neither Zoroaster nor Oromazes (the Hellenized form of Ahuramazda, the supreme god of the Persians) is named in Greek texts until considerably later, and any allegations that Aeschylus includes details about the Persians' religion which mark it off from Greek practice must be treated with caution, especially since the implication of religious differences between Greeks and barbarians is in tragedy a rarity (see below chapters 3. 7 and 4. 4). The text of *Persae* has, however, been ransacked by scholars who believe that Aeschylus

---

[134] Bacon 1961, p. 3.
[135] Olmstead 1948, p. 199 n. 12; p. 232.
[136] On this process see Boyce 1982, pp. 14–48.
[137] M. L. West 1971; Boyce 1982, pp. 153–61.

was attempting to portray Persian religion. Their observations have centred on four main features.

The first aspect of the play which has been thought to reveal Zoroastrian doctrine is its supposed emphasis on the sanctity of the elements. Herodotus observes that the Persians worshipped the sun, moon, earth, fire, water, and wind (1. 131), and his information is confirmed in the Zoroastrian texts, especially in the list of day dedications in the Zoroastrian calendar probably consolidated by Artaxerxes II and preserved in the 16th *Yasna*, which includes, after days dedicated to Ahuramazda and his Aməša Spəntas ('Bountiful Immortals'), Fire, the Waters, sun, moon, and wind divinities.[138] In the queen's dream an eagle, representing Xerxes/Persia,[139] is pursued by a hawk to the hearth of Apollo (205-9), but there is no reason to suppose that the hearth was identified by Aeschylus' audience as the Persian fire-altar of either Mithra or Ahuramazda.[140] Apollo was identified with Helios by the time of Euripides' *Phaethon*,[141] and there is evidence that Mithra's name was later 'translated' as Apollo or Helios.[142] But Apollo is an eminently suitable god from a *Greek* point of view to appear in this prophetic context, and an omen in the *Odyssey*, on which the passage seems to be partially dependent, entails the pursuit of a dove specifically described as the messenger of Apollo (15. 525-8).[143] It is not necessary, therefore, to infer that Apollo in the tragedy signifies Mithra, any more than to identify the Zeus of the play with Ahuramazda; Herodotus, who had lived at much closer quarters with the Persians than Aeschylus, was convinced that Mithra was a female deity, equivalent to Aphrodite (1. 131)![144]

It has been thought that the respect shown towards the earth and sky by members of the Persian army in Thrace (499) is a sign of recognizably Persian religion.[145] But both Gaia and Ouranos were

[138] Boyce 1982, pp. 245-6. *Yasna* 16 is published in English translation in *SBE* xxxi.

[139] The eagle was falsely believed by the Greeks to be the emblem of Persian royalty. See Xen. *Cyr.* 7. 1. 4, and Gow 1928, pp. 138-40.

[140] Suggested by e.g. Stanley (cited by Broadhead 1960, pp. 82-3), and Rose 1957-8, i, p. 106.

[141] See below, ch. 3. 7.

[142] Boyce 1982, pp. 226-7.

[143] Sideras 1971, p. 199.

[144] The name *Mētrogathēs* at *Pers.* 43 may be meant to be a theophoric, and could have arisen from a confusion of Mithra with the Phrygian Mother goddess. See Schmitt 1978, pp. 63-4.

[145] See von Wilamowitz-Moellendorff 1914a, p. 152.

Greek divinities, invoked elsewhere in tragedy (Eur. *Med.* 148), and
even those willing to find evidence of Persian religion in *Persae* have
usually admitted that the practice here referred to is unexceptional.[146]
The descriptions of the river Strymon as 'sacred' (*hagnos*, 497) and the
sea as 'undefiled' (*amiantos*, 578) have both been thought to suggest the
Persians' reverence for water, represented by the Apas, the 'yazatas'
(divine beings) of that element.[147] But the epithet *hagnos* is found both
in Pindar and elsewhere in tragedy applied to rivers in entirely Greek
contexts (*Isthm.* 6. 74, of the Dirke; Aesch. *Supp.* 254-5 in the Greek
Pelasgus' mouth, of the Strymon; see also *PV* 434), and Zoroastrians
actually regarded sea-water as 'sweet water tainted by the assault of the
Hostile Spirit'[148] (Ahriman, the divinity who opposes Ahuramazda in
the dualistic Zoroastrian belief-system). The epithet *amiantos* should
therefore probably be referred to the *Greek* belief that sea-water could
wash away pollution (see *IT* 1193).[149] None of the alleged evidence for
Aeschylus' presentation of Persian belief in the sanctity of the elements
therefore stands up to examination.

The second aspect of the play's theology which has been supposed
to reflect Zoroastrian ideas is the recurrence of references to a *daimōn*
of malevolent intent towards the Persians (345, 472, 515-16, 725, 911).
Sole saw in these a clear poetic appropriation of the army of evil spirits
led by Ahriman (the principle of evil in Zoroastrian religion),
described, for example, in the *Vendidad*.[150] By pointing to this Persian
belief, she argued, Aeschylus is demonstrating the superiority of the
ethical aspect of Greek religion in accordance with the play's patriotic
tendency. But the belief in the malevolent activity of *daimones* was
common enough in Greek religious thought, especially when accompanied by the indefinite *tis* as often in *Persae* (345, 724, 725), and seems
to be interchangeable with the frequent Greek formulations *theos*, *theos
tis*, or troubles which come *ek theōn* (see *Pers.* 598-604).[151] This is not to
underestimate the effect of the accumulation of passages in the play by

---

[146] Keiper 1877, p. 10; Gow 1928, p. 142.

[147] Kranz 1933, p. 86; Headlam 1902, pp. 55-6, after Hermann.

[148] Boyce 1982, p. 166. This explains Xerxes' famous lashing of the waters of the
Hellespont in Hdt. 7. 35.

[149] Blomfield 1818, p. 165. See Parker's remarks on the cathartic properties of seawater
in Greek religious belief (1983, pp. 226-7).

[150] Sole 1946. The *Vendidad* is translated in *SBE* iv.

[151] Broadhead 1960, pp. 116-17. Popular religious thought often attributed failures or
disasters to the workings of *daimones*: see Mikalson 1983, pp. 19, 59-60.

which Aeschylus implies that divine intervention had time and again proved detrimental to the Persians, but rather than reflecting Zoroastrian belief, it is part of the process by which the Persian defeat was theologically explained in *Greek* terms, for it is the *daimones* who effect the *atē* concomitant upon Xerxes' excess and transgression; on one occasion the *daimōn* is, significantly, said to be an 'avenger' (354).

Gow also finds Ahriman in the *thrēnos* (950–4), where Xerxes laments that 'the embattled array of Ionian ships, turning the tide of battle, robbed us [of our men], ravaging the dark surface of the sea (*nuchian plaka*) and the ill-starred shore' (*dusdaimona t' aktan*). Zoroaster distinguishes Ahuramazda and Ahriman at Plut. *de Is. et Os.* 369e, and the latter is associated with darkness (*skotos*); Gow therefore argues that the adjective *nuchian* is connected with the idea of a malevolent *daimōn* in *dusdaimona*, and signifies 'pertaining to Ahriman'.[152] But there is a sound parallel to the expression in the mouth of a Greek chorus at *Medea* 211 (*hala nuchion*) and it is therefore difficult to accept that in this passage the poet is doing anything more than expanding the play's images of light and dark, which point up Greek victory and Persian defeat respectively.[153]

Thirdly, it has been argued that the raising of Darius' ghost would have had a distinctively 'oriental' significance for Aeschylus' audience. There is no need to linger on Headlam's comparison of the queen's sacrificial offering with the Persian water sacrifice mentioned by Strabo (15. 3. 14).[154] In the list of materials she has gathered for her offering—milk, honey, water, wine, oil, and flowers (609–18)—there is absolutely nothing not typical of Greek offerings of the period, indeed of Greek offerings to the dead.[155] The song she then tells the chorus to take up in invocation of her husband's spirit is in technical terms an orthodox *humnos anaklētikos*, and is as nearly so described by her as the poetic diction permits (620–1).[156] But the anacletic hymn which follows (623–80) has been adduced as evidence that in *Persae* Aeschylus represented specifically Persian magic ritual. Headlam argued that necromancy was always performed with the aid of magic powers (cf. Circe's instructions in the *Odyssey*), in later literature especially

[152] Gow 1928, p. 155.
[153] Kakridis 1975.
[154] Headlam 1902, p. 54.
[155] Rose 1950, p. 263; Burkert 1985a, p. 194.
[156] Rose 1950, pp. 263–4.

through *magoi* who originally derived their name from the Persian
Magoi, members of a Median tribe who in ancient Iran formed an
important priestly caste.[157] In *Persae*, he deduced, the chorus are
'supposed to be endowed with the *magic* functions of Persian magi'
which they deploy in the evocation of Darius.[158] He claimed therefore
that between 632 and 633 the chorus uttered spells in unintelligible
jargon which have not been preserved: the reference to 'clear cries in
barbarian tongue' at 635 he unnecessarily altered to read *barbar'
asaphēnē*, mumbo-jumbo of the kind now familiar from the magical
papyri. But his whole thesis rests on an untenable distinction between
magic and ritual, and inferences from much later sources (especially
the necromancer Mithrobarzanes in Lucian's *Menippus*); it was quite
rightly suspected by Eitrem and refuted by Lawson, who showed that
the chorus are not magi, their utterances are genuine prayers, and that
there is no reason to assume that appeals to the dead of this kind were
in any respect 'not Greek'.[159]

Even the idea of raising a ghost cannot in itself have been alien to
Greek religious sensibilities: besides the literary evidence of the nekyia
in the *Odyssey*, the kommos in *Choephoroe*, Aeschylus' *Psychagogi* (see
fr. 273a), and the story of the appearance of Melissa's ghost to
Periander's messengers at the oracle of the dead in Thesprotia (Hdt.
5. 92), there is now archaeological evidence from the Nekyomanteion
which dates from the third century BC but was built on the same site as
the much older chthonic cult.[160] The libations and sacrifices performed there for the dead seem closely to have paralleled Odysseus'
rituals in *Odyssey* 10. Necromancy could hardly have been seen as an
identifiably Persian affair: that Darius actually appears, unlike
Agamemnon in *Choephoroe*, can be explained in dramaturgical
terms.[161]

There may, however, be a difference between the status of Darius
and that of the dead Agamemnon in *Choephoroe*, for it has been argued

---

[157] For the magoi see Boyce 1982, *passim*; below, ch. 4. 5 with n. 107.

[158] Headlam 1902, p. 55.

[159] Eitrem 1928, pp. 6, 10; Lawson 1934.

[160] For a summary of the excavations, discussion of the ghost-raising rituals, and further
bibliography, see Dakaris 1963, pp. 51–4.

[161] Alexanderson 1967 shows that Darius' appearance is dictated by the need for an
adviser to point out the theological significance of the disaster, for Aeschylus to dwell on
certain aspects of the enterprise which have not yet been covered, and for the revelation of
oracles, especially concerning Plataea.

that Aeschylus presented his Persians as believing in the divinity of
their kings. Olmstead, for example, writes that in *Persae* the queen 'is a
wife of the Persian god and also mother of a god . . . When dead, her
husband rules the underworld gods; no clearer proof could be found
that the Persians had adopted king worship from their predecessors.'[162]
The popular view that the Persians worshipped their kings rests,
however, almost entirely on the evidence of *Persae* and is incorrect.
Darius undoubtedly used propaganda to imply that his sovereignty
was divinely *sanctioned*, by suggesting an analogy between his own
kingship, aided by his six noble conspirators, and the divine order of
Ahuramazda and his six great Aməša Spəntas.[163] But nowhere in the
Persian texts is there any evidence that the Persian kings were regarded
as divine or worshipped as such.[164] If in *Persae* Aeschylus implies that
the king was thought by his subjects to be a god, the view he presents is
therefore incorrect, and probably to be explained by Greek misunderstanding of the outsize figures of the kings of Persian art in comparison
with those of their subjects, and the elaborate gestures of obeisance,
especially proskynesis, performed before them, which the Greeks
confused with their own ritual genuflections before the images of gods
(see below). Gorgias called Xerxes 'the Persians' Zeus' (82 B 5a *DK*),
which, if not merely rhetorical hyperbole, might suggest that the
Greeks wrongly believed that the Persian kings encouraged ruler-cult,
or even wilfully misrepresented them as so doing. But what is the
evidence that Aeschylus suffered from or encouraged this misappre-
hension?

At 74–5 Xerxes drives his 'divine flock' (*poimanorion theion*) of men
through every land, and Kranz understood this to mean that Xerxes is
himself a god.[165] But the words are describing *in epic style* a magnifi-
cent army.[166] Nor is the description of Darius as a *daimōn* (620, 642)
evidence for king-worship in *Persae*: in Euripides' *Alcestis* the heroine
after death becomes a *makaira daimōn* (1003). More plausibly, Kranz
and Olmstead cite the words addressed by the chorus to the queen
(157–8): 'you are wife of the Persians' god (*theou*) and mother of a god,
if some ancient *daimōn* has not withdrawn favour from the army'.[167]

[162] Olmstead 1948, p. 270.
[163] Boyce 1982, pp. 91–3.
[164] Cook 1985, p. 225; Duchesne-Guillemin 1979.
[165] Kranz 1933, p. 87.
[166] See above, n. 104.   [167] Kranz 1933, p. 87; Olmstead 1948, p. 270.

Broadhead tries to explain away the uses of the word 'god' here by claiming that in neither instance, of Darius *or* Xerxes, is it to be taken literally.[168] But on no other occasion in extant fifth-century tragedy is any king called *theos* (though see *Rhesus* 385-7 for a dangerously hubristic comparison of the hero with Ares), and it must have jarred badly on democratic Athenian ears. Gow therefore suggested that the implication is that the Persian kings were deified when they died.[169] According to his argument, the chorus are saying that the queen was born to be the wife of a god, Darius, and to be the mother of a god, Xerxes, *provided that* some daemon has not reversed the fortunes of the army: Darius ruled successfully, is dead and undoubtedly divine, while Xerxes' divinity is not a foregone conclusion and is dependent on the successful accomplishment of his imperial mission as heir to Cyrus and Darius. This interpretation, though along the right lines, scarcely does justice to the ambiguity of the language used in evocation of the Persian kings' status during their lifetimes; the wording of the queen's address to Darius' ghost at 711 is also highly ambivalent: she says that while alive he had lived an enviable life either '*like* a god', or '*as* a god'. This ambiguous use of language underlines the charisma surrounding the living Persian kings, although leaving their exact status—neither mortal nor certainly immortal—significantly inexplicit. But the dead Darius' divinity is unequivocal: he is the 'Susa-born god of the Persians' (643).

The question is therefore whether the posthumous deification of a king in tragedy would have struck Aeschylus' audience as distinctively Persian. Calmeyer, an Iranologist, has argued that rituals depicted on tombs of royalty at Persepolis and elsewhere indicate that although Persian kings were not worshipped during their lifetimes, when dead they received a formal cult.[170] He concludes that in setting his play before the tomb of Darius Aeschylus reveals knowledge of this Persian religious practice: 'The deified king comes out of the nether world and prophesies to and gives advice to the queen. So even Aeschylus ... already knew precisely what the tomb of an Achaemenid king was: a place to visit the dead monarch, to venerate him, and speak with

[168] Broadhead 1960, p. 69.

[169] Gow 1928, p. 136.

[170] Calmeyer 1975. Polyaenus 4. 2 indicates that there was a ritual of homage performed for the dead Alexander the Great, who as conqueror of Persia had inherited the title 'king of kings'. See further Badian 1981.

him'.[171] There is admittedly plenty of evidence that the Greeks honoured their forefathers with prayers, libations, sacrifices, and even special festivals of the dead, at which, it was believed, they might return from the underworld and haunt the city.[172] But the references made in *Persae* to the dead Darius' divinity imply that while there is little evidence for evocation of Zoroastrian element-worship, belief in hostile spirits, Magian sorcery, or even ruler-cult, Aeschylus may have been trying to suggest the ritual honours paid to the Persian kings after death. There is no parallel in tragedy for any king, living or dead, being described as a *theos*.

(e) Politics

If the differentiation in terms of the Persians' religion is slight and ambiguous, the characterization of their empire and political psychology is pervasive and explicit. The empire inherited from Darius by Xerxes was of almost inconceivable size, ranging from Sogdiana in central Asia to Ethiopia, and from Sardis to the Indus:[173] the tour of the imperial lands in the parodos (33–58) reveals an accurate assessment of the extent of the dominions. Only three and a half lines are however devoted to the whole of the eastern empire (52–5), which probably indicates that Aeschylus knew little about it except the name Babylon itself. The empire required a fast and efficient courier-system, the *angareion* (Persian loan-word) described at Herodotus 8. 98; the chorus' statement that neither messenger nor horseman has arrived with news (14) suggests that Aeschylus knew of this system, since the normal tragic messenger arrives on foot, a suspicion perhaps corroborated by his actual use of the word *angaros* in reference to the beacon fires in *Agamemnon* (282). The messenger who begins speaking at 249 is not mounted, but the pointed description of his gait as that of a Persian (*dramēma phōtos Persikon*, 247) implies that the poet was at least aware of the importance the Persians attached to the speed of their couriers. Aeschylus' topography of the royal cities is, however, weak: Darius' tomb is incorrectly sited, for the play is set in Susa, whereas Darius was buried at Persepolis.[174] Cissia and Susa, moreover, were not separate

---

[171] Calmeyer 1975, p. 242.

[172] See Hdt. 4. 26; Jacoby 1944a; Mikalson 1983, pp. 96–7; Burkert 1985a, p. 194.

[173] See Kent 1953, pp. 186–7.

[174] There is no need to dwell on the attempt of Sakalis 1984, p. 64, to argue that the play is actually set at Persepolis, nor on Kierdorf's suggestion (1966, p. 52) that Aeschylus knew that Darius' grave was in Persepolis but for dramatic reasons removed it to Susa.

places (16–17): the former was the district within which the latter was situated (Hdt. 5. 49).

An imperial administration requires legislation; under Darius, the chorus sing, his people enjoyed among other blessings strong armies and *nomismata purgina* (858–60), an expression commonly emended, or interpreted as meaning 'a system of laws firm and protective as towers'. But there is no satisfactory parallel for this meaning of *purginos*, which makes it more likely that Aeschylus is referring to the laws which the Persian kings had inscribed conspicuously on the bases of towers erected at their palace doors and city gates.[175] The kings named their close advisers by an Iranian term meaning 'the Faithful' (Hdt. 1. 108, Xen. *Anab*. 1. 5. 15), and so Aeschylus' chorus of counsellors, in describing themselves at the opening of the play as the *pista* ('the faithful', 2)[176] are at least as ethnographically plausible as the eunuch who delivered the prologue of Phrynichus' *Phoenissae*.[177] Aeschylus also seems to have heard the popular rumour—which was probably untrue—that the king's particularly trusted confidants were called his 'Eyes' (987, or 'Ears').[178] The army was divided into units in multiples of ten (Hdt. 7. 81), and accordingly Aeschylus uses titles (unheard of elsewhere in tragedy) for the barbarian officers such as *chiliarchos* (304) and *muriontarchos* (314, see also 302, 993), thought to be translations of the Persian *hazārapatiš* and **baivarpatiš*.[179] The title *hupochoi* in the parodos (24) almost certainly refers to the satraps, the powerful

---

[175] Rogers 1903. Darius recognized the importance of codified law and was concerned to get the regulations written down, especially in the socially advanced provinces such as the Greek cities: see Cook 1985, p. 221.

[176] See also 171, 441–4, 681 (*pista pistōn*, 'faithful of the faithful').

[177] It is, however, unlikely that *skēptouchia* ('royal command') at *Pers*. 297 has any reference to the royal eunuchs, as has been alleged. See Broadhead 1960, p. 106. On eunuchs see below, ch. 3. 8.

[178] While the office of King's Eye is nowhere attested in the Persian texts, there is some evidence that the Old Persian for 'King's Ear' was **gaušaka*: see Eilers 1940, pp. 22–3. But this claim has been disputed, for the term can only be derived from a posited Persian word via an Aramaic papyrus. It is quite possible that Xen. *Cyr*. 8. 2. 10–12 holds the truth: Xenophon argues that the king only had 'eyes' and 'ears' in a metaphorical sense, i.e. that many people were looking out for his interests. Hirsch 1985, pp. 101–39, discusses in detail the Greek notion that the king had officials called Eyes and Ears, and concludes that this was a fiction derived from the Persians' own concept of Mithra, the god of 'a thousand ears ... ten thousand eyes ... with full knowledge, strong, sleepless, and ever awake' (*Yašt* 10, translated in *SBE* xxiii, p. 121).

[179] See Schmitt 1978, p. 20. There is controversy about the extent of the chiliarch's responsibilities: see Lewis 1977, pp. 17–18.

governors of the Persian provinces, especially since those listed immediately before are Persian (rather than, for example, Lydian or Egyptian) commanders.[180] The expression 'great king of kings', used first here in extant Greek literature, is itself known to be a Greek translation of a Persian title.[181] Indeed, several passages reflect the Greeks' fascination with the protocol of the Persian court, especially in the quasi-religious respect paid to the members of the royal family. The queen, for example, is once reverentially apostrophized as 'mother' (*mētēr*, 215), rather than the standard 'woman' (*gunai*).[182] It has often been observed that Aeschylus overlooks the fact that Xerxes left Artabanus in charge of governing the empire in 480 (Hdt. 7. 52). This may simply be because it was a 'law' of Greek ethnography that the more barbarian a community the more powerful its women (see below, chapter 5. 1).[183] But it is just possible that he was aware of the influential role (by Greek standards) royal Persian females really did hold in the life of the court; evidence on cuneiform tablets shows that they held extensive property of their own.[184] Xerxes' mother is however not named in the play.[185]

The queen made her first entrance at 150–8 in splendour, and on a chariot (see 607–9): Xerxes almost certainly arrived in the same kind of vehicle at 908, his pathetic appearance posing a brutal contrast with the pomp implied by his conveyance.[186] These chariots are normally

[180] The word *satrapēs*, the Hellenized form of the Iranian *xšaçapāvā*, is not attested until the beginning of the fourth century. Herodotus and Thucydides use *huparchos*.

[181] See Schmitt 1978, p. 19; the Old Persian title was *xšāyaθiya xšāyaθiyānām*. It had Assyrian and Median antecedents: see Frye 1964, pp. 34–46. See also Dindorf's emendation *despota despotan* at 666.

[182] Darius is addressed as 'father' by the chorus at 663. In Timotheus' *Persae* when a barbarian supplicates a Greek, he calls him 'father' (fr. 791. 154 *PMG*). From Sumero-Akkadian times Asiatic kings could be addressed in this way: see Hallo 1957, pp. 127–8.

[183] The role of oriental queens and princesses exerted a fascination over the Greeks, later fed by the lurid stories of harem intrigue in Ctesias, who as a source has at last been thoroughly discredited. See Sancisi-Weerdenburg 1983.

[184] Especially Artystone and Parysatis, consorts of Darius I and Darius II respectively. For Artystone's various economic transactions see Hallock 1969, nos. 1236, 1454, 1795, 1835–9.

[185] Atossa has surprisingly not turned up in the Persian texts. She is not named in the play, and therefore her name in the list of characters is probably a later import from Herodotus or the scholia. On the queen's role in the play see Kierdorf 1966, pp. 62–6, and the remarks of Edward Said 1978, p. 57, about the way that Aeschylus makes defeated, distant Asia 'speak in the person of the aged Persian queen' in his celebration of Greek (male) victory.

[186] Taplin 1977, p. 123, argues that Xerxes arrived on foot, but the text indicates the contrary (1001).

identified with the *harmamaxa*, an Asiatic wheeled tent with awnings
used by Xerxes on his journey from Sardis to Greece (Hdt. 7. 41),
which was at least in Aristophanes' day regarded as extravagantly
luxurious and effeminate (*Ach*. 69–70). But Taplin argues that chariot
entrances were common enough in the early theatre. Further emphasis
should probably be placed on his passing observation that they were
especially suitable for *oriental* royalty:[187] all the other firm examples in
fifth-century tragedy pertain either to a barbarian character or to one
of the 'barbaric Greeks' to be discussed in chapter 5, Greeks portrayed
as lapsing into the excessive luxury or despotism appropriate only to
barbarians—Agamemnon in *Agamemnon*, Clytaemnestra in Euripides'
Electra, and so on. Entrance on a chariot may have been one of the
Aeschylean complex of dramatic 'danger signals', the significant
vocabulary and symbolic acts by which the other tragedians also
learned unmistakably to connote the 'otherness' of the barbarian
character.

An aspect of Persian court behaviour vividly exploited by the poet is
the practice of proskynesis, low bowing or prostration before a social
superior. The composite verb *proskunein* is not found in Greek sources
before the Persian wars; it is probable that since the Greeks genuflected
before the images of gods (see *PV* 936, Soph. *Phil*. 776, Ar. *Plut*. 771),
when they encountered the Persian act of obeisance towards mortal
superiors, the two gestures were identified.[188] It is from Herodotus'
story of Sperchias and Bulis, Spartan emissaries at the court of Xerxes,
that the Greek attitude to the Persian custom emerges most clearly
(7. 136):

As soon as they arrived at Susa and entered the presence of the king, the royal
guards ordered them to fall to the floor and *proskunein* before the king, and
tried to force them to do so; but they said they never would, even if the guards
should press their heads down. Where they came from, they said, it was not
customary to *proskunein* before a mortal, and it was not for this that they had
come.

[187] Taplin 1977, pp. 76–8.

[188] Horst 1932, pp. 20–1, 44–91. See also Schnabel 1923–5, pp. 118–20. The Persians
inherited proskynesis from the Babylonians: see Duchesne-Guillemin 1979, p. 381. There
is now a large literature on this topic, for which see Frye 1972, p. 103 n. 2. There are only
two tragic references to proskynesis before mortals in *Greek* contexts: (1) *OT* 327. The
recipient is Teiresias, and the allusion is explained by his special status as intermediary
between man and Apollo (at 284 he is given the honorific *anax*). (2) Clytaemnestra's
prostration in *Agamemnon*, for which see below, ch. 5. 1.

There has been controversy as to the exact form the proskynesis took: it has often been taken to signify the full prostration or 'salaam' paralleled on Persian monuments, where a rebellious vassal is represented grovelling before a victorious monarch. But can this be a ceremonial gesture performed every day?[189] Plato calls the full prostration the *proskulisis*, which suggests rolling the body out in the recipient's direction (*Leg.* 10. 887e 3); Plutarch, in a passage which lists the many disgraceful religious practices the Greeks have acquired from the barbarians, distinguishes the proskynesis from the full prostration, the *rhipsis epi prosōpon*, in which the face touched the floor (*de Sup.* 166a). It may well be that the gesture normally took the form of a low bow, perhaps dropping on to one knee, while lowering the head.[190] The messenger in *Persae* tells of a soldier who prayed to the earth and sky, *proskunōn* (499), but the chorus also actually prostrate themselves (or perform a slighter gesture suggestive of prostration) when the queen appears (*prospitnō*, 152), and probably before the ghost of Darius (see 694–6):[191] it is conspicuous that they do not honour in this way the 'failed' king Xerxes.

The inclusion of details about the Persian administration and the overall impression of extravagant protocol add up to much more than a picturesque tableau; they create an antithesis between east and west predicated on differences in political psychology.[192] A crude contrast of Persian monarchy and Greek (i.e. Athenian) democracy was precluded by the poet's desire to contrast within that framework good monarchy under Darius with the irresponsible despotism of Xerxes. But in several passages the intangibly un-Greek ambience created by more subtle means *is* penetrated by explicit political comments; the underlying assumption is that the Persian administration is the exact opposite of the Athenian democratic system. There is no doubt, for example, that the despotic attitude of Persian royalty towards its subjects is to be inferred from the queen's assertion that her son, whatever his failures, is not answerable to the state (*hupeuthunos*, 213): this can only be a conscious contrast with the accountability of

---

[189] Persians performed a variety of gestures ranging from the full prostration to kissing their hands in the direction of the superior. See Frye 1972.

[190] Richards 1934. See Hdt. 2. 80; Sittl 1890, pp. 149–60 with fig. 15.

[191] Kranz 1933, p. 87.

[192] On the political distinctions drawn in the play see also Delcourt 1934, pp. 251–2; Goldhill 1988.

Athenian magistrates, who were obliged to submit annually to *euthunai*, examinations of their conduct in office (Hdt. 3. 80).[193] The contrast is confirmed by her surprise when informed by the chorus that the Athenian state and army are under the unchallenged command of no one man (241–3), and especially by the wording of the chorus' response here, which implies that it is normal for the inhabitants of cities to be enslaved or subjected to a single individual. Even the lieutenants of the king were called his 'slaves', *doulos* in epigraphy being attested as a translation of the *bandaka* occurring on the Behistun inscription;[194] it is the yoke of slavery which the Persians intend to cast upon Hellas (50).[195]

The fullest exposition of what the Greeks thought Persian rule meant to her subjects is expressed by the chorus after they have heard about the catastrophe at Salamis (584–94):

Not for long now will the inhabitants of Asia abide under Persian rule, nor pay further tribute under compulsion to the king, nor fall to the earth in homage, for the kingly power is destroyed. Men will no longer curb their tongues, for the people, unbridled, may chatter freely.

The three distinguishing features of life under Persian rule are formulated here from a clearly democratic perspective. The exaction of tribute contrasts with the Athenian system under which taxes were payable to the state, not to an individual; at least in theory the rich were supposed to support the poor. The performance of proskynesis suggests the exact opposite of the Athenian ideal of political equality. The implication that the Persian constitution suppressed dissent is an expression of pride in the important concept of *parrhēsia*, the freedom of speech for citizens which was so highly valued at Athens.[196] The play's conceptualization of the barbarians' political institutions and psychology is therefore of paramount importance to its overall impact and direction; in the hands of the tragedians even Persia could be made to serve the interests of the Athenian democracy.

---

[193] On the importance of the principle of accountability to the democracy, see de Ste. Croix 1981, p. 285.

[194] Cook 1985, p. 224 n. 1.

[195] On the recurrence of the symbol of the yoke in the play see Hiltbrunner 1950, p. 44.

[196] On the democratic ideal of freedom of speech, probably introduced in the wake of the Cleisthenic reforms, see Momigliano 1971, pp. 513–18; Loraux 1986, pp. 210–11.

5 ORIENTALISM

In *Persae* Aeschylus was using a powerful new range of effects to characterize a foreign people and culture; his barbarians are simultaneously anti-Greeks and anti-Athenians. A dazzling variety of methods obscures the fact that they are speaking Greek: use of foreign names and vocabulary, cacophony, repetition, a proliferation of 'meaningless' cries, and Ionic forms, especially epicisms. The presentation of the Persians is predicated on the antithesis of Hellene and barbarian; the barbarian character is powerfully suggested not only by the elaborate rhetorical style but by the use of a distinctive new 'vocabulary' of words (*ploutos*, *chrusos*, *habro-* compounds, *chlidē*), symbols (the bow, the chariot), significant actions (prostration), possibly rhythm (Ionic *a minore*) and by the emotional excess, especially in the closing scene. Cultural differentiation is expressed primarily in terms not of religion but of political psychology, formulated in opposition to Athenian political ideals, and backed up by extensive references to the protocol of the court and the administrative apparatus of the empire. The passages illustrating the use of differentiation are so numerous and the effect so pervasive that it is totally inadequate to describe them as 'eastern touches', the opinion of those who see the play's ethical interest as paramount. The tragedy is not ornamented by oriental colouring but suffused by it, indeed it represents the first unmistakable file in the archive of Orientalism, the discourse by which the European imagination has dominated Asia ever since by conceptualizing its inhabitants as defeated, luxurious, emotional, cruel, and always as dangerous.[197] This powerful idea of 'The Orient'—which is a social notion rather than a fact of nature—has been of incalculable influence, from the Greek, Roman, and Christian characterization of Asiatic mystery religions, through the Crusades, the Renaissance, and the imperialist movements of the nineteenth centuries, to modern representations of the Moslem world.[198] The

[197] See Edward Said's important book *Orientalism* (1978), especially his discussion of *Persae* (pp. 56-7).

[198] Renaissance Orientalism reached its culmination in *Gerusalemne Liberata*, Torquato Tasso's epic account, published in 1575, of the crusaders' conquest of Jerusalem in 1099. Representations of the Turks right through until the seventeenth century owed much to the ancient European view of Asiatics, focusing on their tyranny and decadence. Cruel Moslems were a popular feature of the London stage; the most conspicuous example is the

language in which *Persae* expresses its Orientalism is a daring result of the poets' search in the years during and after the Persian wars for a new literary language in which to imply the ascendancy of Hellas and express the 'otherness' of the invader. But this marked 'barbarism' coexists with the narration of a genuinely tragic *pathos*, which precludes the nineteenth-century interpretation of the drama as mere xenophobic self-congratulation.

Some scholars have tried to reconcile these conflicting interpretations. Gagarin, for example, argues that the play's merit lies in the dramatic tension consciously created between the Athenian and Persian perspectives.[199] But even he underplays the 'oriental' element, in which the clue to solving the problem lies: Aeschylus presents Persian characteristics as vices exactly correlative to the cardinal democratic Athenian virtues. Portrayal of the enemy has thus become self-definition and self-praise. A more successful approach, therefore, is to view the poet's theological motive for the fall of Persia, about which so much has been written, as inseparable from the 'ethnological' explanation so well understood by Kranz.[200] Aeschylus' poetic enco-mium of the victorious Hellenes implies that the Persians' greatness held within it the seeds of its own destruction, as their ethnic tempera-ment was liable to despotism, slavishness, excess, and their con-sequences. On the other hand, Greek, and especially Athenian greatness, built on the virtues of equality, freedom, and austerity, is smiled upon by the gods and destined to last forever. It is the play's spirit of antipathy towards the enemies of Hellas which Aristophanes, at least, seems particularly to have remembered; he made his Aeschylus proudly proclaim, 'and then again by putting on my *Persians*, an excellent work, I taught my audience always to yearn for victory over their enemies' (*Ran.* 1026–7).

Sultan Bajazet in Marlowe's *Tamburlaine the Great*. See Chew 1937, pp. 469–540. On the whole history of Orientalism up to the contemporary western stereotypes of the Arab and Moslem worlds see Edward Said 1978 and 1986; Kabbani 1986.

[199] Gagarin 1976, pp. 29–56.
[200] See above, n. 60; Deichgräber 1974, pp. 57–8.

3

The Barbarian Enters Myth

1 INTRODUCTION

THE tragedians invented a new 'vocabulary' of significant words, themes, symbols, and actions with which to characterize the Persians of historical tragedy. Of the techniques creating the distinctive barbarian effect, which Kranz called 'das Nichthellenische', none was detected to any significant degree in the portrayal of the foreigners of myth in pre-tragic poetry. It is the aim of this chapter to show how the tragedians' presentation of these mythical figures was profoundly different from that of the earlier poets. It is rarely remembered that Aeschylus, like Pindar and Bacchylides, could have followed the literary tradition and presented his mythical foreigners in more or less the same way as his Greeks, ignoring the new ethnocentric ideology and the findings of the new science of ethnography. But tragedy's perspective on heroic myth is that of the fifth-century city-state, and Aeschylus' audience had turned to democracy, had won a victory over Persia at the same time as the Greeks in the west had defeated the Carthaginians, and had founded the Delian league: another factor was slavery. The democratization of the political system at Athens was made possible only by expanding the slave sector,[1] and almost all Athenian slaves were barbarians. 'Free' was becoming synonymous with 'Hellenic', 'servile' with 'barbarian'.[2] The fifth century also saw the Athenians organizing numerous new colonies and cleruchies abroad, a process which underlined the feeling that they had the right to sovereignty over barbarian peoples on distant shores.[3] All these circumstances combined to confirm the collective orientation and the belief in Hellenic superiority, providing the external historical catalyst for the imaginative leaps now to occur in the poetic medium of tragedy. The ethos of the 'here and now' was to be reflected on to

[1] See de Ste. Croix 1981, pp. 141–2.
[2] See further Dörrie 1972, pp. 152–4.
[3] See Brunt 1966.

stories from the world of heroes; one result was that mythical foreigners came to be presented from an ethnocentric viewpoint radically different from that of earlier poetry. The time had come for the tragic poets, as witnesses to Athenian democratic ideology, to invent the mythical barbarian.

The bridge between the 'historical' and the 'mythical' barbarian was the parallel drawn between the Persian and Trojan wars. The battles of the wars against Persia were assimilated to the mythical archetypes of the Amazonomachy and Centauromachy, and began to appear alongside them in the self-confident art of fifth-century Athens as symbols of the victory of democracy, reason, and Greek culture over tyranny, irrationality, and barbarism. But the narrative of the Trojan war now came under the spell of the new *logos* which commemorated the battles against the Persians, and like it was reshaped along lines analogous to the patriotic Amazonomachy. Later in the century the Parthenon reliefs were to portray scenes from the Trojan war alongside the struggles with Giants, Amazons, and Centaurs; Trojans were now orientalized, and assumed defeated postures which echoed the sixth-century conceptualizations of the deaths of Amazon queens. In tragedy the story of Troy was to be radically reinterpreted; the manner in which the tragedians began to focus on their mythical foreigners' different languages, conduct, and cultures after the manner of their dramatic Persians will occupy sections 4-8 of this chapter. First, however, it is important to look at some of those figures whose barbarian provenance was itself 'invented', for it is they in whom the tragic genre's Hellenocentric emphasis is most overtly manifested. This procedure has another advantage. For obvious reasons much of this book dwells on eastern barbarians and Orientalism, but there was no dearth of barbarians on the tragic stage who came from the north or from Africa, even from the west (see below, chapter 4. 2). Sections 2-3 therefore turn away from Asia, and look elsewhere, especially at Thrace; this country was of enormous concern to the Athenians, and prominent in their mythology.

2 STEREOTYPES

Stereotypes are codes by which perceptions are organized. The idea of the stereotype was first proposed in 1922 by a journalist, Walter

Lippmann, in a book on the organization of public opinion. He argued that there is a 'quasi-environment' which forms a cognitive barrier between people and the real environment; the barrier is composed of mental pictures or 'stereotypes' of 'real' phenomena. Perceptions must conform to these stereotypes. But stereotypical images are culturally variable and culturally determined; in the case of ethnic stereotypes, for example, the character traits imputed to other ethnic groups are usually a simple projection of those considered undesirable in the culture producing the stereotypes. Thus in forming an opinion 'we pick out what our culture has already defined for us, and . . . perceive that which we have picked out in the form stereotyped by our culture'.[4] The results of ethnic stereotypes are disastrous; there is a close relation between them and oppressive behaviour.[5] If the stereotype of Irish people conceives them as stupid, violent, and lazy, then stupidity, violence, and laziness are more likely to be perceived in any particular Irish person than intelligence, self-control, and industry. This perception is then thought to constitute empirical 'proof' of the verity of the stereotype and legitimizes discrimination.

The chauvinist ancient world, however, had few doubts about the accuracy of its cognitive powers, at least when the object was a barbarian. The 'truths' that Thracians were boors, Egyptians charlatans, and Phrygians effeminate cowards were deemed self-evident, and came to affect the tragedians' recasting of myth; tragic drama therefore provided in its turn cultural authorization for the perpetuation of the stereotype. The 'grammar' of associations between barbarian peoples and character traits or abstractions is particularly clear in those cases where the poets altered altogether the ethnicity of heroic figures or the setting of the story. It was briefly observed in chapter 1. 5b how some mythical figures were 'barbarized' in tragedy—the Trojans became Phrygians, and Medea turned into a Colchian. Further striking examples of this tendency are provided by several mythical figures connected with Thrace. The story of the Thracian king Tereus, for example, was dramatized in a famous play by Sophocles. A fair amount about the drama is known. Tereus married Procne, an Athenian princess, who bore him a son named Itys. The Thracian king subsequently raped his wife's sister Philomela, and cut out her tongue to prevent her from communicating his adultery to her sister. She

[4] Lippmann 1922, p. 148.
[5] On the social function and unfortunate effects of ethnic stereotypes see Brigham 1971.

foiled him, however, by embroidering a message on a robe. Together the two sisters plotted revenge, killed Itys, and served him up to his father. On learning what he had eaten, Tereus pursued his wife and sister-in-law, but the three were transformed into a hoopoe (*epops*), a nightingale, and a swallow respectively. The nightingale's song is explained as Procne's ceaseless laments for Itys; the swallow can only twitter because Philomela had lost her tongue.

Tereus, however, had not traditionally been Thracian but a *Megarian* cult hero.[6] His assimilation to the story of Procne and Philomela is not attested until Aeschylus' *Supplices* (58–62), and even in this passage there is no hint that he was not Greek before his metamorphosis into a bird. He was attracted into Attic saga at a late stage (probably by a deliberate manipulation of myth resulting from Peisistratus' attempts to justify Athenian interests in Megara)[7] simply because his name was suitable for the sharp-eyed bird which pursued the nightingale and the swallow.[8] But his *ethnic* redefinition was probably a Sophoclean innovation. This radical change partly depended upon the similarity of the name *Tereus* and that of the famous fifth-century Odrysian king *Teres*, within whose realm in eastern Thrace the play was almost certainly envisaged as being set.[9] But this does not mean that it necessarily reflected a manipulation of Athenian

---

[6] Paus. 1. 41. 9. See Burkert 1983, p. 182.

[7] Halliday 1933, pp. 104–5.

[8] *Tēreus* means 'watcher-over', *hos tērei*. At first Tereus was changed into a hawk, but the hoopoe (*epops*) must have been suggested by the word *epoptēs*, 'overseer'. See Burkert 1983, p. 183.

[9] A passage in Thucydides has, however, been used to argue that the action of the drama took place not in Thrace but at Daulia (see e.g. Burkert 1983, pp. 180–2), in accordance with the fifth-century belief that there had been a Thracian presence in central Greece in prehistoric times (Hellanicus 4 *FgrH* F 42b. See Stanley Casson 1926, pp. 102–8). Teres, Thucydides asserts, had nothing to do with Tereus, who 'lived in Daulia, which is now Phocis, but used then to be inhabited by Thracians' (2. 29). But several factors support the view that the *play* was set in Thrace: (*a*) The papyrus text which is almost certainly a hypothesis to the play confirms the mythographers' setting in Thrace (*Pap. Oxy.* 3013; see Parsons 1974, pp. 46–50). (*b*) Thucydides does not have to be defending Sophocles' version of the myth; he could equally well be arguing against a popular misconception arising from the play. (*c*) None of the later versions mentions the Daulian connection: Tereus is always simply king of Thrace (e.g. Ovid *Met*. 6. 424–74; Apollod. *Bibl*. 3. 14. 8). (*d*) Procne's lament about being married into a barbarian household far from her home (fr. 583) has much more point if she is in distant Thrace rather than at Daulia, which, as Thucydides says (ibid.), was only 'a short distance from Athens'. For other bibliography on this question see Cazzaniga 1950, p. 47 n. 1.

genealogy designed to *flatter* the Thracian royal family.[10] Teres' son Sitalces, who was probably the king on the Odrysian throne when the play was produced, could hardly have construed Tereus' treatment of his wife's sister as a compliment. It is far more likely that the ingredients of the story—rape, mutilation, infanticide, the eating of human flesh, and possibly a Dionysiac festival[11]—were suggestive of a barbarian context, and even amongst barbarians, the Thracians were particularly often accused of deeds of outrageous violence.[12] In reporting the massacre in 413 by Thracian mercenaries of the entire population of Mycalessus in Boeotia Thucydides calls the Thracians 'most bloodthirsty' (*phonikōtaton*, 7. 29).

The belief in the Thracians' propensity to violence was also to influence Euripides' *Erechtheus*, a dramatic realization of the struggle between Athena and Poseidon, and a celebration of the building of the Erechtheion: it was probably performed between 423 and 421 BC.[13] Poseidon had brought his Thracian son Eumolpus to support his claim to tutelage of Athens; the young man was killed by the Athenian king Erechtheus in the mortal battle which in this version replaced the divine conflict, and Athena mollified the sea-god by prescribing a cult of Poseidon-Erechtheus (fr. 65. 90–4). But Athena's speech *ex machina* referred also to the foundation of the mysteries of Eleusis by a homonymous descendant, perhaps in the fifth generation, of the dead Thracian warrior (fr. 65. 100–2). Here the playwright differed from previous versions of the tale, which apparently knew but one Eumolpus, an Eleusinian founder or minister of the mysteries who led the people of Eleusis in the war with Athens which served as the mythical *aition* for the Athenian appropriation of the coveted cult.[14] In introducing an original Thracian Eumolpus Euripides was therefore departing from this tradition.

But the pervasiveness of the connection of Eumolpus with Eleusis in other versions of the myth has led to the assumption that the Eleusinians must have figured in this play. The case for the Thraco-Eleusinian military alliance in it rests solely on the tenuous evidence of

[10] Linforth 1931, pp. 10–11.
[11] Some scholars (e.g. Burkert 1983, p. 181 n. 11) believe that the Ovidian version's backdrop of the trieteric festival of Dionysus stemmed from Sophocles' tragedy (Ovid, *Met.* 6. 587–605). But see the reservations of Cazzaniga 1950, pp. 52–4.
[12] See Halliday 1933, p. 104.
[13] See Calder 1969.
[14] See *Hymn. Hom. Cer.* 154, 473–6.

a *heavily supplemented* papyrus scholion on Thucydides (fr. 63).[15] On the other hand, Treu has convincingly argued that Euripides' Eumolpus had no connection with Eleusis at all except as *ancestor* of the founder of the mysteries.[16] The fragments otherwise show no vestiges of the Eleusinians. When the Athenian queen Praxithea announces that no Thracian shall worship Poseidon in her city (fr. 50. 46–9), when someone remarks on the proximity of the 'barbarian' camp (fr. 57), when the chorus say that they want to dedicate a Thracian shield (*peltē*) in the temple of Athena (fr. 60. 4–5), when the messenger reports that Erechtheus has set up a trophy won 'from the barbarians' (fr. 65. 12–13), there is no sign of the alleged Eleusinians. When Athena in her speech *ex machina* refers to Eumolpus' descendant there is insufficient space in the lacunose papyrus for her to mention Eleusinians before she passes on to the cult of the Hyades, Erechtheus' daughters (fr. 65. 100–7). The fourth-century orator Lycurgus makes no mention of Eleusinians in his summary of the play (*Leoc*. 98–9). It was only the syncretism of mythography which overlaid Eumolpus' association with Eleusis on to the innovative Euripidean version of the struggle for Athens between Athena and Poseidon (e.g. Apollod. *Bibl*. 3. 15. 4).

The removal of the Eleusinians from the list of the prehistoric enemies of Athens may have been intended as a compliment: Eleusinian reinforcements had come to the aid of Athenians fighting at Megara in 424 BC (Thuc. 4. 68). But this alteration in the myth also affected the thematic oppositions established in the course of the drama. Stripped of his priestly role, Eumolpus is turned into the barbarian son of a violent god, whose invasion of Attica is not only analogous to the incursion of the Amazons, but mythically prefigures the Persian wars and the recent Spartan invasions during the Archidamian war. The Thracians, led by Eumolpus, are associated with Poseidon, invasion, and aggression: the Athenians, in the family of Erechtheus, with Athena, autochthony, patriotism, and peace. Athena's defeat of Poseidon thus becomes yet another mythical expression of the Athenians' subordination of barbarism.

Eumolpus the aggressive warrior remained, however, the ancestor of the founder of the mysteries, and the associations of Thrace with mystery religions, particularly with the figures of Orpheus and

---

[15] Σ Thuc. 2. 15. 1, in *Pap. Oxy*. 853 col. x. 2.
[16] Treu 1971. See especially his discussion of fr. 63 (p. 116).

Dionysus, are as important in myth as the theme of Thracian violence. Aeschylus' tetralogy *Lycurgeia*, which centred on the king of Thracian Edonia, brought the 'Thracians' Orpheus and Dionysus together.[17] It is not clear who first made Lycurgus a Thracian, but it is possible that it was Aeschylus.[18] In the *Iliad* his story is told as a negative exemplum; if a mortal fights with a god, he incurs divine punishment, as Lycurgus did when he drove Dionysus and his nurses from the *nusēïon* (6. 130–40). There is no reason to suppose that the *nusēïon* was already associated with Mount Pangaion, nor that Lycurgus was already envisaged as a Thracian:[19] other Homeric Thracians (Rhesus, Thamyris, Asteropaeus) are always labelled as such. The ritual story of resistance to the god, though probably *Argive* in origin, was a 'roving legend',[20] as the later proliferation of Mounts Nysa indicates.[21] But in the period after the Persian wars Athens was concerned to build up her colonies in Thrace, and suffered catastrophic losses in 465 at the Edonian town of Drabescus (Thuc. 1. 100). A Thracian setting for a trilogy involving both Dionysus and Orpheus is not remotely surprising (see section 7), but the choice of a specifically *Edonian* kingdom may have been connected with contemporary history.

Some barbarians of tragedy did not merely change their ethnicity but were quite literally 'invented'. Three of Euripides' barbarian kings seem to have been created precisely in order to provide an opportunity for exploring vices stereotypically imputed to the barbarian character. It is unlikely that the Polymestor of Euripides' *Hecuba* was a legacy of the epic cycle, for in the *Iliad* Polydorus is Priam's son not by Hecuba but by Laothoe, and he is slain before the fall of Troy by Achilles (20. 407–18). By making him Hecuba's son Euripides provides the motive for the act of vengeance leading to the *agōn* between two barbarians under Greek arbitration which constitutes the epideictic climax of the play. It has been argued that the story of Hecuba's revenge and her transformation into a dog had reached Euripides' ears from the Athenian cleruchy in the Thracian Chersonese where the

[17] On the reasons for Dionysus' association with Thrace see below, section 7.

[18] Eumelus (*Europia* fr. 1 Davies) and Stesichorus (fr. 234 *PMG*) both referred to his story.

[19] Assumed by e.g. von Wilamowitz-Moellendorff 1931-2, ii, p. 60. For a refutation see Otto 1965, pp. 52-64.

[20] See Kerényi 1976, pp. 177-8. On the mobility of the Dionysus cult see Henrichs 1982, pp. 151-5.

[21] See Hermann 1937.

play was set, and was a local legend arising from the hatred felt by the Greek settlers towards the neighbouring Phrygians and Thracians.[22] But Polymestor has no forebears, no place in the Thracian mythical stemmata at whose heads stand Boreas or Ares.[23] Such genealogical isolation is usually a sign that a character was a tragedian's own invention. The creation of a new character such as Polymestor might owe something at least to Greek apprehension of contemporary barbarian figures. Crude equations such as that of Rhesus with Sitalces or Cersebleptes rely on the reductive and untenable assumption that tragedy was customarily a vehicle for wholesale historical allegory,[24] but the Greeks' stereotypes of different peoples were products of inter-action with them, and such stereotypes did influence the poets' inter-pretation of myth as has already been seen in the cases of Tereus and Eumolpus.

The fullest study of the character of Polymestor is that in Delebecque's treatment of *Hecuba*.[25] He argues that Polymestor is a thinly disguised caricature of Seuthes, Sitalces' nephew, who had persuaded his uncle to abandon the Athenian cause prior to the fall of Amphipolis in 424 BC. Euripides is supposed to have first conceived a *Polyxena* and then turned half-way through its composition to a denunciation of the Odrysian monarchy. His theory leads Delebecque to the absurd deduction that in the collusion of Agamemnon and Hecuba against Polymestor there can be seen a warning to both Athenians and Spartans against entering alliances with Thrace. It need hardly be said that such polemic was not the task of the tragedian but of the speaker in the assembly. But some of Delebecque's observations are suggestive. Polymestor is the only tragic criminal motivated solely by avarice (25-7), rather than by a desire for vengeance, obedience to oracles, lust, or hunger for power. The chorus assume that it was the Thracian's greed for gold which had made him murder Polydorus, and Agamemnon later jumps to the same conclusion (713, 774-5). It is only by tempting him with talk of hidden treasure that he can be lured into

----

[22] Pohlenz 1954, p. 277. Stephanopoulos 1980, p. 32, discerns old folklore elements in the story of Polydorus and Polymestor.

[23] It is, however, possible that Polymestor's name ('much-counselling') connects him with Ares, who is entitled *pammēstōr*, 'all-counselling', in fr. adesp. 129. 9.

[24] Goossens 1962, pp. 255-61, considers that Rhesus' character is a 'masque' for Sitalces; Sinko 1934, pp. 423-9, prefers the fourth-century Odrysian king Cersebleptes: both use such equations as arguments for the play's date.

[25] Delebecque 1951, pp. 147-64.

Hecuba's tent (1013). Given the emphasis laid on his avarice, it can scarcely be a coincidence that Thucydides comments on the Odrysian kings' extraordinary appetite for treasure (2. 97).

Another feature Polymestor seems to derive from the Athenians' stereotype of the contemporary kings of Thrace is his equivocation. Although a guest-friend of Priam (19), he did not fight for him in the war; the situation is encompassed in his own words to Hecuba, 'you are my friend, but the Achaean army here has a friendship with me too' (982–3). To the ambivalence of this position, and the postponement of the murder of Polydorus until the outcome of the Trojan war became clear (see 1208–29), Delebecque referred the Odrysians' equivocal attitude towards the interests of Sparta and Athens in Thrace, and the delay of Sitalces' abandonment of the Athenian cause until Brasidas had actually set foot in Chalcidice.[26] Here Delebecque is on reasonably firm ground; this aspect of Polymestor's characterization is unusual, as is clear from the flustered attempts in the scholia to explain whose side he was really on (Σ 982, 1114), and *Hecuba* was indeed probably produced around the time of the fall of Amphipolis. But his attempt to link Hecuba's scornful suggestion that Polymestor had hoped to marry into a Greek family with Seuthes' (undatable) marriage to a Greek woman from Abdera pushes the Polymestor/Seuthes equation much too far. Pericles' citizenship law, comedy, and oratory provide abundant evidence that the supposed desire of foreigners (especially Thracians) to marry into citizen families was an Athenian obsession (see chapter 4. 3).

Polymestor's mendacity is breathtaking (see, for example, 953–5, 993), and he had broken the law of guest-friendship: Thracian untrustworthiness was proverbial (see the proverb 'Thracians do not understand oaths', Zenobius 4. 32).[27] It is also conspicuous that Euripides scarcely grants him the status of a king. He is called 'stranger' and 'man', 'barbarian' and 'you there' (*xenos, anēr, barbaros, houtos su*, 710, 790, 877, 1280), but only once does he merit the title 'king' (*anax*, 856), and then it is in the mouth of Agamemnon who at this point has a particular reason for magnifying his status. He is however no fewer than nine times simply called 'the Thracian' or by a noun qualified by 'Thracian'. The sound *Thrēix* or *Thrēikios* beats insistently on the ear,

---

[26] Ibid., pp. 158–9.

[27] Apte 1985, pp. 118–19, discusses the importance of proverbs to the perpetuation of ethnic stereotypes.

much as do Shakespearean characters' repeated references to Aaron and Othello as Moors, or to Shylock as a Jew.[28] This emphasis on Polymestor's ethnicity must reflect contemporary Greek derision of the kings of the barbarian north, but it also suggests that Euripides was playing an associative game. Vast numbers of slaves came from Thrace,[29] and the prosaic version of the very word *Thrēix* by which Polymestor is so frequently designated was therefore one of the commonest slave names, an almost exact equivalent of *doulos*, 'slave', which could stand alone as an insult.[30] Similar stress is laid on the ethnicity of the Phrygian in *Orestes* (1351, 1417, 1518); numerous Athenian slaves came from Phrygia.[31] But this play was produced in 408, and the vilification of the Phrygian in the Spartan Helen's entourage may, like the treatment of Polymestor, reflect in a fairly uncomplicated way the Athenians' frustrations in their current dealings with barbarians. Pharnabazus, the satrap of Hellespontine Phrygia, had recently been lending assistance to Sparta.[32]

Thoas in *IT* like Polymestor has no ancestors, and it is probable that Euripides invented the whole myth in which Orestes and Pylades are sent to the Black Sea in order to rescue Iphigeneia from the Taurians.[33] Indeed, it is unlikely that before Herodotus' *Histories* the Greeks could distinguish the Taurians as an ethnic group from the Scythians or Cimmerians. The fragments of Hecataeus which deal with Scythia and northern Europe reveal no mention of Taurians (1 *FgrH* F 184–94). One of Sophocles' 'Phineus' plays locates the Cimmerian Bosporus, whose northern shore was the Taurian Chersonese, 'among the Scythians' (fr. 707), for in the fifth century as throughout antiquity the term *Skuthai* often embraced all peoples to the north of the Danube.[34] It was Herodotus who argued for a stricter classification of the northern tribes, and insisted that the Taurians were a different people

---

[28] See Fiedler 1974, pp. 16, 88, 149, 160–1.

[29] See Pritchett 1956, p. 278; Velkov 1967; de Ste. Croix 1981, p. 163. Thracians outnumber any other ethnic group in the remains of the list of the metic Cephisodorus' slaves, confiscated and auctioned in 414 BC (Meiggs and Lewis 1969, no. 79, A. 33–49). All the slaves are barbarians.

[30] Σ Plato *Lach*. 187b; Antiphanes' *Turrhenos* fr. 211. 3 Kock. See Pritchett 1956, p. 280 and nn. 31–2; Velkov 1967, p. 72.

[31] See Carl W. Weber 1981, p. 109.

[32] See Willink 1986, p. xlv; Lewis 1977, p. 127.

[33] See von Wilamowitz-Moellendorff 1883, p. 257.

[34] M. I. Finley 1962, p. 56.

from the Scythians (4. 99). The historical Taurians were either remnants of the Cimmerians or survivors from an aboriginal pre-Cimmerian civilization around the Sea of Azov.[35] Recent excavations have begun to throw light on these inhabitants of the Tauric Chersonese, where native settlements of great antiquity have been found.[36] But there is only one piece of evidence to support the view that the Athenians would even have heard of the Taurians before Herodotus, and that is a short phrase in Proclus' epitome of the *Cypria* describing Iphigeneia: 'Artemis seizes her and removes her to the Taurians' (p. 32, Davies). But this is tenuous evidence, for *IT* was always a popular play in antiquity, and the epitomizer may well have been influenced by Euripides' version of the story.[37] Even Herodotus does not refer to the story of Iphigeneia's kidnapping, but merely states that the Taurians call their maiden goddess by her name (4. 103); this claim is probably a result of a false connection of Artemis' cultic title *Tauropolos*, 'bull-hunting', with the Taurians.[38] For Euripides it would then have been a short step to translate his Argive princess to the northern tribe, and to specify that it was the Black Sea from which she brought the wooden image of Artemis to Attica.

It must be doubted, therefore, that Euripides had any dramatic precedent for his evocation of the Taurian land and people, but his debt to Herodotus was considerable. Following the historian's insistence that the Taurians were altogether a different people from the Scythians, Euripides never suggests that Iphigeneia's hosts are Scythian, or adds any Scythian ethnographic detail; the only archers in the play are Greek (1377). Much of the historian's language in his discussion of the Chersonese and the Taurians in 4. 99 and 103 reappears in poetic disguise. The goddess's temple, in Herodotus situated on a cliff-top, is in the play also immediately beside the sea (1196). Herodotus had called the Chersonese 'rugged' (*trēcheē*, 4. 99), and indeed it is combed with rocky promontories, precipices, and cliffs.[39] Euripides cumulatively evokes

[35] See Rostovtzeff 1922, p. 34; Baschmakoff 1939, p. 11.

[36] See Hind 1983-4, p. 85.

[37] Bethe 1966, p. 93; Burnett 1971, p. 73. It is to be noted that Baschmakoff 1939 argued strongly to the contrary. He believed that settlers in the Black Sea in the sixth century had been inspired by the *Cypria* to identify the indigenous maiden goddess they found there with Iphigeneia, and that the myth contained ancient 'pre-Aryan' elements from Taurian tradition associated with the human sacrifices which have been attested by the excavation of necropoleis in the northern Black Sea area.

[38] Lloyd-Jones 1983a, p. 96.

[39] See W. Smith 1870, p. 1110.

the savage shoreline of the Taurians' land (107, 260-3, 324, 1373). When
Iphigeneia regrets the 'barbarian tribes' and trackless paths which
obstruct the land route through Scythia back to Greece (886-8), she
seems to recall the catalogues of tribes inhabiting the Scythian waste-
land which recur in Herodotus' fourth book (e.g. 4. 16-29, 99-109).
Euripides' Pontic geography, far from being vague, exactly mirrors the
information given by the historian.[40] Herodotus describes how the
Taurians dealt with their sacrificial victims: their bodies were pushed
over the cliff on which the temple stood, while their heads were
impaled (4. 103). These twin practices surely suggested to the playwright the punishments for the Greek miscreants planned by Thoas:
'Let us seize them and hurl them from a rocky cliff, or fix their bodies on
stakes' (1429-30). The heads of the Taurians' enemies which Herodotus
had said were stuck on poles above their homes are perhaps
remembered in the trophies (*skula*) of the victims which made the
copings of Euripides' Taurian temple red with blood (73-5): these are
probably supposed to be skulls (see Amm. Marc. 22. 8. 33, '[*Tauri*]
caesorum capita fani parietibus praefigebant'). But most of all, the wording
of Herodotus' statement that the Taurians sacrifice shipwrecked sailors
and Greeks (4. 103) informs many lines in the play where this gruesome
subject is discussed (see 38-41, 72, 276-8, 775-6). The coincidence of
language and material in the two writers is far too great for it to be
supposed that Euripides was not enormously indebted to the historian;
indeed, it is most likely that the poet's barbarous Taurian society
constituted a dramatic bringing to life of chapters in Herodotus, and
was therefore entirely new to tragedy.

Theoclymenus in *Helen* was also probably new to Euripides'
audience. Indeed, this is the first and only fifth-century tragedy known
to have been set in Egypt.[41] Euripides could take Helen there because
Stesichorus had forever cast doubt on Homer's version of her story. In
his famous *Palinode* Helen never went to Troy, but stayed with Proteus
in Egypt while an image of her absconded with Paris (frr. 192. 2-3;
193. 14-16 *PMG*). Stesichorus thus exculpated Helen. The adapted
version of the myth which Herodotus claims to have heard from

---

[40] It used to be fashionable to describe Euripides' Taurian geography as vague or even
fantastic. But this view rested largely on the passage at 132-6 where the chorus claim to
have left Europe, for the Tauric Chersonese was undoubtedly regarded as European in the
fifth century. *Eurōtan* should be read instead of *Eurōpan*: see Hall 1987b.

[41] Satyr plays set in Egypt are attested, such as Aeschylus' *Proteus* and Euripides' *Busiris*.

Egyptian priests omitted the image of Helen and concentrated on Proteus' virtue (2. 112–15). But Euripides wanted to write another play like *IT*, whose underlying premise was the ascendancy of Hellas over the barbarian cultures at the edges of the earth, and he was therefore forced to invent a barbarous son Theoclymenus with whom to replace the noble Proteus. Theoclymenus is an amalgam of the Taurian Thoas and the stereotypical Egyptian xenophobia mythically personified in Busiris. Like both these figures he outrages the Greek law of *xenia* by slaughtering strangers who set foot on his land, but he is motivated not by a requirement for ritual sacrifice, but by sexual desire for Helen (1173–6). His obsession is conveyed by hunting imagery nearly every time his name is mentioned: *thērai gamein me* (63), *ho thēreuōn gamous* (314). The metaphor is reflected in circumstantial detail; at the beginning of the play he is away hunting (154), and when he finally appears he is attended by guards with hunting gear and hounds, who physically substantiate the metaphor of pursuit (1169–70). The tragedians elsewhere manipulated myth in such a way as to imply the barbarian male's generic lust for Greek females, just as whites in the deep south of America fostered the belief in the black man's desire for their wives and daughters (see below, section 5).

3 BARBARIAN SETTINGS AND CHORUSES

The Hellenocentric viewpoint of the tragic poets therefore led them to reinterpret myths by turning heroic characters of Hellenic or indeterminate ethnicity into barbarians, and by inventing other barbarian figures altogether. The invented barbarian world of Greek literature had developed an internal dynamic, and became in its own right a source of theatrical inspiration. There are cases where the Greeks' conception of a particular land or people might lead a myth to be located far afield and for the tragedians to exploit ethnographic material even where no barbarians actually appear. The myth recounted in *PV*, for example, was translated (if not by the mythographers then perhaps first by the playwright himself)[42] to the northern edges of the world, in Scythia: Hesiod had not specified where in his universal mythical landscape Zeus had bound the

---

[42] Although see M. L. West 1966, pp. 314–15. He defends the theory that the story of the punishment of Prometheus originated in Caucasian myth.

subversive Titan for punishment (*Theog.* 521–2). Prometheus predicts
that Io will conceive Epaphus at the mouth of the Nile (848–9), and the
choice of location was therefore partly dependent upon the popular
ethnographic opposition of Scythia and Egypt; the Hippocratic treatise
de Aëribus originally contained an excursus on Egypt to complement
the surviving chapters on Scythia by contrasting the cold damp north
with the warm land of the Nile (13. 1–2). The rocks of Scythia, the
'mother of iron' (301), are a fit choice of background for the portrait of
the indomitable Titan, himself likened to iron and rock (242), for the
Scythians, along with the Chalybians who lived on the southern shore
of the Black Sea, had long been associated with metallurgy.[43] A
Hesiodic fragment attributes the discovery of bronze to *Skuthēs*
(fr. 282), and Aeschylus recalls a similar tradition at a climactic
moment in *Septem contra Thebas*: the chorus use a startling personification of iron to represent the armed struggle which will kill both
brothers, calling it a 'Chalybian settler from Scythia' (728).

Perhaps more important was the correspondence between Scythia
and the abstractions which dominate *PV*. On the one hand the
Scythian hinterland was seen as a remote, desolate, intractable region
which Greek colonists had never been able to penetrate,[44] and so the
untamed land is thematically linked with Prometheus' advocacy of
technological progress, for the 'pioneer in man's conquest of nature'[45]
is tortured in a land where nature can never be conquered. Prometheus
predicts that the Scythians themselves are the first people whom Io will
reach (709–12): 'You will come to the nomad Scythians, who live high
above the ground on strong-wheeled carts with wattled roofs, and are
armed with powerful bows. Do not approach them.' But the Scythians,
paradoxically, were also seen as unspoiled innocents living in a well-
governed utopia (see *Prometheus Unbound* fr. 198),[46] a theme which
complements the role of Prometheus as civilizing hero. The Scythian
setting of *PV*, whether or not it was an invention of tragedy, allowed
the poet to indulge in some of the most spectacular poeticized

[43] Phillips 1955, pp. 171–2, discusses the bronze age mineworks in central Asia which
may have led to this reputation.

[44] This is the basic premise of Herodotus' Scythian *logos*, for a brilliant analysis of which
see Hartog 1988, part 1.

[45] Thomson 1973, p. 299.

[46] The image of the well-governed nomads of the north stems ultimately from Homer's
Abii (*Il*. 13. 6); see Lévy 1981. On the sources for the Scythians as 'noble savages' throughout
antiquity, see Lovejoy and Boas 1935, pp. 315–44.

geography and ethnography in the genre, especially in the first stasimon, where the chorus lists the peoples who lament Prometheus' sufferings, the Asiatics, Colchians, Scythians, and Arabians (406–24), and in Prometheus' accounts of Io's past and future wanderings (707–35, 790–815, 829–52). The fragmentary evidence for the lost *Prometheus Unbound*, which was set in Scythia or the Caucasus,[47] is sufficient to show that it continued the interest in cartography and ethnography (frr. 192. 4, 196–9).

The tragedians did not only relocate myths and invent mythical barbarian individuals. They also imported foreign choruses into plays with Greek characters. The reason for the prevalence of foreign choruses may originally have been connected with the rituals from which tragedy emerged. The theory that its roots lay in the goat sacrifice, eloquently defended by Burkert, has the advantage of explaining both the use of masks and the 'anonymity' of the chorus; the male citizens who originally performed such sacrifices may have ritually disguised themselves in order to disassociate the community from the violence of the action, and to displace their individual personae.[48] Burkert suggests that this might throw light on the popularity of female and foreign choruses.[49] But as tragedy developed the foreign chorus became conventional in its own right—especially the female barbarian chorus—and the reasons for this lie rather in the chorus' function as plural lyric voice, distanced from the individual actors both physically and in role. On one level, of course, the chorus is the voice of the collective, whose well-being is dependent on and jeopardized by the individual characters, but it is paradoxically also estranged from the central *pathos*. It rarely participates or influences decisions and events, for its members remain marginal, standing and dancing on the edges of the actors' space; their medium is song rather than speech, and their role—usually that of social inferior—to sympathize and lament. The chorus' relation to the central figures, simultaneously dependent and marginalized, is thus almost a cultural paradigm of the relation borne in the Greek city-state by women, slaves, and metics to the body of male citizens.

The threnodic role of the chorus was particularly suggestive of femininity and barbarism. This can be no better illustrated than by

---

[47] See Griffith 1983, p. 294.
[48] Burkert 1966.
[49] Ibid., p. 115.

Aeschylus' choice of chorus for his dramatic realization of Ajax's suicide at Troy. Sophocles preferred Salaminian sailors, but Aeschylus selected Thracian women after whom the tragedy, *Threissae*, was named. It has been suggested that he was prompted by an account of Ajax's attack on the Thracian Chersonese in the *Cypria*,[50] but the only evidence for such an exploit is a reference in the late Dictys of Crete (2. 18). It is quite unnecessary to vindicate Aeschylus' choice by such a tenuous hypothesis, for barbarians were of course especially suited to the delivery of laments; a scholion on Sophocles' *Ajax* 134, though disapproving in other respects of Aeschylus' Thracian chorus, says that they were 'solicitous' (*kēdemonikon*), a word which had particular affinities with burial and mourning. It is also likely that the chorus of the first play of the trilogy, *Hoplōn Krisis*, was composed of Trojan captives in the Greek camp.[51]

It has been denied recently that the libation bearers of *Choephoroe* are Asiatic,[52] but the text implies otherwise. They lament in 'Aryan strains of Cissia' (423–4), and lay emphasis on their status as prisoners-of-war (75–7); it is obvious that they were assumed to have been brought back from Troy, like Cassandra, by Agamemnon. It is also likely that Euripides was looking back to these captive Asiatics at Clytaemnestra's court when he twice discusses her retinue of Trojan women in *Electra* (998–1003, 1008–10).[53] Certainly his taste for archaizing is reflected in his introduction of a barbarian female chorus into his Theban tragedy *Phoenissae*: although it is modelled in part on Aeschylus' *Septem contra Thebas*, Euripides externalizes in the ethnicity of his chorus-members the timorousness and threnodic lyricism which Aeschylus had related exclusively to their gender. Even where the plays of Euripides are composed of Greeks he sometimes imports barbarian characters by his own particular interpretation of myth. A famous example is the Phrygian slave in *Orestes*, but he also provided 'barbarian' interest in his *Philoctetes*, produced in 431 in a group with *Medea* (another play where the Hellene–barbarian antithesis is prominent): he introduced Trojan ambassadors intent on preventing Philoctetes from destroying their city (Dio Chrys. *Or*. 52. 13).

---

[50] Martin 1975, p. 178 n. 116.
[51] Ibid., pp. 130–2.
[52] Garvie 1986, pp. 53–4.
[53] In his *Electra* Euripides frequently referred back to Aeschylus' *Choephoroe*. See Winnington-Ingram 1969, pp. 129–32.

4 LANGUAGE

The conceptualization of different peoples in the Greek imagination therefore inspired the poets on occasions to relocate some myths to foreign lands, turn some mythical figures into barbarians, and invent other barbarian characters and choruses altogether. But by far the most common innovation was the 'barbarization' of mythical figures already not Greek in the literary tradition. In *Persae* Aeschylus used a variety of techniques to obscure the fact that his barbarians were speaking Greek: none of these was found in pre-tragic poetry on mythical themes, nor for that matter to any great extent in the poetry of the 'here and now' before Hipponax. But drama presented its audience with characters dressed up as barbarians, thus vastly increasing the incongruity of the Hellenophone foreigner, an incongruity which could be almost ignored by the epic poets because they demanded so much greater an imaginative response from their audience. The tragic poets' answer to the problem must not be exaggerated, for their conservatism becomes apparent if their techniques of linguistic differentiation are compared with the far more adventurous carica-tures in less serious Greek literature, especially the Scythian archer's mangled Greek in *Thesmophoriazusae*,[54] or the gibberish in the later 'Charition Mime' which may be based on an ancient Indian dialect.[55] The tragedians were certainly not interested in having languages inter-preted on stage,[56] although in reference to Cassandra Aeschylus ironically exploits the ambiguity of the word *hermēneus*, which can mean an interpreter either of foreign languages or of obscure oracles

[54] Friedrich's discussion of the Scythian archer's language concluded that the poet had made a real attempt to reproduce a Scythian accent on Attic Greek (1919, pp. 300–1). On the Triballian god in *Aves* see Whatmough 1952. There is controversy over Pseudartabas in *Acharnenses*: is he speaking near-Persian (Dover 1963, pp. 7–8), or is he an Athenian impostor talking gibberish (M. L. West 1968, p. 6)?

[55] The mime, published in Page 1941, pp. 336–49, seems to have been a loose parody of Euripides' *IT*. The dialect was Kanarese, one of the ancient pre-Aryan Dravidian dialects of southern India: see Hultzsch 1904. But Page was convinced that the similarities in vocabulary were coincidental (ibid., p. 337).

[56] Gorgias, on the other hand, exploited the problem involved in making mythical Greeks and barbarians communicate with one another. See, for example, the argument he invented for Palamedes (82 B 11a. 7 *DK*): 'Nor was direct communication possible between myself, a Greek, and the enemy, a barbarian, since we did not understand each other's language, and an interpreter would have meant having an accomplice.'

(*Ag*. 1062-3, see also 615-16, 1254), and a Phrygian shepherd in *Rhesus* claims to be proficient in Thracian (297). It is also unlikely that foreign accents were assumed in tragedy as they were in comedy, where even Greek dialects other than Attic are caricatured. A scholion on *Phoenissae* 301, where Jocasta claims to have heard the chorus utter a 'Phoenician cry', quotes a fragment of Sophocles (176) in which someone's speech is said to 'smell' Spartan, and comments that even though dramatic characters spoke Greek, they preserved the 'echo of their national speech'. But what source of information could the author of this scholion have had? In Aeschylus' *Choephoroe* although Orestes *says* that he and Pylades must feign a Phocian accent (564), there is no observable difference in their language when the time comes for them to approach the palace (653-6, 658-706).[57]

All through the genre there is, however, an uncomfortable aware-ness that mythical foreigners should be heterophone, though the tragedians favoured the more poetic techniques developed for the Persians of historical tragedy, rather than the 'realistic' imitation of other tongues suitable for comedy. An Aeschylean fragment mentions an 'Ethiopian voice' (328) and his Egyptians are wary about the hostility their literal 'barbarism' may cause: 'everyone is quick to cast reproaches against those who speak another language' (*Supp*. 972-4). The suppliants had earlier used in references to their alien speech an unusual word, *karban*, apparently equivalent to *barbaros* (119, 130). It has been thought that the word itself sounded foreign to Aeschylus' audience, for it may be Egyptian or Hebrew in origin and therefore particularly suitable for these barbarians. But another form of the same word, *karbanos*, is used with the same meaning in *Greek* mouths at 914 and *Ag*. 1061 (see also Soph. fr. 269a. 54). Euripides normally prefers to remind his audience that his foreigners are uttering barbarian cries, prayers, or songs, or have heard in their homeland a 'barbarian story' (*Or*. 1385; *Phoen*. 819, 1301, 679; *Bacch*. 1034), and leaves them to supply the rest from imagination.

Nowhere in extant tragedy are there exact parallels to the acoustic effects produced by the catalogues of barbarian names and the frequent Ionicisms in *Persae*, but in the mythical context of *Supplices* Aeschylus used cries, repetition, and alliteration to substantiate his Egyptians' claim to be heterophone: see '*o o o a a a*' (825), '. . .

---

[57] But see Stevens 1945, p. 96, who believes the scholion on *Phoen*. 301, and thinks that there are unusual dialectal forms in Orestes' speech in *Choephoroe*.

bathuchaios/bathreias bathreias/. . . naï naï/basēi tacha/theleos atheleos/biai biai . . ./bateai bathumitrokaka . . .' (858–64), and '*ma Ga ma Ga boan/ . . . ō ba Gas . . .*' (890–2, 900–2). The same poet's *Edoni* included a drumming anapaestic passage (in the parodos?) describing the rites of the votaries of Dionysus, whose concert of exotic instruments—reed pipes, cymbals, and the bull-roarer—creates an impression 'more savage and onomatopoeic than anything in *Bacchae*'[58] (fr. 57). The repetition and cries in the threnodic passages of *Persae*, suggesting lack of restraint as much as barbarian diction, find close parallels in *Troades*: the great lament shared between Hecuba and the chorus is rich in cries and repetition (1310, 1312). Similar reiteration is found in the songs of the barbarian chorus of *Phoenissae* (679–81, 818–19). But by far the most extensive use of lyric repetition in the mouth of a barbarian character is in *Orestes*, probably produced the year after *Phoenissae*. Here the Phrygian slave's florid monody may owe much to Timotheus' extraordinary dithyramb *Persae*, a poem in which Phrygian and Persian voices are heard, and which is also full of repetition and exotic vocabulary (frr. 788–91 *PMG*; see *Or.* 1373, 1381, 1426–8).[59] The Phrygian in *Orestes* is already anomalous since he is one of the only two minor characters of low social status to break Maas' 'law' by singing in tragedy;[60] the other, the herald in Aeschylus' *Supplices*, is significantly also an overwrought barbarian.[61]

In *Persae* translations of foreign titles and actual foreign vocabulary were found; these techniques of suggesting foreign diction were transferred to the barbarians of myth. Hector was once the 'great . . . king' of Troy (*megas . . . anaktōr*, *Tro.* 1217), as Rhesus is 'great king' of

---

[58] Bacon 1961, p. 41. On the characterization of sound in this fragment see Kaimio 1977, p. 172.

[59] For a discussion of the resemblances between Timotheus' *Persae* and Euripides' Phrygian's monody see Bassett 1931, pp. 160–1. Janssen 1984, p. 22, argues that *Persae* was first performed in around 408/7 BC, but it is impossible to be sure whether the dithyramb influenced the tragedy or *vice versa*. It is known from Dion. Hal. *Comp.* 11 that the actor playing Electra in *Orestes* was probably required to sing in a high voice. As the same actor took the part of the Phrygian, this suggests that he was portrayed with a high, effeminate voice (the 'chariot melody' he refers to at 1384 was in the high-pitched Phrygian mode). This would have been particularly apt if he was a eunuch: see below, section 8. The orientalized Menelaus will also have been played by this actor: see below, ch. 5 n. 33.

[60] See Maas 1962, pp. 53–4.

[61] For a refutation of the theory that the herald's side of the lyrics at 836–65 was sung by a secondary chorus constituted by his attendants see Taplin 1977, pp. 216–17. On the contrast of the barbarian singing voice with the Greek spoken trimeter see below, section 5.

Thrace (*megas basileus*, *Rhes*. 379), in contrast with the Greek leaders who are democratically styled 'generals' (*stratēlatai*, 173, 495). A few actual foreign words were used by Aeschylus in mythical contexts: the Asiatic term for a king, *palmus*, appears in an Aeschylean fragment (fr. 437). There is a scattering of similar words in *Supplices* calculated to lend a foreign effect; *baris*, occurring now in an Egyptian context (836, 873), and *bounis*, 'hilly', perhaps a Cyrenean word (117, 129, 776). But there is no need to assume that the corrupt state of the text at 825–902 is the result of a large amount of Egyptian vocabulary baffling to scribes.[62] This theory has led to many proposed emendations involving barbarian words, for example *champsa* in Ellis's emendation of *perichampta* at 878. The proposed *champsa* is an Egyptian word meaning 'crocodile' known by Herodotus probably from Hecataeus (Hdt. 2. 69; see 1 *FgrH* F 324a). But there is not enough evidence to support the 'Egyptian vocabulary' theory; what can be made out of the words suggests that they implied barbarian speech by being unusual, archaic, and cacophonous, but there is not one certainly non-Greek term other than *baris*. Aeschylus may have used scattered items of foreign vocabulary here, but there is no parallel in Greek tragedy, even in *Persae*, for continuous language imitation in the manner of Hanno's 'Carthaginian' speeches in Plautus' *Poenulus*, and the state of the text in *Supplices* must not be used to argue that the play provided an exception to this rule. None of the Aeschylean texts except that of *PV* can be described as well preserved.

Sophocles' Trojans, however, seem to have been considerably 'barbarized' in the linguistic sphere, which is perhaps surprising in view of the relative unimportance of the Phrygian Tecmessa's ethnicity in *Ajax*. Like the Cissian mourners in *Persae*, Aeneas in *Laocoon* wore a *bussinon pharos* (fr. 373. 3); like Darius, someone in *Poimenes* (perhaps Priam) was addressed by the oriental honorific *iō balēn* (fr. 515). In the same play the Persian word *parasangēs* (a measure of distance) was heard (fr. 520), and like the Greeks referred to in *Persae* as 'Ionians', a Greek woman, perhaps Helen, was called *Iaina* (fr. 519).[63] In *Troilus* the 'barbarian lament' *iai* was uttered (fr. 631), as was the title *orosangai* attested in Persian texts (fr. 634).[64] Herodotus explains

---

[62] This was Gilbert Murray's verdict; see his app. crit. to *Supplices* (1947, n. *ad loc*.)

[63] See also Soph. fr. 56 with Radt's comments.

[64] See Herzfeld 1938, p. 195, who sees the *orosangai* in the *huvarzyanhō*, a word whose meaning is approximately equivalent to that of *euergetai*. On the other hand it may have

that an *orosangēs* was one who had been enrolled in the Persian king's
'Order of Benefactors'; the Samians Theomestor and Phylacus who
fought for Xerxes at Salamis were made *orosangai* in recognition of
their services and received large estates (Hdt. 8. 85). But Sophocles
imported this Persian office into his mythical Trojan past.[65] Even
Euripides, who is less interested in foreign vocabulary than his
predecessors, kits out his Phrygian slave in *eumarides* (*Or*. 1370–1), the
Persian slippers previously named in *Persae* (660). Aeschylus' play had
been a product of the process by which the Persian wars were turned
into myth; by the reverse process the tragedians suggested that the
language of their mythical Trojans was that of the Persian court.

5 BEHAVIOUR

Stereotypes project on to target groups characteristics which are the
opposite of qualities admired in the group creating the stereotypes.
The cardinal Hellenic virtues as defined in fourth-century philosophy
(see, for example, Plato, *Resp*. 4. 427e 10–11) normally included
wisdom or intelligence (*sophia* or *xunesis*), manliness or courage
(*andreia*), discipline or restraint (*sōphrosunē*), and justice (*dikaiosunē*).[66]
Sometimes they are listed in the form of a 'canon', though in the earlier
Platonic dialogues a particular virtue may be the principal subject
under discussion.[67] The *Laches*, for example, attempts to define
courage. The third virtue, *sōphrosunē*, was perhaps the most important;
it tempered *all* the passions and made possible the observance of
measure (*mesotēs*) in all actions, and the avoidance of extremes. It was a
concept integral to fifth-century tragedy, where so often extreme
personalities and unbending wills are on a collision course with
catastrophe.[68] But all of Plato's virtues are already in a process of
canonization in tragedy,[69] and they can help to illuminate the portrayal
of barbarians. At *Resp*. 4. 444b 7–8 Plato provides a list of vices which

been connected with a Median word *varusanha*, 'widely-renowned' (Wiesehöfer 1980, p. 8
and n. 5), or with the Hittite UR.SAG (Armayor 1978b, p. 155).

[65] For a detailed discussion of the offices of King's Friend and King's Benefactor see
Wiesehöfer 1980.
[66] In general see Kunsemüller 1935.
[67] Ibid., pp. 8–9.
[68] On *sōphrosunē* in tragedy see North 1966, pp. 32–84.
[69] See e.g. *Septem* 610; Kunsemüller 1935, pp. 35–43.

correspond with the virtues; stupidity (*amathia*), cowardice (*deilia*), abandonment (*akolasia*), and lawlessness (*adikia*): barbarian characters are often made to manifest one or more of these vices, thus helping the tragedian to define the nature of Greek morality.[70]

The vice corresponding to intelligence is defined by Plato as 'ignorance', *amathia*; in comedy the adjective *amathēs* appears in conjunction with *barbaros* (Ar. *Nub*. 492). Euripides' escape dramas *IT* and *Helen* both include long deception scenes in which Greek characters (Iphigeneia, Helen), demonstrate their intellectual ascendancy over barbarian foes (Thoas, Theoclymenus), just as Odysseus had outwitted the monstrous Cyclops. In such dramas the parallel between the more primitive type of stage barbarian, and the Cyclops or satyr as the supernatural projection of primitive man, is at its clearest (see also above, chapter 1. 7 and below, n. 91): Euripides' Taurians blow conch shells, regarded as the instruments men used *before the invention* of trumpets (*IT* 303; Hesychius s.v. *kochlos*). Thoas unwittingly verbalizes the premise of the entire sequence while Iphigeneia persuades him to let her take away the image of Artemis by admiring her foresight (*promēthia*) even as she lies to him (1202). During this scene she and the chorus and the audience form a Hellenic conspiracy; the chorus has already sworn to assist in the subterfuge (1075–7), and Iphigeneia's words, rich with ambiguity, implicate the audience in the baiting of the foreigner. Helen's deception of Theoclymenus follows exactly the same pattern. The popularity of these deceiving-the-barbarian scenes is reflected in Aristophanes' choice of a Scythian archer as a substitute for the barbarian kings of tragedy in the send-up of Euripidean escape-plots constituted by *Thesmophoriazusae*.[71]

In *Rhesus* the Thracian king's error was his imprudent failure to set a night watch over his sleeping troops, an oversight stressed by the Thracian charioteer who reports the disaster (763–9).[72] In this rashness lies a clue to Rhesus' characterization, for an opposition is established between the blunt and unsophisticated barbarian intellect and the

---

[70] The discussion of *dikaiosunē* is reserved until ch. 4. 4 and 5.

[71] See Hall 1989.

[72] The Thracians, though seen as 'spirited' (Plato *Resp*. 4. 435c 6), were considered to be particularly stupid. An Aristotelian text explains that they are the only people in the world to use a numerary unit of four rather than ten 'because like children they cannot remember very far, nor have they any use for any large number' (*Pr*. 15. 3 = 911a 2). Androtion was so struck with their backwardness that he claimed Orpheus' Thracian provenance was a lie (324 *FgrH* F 54)!

covert and cunning activities of the Greeks. Rhesus' response to the story of Odysseus' former sly raid on the Trojan camp is that no brave man kills furtively, but 'face to face' (511). 'I speak the truth always and am not a man of double tongue' announces the Phrygian Hector (394–5). 'I am the same, a man who cuts a straight path in my words', responds his Thracian ally (422–3). The charioteer asks Hector why, speaking *as one barbarian to another*, he twists his words (833–4). 'Thracian' Ares, with whom Rhesus himself is equated (385), was Athena's traditional enemy, and in this play he is set in opposition to her in her role of heavenly ally of the clever Greeks, the goddess of mental rather than physical prowess. For Odysseus' and Diomedes' subterfuge and machinations (512–13) the outdated machismo of the barbarian monarchs can be no match.

The criticisms ranged against the barbarian intellect are not the same in every tragedy, however, for elsewhere they are not portrayed as deficient in intelligence but excessively cunning. In Aeschylus' *Supplices* the length and detail of Danaus' prescription to his daughters for their appeal to the Argives indicates that the audience is supposed to take note of his calculated 'stage management' of the scene. The Danaids are to arrange themselves piously around the altar (186–90). Their words are to be modest, mournful, and plaintive (194). He gives advice on their facial expression (198–9). Shrewdly assessing the 'laconic' Argives, he warns his daughters against loquacity (200–1); since they hold the weaker hand they must not speak too boldly (203). Aeschylus is here surely implying that Danaus has astutely assessed the circumstances and wishes to manipulate the Argives; it was precisely the supposed generic cunning of the Egyptians which was used against them in comedy and oratory.[73] Cratinus, for example, used the verb 'to Egyptianize' as an equivalent of 'to be villainous and malicious' (*panourgein kai kakotropeuesthai*, fr. 406 *KA*), and Hyperides' speech in prosecution of an Egyptian perfumier from the Piraeus stresses not only his ethnic origin but his sophistication, wiliness, and duplicity (Hyperides 3. 3, 13, 23). It is especially significant that a line attributed to Aeschylus himself, perhaps from the same trilogy as *Supplices*, already reflects this stereotype: 'Egyptians are terribly good at weaving wiles' (fr. 373); Danaus is a personification of Egyptian cunning.

A similar pattern establishes itself with respect to *andreia*, manliness

---

[73] See Froidefond 1971, pp. 93–5, 225–6; Whitehead 1977, p. 112; Long 1986, p. 140.

or courage. The barbarians' failure in this virtue may take one of two forms; they may be cowards who embody the Platonic opposite of courage, *deilia*, or excessively confident boasting warriors who adumbrate the *alazones* of New Comedy. The ideal mean between these extremes, defined in Plato's *Laches* as courage tempered with prudence (197b), is normally reserved for Greeks. In *Persae* the messenger's speech implied a contrast between barbarian cowardice and Greek bravery, for statements about Greeks formulated in barbarian mouths, though often hostile, are never belittling; two speeches in Euripides' *IT*, produced nearly sixty years later, are modelled along the same lines. Just as Iphigeneia's deception of Thoas celebrates the ascendancy of the Greek intellect, so the messenger speeches celebrate the superiority of the Hellenes in the physical sphere. The first speech, delivered by a Black Sea cowherd, is a eulogy of Greek valour. Despite being heavily outnumbered, Orestes and Pylades were too athletic-looking to be attacked (304–5). The cowherd admits that they were finally captured not because the Taurians were courageous (*tolmēi men ou*, 330), but by force of numbers. In the second messenger's speech the account of how the heroes, once again outnumbered and unarmed, fought off the Taurians is informed by the Greeks' pride in their athletic prowess, for skills from both boxing and the *pankration* were used against the barbarians (1369–70).

Barbarian timidity is stressed above all in *Orestes* where Euripides introduces in his eunuch an incarnation of the proverbial cowardice of the Phrygians, an eternally popular topos in comedy;[74] Tertullian, who regarded the ethnic determination of character as a matter of universal knowledge, headed his list of stereotypes by remarking on the comic poets' caricatures of timid Phrygians (*de Anima* 20. 3), and Aristophanes' *Aves* already supplies evidence to support his remarks (1244–5). Euripides' *Orestes* treads a precarious boundary between tragedy and comedy, and Tertullian might have added the tragic poets had he recalled it. 'Let Menelaus see that it is men he has to deal with, not cowardly Phrygians,' says Electra (1351–2); Pylades ordered Helen's slaves to clear off, calling them 'cowardly Phrygians' (1447), and the slave himself comments that Phrygians are born greatly inferior to Hellenes in terms of martial prowess (1483–5). He is also conspicuously made to admire Pylades' strictly Hellenic virtues of intelligence, loyalty, and courage (1405–6).

---

[74] On this stereotype see Long 1986, p. 141.

At the other end of the scale, however, two of the allies who came to the aid of Troy only to die at Greek hands were portrayed as vaunting barbarian monarchs whose boasts precipitated their downfall, Cycnus, the hero of Sophocles' *Poimenes* (see his boast in fr. 501), and especially Rhesus, whose *alazoneia* is breathtaking.[75] The Trojans have been fighting the Achaeans for ten years, but Rhesus claims that he will single-handedly defeat them in a single day (444–9); he wants to face Achilles and his army alone (488–91), and intends to follow up his victory by invading and conquering Hellas (471–3). But Rhesus' bravado is not tempered by caution, and he dies in his bed before he can even take the field. Perhaps the other plays in this category which dealt with Memnon, Sarpedon, and Eurypylus likewise implied that the confidence of these barbarian princes was nearer to *alazoneia* than to *andreia*.

The third great Platonic virtue, *sōphrosunē*, entailed the proper restraint of the passions, and many of the barbarians of tragedy are invested with an overbearing temper or wild *ēthos*, thus demonstrating *akolasia*, the philosophers' opposite of *sōphrosunē*: Medea is a perfect example (see *Med*. 103–4). This was of course not restricted to non-Greeks: even Medea is in part modelled on the heroic type exemplified by Prometheus, Ajax, and Antigone. But the invention of the barbarian provided a new frame of reference for such psychological portraits, and in many cases the unfettered passions of barbarians come to be closely associated with their ethnicity. The Egyptian herald in *Supplices* threatens far greater violence against his countrywomen than even the most uncouth Greek abductors in tragedy (838–41); the Danaids who reject and later murder their cousins (one of the few constants in this highly variable myth), are no less guilty of unrestrained emotions.[76] In

---

[75] Pohlenz 1954, p. 473, connects the characterization of Rhesus with that of Theorus, the Thracian emissary in *Acharnenses*, in whose unfulfillable promises the Odrysians' betrayal of the Athenian cause before Amphipolis is acerbically caricatured. But he also sees Rhesus as the direct precursor of the *miles gloriosus* of New Comedy. On the vice of *alazoneia* see Theophr. *Char*. 23 and Ribbeck 1882.

[76] Some scholars have seen a distinction between the barbarism of the sons of Aegyptus, represented in *Supplices* by the herald, and the modesty and *sōphrosunē* of the Danaids. Couch 1932, p. 55, went so far as to argue that while the sons of Aegyptus are of 'an impious and insolent race', the Danaids represent the 'persistence of Greek tradition in an alien environment', and that they 'count the cost of flight to a strange land not too great a price to pay for the preservation of Greek tradition and worship'. But whatever else happened in the rest of the trilogy, the Danaids (except for Hypermnestra) must have killed their cousins, and therefore been guilty of a violent crime; see Garvie 1969, pp. 206–7. More importantly,

Sophocles' *Tereus* the Thracian king's error was his failure to control his sexual desire for the Greek Philomela, just as Theoclymenus lusts after Helen; this appears to have been a standard trait of the barbarian male in Greek writers, for one of the reasons Iphigeneia gives for agreeing to die is that she must protect Greek women from forcible abduction by barbarians (*IA* 1380–1).

Polymestor's terrible song after being blinded delineates the wild barbarian character at its most uncontrolled;[77] he has crawled out of the tent on all fours, like a 'mountain beast', and even threatens to eat the corpses of the women who have punished him (*Hec.* 1057–8, 1070–2). Here Euripides seems to foreshadow Aristotle's illustration of the moral vice of 'brutishness' or 'bestiality' with the ethnographic example of the Pontic barbarian tribes who practise cannibalism (*Eth. Nic.* 7. 1148b 19–24). But it is not only the ethnographers' banishment of bestial behaviour to the lands of the barbarians which lies behind Polymestor's actions here; cannibalism, like incest, rape, and parricide, were especially associated with the tyrant, who lets loose the savage appetites in his soul.[78] Vocabulary suggestive of animal nature or appetites is often used in the characterization of barbarians; in *Supplices* Aeschylus used a wide range of animal images in his delineation of the herald and his retinue; the crow, dog, monster, spider, and snake (751, 758, 762, 887, 895).

In the Egyptian herald, Tereus, Theoclymenus, and Polymestor, the lack of *sōphrosunē* in the barbarian personality is expressed in its savagery and wildness, *agriotēs*; this type of barbarian is rarely portrayed as effeminate. In others, however, the fault is not savagery but the excessive refinement and luxury, *habrotēs* (the vice of the soul which Aristotle calls *malakia* or *truphē*, *Eth. Nic.* 7. 1145a 35–6), and in this form of deviation from Hellenic self-restraint there is often an element of effeminacy. Both *agriotēs* and *habrotēs* are opposed to the Greek ideal, but they are also opposed to one another and it is therefore necessary to modify the view which sees the barbarian in Greek literature as a simple anti-Greek. Only the idea of the mean between

---

their contempt for democracy, and as women their rejection of the married state, are both typical signs of 'barbarism'.

[77] See further Blaiklock 1952, p. 114.

[78] Plato *Resp.* 9. 571c–d; 10. 619b–c; Detienne 1979, pp. 58–9. On the view of barbarians as occupying a position somewhere between beasts and 'human beings' see Wiedemann 1986.

two extremes, later formulated in abstract philosophical terms by Aristotle, can provide the conceptual structure within which to locate the Greek appropriation of moderation, and the different kinds of extremism—stupidity or excessive cunning, cowardice or bravado, primitivism or luxuriousness—manifested in the barbarians of tragedy. Aeschylus' *Edoni* actually brought into conflict a savage barbarian and a luxurious one. Lycurgus, king of one of the most warlike tribes known to the Athenians, interrogated Dionysus, disguised as an Asiatic 'soft-stepping prophet' (*mousomantis . . . habrobatēs*, fr. 60)[79] in a trailing Lydian robe (frr. 59, 61). This famous scene was parodied in Aristophanes' *Thesmophoriazusae*, where the part of Dionysus was taken by the effeminate Agathon, and imitated in the confrontation between Pentheus and Dionysus in *Bacchae*.[80]

The vocabulary signifying barbarian luxury recurrent in *Persae* (*habro-* compounds, *ploutos*, *chrusos*, *chlidē*) is used in tragedies on mythical themes to evoke the same associations. Hecuba's foot once walked 'delicately' in Troy (*habron . . . en Troiai poda*), and Ganymede, the Trojan boy loved by Zeus, treads 'delicately' amidst the golden wine-cups (*Tro.* 506, 819–22). The long effeminate hair of the Lydian Dionysus is a 'luxurious' fashion (*Bacch.* 493, *habron bostruchon*). The wealth, *ploutos*, so intimately connected in the Greek mind with tyrannical forms of government (see *OT* 380–1), was associated by the tragedians quite as much with mythical Troy and Egypt as with contemporary Persia: Euripides' Hecuba speaks of the opulence of her palace and the unsurpassed wealth of her son Hector (*Hec.* 624, *Tro.* 674). Helen's reluctance to sit at table beside a barbarian is not diminished by her awareness of his riches, and Teucer likens Theoclymenus' palace to that of Ploutos himself (*Hel.* 295–6, 69). *Persae* had stressed the gold of the eastern empire, and gold, though of course found also in Greek contexts, becomes a symbol of barbarian luxury predominating in accounts of foreign costumes, armies, and palaces. In Aeschylus' *Phryges*, the third play of his so-called 'tragic Iliad', a trilogy dealing with Achilles' revenge on Hector, Hermes led in Priam and his Phrygian retinue, and the gold of the ransom money, that hallmark of eastern splendour, was weighed out on stage before the spectators' eyes (*Σ A Il.* 22. 351).

---

[79] The reading *habrobatēs* was Hermann's; he however believed it to refer to Orpheus.

[80] For a discussion of the parody in *Thesmophoriazusae* see Rau 1967, pp. 109–11. Eubulus also seems to have parodied part of this famous scene: see Kassel 1966, pp. 10–12.

In Sophocles gold is claimed to come from as far east as India (*Ant.* 1038-9), but in Euripides it is associated with Asia and Thrace. It is perhaps particularly apt that Medea is described as being born of the 'golden race' of the sun (*Med.* 1255-6), for there was a famous and brilliant school of goldwork around the Phasis in the fifth century.[81] The Euripidean Paris is usually said to be decked in gleaming gold (*Tro.* 992, *IA* 74), Hecuba was once queen of the 'golden Phrygians', the 'Phrygian city' runs with gold, and the Phrygian gods have golden images (*Hec.* 492; *Tro.* 995, 1074-5). But nearer to home were the ore-rich regions of southern Thrace and its great rivers which fetched down the alluvial gold so coveted at Athens; thus the Thracian Polymestor's crime in *Hecuba* was motivated by lust for gold, the Thracian army is clad in golden armour, Rhesus lives in 'golden halls', and the Muses' singing competition with Thamyris took place on the gold-rich soil of the Pangaion mountains (*Rhes.* 382, 439, 921-2).

Another term found in the eastern context of *Persae* to be inextricably bound up with the notion of barbarian luxury, *chlidē*, enters the semantic field surrounding mythical barbarians. The Egyptian Danaids 'luxuriate' in their exotic clothing (Aesch. *Supp.* 235-6), Paris is dressed in gorgeous barbarian luxury (*barbarōi chlidēmati*, *IA* 74), and the funeral of the Thracian Rhesus at Troy is to be honoured by the immolation of the *chlidē* of a thousand gowns (*Rhes.* 960). A word embracing much the same concepts as *habrosunē* and *chlidē* was *truphē*, used of an excessively dainty or comfortable way of life;[82] wealth and *truphai* are said to be a bad education for masculinity and courage (Eur. fr. 54. 1-2, from his *Alexander*). This term enriches Euripides' 'vocabulary of barbarism'. Helen has come back to Greece with 'Trojan luxuries' (*truphai*, *Or.* 1113), and the Asiatic maenads toss their 'delicate locks' into the air (*trupheron . . . plokamon*, *Bacch.* 150).

The evocation of eastern *habrosunē* in *Persae* had relied not only on the implementation of key vocabulary. It also involved the suggestion by various other means of both the material comforts enjoyed by the Persian ruling class, and their psychological tendency towards unrestrained emotionalism, particularly excessive displays of grief. Both of these techniques are echoed in the portrayal of mythical societies, especially Troy. In Sophocles' *Laocoon* a Trojan altar steams with drops

---

[81] Lordkipanidze 1985, p. 19.

[82] *Truphē* is paired with *malthakia*, 'softness', at Plato *Resp.* 9. 590b 3, and with *akolasia*, 'intemperance', at *Grg.* 492c.

of myrrh, 'barbarian fragrances' (fr. 370); the Asiatic maenads of *Bacchae* sing of 'Syrian incense' (144, see also fr. adesp. 656. 30–1). Helen in *Orestes* has brought back with her from Troy valuable mirrors and scents besides which the amenities available in Hellas seem humble indeed (*Or*. 1112–14). In a passage of particularly subtle exoticism the Trojan chorus of *Hecuba* sing that on the night Troy fell they had been arranging their hair under their *mitras*, and 'gazing into the endless reflections' of their golden mirrors (923–5).

The poets often used allusions to foreign music to evoke the associations of the exotic lifestyle and unrestrained *ēthos* of the barbarians; a fragment of Sophocles' *Mysi* speaks of the antiphonal tunes of the 'Phrygian triangle' and 'Lydian pectis' (fr. 412), *Troades* 544 of Libyan pipes used in celebrations at Troy, and Paris in *IA* once played 'barbarian' melodies on his pipes while tending his herds on Ida (576–8). Certain instruments are especially associated with the rites of Demeter-Cybele (see further below section 7); the chorus of Sophocles' *Tympanistae* was composed either of Bacchants or devotees of the Mountain Mother, and the play referred to *elumoi* (fr. 644), narrow pipes used in the worship of the 'Phrygian' goddess (Pollux 4. 74), probably to be identified with the 'loud and deep-toned' Phrygian pipes discussed by Athenaeus (*Deipn*. 4. 185a). An anonymous fragment speaks of the Phrygian pipe, castanets, and tympani beloved of the Mother (fr. adesp. 629. 5–9): significantly, it is in Ionics and Anacreontics, the only metres which can almost certainly be claimed to have a thematic association with barbarism. It was seen in chapter 2. 4b that Ionics *a minore* seem to have been used to support exotic atmospheres conjured up by oriental themes and significant vocabulary; it is just possible that the use of Ionics in *Agamemnon* is designed to evoke similar associations. Ionics are interspersed with other metres in a section of the great second stasimon where the theme is first the crime of Paris and Helen, who left her 'delicate draperies' (*habrotimōn/prokalummatōn*), and then the loud lamentations of Troy caused by that crime (690–5, 708–13).[83]

Barbarian music was especially important in Sophocles' *Thamyris*, which recounted the story of the Thracian citharode, already mentioned in the *Iliad*. He travelled in the Peloponnese from Oechalia to Dorium, where the Muses met him (*Il*. 2. 595–600),

---

[83] See Scott 1984, pp. 53–5.

and put an end to his singing ... for he boasted that he would be victorious if the Muses themselves were to sing against him, the daughters of Zeus who wears the aegis, but in their anger they maimed him and deprived him of his wonderful singing and made him forget his lyre-playing.

In myth he is a kind of *Doppelgänger* of the Thracian singer Orpheus; his name may have originated as that of a *daimōn* of feasts and festivals, for Hesychius glosses a noun *thamuris* (s.v.) with *panēguris*. The etymological root is Greek enough,[84] but his name may have sounded foreign to Sophocles' audience by association with the truly barbarian name *Tomyris* borne by a famous Massagetan queen (Hdt. 1. 205). Thrace was especially associated with music (the Muses are usually located in the north of Greece): in Aeschylus' *Lycurgeia* the calming music of Orpheus, the disciple of Apollo, was no doubt contrasted with the furore of the songs of Dionysus' *Bassarae*.[85] The fragments of *Thamyris* not only suggest that the poet transported the setting of the singing competition from the Peloponnese to Thrace,[86] but that it reflected interest in the exotic melodies played on Thamyris' lyre (see frr. 241, 245), and in foreign musical instruments, the *magadis*, triangle, and phoenix (frr. 238, 239, 239a), the latter said to have been used specifically 'by Thracian princes at their feasts' (Nicomedes ap. Ath. *Deipn*. 14. 637a–b).

In many tragedies the contrast between singing and speaking voices reinforces the antithesis between barbarian abandonment and Greek self-restraint. In Aeschylus' *Supplices* only barbarians sing. During the suppliants' altercation with Pelasgus the despotic and transgressive sentiments of the chorus are expressed in song; the Greek's democratic and prudent responses emerge in the iambic trimeter (348–437). A similar pattern is clear in the cases of the barbarian choruses of *Choephoroe* and of Euripides' *Phoenissae* and *Bacchae*. Emotional lyricism becomes the vehicle for barbarian—especially female

---

[84] See von Kamptz 1982, p. 113.

[85] See Burkert 1985a, p. 224: 'An opposition between Apollo and Dionysus was first sensed in music: their cult hymns, the paean and the *dithyrambos*, are felt to be incompatible in harmony and rhythm and also in ethos; clarity is opposed to drunkenness.'

[86] Fr. 237 refers to the 'Thracian peak of Zeus' Athos'. The setting may therefore have been the coastal region around Mount Athos on the eastern promontory of Chalcidice; Strabo records a tradition in which Thamyris ruled over this area (7. fr. 35 Meineke). A passage in *Rhesus*, however, clearly identifies Mount Pangaion as the scene of the contest (921–2).

barbarian—self-expression; the spoken trimeter is the medium of Hellenic 'reason'. The singing voices of several barbarian individuals also weld emotional content to lyric form by interacting with the measured tones of Hellenic characters. The Trojan Cassandra's kommos in *Agamemnon* violently irrupts into the tense spoken dialogue of the preceding scene (1072). The savage song of the Thracian Polymestor, as he crawls blinded around the stage, has already been discussed; in *Orestes* the two singing characters are the female Electra and the Phrygian slave.

Xerxes' sung exchanges with the chorus had brought Aeschylus' enactment of the oriental pathos in *Persae* to an almost hysterical close, and it is in scenes of mourning that the barbarian singing voice is most often heard. The Asiatic chorus of *Choephoroe* describe in grim detail the mutilations they inflict upon themselves, the gashing of their cheeks into 'fresh-cut furrows' until they run with blood (23–5), the tearing of their robes and pounding of their breasts (28–31), the clenched fists which rain down blows on their heads until they resound with the strokes (425–8): it was exactly these excessive customs which were regarded as 'barbaric' at Athens. The deaths of heroes fighting for Troy provided the tragedians with particularly good opportunities for the presentation of laments by eastern characters. Aeschylus' *Cares* dealt with the death of Europa's son, Lycian Sarpedon, who fought and died at Troy. The poet's choice of a Carian rather than a Lycian chorus is perhaps illuminated by Strabo's observation that the Lycians were often subsumed to the Carians by the poets (14. 5. 16); after all, they were neighbours and both spoke daughter dialects of Luwian. But a chorus of genuine male Lycians seems to have appeared in Euripides' *Bellerophon*; in choosing a Carian chorus to bewail Sarpedon's death in his *Cares*, therefore, Aeschylus may have been prompted rather by the fame of the Carian epicedian lament. Plato speaks of hiring mourners to sing 'Carian dirges' at funerals (*Leg*. 7. 800e 2–3), and Menander wrote a *Karinē* about one such wailing-woman. Perhaps Europa sang laments similar to those delivered by Astyoche for her Mysian son in Sophocles' *Eurypylus*; a section of this play involving a threnodic interchange with the chorus in both lyrics and iambics survives on a papyrus (Soph. fr. 210. 30–48).

It was the death of Hector and the fall of the city of Troy itself which provided the fertile mythical material most frequently converted by the playwrights into long songs of grief, usually delivered by

Andromache, Hecuba, or a chorus of Trojan widows.[87] Asia, defeated, addresses the Greek audience in the female singing voice. Either Andromache or Hecuba uttered a long semi-lyrical *thrēnos* at Hector's tomb in a play of unknown authorship, recounting the sufferings of the land of Ida and the destruction of the Trojan citadel (fr. adesp. 644. 20–49). There are similar passages in *Andromache* (see especially the heroine's elegiacs at 103–16). After the prologue of *Hecuba* there follows a long section of Trojan recitative and singing, performed by Hecuba, the chorus, and Polyxena (59–215): it is Odysseus' appearance which disrupts the threnodic mood and asserts the primacy of the Greek, male, spoken, voice of cynicism and reasoned argument.

The plangent *thrēnoi* of *Troades* nearly equal the inconsolable grief expressed by Xerxes and the chorus in *Persae*, and at times seem deliberately designed to echo passages from the earlier drama. Just as the Greek paean had been contrasted with the barbarian lament in Aeschylus' play, so Hecuba contrasts her *thrēnos* (98–152) with the Hellenic paean (126), and subsequently with the joyful choruses which used to be danced at Troy 'to the Phrygian gods' (151–2). At the heart of the play there is another lament, when the chorus invoke the Muse to weep and sing an 'epicedian ode' (512–14), and later Hecuba and Andromache sing a dirge for their family and city, reiterating the perfect tense perhaps traditional in the threnodic genre: 'our prosperity has gone, Troy has gone' (*bebak' olbos, bebake Troia*, 582);[88] Phrynichus had opened his *Phoenissae* with a participle form of the same verb (*Tad' esti Persōn tōn palai bebēkotōn*, fr. 8), and Xerxes and the chorus in *Persae* had lamented the extermination of the barbarian army, 'they have gone ... gone', 1002–3). The dirge concluding *Troades* (1287–332) seems to recall that at the end of *Persae*, with its frequent repetitions, emotional cries, and Hecuba's orders to the chorus to practise a ritual gesture of mourning, the beating of the ground with their hands (1306).

Barbarian abandonment elsewhere found a medium in gesture and even in dance. The chorus of Aeschylus' *Persae* had clapped their hands

---

[87] On the significance of the fall of Troy in archaic and fifth-century Greek poetry see Fittipaldi 1979.

[88] Alexiou 1974, pp. 83–5, discusses the traditional form of the ancient Greek lament for cities. For its eastern antecedents see the patterns of repetition and refrain, the motif of abandonment by the gods, and the traditional comparison of former peacetime revelry with the prospect of exile and slavery in *The Lamentation over the Destruction of Ur* (Kramer 1940, pp. 21–5, 29, 35, 39–40, 43, 55, 59).

(Ar. *Ran*. 1029), but the chorus in his *Phryges* performed unusual dance movements. In an Aristophanic fragment which refers to this play, a character remembers seeing the Phrygians who came with Priam to ransom Hector's corpse 'making many gestures (*polla*...*schēmatisantas*) in one direction, and another, and another' (fr. 696B. 3 *KA*); perhaps they were dancing a *schēma* which is illustrated in ancient art performed by dancers in Persian or Phrygian costume who clasp their hands over their heads and bend repeatedly to right or left, pointing the elbows as they go. Again, Hesychius records the existence of a dance called the 'fox' (*alōpēx*, s.v.), performed by the Bassarae, votaries of the 'Thracian' Dionysus, which imitated the movements of the fox; it has been thought that Aeschylus' Thracian Bassarae danced the 'fox' in the *Lycurgeia*.[89]

6 ETHNOGRAPHY

The researches of the Ionian geographer Hecataeus and those of his contemporaries and successors, especially Herodotus, exerted a profound influence on the tragedians. Observations about the lands and customs of contemporary barbarians were often lifted from the prose writers to add picturesque detail to the presentation of the non-Greeks of heroic tradition. The tragedians took up Anaxagoras' theory about the Nile's emanation from the melting snows of Ethiopia (Aesch. fr. 300; Eur. *Hel*. 1–3; *Archelaus* fr. 1). Hecataeus' cartographic material almost certainly inspired various passages of poeticized geography in Aeschylus and Sophocles (see above, chapter 2. 3). The Danaids had been discussed by Hecataeus (1 *FgrH* 19–22), but he had also referred to Egyptian bread and beer (F 322–3), an interest which reappears in Aeschylus' *Supplices* transformed into claims that the Egyptian diet and ale are inferior, and not as conducive to manliness as Greek fare (761, 953). But although the barbarians' supposed generic greed and predilection for alcohol were commonplaces in ancient authors (in tragedy see, e.g., Eur. fr. 907), the Thracians were especially prone to such accusations. In comedy the Odrysian king Medoces was pilloried

[89] On the dance with hands joined performed by Phrygian votaries see Lawler 1964, pp. 114–15 and fig. 47; on the 'fox' dance, ibid., pp. 69–70. In Egyptian art there is a clear distinction between the unrestrained gestures of foreigners and the controlled movements of even the lowliest Egyptians (Helck 1964, p. 105).

for his greed,[90] and Plato paints a repellent picture of Thracians of both sexes drinking their wine neat and tipping it down their clothes (*Leg*. 1. 637e).[91] It is interesting to find a similar criticism being levelled at the Thracian king in *Rhesus* (418–19), a perfect example of an ethnic stereotype affecting the rhetoric with which a tragic poet brought a myth to life.

Euripides' *IT* was profoundly influenced, if not actually prompted, by Herodotus' account of the Taurians. But perhaps it was the historian's Egyptian *logos* which was most often echoed in passing allusions by the tragedians. The reverberations of his second book were to be felt in all literary genres; the stir it caused has been likened to the effect of Marco Polo's travelogue on medieval Europe.[92] Among the historians Herodotus' near contemporary Hellanicus wrote an *Aiguptiaka*; Aristophanes' *Aves* and *Thesmophoriazusae*, and Euripides' *Electra* and *Helen*, all reflect the new interest in Egypt, especially in Herodotus' discussion of the Helen myth (see above, section 2). But Sophocles preferred to use Herodotus' Egyptian enquiries to sharpen his rhetoric (see *OC* 337–41), or for metaphorical effect; someone, probably Phineus after his long starvation, was said to resemble an Egyptian mummified corpse (fr. 712), a comparison most likely to have been influenced by Herodotus' account of Egyptian mummification practices (2. 86–90; see also Soph. fr. 395. 3).[93]

Both playwrights also reflect knowledge of Thracian customs described by the historian. Sophocles' *Thamyris* mentioned cannabis (fr. 243), a plant Herodotus had said was used by the Thracians; they made cloth out of it and like the Scythians probably enjoyed its

[90] On Thracian stereotypes in comedy see Yarcho 1982.

[91] Just as the traditional Amazonomachy scene influenced artistic portrayal of the Persians, so the stereotypical view of primitive peoples borrowed features from other mythical tribes, the Cyclopes and Centaurs. Besides sharing a propensity for heavy drinking, the Thracians and Scythians were associated, like the Cyclopes, with the use of dairy products. See 1 *FgrH* F 154, Eur. *Cyc*. 134–6; Seaford 1984a, pp. 127–8; Hartog 1988, pp. 166–70. The process was reciprocal, for 'supernatural barbarians' took characteristics from the ethnography of primitive tribes; the portrayal of Amazons was affected by the iconography of the Scythians and Thracians (Shapiro 1983). Aristotle talks of the 'Thracian Cyclopes' (*de Mir*. 121 = 842a 11), and satyrs appear on vases in Thracian costumes, sometimes holding a *peltē*. On a psykter by Douris in the British Museum (E 768 = *ARV*², p. 446, no. 262) a satyr wears the geometrically patterned Thracian *zeira*. See Raeck 1981, pp. 84–5.

[92] Froidefond 1971, p. 209.

[93] For a discussion of Sophocles' debt to Herodotus see Rasch 1913.

narcotic properties (see Hdt. 4. 74–5). Herodotus had also insisted that the Thracians were polygamous (5. 5), a custom for which they were derided in Euripides' *Andromache* (215–17) and later in Menander (frr. 794–5). But Aeschylus may have drawn his audience's attention to this practice long before Euripides or Herodotus, for there is a strong possibility that he composed a *Thamyris* which ingeniously connected the story of the singer's quarrel with the Muses to the alleged Thracian practice of polygamy. The scholiast on *Rhesus* 916, whose remarks are preserved on a leaf of a Vatican manuscript,[94] records this tradition, introducing it by naming as his source a work of the fourth-century Asclepiades, probably his *Tragodoumena* (= 12 *FgrH* F 10):

... there are those who say that there were two Thamyrises ... but [in Aes]chylus the story of Thamyris and [the Muses] is more [precisely] explained. At any rate (*goun*) Asclepiades in his Tra[godoumena] says the following about them.

A synopsis of the plot is then provided:

They say that Thamyris was wonderful in appearance, his right eye being blue and his left black, and that he thought that he excelled all others in singing. When the Muses came to Thrace, Thamyris became angry with them because he wanted to cohabit with them all, saying that it was a Thracian custom for many women to live with a single man. So they challenged him to a singing contest on these terms: if they were victorious, they should do whatever they wished with him, but if he won, he could take as many of them as he chose. This was agreed, but the Muses won, and put out his eyes.

It has been customary to assume that such a bizarre storyline could only be derived from comic travesty of myth, perhaps Antiphanes' *Thamyras*,[95] rather than from the tragedy suggested by Asclepiades' interests. But the quotation from his work follows a statement about Aeschylus, and the introductory *goun* looks suspiciously as if it is functioning 'in part proof',[96] which would mean that the scholiast was producing the version in Asclepiades precisely in order to illustrate the statement about Aeschylus' play. Jacoby suggested, with such an interpretation in mind, that 'more [strangely]' (*xenikō]teron*) should be read instead of Rabe's supplement 'more [precisely]' (*akribes]teron*). Scholars

---

[94] Published by Rabe 1908.

[95] Lesky 1951, p. 102. (Different traditions prefer to spell the name either as *Thamyris* or *Thamyras*.)

[96] See Denniston 1954, pp. 451–3.

who feel that Aeschylus must at least have referred to Thamyris' story assume that he was the subject of a choral ode, perhaps in *Edoni* or *Bassarae*.[97] But this does not solve the problem of the apparently untragic nature of the story recorded by Asclepiades.

Is it possible that Aeschylus did not merely introduce the story of Thamyris as a mythical exemplum, but produced a *Thamyris* himself, from which the version in Asclepiades is derived? So little is known about early tragedy that it is hazardous to assert that a story is inappropriate for tragic dramatization according to some subjective criterion of seriousness or 'good taste'. The effect of ethnic stereotypes on Aeschylean tragedy is clearly demonstrated in *Persae*, *Supplices*, and the fragmentary *Lycurgeia*. The Thracian Tereus was portrayed by Sophocles as the rapist of his own wife's sister, which must have emphasized his libidinousness, even if no references were actually made to Thracian polygamy. One scholar has tried to bring the story into line with what he perceived to be a 'tragic tone' by suggesting that Thamyris had demanded but one of the Muses.[98] But in the absence of any other evidence for this play it is perhaps safer to refer the story from Asclepiades to a satyr drama.

Aeschylus referred to his Persians' foreign costumes; his mythical barbarians were characterized in the same way. The Egyptian Danaids are dressed in barbarians gowns and headgear by which Pelasgus can immediately tell that they are not Greek (*anellēnostolon*, *Supp.* 234–7), and the Thracian maenads in *Bassarae* took their name from distinctive cloaks made or trimmed with fox fur.[99] Sophocles did not neglect barbarian costumes: in his *Andromeda* someone mentioned or wore a striped white Persian gown (the *sarēton*, fr. 135), and in his *Aechmalotides* a fabric was described as 'foam of a Lydian shuttle' (fr. 45). In Euripides' plays the gorgeous garments of his eastern barbarians are mentioned on several occasions; Agamemnon can tell that the clothes covering Polydorus' corpse are Trojan rather than Argive (*Hec.* 734–5), and Hecuba wraps Astyanax's body in the 'splendid Phrygian robes' he should have worn to his wedding (*Tro.* 1218–20). Polyneices can see

---

[97] Radt prints the passage as Aeschylus fr. inc. 376a. Mette thought it came from *Bassarae* (1963, p. 139), while Höfer attributed it to *Edoni* (1916–24, col. 472).

[98] Otto 1955, p. 48.

[99] Zoomorphism played an important part in Thracian religion: see Hoddinott 1986, p. 27. On the possible religious significance of the fox, see Kazarow 1954, p. 547. For the Bassarids see also Anacreon fr. 411b *PMG*; Euripides' *Hypsipyle* fr. 64. 50–1 Bond. Pisani 1934, pp. 217–24, discusses the whole subject.

from their appearance that the chorus of *Phoenissae* are not Greek (277–9). Paris in particular is said to have worn clothes of great opulence, for Hecuba remarks that at the mere sight of him in his 'barbarian robes' and gleaming gold Helen lost her wits (*Tro.* 991–2). In *IA*, where references to Paris portray him as the quintessential *habros* eastern barbarian, his clothes are embroidered with flowers (73).

The northern barbarians were more famous as fighters than lovers, and the visual images of the Thracian peltast and rider and the Scythian archer, popularized by the vase-painters, affected the tragedians' recasting of myth. In the *Iliad*, of course, the Thracians' fighting methods had been indistinguishable from those of other peoples, but once Peisistratus had hired a contingent of mercenaries from the Pangaion region in Thrace they had appeared on numerous vases in their unmistakable short patterned cloak (*zeira*), peaked cap (*alōpekis*), spear, and distinctive shield (*peltē*).[100] Tragedy uses this shield as a symbol of Thracian martial prowess. Ares, the divine embodiment of Thracian bloodthirstiness, is 'lord of the golden Thracian *peltē*' (Eur. *Alc.* 498), and mythical kings are anachronistically conceived in the gear of the contemporary Thracian peltast. Lycurgus wears a short *zeira* on a vase probably illustrating a scene from the *Lycurgeia*,[101] and a Thracian is described in *Lysistrata* as 'waving his *peltē* and spear like Tereus', almost certainly in reference to Sophocles' tragedy (Ar. *Lys.* 563). The likelihood that Tereus was cast in the mould of the Thracian soldier is even greater if Sophocles made use of the tradition that he had previously afforded military aid to Athens (Thuc. 2. 29; Ovid *Met.* 6. 424–6), as so many troops of Thracian peltasts were to do from the time of Peisistratus onwards. Polymestor was also conceived as a Thracian soldier. When Hecuba and her women literally disarm him, they take away his 'twofold equipment' (1156); this may mean both his spear and shield, or the twin spears with which Bendis, the great Thracian goddess, was represented (Cratinus fr. 85 *KA*), and which were carried by one of the most familiar types of peltast.[102] But the women also admire the fine fabric of his clothes, made by a 'shuttle in an Edonian hand'

---

[100] For a full description of the Thracian (Bithynian) costume see Hdt. 7. 75. On Peisistratus' mercenaries see Best 1969, pp. 6–7.

[101] An Attic red-figured hydria by a late mannerist, 450–25 BC. See Trendall and Webster 1971, p. 49, no. III. 1. 13 (= *ARV*², p. 1121, no. 17).

[102] Best 1969, p. 141.

(1153), for Thracian textiles were famous;[103] the dead hero's linen shroud in Sophocles' *Eurypylus* was woven by women of the Ister (Danube), which constituted the northern boundary of Thrace (fr. 210. 67–8).

It is perhaps in his equestrianism that Polymestor is most recognizably Thracian. The androphagous mares whom Heracles subdues belong to another Thracian, Diomedes (Eur. *HF* 380–6), and art represents the Thracian Eumolpus riding beside his father Poseidon, the patron and parent of horses.[104] Horses played an essential role in both the solar and the rider cults in Thracian religion, and kings were buried with their horses.[105] Euripides therefore ensures that Polymestor is cast in the mould of the mounted warrior, as the 'Thracian rider' (710), who rules the 'horse-loving people' of the Chersonese (9, see also 1090). In *Rhesus* there is a list of the contingents of horsemen, peltasts, archers, and javelin-throwers the poet imagines arriving to fight at Troy in their 'Thracian gear' (309–13): it is in this play, where a full epic prototype has survived, that the process can best be seen by which 'the military relationships of the time of writing ... are obviously projected on to those of a distant past'.[106]

Much the same pattern is found with the Scythian bow. Scythians do not appear in Homer, but Peisistratus had hired a troop of Scythian archers who provoked an efflorescence of portraits in sixth-century vase-painting, and in the fifth century Scythian archers worked as public slaves at Athens.[107] Their composite bow, so different from the

---

[103] On Thracian textiles see Kazarow 1954, p. 543. The shuttle was prominent in myths dramatized by the tragedians which were connected with Thrace. In one version of the Phineus story the Phineids' stepmother blinded them 'with a shuttle for a dagger' (Soph. *Ant*. 973–6); in Sophocles' *Tereus* Philomela communicated with her sister by the ruse of a false message embroidered on a robe, the 'voice of the shuttle' (fr. 595, see Arist. *Poet*. 1454b 36–7). Kiso 1984, pp. 77–8, thinks that Philomela's weaving skills were a sign of the superior level of civilization introduced by the Athenian sisters to Thrace.

[104] A vase from Policoro of the late fifth century almost certainly illustrating Euripides' *Erechtheus* portrays Eumolpus as a rider, a characterization which Weidauer thinks was lent special meaning by his Thracian provenance (1969, p. 93 with fig. 41).

[105] See Hoddinott 1986, pp. 27, 29, and the fifth-century evidence for the Thracian hunter-hero cult in the figure of a mounted hero on a silver belt clasp in Hoddinott 1981, p. 108.

[106] Best 1969, p. 12.

[107] For a comprehensive discussion of Scythians in archaic Attic vase-painting see Vos 1963. On the function and image of Scythian state slaves in fifth-century Athens see Plassart 1913; Jacob 1928, pp. 53–78; Hall 1989.

Greek segmented version, attracted much attention.[108] Although no Scythians except the chorus of Sophocles' Argonautic play *Scythae* are known to have appeared in the tragic theatre, in *Choephoroe* the chorus longs for Ares to come and deliver the house, wielding his Scythian bow (161–3), and in a fragment of Agathon an illiterate man describes the shape of the letter Σ by comparing it with a Scythian bow (fr. 4. 3). But in *Persae*, by calling Darius *toxarchos* (556), Aeschylus had turned the bow into a powerful symbol of barbarism in general, and Euripides is looking as much to Persia as to Homer in entitling Paris *ho toxotas* (*Or.* 1409). As Lycus' famous sophistries in *HF* demonstrate (159–64), the archer, unless divine, was considered in the fifth century to be considerably inferior to the Hellenic hoplite.

There are few references to the different physical appearance of barbarian characters in tragedy except in the case of blacks, also familiar from their visual images in sixth-century art. The Danaids refer to their own skin as darkened by the sun (*melanthes/hēlioktupon genos*, Aesch. *Supp.* 154–5), and Pelasgus likens them to 'Indian nomad women . . . who live in the neighbourhood of the Ethiopians' (284–6). It is the dark skin of the Egyptian sailors showing against their white clothing which strikes Danaus when their ship heaves into view (719–20),[109] and the women use the same word, *melanchimos*, of their antagonists (745). The dark Egyptian skin affects the imagery with which they express their fear of their attackers (*onar onar melan*, 888).[110] But did they wear masks which supported these claims to a dark skin? Pickard-Cambridge concluded that 'where the complexion of foreigners was in question, the mask-maker could doubtless oblige',[111] and there is no reason to doubt this. It may be relevant that according to the Suda Aeschylus (s.v.) was the first 'to introduce fearsome masks which were painted with colours', but the more important evidence is circumstantial. Given the popularity of blacks in Greek vase-painting from the first half of the sixth century, and the care with which they

[108] When Plato discusses ambidexterity he illustrates his argument by allusion to the archers of Scythia, trained to use both hands (*Leg.* 7. 795a 1–3).

[109] This passage seems to owe something to the Athenians' experiences of Xerxes' fleet, which had included a task force of two hundred Egyptian triremes commanded by Xerxes' own brother Achaemenes (Hdt. 7. 89, 97). At the battle of Artemisium it was the Egyptians who of all the imperial navy had emerged with the most glory, by capturing five Greek ships with their crews (Hdt. 8. 17). See also *Persae* 33–40.

[110] On the white/black and light/dark antitheses in *Supplices* see Irwin 1974, pp. 130–1.

[111] Pickard-Cambridge 1968, p. 192.

were portrayed, it seems unlikely that the mask-painters would not
have been prompted to borrow the same artistic techniques.[112] It is
even possible that the frequent selection by the dramatists in the first
half of the fifth century of the stories of the Egyptian Busiris and the
descendants of Io, of the Libyan Antaeus and Ethiopian Memnon,
reflects a similar interest in the visual possibilities of contrasting the
black and white complexion as that evidenced in sculpture and vase-
painting.

Besides Aeschylus' Danaid trilogy and Memnon plays, Phrynichus
composed a *Danaides*, he and Aristias both wrote dramas, whether
tragic or satyric, about Antaeus, and the shadowy Sicilian Epicharmus
is credited with a *Busiris*. It is also possible that Zeus appeared in the
guise of a black stranger at the Argive court in Sophocles' probably
tragic *Inachus* (see fr. 269a. 53-4, *ho polupharm* [*akos*]/*karbanos aithos*), and
having stealthily made Io pregnant with a son Epaphus, the founder of
the Egyptian people, turned her into a cow. It has been argued that his
dark skin and covert activity in the play offered an aetiology for the
Egyptians' appearance and supposed generic cunning.[113] But it is
difficult to be sure how the physical appearance of the *Ethiopians* of
tragedy was visualized. Homer's Ethiopians, of course, live on the edges
of Ocean, in both the east and the west (*Od*. 1. 22-4), and are an
idealized semi-fabulous people enjoying a special relationship with the
gods (*Il*. 1. 423).[114] It is not even clear that the customary interpretation
of the name *Aithiopes* (which derives from *aithō* and *ops*) as 'burnt-
faces' reveals the whole truth:[115] it has been suggested that the *aith*-
element originally implied, rather than tanned or pigmented skin,
either brilliant eyes or a radiance reflected by dwellers in the east from

---

[112] See Snowden 1970, pp. 158-9, and 1983, pp. 63-4. He presents reasons for believing
that the appearance of blacks was much admired.

[113] Stephanie West 1984, p. 297. Seaford 1980 wants to connect Zeus' dark colour with
his role as Zeus Chthonios, king of the dead; he suggests that this may have concealed an
allusion to the Egyptian god Osiris. The dark stranger may, however, be Hermes, and the
tragedians only rarely alluded to non-Greek religion: see below, section 7 and ch. 4. 4.

[114] The utopian view of the Ethiopians in Homer was influential throughout antiquity.
See Lovejoy and Boas 1935, pp. 348-51; Lonis 1981.

[115] See Dihle 1965, pp. 67-9. He shows that the word *Aithiops* is purely Greek; it has no
connection with either the Egyptian *kuš*, or the Arabic plural *Atāyib* ('good'). The personal
name *ai-ti-jo-qo* appears already in the Pylos tablets, but although there are blacks in the
Minoan frieze at Knossos, there is no indication in epic that the *Aithiopes* are supposed to be
dark-skinned; Dihle suggests that this could be a later development and have nothing to do
with the original meaning.

the morning star.[116] But already in the *Odyssey* there is a passage which presents the Ethiopians as a relatively identifiable ethnic group living somewhere near Africa, between Syria and the Nile. Menelaus reports that his travels took him 'to Cyprus and to Phoenicia and to Egypt, to the Ethiopians, Sidonians and Erembi [Arabs?], and to Libya' (4. 83-5). It is not, however, until Herodotus' *Histories* that extant Greek literature provides a clear distinction between Ethiopians living in Africa ('upper Egypt' or 'Libya') and those in the east (Hdt. 7. 69-70); the 'Libyan' Ethiopians have, he says, the tightly curled hair which might be expected in the African black, while the eastern Ethiopians had the straight hair of some dark-skinned Asiatic peoples.

Not one of the numerous Greek tragedies involving Ethiopians survives intact, and it is difficult to ascertain where the dark-skinned peoples mentioned in fragments were envisaged as living, or how their physical appearance was conceived or dramatically exploited. Euripides' *Archelaus* (fr. 1. 3-4) refers to dark-skinned Ethiopians living, apparently, in Africa at the source of the Nile, like Herodotus' Ethiopians of 'upper Egypt', but other fragments mentioning dark-skinned peoples or Ethiopians seem to refer them, like Homer, either to the far east where the sun rises, or to the south-east corner of the Mediterranean, approximately in the region of modern Syria/Lebanon/Israel. Euripides' *Phaethon*, for example, is set at the court of Merops, king of a dark-skinned people in the furthest east, who are the first to be struck by Helios' rays each morning (line 4, Diggle). But although the chorus and probably Merops were presumably presented as blacks, Phaethon as the son of Helios, and his mother Clymene as an Oceanid nymph, will almost certainly have been white.[117] It is not clear exactly where Sophocles' and Euripides' plays entitled *Andromeda* were thought to have been set; both of them recounted the story of the princess chained to a rock by her father Cepheus, king of the Ethiopians, to be devoured by a sea-monster, but rescued by the Greek hero Perseus. Tradition was to locate the rock at Joppa in Phoenicia (now Israel, see Strabo 16. 2. 28), and later writers regarded Cepheus as king of the *African* Ethiopians (e.g. Pliny *HN* 6. 35. 182), but there is not enough evidence about either tragedy to be certain even that the

[116] Forsdyke 1956, p. 97.

[117] See Diggle 1970, pp. 80, 82. But on an Apulian volute-krater depicting a dramatic scene not from *Phaethon* (Bari 3648), Merops is white. See Trendall and Webster 1971, p. 110, no. III. 5. 5.

exact location was specified. Andromeda herself, of course, as the mother by Perseus of the Persians (Hdt. 7. 61) elsewhere has strong oriental affinities, and indeed on vases portraying the myth recounted in the tragedies she is always white. On the same vases, however, attendants, and on one occasion figures perhaps representing the chorus and Cepheus himself, are portrayed as flat-nosed and curly haired 'African' blacks.[118] This supports the view that black masks were in use, but it does not help to pin down the exact geographical or ethnic specifications given by the tragedians, and indeed their poetic vision of Ethiopia may have been little more than a vaguely exotic locale, almost indistinguishable from, say, the Egypt of Euripides' *Helen*.

An even more intractable problem is that of Memnon, the son of the Dawn, whose defeat while at Troy was famous from the cyclic *Aethiopis* and adapted to the tragic stage by Aeschylus in his *Memnon* and *Psychostasia* and by Sophocles in his *Aethiopes*. The ancients debated whether he was an eastern or African Ethiopian, and the question has never been fully clarified. His father Tithonus *may* be a Hellenized version of the Nubian god Didun,[119] and two vases *may* represent Memnon as an 'African' black,[120] but all the literary sources until Hellenistic times clearly view him as Asiatic: rumours that he was an African first appear in the second century BC.[121] It is therefore likely that the tragedians presented him as an Asiatic: Strabo says that Aeschylus actually made his mother a native of Cissia (15. 3. 2), for all the world as if he were related to the contemporary Achaemenid dynasty in Persia, and Herodotus certainly associated him with Susa (5. 53–4; 7. 151). But what does this reveal about the appearance of the characters in the Memnon plays? From the testimony it is only clear that Aeschylus made him an imposing horseman (Ar. *Ran*. 961–3). An unplaced fragment of Aeschylus refers to an 'Ethiopian woman' (fr. 329); was Memnon's Cissian mother (as opposed to Eos, identified with Eos, or Eos in disguise?) a dark-skinned Asiatic Ethiopian? But

[118] See Trendall and Webster 1971, pp. 63–5, 78–82, nos. III. 2. 1–3; Snowden 1970, pp. 157–9.

[119] Forsdyke 1956, p. 101.

[120] See Snowden 1970, p. 152 and figs. 15a–b, 21. In neither case is it at all certain that the black warrior represented is Memnon.

[121] See Drews' analysis of the sources (1969). As Lesky says (1959, p. 31), it was self-evident that Memnon, as son of the Dawn, should come from the east.

often in art a white Memnon, though in oriental clothing, appears like Andromeda attended by 'African' blacks. It may be that it is fruitless to attempt a systematization of the ancient evidence even according to Herodotus' classifications; the functions performed by the new exoticism of the tragic theatre were not identical with those served by contemporary anthropological enquiries. Perhaps the tragedians, like the vase-painters, though manifestly exploiting the contrast between black and white skins, did not concern themselves with distinguishing between the different sub-categories of black barbarian.[122]

7 RELIGION

Aeschylus did not explicitly differentiate the religious beliefs of his Persians from those of Greeks; the same principle usually applies to the foreigners of myth. Awareness of a small number of distinctively barbarian recipients of worship is however discernible in the tragic texts. In Aeschylus' *Edoni* reference was made to the instruments (*orgia*) of Cotys or Cotyto, an indigenous Thracian goddess,[123] which perhaps have been taken over by the Dionysiac votaries who have arrived in Thrace (Aesch. fr. 57. 1).[124] The plot of the *Lycurgeia*, from which *Edoni* came, may have hinged on Thracian heliolatry, a practice to which Sophocles alluded in his *Tereus*: 'Helios, most venerable and awesome to the horse-loving Thracians' (fr. 682). The second play of the Aeschylean tetralogy, *Bassarae*, saw the maenads' destruction of Orpheus, who would not accept or seceded from Dionysiac religion, preferring the cult of the sun.[125] Apollo was certainly identified with

[122] Though see Snowden 1970, p. 157. He thinks that Aeschylus does distinguish the appearance of the Danaids in *Supplices* (who are, he suggests, of a black/white ethnic mixture) from that of their black cousins. I am not sure that the text can support this distinction.

[123] Although Cotyto's rites were introduced to Athens by Eupolis' time, for he parodied them in his *Baptae* (see *KA* v, pp. 331-3).

[124] For this interpretation of the *orgia* (not *organa*) mentioned in Aesch. fr. 57. 1 see Henrichs 1969, p. 227 n. 13. The musical instruments—pipes, cymbals, and the bull-roarer—are enumerated in the following lines.

[125] Until recently the orthodox reconstruction of the *Lycurgeia* was that of Deichgräber 1939. According to his view the trilogy enacted the rejection of Dionysus by both Lycurgus and Orpheus, their punishment, and Thrace's reconciliation with the newly arrived god. But M. L. West 1983a has proposed an interpretation which makes the fundamental

Helios by the time of Euripides' *Phaethon* (and perhaps of Aeschylus' *Supplices*—see below), and some fringe intellectual groups, whom Sophocles calls 'the wise' (fr. 752. 2) revered the sun.[126] But although the Greeks might invoke Helios or swear oaths by him (see *PV* 91, *OT* 660-1), outside of Rhodes and Crete they did not normally practise heliolatry, which they regarded as a cult fit for primitive man or for barbarians (Plato *Cra*. 397c-d; Ar. *Pax* 406-11).[127] In making his Thracian Orpheus a sun-worshipper Aeschylus does therefore seem to have been exploiting ethnographic theories about Thracian religion; his view is supported by the increasing evidence that it shared features with Persian Zoroastrianism, especially the cult of the sun practised from mountain peaks. Disc-shaped niches for this purpose have been found cut in the hills of southern Bulgaria, and sun motifs are widely evidenced in Thracian pottery and metalwork.[128]

Aeschylus' *Supplices* may also reflect knowledge of barbarian gods. The Danaids' praise of the Nile (561, 854-7) led Kranz to propose that Aeschylus was familiar with ancient Egyptian hymns to Hapy, the personified Nile.[129] Plato certainly knew about Egyptian religious literature (*Leg.* 2. 657a-b), and there is no reason to exclude the possibility that Kranz was right: the Egyptian herald, though he invokes Hermes (one of the few Greek gods believed by Herodotus *not* to be a barbarian import) nevertheless implies that the Argive gods carry no weight with him, for *his* gods 'live beside the Nile' (922). But the most intriguing possibility is that the 'bird of Zeus' which the Egyptians invoke is none other than Amun-Re (212-14):[130]

movement of the trilogy a Nietzschean struggle between Dionysus and Apollo. The story of Orpheus' destruction by the Bassarae is reported in the *Catasterisms* of pseudo-Eratosthenes (no. 24, *The Lyre*), at least some of whose syncretistic version of Orpheus' story is referred to Aeschylus. West argues from two details preserved in a Venice MS containing excerpts from the *Catasterisms* that in *Bassarae* Orpheus had been a disciple of Dionysus, but rejected him after a visit to the underworld, where he underwent a *conversion* to the worship of Helios-Apollo.

[126] The sixth-century Pherecydes of Syros, for example, was thought by Lydus to have identified Zeus and Helios (*de Mensibus* 4. 3); see A. C. Pearson 1917, iii, p. 11. But M. L. West 1971, p. 10 and n. 2, is sceptical about Lydus' testimony. See also Ar. *Nub*. 571-4.

[127] See von Wilamowitz-Moellendorff 1931-2, i, pp. 249-52.

[128] See Hoddinott 1981, p. 17, and 1986, p. 26.

[129] Kranz 1933, p. 101. There is an English translation of a popular Middle Kingdom hymn to Hapy, of the kind Kranz had in mind, in Lichtheim 1973-80, i, pp. 205-9.

[130] The text reproduced here is that of Johansen and Whittle 1980.

⟨*ΔA.*⟩ καὶ Ζηνὸς ὄρνιν τόνδε νῦν κικλήισκετε.
⟨*XO.*⟩ καλοῦμεν αὐγὰς ἡλίου σωτηρίους.
⟨*ΔA.*⟩ ἁγνόν τ' Ἀπόλλω, φυγάδ' ἀπ' οὐρανοῦ θεόν.
[*Danaus*: Call also now upon this bird of Zeus.
Chorus: We call on the saving beams of the sun.
Danaus: And on holy Apollo, a god once exiled from heaven.]

In the art of Mesopotamia and Syria the sun-disc was often portrayed with large wings,[131] but Aeschylus may have been aware that in specifically Egyptian iconography Re or Amun-Re, the sun-god, is portrayed as a hawk or with a hawk's head, which either consists of the sun or supports it. The sun-disc had distinctive long beams radiating outwards.[132] Herodotus identified Amun-Re with Zeus (2. 42); an artistic representation of Zeus with his eagle might therefore be 'identified' by the Egyptian characters as Amun-Re and the sun-headed hawk.[133]

Many editors have however accepted Bamberger's substitution of *inin* ('child') for *ornin* ('bird') at 212, and Page altered the *t'* ('and') at 214 to *g'* ('indeed') in order to extract from all three lines taken together a reference to Helios-Apollo.[134] If *ornin* is to be removed this additional emendation becomes necessary, for if Apollo has already been mentioned at 212, the *t'* is superfluous: it certainly cannot be explained as 'epexegetical' (Tucker's view). It is however difficult to see how the unusual *ornin* can have replaced the ordinary *inin*, a word often used in tragedy for Zeus' children, especially Apollo and Artemis: *difficilior lectio potior*. The question cannot be decisively settled, but the text should certainly not be emended *twice* simply because it does not conform with Greek religious orthodoxy. If Aeschylus could refer to Cotyto by name he might indeed point to Amun-Re by implication,

---

[131] See Pritchard 1954, nos. 447, 477.

[132] See Frankfort 1948, p. 15; Pritchard 1954, no. 320.

[133] For the Amun-Re allusion see Pasquali 1924, p. 246; Horus is preferred by Rose 1957-8, i, p. 30. Defenders of *ornin* have tried various other explanations. A scholion on 212 glosses it rather lamely as 'the sun: for it wakes us up like the cock'. Others have tried to make a connection with the word *alektōr* ('cock'), or with *Ēlektōr*, a Homeric name for the sun, or seen a reference to a statue of Helios (complete with attendant cock), who Pausanias said had an altar by the river Inachus (2. 18. 3). For refutations of these interpretations see Tucker 1889, pp. 48-9; Johansen and Whittle 1980, ii, pp. 170-2.

[134] Diggle accepts Page's emendation and sees in this passage the earliest literary equation of Apollo and Helios; he describes the text's *ornin* as 'grotesque' (1970, p. 147).

especially during a period when the Athenians were beginning to cast interested and acquisitive eyes on the fertile land of the Nile.[135]

Outside Aeschylus there are few signs that recognizably barbarian gods were admitted into the pantheon of tragedy, but there is a small number of allusions to practices associated with non-Greek religion. Sophocles' interest in Egyptian funerary rites, probably inspired by Herodotus, has already been mentioned. Euripides just occasionally suggests that he is exploiting ethnographic rumours. Herodotus often conceptualized barbarian customs as the mirror image of Greek practice. He observed, for example, that the Thracian Trausi inverted normal custom by lamenting births and celebrating deaths (5. 4); a character in Euripides' *Cresphontes* recommends exactly these unconventional rites of passage (fr. 67). In his *Troades* the chorus' sad song about the festivals of Idaean Zeus mentions golden votive images of the gods and the twelve sacred cakes 'of the Phrygians' which may perhaps point to some particular custom (1074–6). The Phrygian in *Orestes* claims—probably wrongly—that *ailinon* is a specifically Asiatic funereal cry (1395–7),[136] and the Egyptian Theonoe may be tinged, for once, with a recognizably Egyptian hue when she is preceded by attendants who waft incense to fumigate her path (*Hel*. 865–7); Plutarch attests that this was a practice of the Egyptian priesthood (*de Is. et Os*. 79).[137] Ion of Chios introduced to his audience a barbarian nurse who had been in the 'mourning pits', where, according to a text attributed to Plutarch, the Egyptians, Syrians, and Lydians spent time after bereavements (Ion fr. 54; see [Plut.] *Cons. ad Apoll*. 22).

One ritual was deliberately associated with barbarian communities by the tragedians, and that was human sacrifice. Socrates' companion in the pseudo-Platonic dialogue *Minos* alludes to different views on human sacrifice amongst Greek and barbarian peoples in order to defend his relativist position on human law: the Carthaginians

---

[135] The chronology of the Egyptian revolt against Persia and the ill-fated Athenian intervention is much disputed, although in Diodorus' scheme the crisis began in 463/2. For a discussion see Salmon 1965, pp. 94–192.

[136] Boisacq proposed a Phrygian origin for the cry, but there is no evidence to support this view: see Aesch. *Ag*. 121; Soph. *Aj*. 627. The expression in Euripides is no proof of etymological origin: see von Wilamowitz-Moellendorff 1895, ii, p. 85. The *linos* song (*Il*. 18. 570), sometimes personified as a mythical singer (Hes. fr. 305. 1), with whom the cry *may* originally have been connected (see Paus. 9. 2. 8), did, however, probably come at an early date from Phoenicia. See Frisk and Chantraine under *ailinos* and *linos*.

[137] On the Egyptians' use of incense see Gwyn Griffiths 1970, pp. 565–71.

consider human sacrifice sacred and lawful, whereas 'we' (by which he means most of the Greeks)[138] regard it as the opposite (315b–c). But Sophocles by and large rejected the relativism developing among contemporary sophists and ethnographers (on which see below, chapter 4. 4). By his 'universal' standards the sacrifice of a human being represented an extreme of human cruelty, and he therefore exploited the opportunity to denounce it as 'barbaric'. Here, as so often, the ethnically other meets the mythical and chronologically prior, for human sacrifice is one of the most important pivots around which Greek mythical complexes revolve. In tragedy there is a plethora of innocent victims sacrificed by Greeks: Iphigeneia, Polyxena, Erechtheus' daughter, and Menoeceus in Euripides' *Phoenissae*.[139] But Sophocles, undeterred, made a character observe in his *Andromeda* that 'the barbarians have always had the custom of sacrificing human offerings to Cronus' (fr. 126. 2–3). He was probably influenced by rumours of Carthaginian or Phoenician child sacrifices,[140] for in accordance with the ethnographers' principle of identifying Greek and foreign gods, the Phoenicians' Ba'al became Cronus.

The Sophoclean character voices what is for once a legitimate complaint against the barbarians from a fifth-century Greek, for to his audience human sacrifice was vestigial and occasional,[141] whereas the evidence that it was widely practised in Middle Eastern religions is growing steadily.[142] The Phoenicians' habit of incinerating their own children spread from the Levant to their colonies all over the Mediterranean; hundreds of urns filled with charred human and animal remains dating from the seventh to the second centuries BC have been discovered in the Tophet precinct at Carthage, gruesomely confirming

[138] He states that human sacrifices are still performed by Greeks in Arcadia and by the descendants of Athamas: see also Hdt. 7. 197.

[139] On the tragedians' exploitation of the paradox in accusing the barbarians of sole rights to atrocities frequently performed by Greeks in myth see further below ch. 5. 2. For a detailed discussion of human sacrifices in Euripidean tragedy see O'Connor-Visser 1987; for a more literary approach see Foley 1985.

[140] Sophocles showed interest in Carthage in his early *Triptolemus* (fr. 602).

[141] A perhaps over-cautious discussion of the literary and archaeological evidence for human sacrifice and ritual killing in Greek religion is given by Henrichs 1981. The assessment of O'Connor-Visser 1987, pp. 211–30, is less conservative. See also Burkert 1983, pp. 84–7, 114–15, and n. 138 above.

[142] Morton Smith 1975 summarizes the evidence. For further bibliography see Henrichs 1981, p. 196 n. 5.

the allegations of ancient historians.[143] There is evidence that this Phoenician custom was the particular predilection of wealthy families, performed especially in times of crisis, and when favours were asked of the gods.[144] This perhaps explains the eastward gravitation of the story of Andromeda, the princess offered as a sacrifice by her Ethiopian father Cepheus to pacify a sea-monster sent by Poseidon.[145] Her rescue by the Hellenic Perseus was also dramatized by Euripides, whose version was parodied in Aristophanes' *Thesmophoriazusae*.[146] Other myths were dramatized in a way which characterized the ritual of human sacrifice as 'not Greek'. In Euripides' *Bacchae* the 'barbarian' influence on Agave induces the madness which leads her to kill Pentheus, an act combining three 'barbarian' crimes in one: human sacrifice, cannibalism, and infanticide.[147] In *IT* human sacrifice is repeatedly denounced as a barbarian custom, though in that play the layers of irony become almost impenetrable, for had not the heroine herself been offered to Artemis by her own Greek father?[148]

These, however, are isolated phenomena; by and large the religious behaviour of non-Greek characters, like that of the Persians and Lydians in Herodotus' more 'literary' passages, is entirely in accordance with their belief in the gods of the Hellenic pantheon and their understanding of Greek rituals. In the Phrygian Tecmessa's indictment of Athena in *Ajax* (952–3), in the Taurian shepherd's prayer to Palaemon and the Dioscuri in *IT* (270–2), in the Egyptian Theonoe's disclosure of the Olympian quarrel between Zeus, Hera, and Aphrodite in *Helen* (878–86), and in by far the majority of passages where barbarians invoke a deity or express a theological opinion, it is apparent that in terms of the gods no tragic convention arose for the differentiation of barbarian beliefs. The few exceptions to this rule do not invalidate it.

---

[143] See Stager 1980. Jeremiah denounced the sacrifices of children performed at the Tophet precinct outside Jerusalem (Jer. 8: 31; 32: 35).

[144] Stager 1980, p. 3.

[145] There is however no reason to suppose that Rebuffat 1972 is right in suggesting that the presence of the Phoenician chorus in Euripides' *Phoenissae* means that Menoeceus' death is modelled on semitic human sacrifices. See O'Connor-Visser 1987, pp. 94–8 n. 13.

[146] On the *Andromeda* parody see Rau 1967, pp. 65–89.

[147] See Detienne 1979, pp. 62–3.

[148] The myth in which Heracles put a stop to Busiris' human sacrifices (a mythical verification of the stereotypical Egyptian xenophobia) was also popular, though not apparently chosen for tragic dramatization; it was treated in hexameters by Panyassis (for a discussion see Matthews 1974, pp. 126–8), in a satyr drama by Euripides, and in comedy by Cratinus and several fourth-century writers. See Long 1986, pp. 56–7.

They show instead what the tragedians might have done if they *had* been concerned to provide their audience with a window on the strange and unfamiliar cults of the world beyond the borders of Hellas.

But the Greeks' view of the barbarian was inherently contradictory, for civilization's notion of itself as in a process of linear progression is never unquestioned; the rise, paradoxically, is seen also as a fall.[149] The retrospective vision incorporates the idea not only of primitive chaos, but of a more virtuous era, when men were nearer to the gods. Since the Greek concept of 'the past' overlaps with 'the elsewhere', the notion of the special spirituality of the men of the golden age, before they were alienated by technological progress, can also be produced in narratives depicting utopian barbarian communities.[150]

This schizophrenic vision of inferiority and of utopia gives rise to an inherently contradictory portrayal of the barbarian world. It is the home on the one hand of tyrants and savages, and on the other of idealized peoples and harmonious relations with heaven. The countries believed to be older than Greece, especially Egypt, become the sources in ethnography of numerous gods, and in Platonic philosophy of primeval wisdom.[151] In this conceptual system, therefore, anarchy and tyranny, cruelty, and deviant social practices all belong to the non-Greek world, but so do mystics like Orpheus and sages like Anacharsis. Although tragedy as a medium for the celebration of civic and civilized values generally defines Hellas' evolution as progress rather than fall, there are aspects of its portrayal of foreign religion which stem from the idea that barbarians are somehow closer to the gods than the Greeks, that they have retained an intimacy with the mystical workings of the universe which civilized Hellas has lost. This idea is particularly expressed in the tendency of a certain category of religious experiences to gravitate in the Greek imagination to the world beyond its boundaries, even though they were central and familiar elements of Greek religion. This is especially clear in the cases of the ecstatic rites of Dionysus and the Mother, and prophecy. Such practices, like abandoned lamentation, were seen as simultaneously belonging to the chronologically past and to the geographically distant—'other' locations which coincided and overlapped.

The ideas of the barbarian seer and barbarian prophecy lie behind

---

[149] See Diamond 1974, p. 207; ch. 1 n. 172 above.
[150] On the 'noble savage' in antiquity see Lovejoy and Boas 1935.
[151] On 'barbarian wisdom' see Dörrie 1972; Momigliano 1975.

much Greek discourse about non-Greek lands; in a lost tragedy the mantic art itself was described as 'Lydian' (fr. adesp. 234a). The tension engendered by the 'double-seeing' and contradictory Greek apprehension of the barbarian is in Euripides' Thracian Polymestor embodied in a single figure; this most villainous of tragic barbarians is transformed at the last minute into a prophet of Dionysus, the deliverer of cryptic predictions, just as Shakespeare's Caliban is simultaneously a savage and a visionary.[152] Rhesus, the vaunting Thracian warrior, is also transformed, though posthumously, into a prophet of Dionysus (*Rhes.* 970–3).[153] In Euripides' *Erechtheus* the tension is resolved chronologically: the Eleusinian priest Eumolpus will one day be born from a line descending from his warlike Thracian ancestor. But often the contradiction is expressed in a pair of complementary barbarians. In *Persae* the wise Darius, deliverer of oracles, is contrasted with the hubristic Xerxes; the decadent and effeminate Paris of fifth-century tragedy has a sister, Cassandra, beloved of Apollo, all-seeing and all-knowing; the libidinous and violent Theoclymenus in Euripides' *Helen* also has a sister, the virtuous and virginal Theonoe, 'Divine Mind', who possesses extraordinary powers of prophecy.

Helen, however, demonstrates the importance of clearly defining the nature of tragedy's treatment of 'barbarian religion'. There is, for example, little justification in seeing the Egyptian Thoth behind the Hermes who delivered a prediction to Helen (57):[154] Hermes in Greek belief is the messenger of the gods, the divine communicator (*hermēneus*). Nor is there any basis for the equation of Proteus' tomb with the 'eternal home' of the Egyptian cult of the dead.[155] The arguments used in chapter 2. 4d to show that addresses to Darius' ghost in *Persae* were comprehensible in Greek terms are equally valid here. Even less convincing is the theory that the figure of Theonoe represents a dramatic appropriation of the '*divines adoratrices*', the 'wives of the gods' in Egyptian state cult, who were important prophetesses of Amun.[156] During the New Kingdom this role was often assumed by the pharaoh's wife and/or sister in order to tighten

---

[152] See Fiedler 1974, pp. 197–8.
[153] It is usually thought that the 'prophet of Bacchus' referred to here is Orpheus or Lycurgus, but see Diggle 1987.
[154] Gilbert 1949, p. 84.
[155] Goossens 1935, pp. 250–3.
[156] Gilbert 1949, pp. 82–3.

the royal family's control over the religious organs of state.[157] But even Herodotus is apparently not aware that these priestesses were royal (1. 182).[158] The point is not that Euripides is incorporating references to specifically Egyptian religion, but that the familiar figure of the barbarian mystic has informed his perception of Helen's myth.

In tragic myth, therefore, prophecy was often hauled outside the spiritual horizons of Hellas. But there was also a tendency to associate certain gods with non-Greek lands. Ares, Dionysus, and the Mother were particularly vulnerable to 'barbarization'. In *Hecuba* Polymestor describes his people as 'possessed by Ares' (1090) and in *Antigone* the tutelary deity of Thracian Salmydessus is also the war-god (970). But Herodotus was wrong in asserting that the Thracians worshipped such a deity (5. 7), and Ares is clearly named, in company with 'all the gods', in Mycenaean Greek.[159] The Greeks did not adopt a barbarian god of combat, but at an early stage located their divine personification of violence in the north as an articulation of their history of conflict with its people,[160] and of Ares' liminality in relation to the major Olympians.

Dionysus is frequently associated with either Thrace or Asia in tragedy as elsewhere: in *Hecuba* he is 'the Thracians' prophet' (1267), and in *Bacchae* his cult is portrayed as an import from Asia. Indeed, scholars used to believe the literary sources which claimed that Dionysus was a late entrant into the Greek pantheon from Thrace or Phrygia,[161] but there is now evidence that a Greek Dionysus cult may have existed as early as the fifteenth century BC,[162] and the god was in any case the recipient of one of the most important Athenian state cults, even in classical times regarded as extremely ancient.[163] In *Bacchae*, the play where his connection with Asia is most explicit, stress is also laid on his Theban provenance and Olympian ancestry.[164]

---

[157] Kees 1953, p. 265.

[158] See Kannicht 1969, i, p. 52.

[159] Ventris and Chadwick 1973, p. 411 (KN 201).

[160] See Hoddinott 1981, p. 169. Ares was also strongly associated with the Scythians, the Thracians' northern neighbours. See Hartog 1988, pp. 188–92.

[161] See e.g. Dodds 1960, p. xxi. A notable exception was Otto 1965, pp. 52–64.

[162] See Burkert 1985a, p. 162. The proper name 'Dionysus' may occur in connection with wine on the Pylos tablets: see Ventris and Chadwick 1973, pp. 127 and 411 (Xa 1419).

[163] Otto 1965, p. 53, points out that the Anthesteria was called the '*Old* Dionysia' (Thuc. 2. 16).

[164] See Arthur 1972, pp. 152–3 and n. 19: 'the exact nature of his foreignness is . . . complex, since the emphasis on Dionysus as the child of Zeus and Semele, born by the river Dirce and washed in its waters, is an insistence upon Dionysus as a Greek and a Theban.'

Several factors contributed to this confusion. First, there is no doubt that the Greek Dionysus was subject to numerous foreign accretions over the thousand years before extant tragedy, especially in the sixth century.[165] His worship was extremely mobile and widespread,[166] and certainly syncretized with various foreign cults, including those of the Asiatic Sabazius and the truly Thracian Hero. But the most important factor in his links with foreign countries is his role in mystery religion. Hoddinott writes of Herodotus' claim that the Thracians worshipped Dionysus (5. 7): 'the underlying implication of ecstasy, fertility and rebirth is almost certainly true of Thracian religion in its mystery aspect, but was not embodied in individual gods and goddesses.'[167] 'Thracian' had come to describe a kind of religious experience, rather than a place of origin: Orpheus, closely associated with shamanism, is also located in Thrace.[168]

In Aeschylus' *Lycurgeia* and in Euripides' *Bacchae* Dionysiac religion was portrayed as coming from the east to Thrace or Thebes.[169] Such myths, however, do not narrate the historical spread of his worship, but articulate his role as the epiphany god—the god who arrives, often from the sea, and meets resistance. In such plays the poets were expressing Dionysus' most fundamental quality in *Greek* religion and literature, his 'dissolution and confusion of basic polarities',[170] not only between Greek and barbarian, but between man and woman,[171] adult and adolescent. He is the recipient both of civic cult and of subversive ecstatic rites whose place was the chaotic natural world extraneous to the polis. By presenting the cult of Dionysus as a barbarian import the

---

[165] See Carpenter 1986, pp. 74–5, 124. He argues that an original mainland Greek Dionysus was conflated with an eastern image of the young male god in the sixth century; the familiar Dionysian imagery of red-figure vase-painting—snakes, maenads in leopard-skins who carry thyrsoi—is not previously apparent in artistic representations of the god.

[166] See above, n. 20.

[167] Hoddinott 1981, pp. 169–70.

[168] On the shamanistic associations of the northern countries in Greek authors, especially embodied in such figures as Abaris, Zalmoxis, and Orpheus, and in Aristeas' journey through Scythia to the Hyperboreans, see Meuli 1935; Eliade 1982, pp. 175–9, 181–3; West 1983b, pp. 4, 146–50. There is now considerable evidence that Dionysiac and Orphic religion in practice overlapped: see West 1983b; Burkert 1985a, pp. 293–5, 300.

[169] Otto 1965, pp. 58–9, suggests that in actuality the opposite process occurred: it was the Greek colonists who translated the myth abroad.

[170] Segal 1978, p. 186.

[171] On Dionysus' ambiguous sexual and ethnic status see Delcourt 1958, pp. 39–43; Kenner 1970, pp. 116, 120–6; Henrichs 1982, pp. 138–9, 158–9.

poets thus found mythical expression for his role as the god of epiphany, and revealed his promise of liberation from the norms of Hellenic *sōphrosunē*, his responsiveness to primeval instinct, and his danger.[172]

Cybele, the great Phrygian mother-goddess, had long been assimilated into mainland Greek religion when Sophocles evoked her in *Philoctetes* (391–402) and Euripides in *Helen* and *Bacchae* (1301–68; 126–9): Pindar had already mentioned her in association with Dionysus and Pan (frr. 70b. 9; 95. 3).[173] She was identified with Rhea, the mother of the gods, or with Demeter,[174] but although the Greeks avoided using her foreign name, preferring to call her 'mother of the gods' or 'mountain mother' (Eur. *Hel*. 1301–2), she brought with her from Asia her exotic musical instruments, the castanets, tympani, and cymbals, and her lions. Even these vestiges of her Asiatic origin were however assimilated to her Hellenic persona.[175] Her acceptability is demonstrated by Agoracritus' famous statue of her, made for the Metroon in the Athenian agora.[176] A fifth-century imitation has been found in Attica, whose austere Hellenic form is nevertheless portrayed with lion and tympanum.[177] Euripides' orientalizing of the Mother finds a close parallel in the fusion of Greek and Asiatic elements in this statue. Cybele's mythical attendants, the Corybantes, likewise became associated with Rhea's Curetes; they in turn are probably to be identified with the initiates of the Cretan Zeus who sing the hymn preserved in a fragment of Euripides' *Cretes* (fr. 79). These Curetes probably owe more to poetic imagination than to any authentic cult.[178] In such passages the tragedians present a profoundly syncretistic view of religion: the barbarian characteristics of Dionysus or Demeter-Cybele, with their entourages of maenads and Corybantes and Curetes,[179]

---

[172] See Winnington-Ingram 1948a, pp. 31–3, 40–1, 154.

[173] See Homer A. Thompson 1937, p. 206; Burkert 1985a, pp. 178–9.

[174] On this syncretism see Henrichs 1976, pp. 256–7.

[175] On the complexities of the Mother's foreignness see further Hartog 1988, pp. 80–2.

[176] See Paus. 1. 3. 5. For discussions of the statue and the Metroon see von Salis 1913; Homer A. Thompson 1937, pp. 140, 203–6.

[177] Published by Papachristodoulou 1973.

[178] Burkert 1985a, p. 280.

[179] See Sutton 1971, p. 399. On Cybele's associations with the Corybantes see Dodds 1951, pp. 77–8 and n. 90. For the conflation of the Cretan Curetes and the Asiatic orgiastic rites associated with the Corybantes, Cabiri, and Idaean Dactyls, see Strabo's famous excursus (10. 3. 6–23), with Jeanmaire's discussion (1939, pp. 593–616). For a general discussion of the Mother in ancient art, myth, and literature see Vermaseren 1977, pp. 71–87.

constitute an *artistic distillation* of the exotic or ecstatic aspects of divinities who, accepted, respected, but suspected, occupied an ambiguous place in the Athenian religious establishment. Tragic evocation of the 'Thracian' or 'Asiatic' Dionysus or of the 'Phrygian' Mother does not represent reference to recognizably barbarian gods, but externalization of the *furor*, strangeness, and wildness, the 'un-Hellenic' and 'irrational' facets of accepted Greek cults. The Greeks may have conceptualized Dionysus and the Mother as imported barbarian gods, but their concepts 'Thracian' and 'Phrygian' had entered the domain of metaphor.

8 POLITICS

A much more significant focus of the 'discourse of barbarism' in *Persae* was politics. This is the single most important area in which the tragedians departed from their epic prototypes, and it has been argued that it is ultimately to be referred to the ideology binding together democratic Athens and her empire. Barbarian tyranny became a rhetorical topos in the repertoire of the tragic poets, and is often discussed in general terms or in plays with no barbarian characters: these phenomena are treated in chapter 4. 5. But even the terminology and ethnographic detail used in the presentation of mythical barbarians were influenced by contemporary beliefs about the Persian monarchy. Had he lived, Hector would have inherited, like Xerxes, a 'tyranny like that of a god' (*isotheos turannis*, *Tro.* 1168-9), in contrast with Agamemnon who, it is stressed in *Orestes*, was 'deemed worthy to rule Hellas and was no *turannos*' (1167-8). In *IT* Agamemnon had ruled the army, but Thoas is a *turannos* (17, 1020). This contrast, apparent in many plays, is most fully developed in *Rhesus*, where the Greek kings are designated either by their names alone (Menelaus, 174; Achilles, 182) or collectively as 'generals' (*stratēlatai*, 173, 495). In contrast, Hector and Rhesus are always *anax* or *basileus*.[180] When Greece is described it is merely 'Hellas' or 'Argos and Hellas' (477), but Rhesus and Hector each rule a *turannis* (406, 484, see also 388). The Greeks' epic kings have become fifth- or fourth-century generals, while the barbarian kings have turned into oriental despots. The poet

---

[180] See 2, 130, 264, 738, 828, 886, 993. *Contra* see only 718, where the Atridae are said to have a 'royal hearth', (*basilid' hestian*).

even draws a distinction between the statuses of the Thracian and Phrygian kings. Rhesus is a petty monarch established on his throne, like a vassal of the Persian empire, by the military intervention of his powerful Phrygian allies (406–11). Thus, like Polymestor, he reflects the low Athenian opinion of the Thracian royal house.

The tragedians had run up against a problem in choosing to celebrate democratic ideology through myths in which the principal characters were almost exclusively members of royal families.[181] Only Aeschylus dared to portray a mythical Athens without a king in his *Eumenides*. The rulers in Greek tragedy range from the wise and benevolent king, equipped with democratic virtues, to the truly decadent despot.[182] The ambivalent status of the tragic king is reflected in the range of terms used almost interchangeably to designate him, and in the ambiguity of their implications.[183] It must be conceded, therefore, that *turannos* and its cognates can in tragedy be used of an almost benign rule, as can *anax* and *basileus*, but they frequently bear pejorative overtones.[184] The implications must be judged in each case according to context. Where a barbarian leader is called *basileus* in contrast with Greek 'generals' it can hardly be coincidental, and where the word *turannos* is used in conjunction with other items from the 'vocabulary of barbarism' the implication is that the ruler, whether or not he is himself a barbarian, is a tyrant after the model of the oriental despot (see further below, chapter 5. 1). Thus in *Agamemnon*, where Priam, it is said, would willingly have trodden the purple carpets (935–6), *turannikou* in reference to his city's blood has a clearly deprecatory meaning (828). In Euripides especially the Trojans' rule is formulated

[181] On the contradictions this engendered, especially in early tragedy, see Podlecki 1986, pp. 83–99.

[182] See Easterling 1984.

[183] Herodotus uses the terms 'tyrant', 'king', and 'despot' interchangeably, and makes little distinction between the behaviour of such rulers: see Hartog 1988, pp. 322–30.

[184] Andrewes 1956, pp. 20–30, discusses the variability of the implications of the term *turannos*. But his view that in the literature of democratic Athens there are instances of the term which revert to its original 'neutral' sense is questioned by Tuplin 1985, p. 374 and n. 83. The important point missed by discussions which attempt to pin down the implications of the word in every single instance is that it was one of the terms most generative of tragic ambiguity; Euripides can make his Athenian chorus in *Heraclidae* call Theseus, the supposed paragon of democratic virtues, *turannos* (111), but there may well be ironic overtones here. Knox 1957, pp. 53–66, perhaps overstates, however, the opprobrious implications of Oedipus' title in *OT*. On the difficult line at *OT* 873 see Lloyd-Jones 1983b, p. 213 n. 23.

as a barbarian tyranny. Priam's hearth was *turannon*, and Hecuba who came from a 'tyrant's home' is now a slave (*Andr*. 3; *Hec*. 55–6, see also 365–6, 809, *Tro*. 474). Astyanax was to have been 'tyrant of fruitful Asia', and Helen claims that she has saved Hellas from subjection by a barbarian army to a barbarian *turannis* (*Tro*. 748, 933–4).[185]

The protocol of the hierarchical oriental court portrayed in *Persae* often reappears in mythical contexts. The Persians' elaborate manner of address to royalty finds a counterpart in the formal language in which the chorus in *Phoenissae* sing to Polyneices, falling to their knees in prostration before him (291–4): 'O offspring of the children of Agenor, kinsman of my *turannoi*, who sent me here—I fall to my knees before you, lord, honouring the custom of my home.' But the Phoenician hierodules are not the only Euripidean barbarians to perform proskynesis like the chieftains on the reliefs at Persepolis, for the Phrygian in *Orestes* collapses in prostration before Orestes, again helpfully informing his audience that this is a barbarian custom (1507). One of the reasons Hecuba gives for Helen's elopement in *Troades* is that she wanted to receive proskynesis from the barbarians (1021). The tradition of prostration by barbarians on the tragic stage was to prove enduring, for in the fragment of the later 'Gyges' tragedy the chorus of Lydian maidservants claim to be performing it before their queen (fr. adesp. 664. 9).

The possession of a personal bodyguard seems to have been another mark of the tyrant, especially the barbarian tyrant: when Thucydides describes how Pausanias succumbed to oriental luxury and despotism he attaches particular significance to the way he isolated himself and flaunted his Median and Egyptian bodyguards (1. 130, see below, chapter 5. 1). In tragedy, therefore, when attention is drawn to someone's personal guards, the playwright seems to be signifying that he is heading towards despotism. It cannot of course be proved that in the later plays of Aeschylus' *Danaid* trilogy Danaus' accession to the Argive throne was portrayed as the coup of a *turannos*, but in *Supplices* deliberate emphasis is undoubtedly placed on the Argives' granting to him of a personal bodyguard, traditionally the first step towards obtaining a formal tyranny.[186] Similar attention is drawn to Polymestor's guards in *Hecuba*, and to his concern for his own safety if left alone without them (979–81).

[185] On Trojan tyranny, pride, and wealth in *Troades*, see Burnett 1977, pp. 308–10.
[186] See Garvie 1969, p. 199; Knox 1957, pp. 60, 214 n. 20.

In the last chapter it was seen that the prologue of Phrynichus' *Phoenissae* was delivered by a eunuch as he prepared the seats for the Persian royal council. Eunuchs appalled and fascinated the phallocentric Hellenes (witness Herodotus' outrage at the castration of Hermotimus, 8. 105), especially those who had become famous by reaching high ranks in the court. The palace eunuch of the Greeks' imagination encapsulates their systematic feminization of Asia; emotional, wily, subservient, luxurious, and emasculated, he embodies simultaneously all the various threads in the fabric of their orientalist discourse.[187] But Phrynichus' choice of character reveals an attempt at realism, for the Achaemenids had indeed taken over from their Assyrian and Median precursors the custom of using eunuchs in large numbers in both administrative and servile capacities (see, for example, Hdt. 1. 117).[188] In the fifth century two are particularly conspicuous, Nehemiah, Artaxerxes I's cupbearer, and Artoxares the Paphlagonian. The latter's extraordinary career is given an improbably lurid gloss by Ctesias,[189] but he may well be the powerful Artaḫsarū who has turned up in several Babylonian texts and who it has been suggested inspired Aristophanes' portrayal of Cleon as a Paphlagonian slave.[190] If this is right, it reflects the fascination with eunuchs which also explains why Sophocles chose as an attendant for the young Trojan prince in his *Troilus* not an ageing paedagogus but a eunuch, whose mutilation was much emphasized in the play. In an astonishing fragment he explains to the audience that it was none other than the queen herself (presumably Hecuba) who had him castrated: *skalmēi gar orcheis basilis ektemnous' emous* (fr. 620).

Some have argued that the Phrygian slaves Helen has brought back with her from Troy in *Orestes* are not eunuchs, for they are never explicitly described as such. Several factors suggest the contrary, however. First, *Orestes* is remarkable for its echoes of previous

---

[187] On the feminization of Asia in the Greek imagination, the equation of the relation of male to female with that of west to east, see Edward Said 1986, p. 225, and below, ch. 5. 1.

[188] Rusa II's court at Urartu had at one time 5,507 retainers of whom no fewer than 3,892 were eunuchs; in Assyria Tiglathpileser III employed only eunuchs as chiefs of provinces; the Persians castrated boys given as tribute from the satrapies (Diakonoff 1985, p. 137). For a discussion of eunuchs in the courts of imperial Rome, China, Byzantium, and Islamic Spain, and the obloquy they attracted, see Hopkins 1963, pp. 72–80.

[189] On oriental palace eunuchs in Greek and Roman historiography see Guyot 1980, pp. 77–91.

[190] Lewis 1977, pp. 20–1.

tragedies,[191] and it has been seen that oriental eunuchs were by no means out of place in the genre.[192] Secondly, the only men allowed in oriental women's quarters, like these Phrygian slaves in attendance on Helen, were eunuchs. Thirdly, their chief representative, who delivers the monody which serves as a messenger speech, reports that the Phrygians were fanning Helen 'in barbarian fashion' with a punkah, a round feather fan used to keep Persian royalty cool (1426–30), and in oriental art such a fan is usually deployed by a eunuch:[193] if Euripides knew about punkah-fanning, he may well have known who performed it. Fourthly, later antiquity certainly envisaged the Phrygians' chief representative as a eunuch.[194] But the most cogent argument is that he is derided by Orestes for being 'neither man nor woman' (1528, see above, n. 59).

In the fifth century accusations of physical cruelty were a commonplace of Greek rhetoric against the barbarians, and amongst cruel punishments impalement was regarded as the most extreme; it was a mark of the tyrant. In *IT* Thoas plans reprisals against the Greeks, *katakrēmnismos* and impalement (1429–30): although the Greeks regularly threw criminals off cliffs, the impalement even of corpses or parts of them was denounced by Herodotus' Pausanias as a barbarous act unfit for Greeks (9. 79). But the Thoas of the tragedy is made to plan not just to stick his victims' heads on stakes, but to impale them bodily (1429–30). Throughout his *Histories* Herodotus' Persians impale their enemies (3. 159, for example): Darius' own words on the Behistun inscription for once confirm the historian's allegations. The king describes the punishment he imposed on a rebellious Sagartian chief (33. 2. 86–91):

Ahuramazda bore me aid; by the favor of Ahuramazda my army smote that rebellious army and took Ciçantakhma prisoner [and] led him to me. Afterwards I cut off both his nose and ears and put out one eye; he was kept bound at my palace entrance, all the people saw him. Afterwards I impaled him at Arbela.[195]

[191] See Zeitlin 1980; M. L. West 1987, pp. 31–2.
[192] On eunuchs in the Greek theatre see also Guyot 1980, pp. 71–2.
[193] See Chapouthier 1944, p. 210. For a barbarian punkah-fanner in *Greek* art, in a scene illustrating Euripides' *IT*, see the cover of this book.
[194] See Terentianus Maurus, *de Metris* (AD second century) vv. 1960–2, in Keil 1874, p. 384: *fabula sic Euripidis inclita monstrat Orestes:/nam tali versu cunctis trepidantibus intus/ Argivum fugiens eunuchus flagitat ensem*.
[195] Translated by Kent 1953, p. 124. See also 32. 2. 70–8 (Phraortes' punishment which

Rhesus, who is modelled in other respects on Persian royalty, is accordingly made to declare that he will take Odysseus alive, and 'having impaled him beneath the spine, set him up at the gates of the city, a feast for winged vultures' (*Rhes.* 513–15).

The Persian kings' practice of mutilation, like that performed on Ciçantakhma,[196] deeply disturbed the Greeks; in classical times they performed mutilations 'only' on slaves, 'for the bodily integrity of the citizen must be preserved'.[197] And so the playwrights recast their myths so as to bring mythical mutilations into association with the barbarian ethnicity of their perpetrators. Hecuba's manservant is castrated (see above), the Egyptian herald threatens to strip, brand, and behead the Danaids (Aesch. *Supp.* 839–41, 904), and the Thracian Tereus tears the tongue from Philomela's head. The savage reprisal which Hecuba and her women take against Polymestor when they blind him is an example of 'barbaric' justice. In at least one of Sophocles' versions of the story of Phineus, his second wife was the Phrygian Idaea, daughter of Dardanus (fr. 704); it was she who took up her shuttles and with them gouged out the eyes of her stepsons, a hideous crime famously recounted by the chorus of *Antigone* (966–76).

also includes the removal of his tongue), and 50. 3. 83–92 (the mass impalement of Arhka's followers). The inscription's term *uzmayā-patiy kar-* was originally understood to mean 'crucify' (see e.g. King and Thompson 1907, pp. 36–7). But the true meaning, 'impale on stakes', was seen by Weissbach 1911, p. 39, after inspecting representations of the punishment in Persian art. See also Kent 1953, pp. 178–9.

[196] The Persians had of course not invented such punishments; prisoners-of-war in Assyria might have expected to be mutilated, blinded, and impaled (Luckenbill 1926, pp. 168–9).

[197] Hartog 1988, p. 142.

4

An Athenian Rhetoric

I A THEATRE OF PANHELLENIC IDEAS

THIS book has argued that since the techniques employed by the tragedians in differentiating their barbarians from their Greeks are scarcely adumbrated in pre-tragic poetry, they must be considered to constitute a dynamic manipulation of myth to suit not only the demands of the dramatic medium but also the political climate of fifth-century Athens. It has shown that the multifarious representatives of the genus *barbaros* in extant and fragmentary tragedy were distinguished in various areas not only from Greeks, but also from other species of barbarian, thus according with the argument of the Eleatic stranger in Plato's *Politicus*, who observes that the normal division of mankind into only two groups is unsatisfactory because it is clear that different barbarian sub-categories are intrinsically dissimilar (262d–e).[1] The distinction between the various kinds of barbarian is in tragedy not confined to material borrowed from the ethnographers, but extends to a character typology based on ethnicity: the presentation of certain figures accords with the pejorative ethnic stereotypes found in comedy and oratory. Particularly clear examples are provided by the cunning Egyptian Danaus, the avaricious and mendacious Polymestor, and the cowardly Phrygian in *Orestes*. The last two show that Bacon was wrong in her diagnosis that in Euripides 'the actual concrete foreigner—Ethiopian, Persian, Egyptian—disappears, and we have instead the symbolic foreigner'.[2] I suspect that what Bacon meant,

---

[1] Elsewhere in Plato the fundamental bipartite division is of course both accepted and justified. Platonic passages discussing barbarians are collected by Vourveris 1938, and discussed by Friedrich Weber 1904, and R. Müller 1980. Newman 1887, p. 430 n. 1, suggested that the Eleatic stranger's refutation of the antithesis in the *Politicus* represented a Platonic 'recantation' which might show that it was written subsequently to the *Republic*, but, as Haarhoff rejoins (1948, p. 67), the objection is made on grounds of formal logic and in no way affects the substance of the opinion. For Persia in the political philosophy of Plato and Xenophon see Hirsch 1985, ch. VI.

[2] Bacon 1961, p. 168.

however, was that the rich ethnographic detail in Aeschylus' *Persae* and *Supplices* begins to give way in the second half of the century to a sophistic examination of the canonical antithesis of Hellene and barbarian and of the paradoxes inherent within it. This move towards a simpler, binary articulation of the Hellenocentric world view is mirrored by the simultaneous evolution in vase-painting of the elaborately differentiated barbarian costumes and even physiognomy—Thracian, Scythian, Persian, Ethiopian—of the first half of the century, into a universal foreign type dressed in a standard barbarian uniform.[3] This chapter therefore moves the focus of the argument away from invention and ethnography towards the rhetorical exploration of the polarity between Greek and barbarian, and all that this polarity entailed.

Tragic rhetoric often treats its invented barbarians as a single category embodying the opposite of the central Hellenic values, for character traits viewed by the dominant ideology of any ethnic group as undesirable in its own members may be projected arbitrarily on to several target groups, or all other ethnic groups, simultaneously.[4] The polarization of Hellenism and barbarism even presupposes that a generic bond exists not only between all Greeks, but between all non-Greeks as well. The queen in *Persae* regrets that troubles have fallen not only on the Persians, but on 'the entire barbarian *genos*' (434). A character in Sophocles' *Tereus* accused 'the entire barbarian *genos*' of avarice (fr. 587), and Euripides' Hermione uses the same collective label in her attack on barbarian sexual and social mores (Eur. *Andr.* 173). Euripides also makes Hecuba articulate this theory of what might be called 'Panbarbarism' when she derides the Thracian Polymestor's claims that he wanted to maintain friendly relations with the Greeks: 'the barbarian *genos*', she declares, could never be friendly towards Hellas (*Hec.* 1199–201). Similarly, two characters in *Rhesus* imply that a family relationship exists between all barbarians (404–5, 833–4).

An extensive 'table of opposites' dependent upon the antithesis of Greek and barbarian evolved. The sophists discussed the issue, for it is touched upon in the surviving fragments of their works,[5] and their

---

[3] Raeck 1981, p. 3.

[4] Apte 1985, pp. 126–8.

[5] See chh. 4 and 5 *passim*; Untersteiner 1954, pp. 283–4; Guthrie 1971, pp. 160–3; Kerferd 1981, pp. 156–60. But their comments on the sophist Antiphon must be read in the light of the new papyrus fragment of his *On Truth*, discussed below, ch. 5. 2.

interest in its diverse ramifications is reflected in many of the Platonic dialogues of the next century. But the substantial evidence for the importance of the debate, and the interest it engendered at Athens, lies in the plays of the tragedians, for they repeatedly explored and sometimes questioned the validity of the polarization of Greek and barbarian from every angle, especially but not exclusively where mythical Greek and mythical foreigner were brought into confrontation. In the remains of the hundreds of tragedies produced during this period contemporary discussion of the world beyond Hellas is repeatedly reflected: the arguments range from unabashed jingoism to debate whether virtue, piety, and respect for law are universal or culturally relative. The barbarian world of the tragic stage had to come to serve as an expression of what structuralists call *l'Autre*,[6] everything that Hellas, and in particular the male 'club' which constituted the Athenian citizenry, was not, for the Greeks' culture was now defined by comparison with and negative illustration from others.[7] Thus even the heroic lays could no longer be interpreted and reformulated in Athenian ideology except from the anachronistic viewpoint of a free and ascendant Hellas.

Several reasons have already been suggested for the tragedians' peculiar attraction to the nexus of ideas surrounding the notion of the barbarian, but there are other factors which must be taken into account. Tragic drama was simultaneously the most patent example of Athenian cultural prestige, and a Panhellenic text designed for export to other Greek cities; Aeschylus' *Aetnaeae* was written for a Sicilian, and Attic tragedies were performed around the Greek-speaking world. But most of them were first produced at the Athenian City Dionysia. This festival presented, of course, an opportunity to vaunt Athenian ascendancy over the other Hellenic states:[8] Isocrates criticizes the spirit of imperial arrogance which led his Athenian forebears to display the

---

[6] For a brilliant analysis of the numerous functions performed by the barbarian 'other' in the ethnographic narratives of Herodotus (as inversion, complement, disjunction; in comparison, polarity, and analogy), see Hartog 1988, ch. VI; see also Rosellini and Said 1978.

[7] See Laurot 1981; Vidal-Naquet 1986, pp. 206–8.

[8] For a discussion of Athenian self-praise in tragedy see Butts 1942, pp. 17–175. Goldhill 1987, pp. 58–64, discusses the importance of the rituals which began the festival in defining Athenian civic ideology, but he perhaps underestimates the inherent contradiction implied by the festival's double role as a celebration of both Athenian power and the Panhellenic ideal which was used to bolster it (see above, ch. I, n. 54), a contradiction frequently reflected in the plays themselves.

annual tribute and city's war orphans during the festival (8. 82) in the same orchestra where the dramatic choruses danced. But Athenian and Panhellenic propaganda were inextricably interlinked, and this show of Athenian hegemony was designed with its Panhellenic audience in mind, for there were many visitors at the Dionysia from other Greek states: Meidias' assault on Demosthenes at the festival was considered to have been particularly outrageous because it was perpetrated in front of many visitors in addition to the Athenians (Dem. *Meid*. 74). The proclamations made at the Dionysia 'in the presence of all the Greeks' (Aeschin. *In Ctes*. 43), and the numerous inscriptions recording the honours conferred at the festival on citizens and non-Athenians alike, bear witness to the sense of collective ethnic identity underlying the City Dionysia, which must have shared something with the exclusively Greek atmosphere of the Panhellenic games (Hdt. 5. 22) or the celebration of the Mysteries, from which all barbarians were prohibited by solemn proclamation (Isoc. *Paneg*. 157).[9]

Some of the visitors were ambassadors from other Greek cities (Thuc. 5. 23), in the fifth century especially from the allied states, and they were treated with great politeness, being granted *proedria*, the right to seats at the front of the theatre (Hdt. 1. 54; Dem. *De Cor*. 28), alongside the descendants of those heroes of the fight for democracy, the tyrannicides (Isae. 5. 46–7),[10] and Athens' own distinguished citizens (Ar. *Eq*. 573–6; *Thesm*. 834). It seems that a Panhellenic spirit pervaded this festival more than the others, for at the smaller Lenaea the audience was exclusively Athenian rather than drawn from all corners of the Greek world (Ar. *Ach*. 504–6). But it was not only on an international level that the City Dionysia confirmed ethnic boundaries. Athens was a complex society consisting of numerous ethnic groups: a large majority of its non-citizen inhabitants were not Greek.[11] At the City Dionysia metics were not permitted to act as *chorēgoi*, whereas there was no such prohibition at the Lenaea.[12] This prohibition underlines the importance of the festival as a celebration of Athenian citizenship, but many of the metics were also barbarians:

[9] For the Panhellenic nature of the audience at the City Dionysia and the inscriptions see Pickard-Cambridge 1968, pp. 58–9, 82 n. 2.

[10] See Taylor 1981, p. 19.

[11] In modern terms, classical Athens was a 'multiethnic society'; Apte 1985, p. 133, shows that ethnic stereotypes and racist discourse are far more prevalent in such communities than in those which are ethnically homogeneous.

[12] Lewis 1968, p. 380.

the Dionysia was therefore one of the social institutions which confirmed ethnic boundaries within the polis itself.

So the City Dionysia, though in one respect a celebration of the cultural and political hegemony of Athens, also presented the chance to pay homage to the Panhellenic ideal.[13] Perhaps the anti-barbarian feeling which breathes from so many dramas constitutes an authorial response, whether conscious or unconscious, to precisely the heterogeneous Greek audience before which they were enacted. Only rarely in tragedy an attack on another Greek state surpasses in acerbity the pervasive critique of barbarian mores, and when it does, it is in invective against Sparta or Thebes at the height of the Peloponnesian war.[14]

Fourth-century texts retrospectively suggest that patriotic eulogy not only of Athens but of all Hellas was perceived to be an important didactic function of the tragic genre, for when an Athenian orator or philosopher wanted to advocate Panhellenist policy, or justify the subjection of barbarian races to the Hellenes, it was more than likely that he would make an appeal to the tragic poets. Some turned to Homer, interpreting the *Iliad* as a celebration of the archetypal victory of Hellenism over barbarism (e.g. Isoc. *Paneg.* 159), but the tragedians were even more susceptible to citation. Lycurgus, a fourth-century orator, quotes a long speech from Euripides' lost *Erechtheus* (fr. 50), delivered by a mythical Athenian queen at a moment when her city was in danger of being invaded by barbarians, in order to illustrate the patriotism he finds lacking in the defendant (*Leoc.* 100-1). The tragedian, he claims, chose the subject of the play in order to increase his spectators' love of their country. When the people of Larissa are threatened by Macedonian expansionism Thrasymachus the sophist, in his speech on their behalf, paraphrases a line from Euripides' *Telephus*: 'Shall we, as Greeks, be slaves to barbarians?' (85 B 2 *DK*, Eur. fr. 127). Perhaps most significantly it is a tragic poet whom Aristotle invokes when he attempts to justify slavery. The ideal community, he explains, is divided by nature into the rulers and the ruled, masters and slaves: those suited by nature to the servile status are,

---

[13] On Panhellenic sentiments in tragedy see Dunkel 1937; A. Diller 1937, p. 30; Delebecque 1951, pp. 407-9; Synodinou 1977, pp. 35-6. For Panhellenism in comedy see Hugill 1936; Dunkel 1937, pp. 3-4.

[14] Especially in Euripides' *Andromache* and *Troades*. See Kitto 1961, pp. 230-6; Stevens 1971, pp. 11-16; below, ch. 5. 2.

of course, barbarians (*Pol.* 1. 1252b 7-9): 'This is why the poets say "it is right that Greeks should rule over barbarians", meaning that barbarian and slave are by nature identical.' The philosopher is quoting Euripides (*IA* 1400). It is thus the poets, and a tragic poet in particular, whom he selects as supreme illustrators of the self-evident 'truth' that all barbarians are naturally inferior to Hellenes.

The classic fifth-century definition of the factors which united all the Greeks was put by Herodotus in the mouth of the Athenians in a speech to the Spartan envoys, who feared that Athens might come to terms with Persia (8. 144):

> There is not enough gold in the world, nor any land so beautiful, that we would accept it in return for colluding with the Persians and bringing Hellas into slavery. There are many important reasons to prevent us from doing so, even if we wished to ... there is the Greek nation—our shared blood and language, our common temples and rituals, our similar way of life.

In blood and language, religion and culture, Herodotus had isolated four ancient criteria of ethnicity which will in sections 3-5 provide a framework around which to construct this chapter's observations about the tragic poets' projection through their invented rhetoric of barbarism of what it meant to be Greek.[15] But first an attempt must be made to determine approximately where the tragic poets envisaged the *physical* borders of Hellas as lying. This procedure will also shed light on the manner in which tragic rhetoric reflected certain ideas about ethnicity circulating at the time.

2 THE BOUNDARIES OF HELLAS

Ethnicity is a process by which a group conceptualizes its difference from others in order to heighten its own sense of community and belongingness. Ethnic boundaries are therefore social constructs, not facts of nature, and as such are liable to be arbitrary and ambiguous.[16] This is especially the case when, as in ancient Greece, an ethnic group's perceived boundaries are not coterminous with clear geopolitical limits; it was suggested in chapter 1. 2 that this can partly explain why

---

[15] For a discussion of the various components of Hellenic collective orientation in the fifth century see Davies 1978, pp. 21-48.

[16] See Barth 1969, p. 10.

the original criterion of Greekness was linguistic. Fifth-century tragedy reflects the vagueness and variability of the physical 'boundaries of Hellas', though it develops poetic landmarks symbolic of the gateway from Hellas to barbarism: in Euripides it is the Symplegades, the 'crashing rocks', which guard the way into the Black Sea.[17] There is also a sense that the physical boundaries of Hellas, however indeterminate, are somehow commensurate with the boundaries of decency (see below, chapter 5. 2). But it will become clear that the poets' treatment of the ethnicity of their mythical characters was generally far from vague; when a character's ethnic origin had not been firmly settled in the mythical tradition they were anxious to resolve the ambiguity (see also above, chapter 3. 2). Tragic drama, as a social institution which buttressed and defined both the citizen status and Hellenic ethnicity, was even used as a medium for 'testing' certain heroes' and communities' claims to be Greek.

The tragic poets attached considerable importance to the ethnicity of their characters, but while most Asiatics, all blacks, and northerners in Thrace and beyond were unquestionably not Greek, the loss of the relevant plays means that it is difficult to ascertain which peoples in the west, where the boundaries were even more ambiguous, were represented by the tragedians as Hellenic. The confusion may reflect the hybrid nature of the populations of Magna Graecia in the fifth century. Mycenaean remains have been found in Sicily, but even in the fifth century there were indigenous communities which, although marginalized by the Greek colonists, had been neither destroyed nor completely Hellenized.[18] Aeschylus' *Aetnaeae*, written to celebrate Hieron's foundation of Etna, is hardly likely to have portrayed its inhabitants as anything other than Greek,[19] and Euripides' Trojans regard both Sicily and Italy as belonging to the Hellenic world (*Tro.* 220–9). But Sophocles' *Camici*, set in Sicily, seems to have portrayed a rare species of barbarian. It probably related the story which became the stock-in-trade of historians narrating the Greek colonization of Italy, namely the pursuit of Daedalus by Minos to Sicily, and the

[17] See e.g. *Med*. 2, 1263-4; *IT* 355, 422, 746. The idea that the Black Sea lay beyond the pale of civilization was behind the Greeks' assimilation of its Iranian name *Axšaina* ('dark'), to the Greek word *axeinos*, 'inhospitable', or the euphemistic *euxeinos* (Allen 1947). Euripides preferred the former.

[18] On the relations between colonizers and colonized in Sicily see e.g. Sjöqvist 1973.

[19] On this play see Gastaldi 1979, pp. 58–68.

murder of the Cretan king by the daughters of Cocalus, king of the Sicanians (see Hdt. 7. 169–70; Apollod. *Epit.* 1. 14–15).[20] The Sophoclean title indicates that the chorus consisted of citizens of Camicus, one of the few Sicilian sites known to have remained a settlement of indigenous Sicanian barbarians (Thuc. 6. 2).[21]

Further north, Polybius asserts that the playwrights told strange stories about the settlement of the 'Veneti' in north-east Italy, adding that these people were like the Celts (2. 17. 5–6)—a people of whom the fifth-century Greeks seem to have been astoundingly ignorant.[22] But the only title which can easily be referred to Polybius' statement is Sophocles' *Antenoridae*, which recounted the escape of Antenor and his Eneti from Troy along the ancient trade route through Thrace to the Adriatic, and which ended in the foundation of Enetica (Strabo 13. 1. 53):[23] it can only be conjectured that these mythical colonizers, as Trojans, were barbarians. Another tantalizing Sophoclean title is *Iberi*: perhaps this play, like Aeschylus' *Heliades* and Euripides' *Phaethon*, recounted the story of Phaethon's crash to earth. In Aeschylus' version the son of the sun fell into the Eridanus, which was identified by the poet with the Rhône in Iberia (fr. 73a = Pliny *HN* 37. 11. 31–2). A fragment mentions mourning women of Adria (fr. 71). Adria was an Etruscan town with a large Greek population, but it is possible that the women were supposed to be Celts, for Hesychius glosses the term *Adrianoi* with *Keltoi*. Euripides, on the other hand, decided in his *Phaethon* that the Eridanus was in fact the Po, and so his protagonist fell to earth from his father's chariot between Venice and Ravenna, rather than near Marseilles (Pliny *ibid.*).[24]

There is also doubt about western Asia, some of the islands, and northern Greece neighbouring Thrace and Illyria. As a general rule, as in the case of the tragedies set in the west, it appears that the playwrights took their cue from fifth-century political geography rather than from epic. For example, in the *Iliad* there are no Greeks resident in Asia Minor, but in *Bacchae* Dionysus describes the

[20] See Vanotti 1979, pp. 112–19.

[21] See A. C. Pearson 1917, ii, p. 4.

[22] The Greek sources remain almost silent about the western barbarians, especially the Celts, until the second century BC (Momigliano 1975, pp. 53–8, 74). For the sparse literary references before then see Rankin 1987, ch. III.

[23] See the discussion by Vanotti 1979, pp. 103–12.

[24] On Euripides' *Phaethon* and the passage at *Hipp.* 732–42 which tells of the hero's fall, see Burelli 1979, pp. 131–40.

populations of the cities on the Asiatic seaboard as mingled Greek and barbarian (17–19). The apostle from Lydia whose guise Dionysus has assumed, though he has brought with him a retinue of Asiatic women who are indubitably barbarians (604), is himself never described as such, but as a *xenos* (453); perhaps his role as *goēs* (234) transcends the question of his ethnicity (see chapter 5. 2), but it is a possibility that he was supposed to be envisaged by Pentheus as one of the eastern Greeks who were thought to have adopted the destructive luxury of the Lydians (see Xenophanes 21 B 3 *DK*).

Tantalus and his children Niobe and Pelops present another problem. Sophocles' *Tantalus* may have dealt with the hero's death and burial at Sipylus in Lydia, and the same poet's Niobe certainly returned to her native land in the course of the play which bore her name (*ΣT Il.* 24. 602); there was plentiful oriental colour in Aeschylus' *Niobe* (see frr. 155, 158), though its setting was probably her marital home in Thebes. In *Antigone*, however, Niobe is envisaged as a Phrygian (824), like Pelops, the Atridae's grandfather who gave his name to the Peloponnese (see Soph. *Aj*. 1292), and it is likely that Pelops' Phrygian origin was stressed in the plays entitled *Oenomaus* by Sophocles and Euripides which recounted the story of his race for the hand of Hippodamia (see Eur. *Or*. 983–94). In the fourth century Athenian propagandists often compared their own autochthonous mythical ancestors with the barbarian progenitors of the Peloponnesians and Thebans—Pelops, Danaus, and Cadmus (Isoc. 10. 68, 12. 80; Plato *Menex*. 245c–d)—and Danaus was certainly portrayed as a barbarian by Aeschylus, so it is safest to assume that the poets gave Pelops and Cadmus the same treatment. In his surviving plays Euripides certainly emphasizes Cadmus' Phoenician origins (see *Phoen*. 5–6, 638–9; *Bacch*. 170–2), a tradition which may have been ancient but perhaps derives from logography (Hdt. 2. 49).[25]

Over Lemnos and Cyprus there also hang question marks: neither is Greek in epic, and Bacon treated them as foreign places in tragedy.[26] These islands often perform a function in Greek thought similar to that served by the barbarian world, but although Herodotus says that Pelasgians had still occupied Lemnos in Darius' day, he implies that it

---

[25] It used to be thought that Cadmus' oriental origin was a fabrication dating from the sixth century or even later (see the discussion of Vian 1963, pp. 52–75). But Edwards 1979, pp. 65–87, concludes that it may be much earlier; see also M. L. West 1985, pp. 149–52.

[26] Bacon 1961, pp. 6–7.

had become Greek by the time he was writing (5. 26), and there is no reason to suppose that the plays which dramatized the story of Hypsipyle and the Lemnian women portrayed the islanders as anything other than Greek:[27] indeed, the murderous women of Lemnos were contrasted with the Thracian slaves to whom their husbands had turned. Aeschylus' Lemnian *Cabiri*, and the Lemnian choruses of his and Euripides' *Philoctetes* plays, may, however, have retained some flavour of their barbarian or Pelasgian origin.[28] The Argive king in Aeschylus' *Supplices* appears to regard Cyprus as outside the Hellenic world (282-3), and historically of course it had a large Phoenician community:[29] as Aphrodite's domain it usually signifies erotic love and sensuality. But nevertheless it is not usually envisaged as a barbarian land: the streams of the 'hundred-mouthed barbarian river' which water Paphos at *Bacchae* 406-8 are those of the Nile.[30]

Bacon also believed that the Crete of tragedy was not Greek.[31] It is true that Herodotus said that prehistoric Crete had been inhabited by non-Greeks (1. 173), but in the fifth century, as in the *Iliad*, it was clearly believed to be Hellenic,[32] and there is no evidence that the tragedians departed from this view in their representation of the mythical Cretan past. In defence of her position Bacon would have been advised to invoke Euripides' *Cretes* fr. 79, where a chorus of initiates sing a hymn to the exotic divinity Zagreus. But even this would not have been decisive, for Zagreus was probably a god from north-west Greece who is being identified with Dionysus.[33] She preferred, however, to argue that the tragedians portrayed Crete as a barbarian land from a passage in Sophocles' *Ajax*. Agamemnon has accused Teucer, the illegitimate son of Telamon by the barbarian Hesione, of being the son of a slave and also of being a barbarian (1228,

[27] See Dumézil 1924, pp. 38, 58.

[28] On Aeschylus' *Cabiri* see Hemberg 1950, p. 167, and Burkert 1985a, p. 281. The fact that Sophocles made Lemnos a desert island in his *Philoctetes* shows how arbitrary all this was.

[29] On Cyprus in the archaic period see Burkert 1984, pp. 15-19. The Phoenicians arrived in the ninth century and remained permanently established at Kition, though Greeks flourished in the north-west of the island. See Karageorghis 1982, pp. 123, 162. On the ambiguity of Cyprus' ethnic status in fifth-century literature, see Yon 1981.

[30] See Dodds 1960, p. 124.

[31] Bacon 1961, pp. 6-7.

[32] Although a passage in the *Odyssey* envisages Crete as inhabited by many different peoples, speaking a variety of languages (19. 175-7).

[33] M. L. West 1983b, pp. 152-4. For another view see Willetts 1962, pp. 203, 240-1.

1263). Teucer defends himself against the latter charge by pointing to Agamemnon's own barbarian ancestor, Pelops (see below), and continues, 'Did not Atreus, your own father, most sacrilegiously serve up his nephews to his brother? Was not your mother a Cretan, whose father discovered her in adultery . . .?' (1293–7). He then demonstrates the royal lineage and honourable careers of his own parents (1299–303). Atreus and Aerope are adduced to testify to the *immorality* in Agamemnon's family, not his barbarian blood, as Bacon implies by misleading use of ellipse in her quotation from Teucer's speech. Like all islanders Cretans were regarded with some contempt. But Teucer is here interested in the history of female sex offenders in the Cretan royal family, not in their ethnicity; there is a similar allusion to Pasiphae in *Hippolytus* (337–8), which at a critical moment during Phaedra's struggle with Aphrodite reminds the audience of the sexual proclivities of her mother. Phaedra is an outsider, a fact exploited by Euripides in underlining her disruptive and transgressive role, but nowhere is it implied that she is not Greek; if Sophocles or Euripides had wanted to call her or Aerope or Pasiphae a barbarian then they would have done so.

The tragedians, then, regarded parts of western Asia and the Aegean islands as Greek, in accordance with contemporary criteria, rather than attempting an accurate representation of prehistorical boundaries, or even of the poeticized geography of epic. But ethnic boundaries become extremely difficult to draw where ethnic groups shade off into one another and interaction and interdependence have led to a high degree of acculturation; the boundary between Hellenism and barbarism which the Greeks always found most problematic was amongst the tribes of the mainland in northern Greece, where Hellenic influence was at its strongest.[34] A passage in Aeschylus' *Supplices* provides a view of the extent of mainland Hellas. The Argive king explains that his people, called Pelasgian after him, occupy all the territory west of Argos (by which he means the whole Peloponnese),[35] and on the mainland their realm extends beyond Pindus and to the west of the

[34] For a discussion of the problem of the northern boundary of Greece in ancient authors, see Kyriakides 1955, pp. 16–17.

[35] See also *Supp*. 117, 129, 260, 262, 269. Aeschylus used an ancient name for the Peloponnese, 'Apia', in order to imply that Pelops had not yet arrived; Pausanias agrees that before the time of Pelops the Peloponnese was called Apia from Apis, king of Sicyon (2. 5. 7).

Strymon, covering Perrhaebia[36] and Dodona, but not Paeonia, where lived a Thracian tribe (250–8). Such a boundary is not very different from that envisaged in the fifth century: it stops short of the Thracians and Illyrians, but includes Aetolians (see below) and Ambraciots. It is not clear whether the Macedonians are supposed to be included.

In this play Aeschylus was attempting to conform with the contemporary theory, perhaps invented by Hecataeus (1 *FgrH* F 119), but later developed by Herodotus (1. 56–8),[37] that Greece had in early times been occupied by the Pelasgians, an indigenous Mediterranean *Urvolk*, speakers of a non-Greek language. They had been supplanted in some areas, especially Sparta, by incursive Dorians, who were the original Hellenes (1. 56). Thereafter, the Hellenic tongue had spread even to the autochthonous Pelasgians in Greece, but not to the vestigial 'barbarian' Pelasgians Herodotus said were still to be found elsewhere in the Mediterranean.[38] Analogous with this theory are Thucydides' observation that many barbarians resembled what the Greeks had been like in former times (1. 6), and the statement in Plato's *Cratylus* that 'the earliest men in Greece believed only in those gods in whom many barbarians believe today' (397c–d), for all these ideas presuppose that the Greeks had developed to a *higher* level of civilization than other peoples. But although all Greeks with a claim to autochthony, the Arcadians or Athenians, might therefore trace themselves back to a Pelasgian origin (Hdt. 1. 146, 56–7; 8–44), Argos was thought to have a particular right to this distinction, partly as a result of its Homeric epithet, 'Pelasgian' (*Il.* 2. 681); the Argive historian Acusilaus ratified Pelasgus' place in his city's mythology by making him brother of Argos and son of Zeus (2 *FgrH* F 25a). Thus Argos in tragedy is frequently described as 'Pelasgian' (for example, Eur. *Heracl.* 316, *Supp.* 368); the hero of Euripides' *Archelaus* elaborates on the theory by arguing that it was his ancestor Danaus who made the previous inhabitants of Argos, the 'Pelasgiots', change their name to 'Danaans' (fr. 1. 7–8), one of the Achaeans' Homeric synonyms. But while in *Supplices* Aeschylus is

[36] Aeschylus wrote a *Perrhaebides*, in which the characters and chorus were at least notionally Greek, however exotic fr. 185 may suggest their presentation was.

[37] This passage is notoriously difficult to unravel and has been thought to be textually corrupt; for a discussion and defence of the transmitted text see McNeal 1985. All the ancient testimony to the 'Pelasgian' theory is assembled in Lochner von Hüttenbach 1960.

[38] In the Hellespont, Thrace, Samothrace, Lemnos, Imbros, and the Troad (1. 57; 2. 51; 4. 145; 5. 26; 7. 42). Hellanicus (4 *FgrH* F 4) and Sophocles (fr. 270. 4) both identified the Pelasgians with the Tyrseni (Etruscans): see Lochner von Hüttenbach 1960, pp. 103–4.

nodding to the ethnographers' theory about the original Pelasgian population of Argos, *his* Pelasgians are of course simultaneously envisaged as 'Hellenes' (220, 237, 243, 914), and the play depends to a great extent on the contrast between their truly Greek language, customs, and institutions, and those of the barbarous Egyptians.

3 PROOFS OF ETHNICITY

The first of Herodotus' criteria of Hellenic ethnicity, shared blood,[39] was of course as inherently unsatisfactory as geography. Some Greek cities were thought to have been founded by visitors from abroad, Argos by Danaus, Thebes by the Phoenician Cadmus, and the Peloponnese took its name from a Phrygian. Conversely, peoples thought to be thoroughly barbaric traced their line to the purest of Greek heroes, the Persians to Perseus, the Scythians to Heracles (Hdt. 7. 61; 4. 10). From the brief pedigrees of the *Iliad* onwards there is evidence that the genealogies of their mythical heroes singularly preoccupied Greek intellectuals, but it was the Hesiodic *Ehoiai* which sought to explain the names and origins of both Greek and foreign peoples by incorporating them into mythical stemmata ultimately deriving from Deucalion or Inachus or Cecrops. The parentage of foreigners had, however, presented little problem to the poets of either heroic narrative or genealogical poetry, for they were hardly differentiated from their Greek counterparts: ethnicity was scarcely an issue in the archaic literary world of heroes. It was not until the tragic poets made Athenian citizens dress up as mythical foreigners, and impersonate them in the theatre, that the problem arose of how to rationalize the physical and cultural differences between, for example, Io's Egyptian or Phoenician descendants, and the Argives or Thebans to whom they were related.[40]

Aeschylus confronted this problem in his *Supplices*, where his barbarous Egyptians are descended through Io from the same line as the autochthonous Pelasgians of Argos (291–320). In *PV* the child whom Io is to conceive at Zeus' touch by the mouth of the Nile,

---

[39] On the importance to subjective ethnicity of the idea of a common descent, see Keyes 1981b, pp. 5–7.

[40] For a discussion of the enormous contradictions entailed in the tracing of barbarian peoples to Greek origins, see Bickerman 1952, pp. 68–78.

Epaphus, will be black, nurtured by the Nile which waters Egypt's soil (851–2): this is stressed to explain why the people who spring from him are dark of skin despite their Argive ancestress. In *Supplices* Aeschylus also brings the Egyptians' different appearance into association with the river and soil which has nourished them: 'the Nile might have nurtured such a growth' remarks Pelasgus on the Danaids' strange appearance (281). Danaus warns his daughters against antagonizing their hosts, for 'the Nile does not nurture the same breed as the Inachus' (497–8). In these words is foreshadowed the 'environmental' explanation of ethnic difference occasionally adopted by Herodotus[41] and expounded by the author of the Hippocratic *de Aëribus*, generally believed to be an authentic fifth-century work. It argues that climate and topography determine not only physiology, but also temperament and political behaviour. The fertility and equable climate of Asia, for example, produce handsome people, who are however deficient in courage and industry, and ruled by pleasure (12. 28–44): this leads to stagnation and is associated with despotic forms of government (16. 3–34). Europeans, on the other hand, on account of the challenges presented by the harshness and variability of their seasons, are less uniform in physique, braver, and do not tolerate monarchies (23. 13–41).[42] But neither in Aeschylus' *Supplices* nor elsewhere in extant tragedy is natural science so invoked to draw *explicit* connections between environment and national character: Sophocles' *Inachus* may have provided a quite different aetiology for the Egyptians' supposed cunning (see above, chapter 3, n. 113). In *Persae* the reason why the playwright invokes the barrenness of the Attic soil (792–4), though he is aware of the contrasting fertility of Asia, is *not* to explain the courage and hardiness of the Athenians, which is the use to which the composer of an epitaphios might have put it.[43] In *Supplices* he only mentions the environmental factor in association with the different *physiology* of the Egyptians; perhaps in describing themselves as a 'black

[41] See Hdt. 3. 12 and Klaus E. Müller 1972, pp. 116, 137–44.

[42] Backhaus 1976 argues that this treatise represents the earliest known attempt to prove that the barbarians are inferior with arguments from natural science. See also Jouanna 1981, pp. 11–15.

[43] See the argument in Plato's 'ironic' epitaphios *Menexenus* (237d): such a speech could invoke the original barrenness of Attica, because the earth was unable to support animals, and was thus forced to restrict its inhabitants to a superior breed of men. But in *Persae* it is not nature but *nomos* which distinguishes Athenians from Persians: see Heinimann 1945, p. 33.

race, struck by the sun' (154–5) the Danaids reflect the theory that dark-skinned peoples are simply more heavily sun-tanned than others (see Hdt. 2. 22).[44]

The Danaids must prove that they are descended from Io if their claim to asylum is to be heard: the arguments of tragedy are elsewhere informed by the question of a barbarian's claim to genealogical connection with a Greek community, or conversely by the suggestion of a barbarian taint in the blood of a seeming Greek. The barbarian chorus of Euripides' *Phoenissae* claim to be Agenorids like their Theban hosts, and *homogeneis* with them (217–19). They are descended, like the Danaids, from Io (248), and therefore share blood (*koinon haima*, 247) with the Thebans, which they invoke to explain their sympathy at the city's plight (249, see also 291). The paradoxical conjunction of their shared blood (Herodotus' first criterion of *Hellenic* ethnicity) and their obviously barbarian appearance, speech, and conduct (278–9, 301, 293–4) is not one Euripides cares to explain, by the 'environmental' or any other theory. In his *Telephus*, however, the protagonist's claim to Hellenic blood was an issue of supreme importance. Telephus was the son of an Arcadian princess and Heracles, but his birth had brought disgrace upon his mother, who had been sent off to marry the barbarian king Teuthras of Mysia. In Euripides' version of the story, Telephus explains in the prologue that he had eventually gone to Mysia, where he had found his mother and succeeded to the Mysian throne, thus becoming, as he puts it himself, a Greek ruling over barbarians (fr. 102. 9–11, 14). Although purely Greek by blood, the question of his ambivalent nationality, which assumes such importance later in the play, is thus established at its beginning.

At the supposed time of the action of the drama, Telephus has been forced to return to the Peloponnese where he was born, because he was wounded by Achilles when the Greeks attacked his city, mistaking it for Troy; an oracle has told him that only the man who inflicted the wound can heal it. But the Greeks are aware of another oracle: without Telephus to guide them they cannot take Troy (see Hyginus *Fab*. 101). The Mysian king arrives at Agamemnon's palace, forced to assume a disguise because he had fought on the barbarians' side in the Teuthranian war. In the course of the drama he must prove that he is no barbarian, or otherwise the Greeks will not accept him as their

---

[44] See also tr. fr. adesp. 161, 'the sun, shining with its light, will turn your skin Egyptian'.

leader. A papyrus has preserved the end of a choral ode from what is almost certainly Euripides' *Telephus*.[45] The chorus predicts that Telephus will steer the Atridae to Troy (fr. 149. 1-6), 'for Tegean Hellas, not Mysia, bore you . . .' (7-8). The stress laid here on the Hellenic ethnicity of Telephus' mother suggests that his Greek blood had been contested and proved during the previous episode.[46] The evidence of another papyrus supports this interpretation, for in it Telephus as a Greek and a citizen (*astos*) appears to be freed from some restriction (fr. 148. 10).[47] That the issue of the unsuitability of a Mysian leading the Greek forces was raised is perhaps further confirmed by the question preserved in a fragment (127), 'shall we, as Greeks, be slaves to barbarians?' It has been suggested that this was asked in indignation by Achilles, when told that the stranger was to lead the Panhellenic army to Troy.[48]

Telephus, the Hellene by blood but Mysian by domicile, was therefore put on trial by Euripides like an Athenian citizen defending himself against charges of foreign parentage. This play was produced in 438 BC, only twelve years after Pericles had passed his famous law of 451/0, by which all but those who could prove that *both* parents were Athenians, and of the citizen class, were now excluded from its privileges (*Ath. Pol.* 26. 4).[49] Citizenship, tied strictly to the descent-group, was of enormous importance both politically and economically; those who enjoyed it seem to have felt a deep anxiety about preserving their special status and went to inordinate lengths to expose 'infiltrators'.[50] The evidence for legal action in the form of a *graphē xenias* being taken against a foreigner masquerading as a citizen is from the fourth century,[51] but an Aristophanic comedy parodied this procedure: several barbarian gods being 'imported' at the time to Athens were tried on a charge of *xenia*, found guilty, and expelled from the city.[52]

[45] *Berlin Papyri* 9908 = fr. 149.   [46] See Handley and Rea 1957, p. 33.

[47] *Rylands Papyri* 3. 482 = fr. 148. See Webster 1967, p. 47.

[48] Handley and Rea 1957, p. 33.

[49] See A. R. W. Harrison 1968, pp. 24-9. Patterson 1981, p. 99, argues that marriages between Athenians and non-Athenians (e.g. Miltiades' marriage to a Thracian princess) had by no means been confined to the aristocracy.

[50] On the importance of descent-group thinking to the Athenian citizenry and therefore to the democracy see Davies 1977-78.

[51] Dem. *Ep*. 3. 29; Σ Dem. 24. 131. See A. R. W. Harrison 1968, p. 165.

[52] See Aristophanes' *Horae* frr. 578, 581. 14-15; T ii *KA*: *novos vero deos et in his colendis nocturnas pervigilationes sic Aristophanes . . . vexat, ut apud eum Sabazius et quidam alii dei peregrini iudicati e civitate eiciantur* (Cicero *Leg.* 2. 37).

Pericles' law had certainly instigated heated arguments, and the contestation of particular citizens' parentage; when Aristophanes wanted to insult Cleophon, he took care to remind his audience that he had a Thracian mother (*Ran*. 679–82).[53] Perhaps this outbreak of litigation was reflected in the *agōn* of *Telephus*, as it surely was in the stress laid on the undesirability of having a foreign wife in *Medea* —see especially 591–2.[54]

Twice elsewhere in tragedy the aspersion is explicitly cast against a Greek that his blood is not entirely free from barbarian taint. In *Ajax* Agamemnon has upbraided Teucer, as the illegitimate son of Telamon by the barbarian Hesione, for failing to appoint a free man (*anēr eleutheros*, in Athens a synonym for 'citizen') to speak on his behalf (1259–61). This is a reference to the Athenian law which permitted non-citizens to plead in court, as Teucer is pleading for Ajax to be buried, only through a *prostatēs*, a citizen appointed to represent him.[55] Other passages in tragedy are formulated in accordance with this law: in Euripides' *Philoctetes* a character expressed outrage that barbarians, presumably the Trojan ambassadors, were allowed to plead their cause (fr. 796). The importance attached to this law is shown by the fact that the punishment suffered by a non-citizen convicted in a *graphē aprostasiou* of having pleaded personally in court was no less than enslavement.[56] But Teucer does not allow Agamemnon to intimidate him, and answers with dignity that his own conduct in the war has been impeccable (1288–9), and then produces one of the most extraordinary arguments in any tragic *agōn*: Agamemnon's lineage is not, after all, so very pure, for was not Pelops, his own grandfather, none other than a barbarous Phrygian? (1291–2).

In *IA* Euripides provides Achilles, as angry with Agamemnon as Teucer was in *Ajax*, with a similar point. Appalled by the plan to sacrifice Iphigeneia he swears to Clytaemnestra that he will save her

---

[53] A. Diller 1937, p. 94 n. 45, collects numerous other insinuations of foreign parentage in Old Comedy and oratory.

[54] Patterson 1981, pp. 99 and 124 n. 73, thinks it likely that foreign marriages were normally restricted to Athenian *men* marrying non-Athenian *women*. Of course it is not only the allegedly or actually barbarian Telephus and Medea whose stories were influenced by this xenophobic Athenian law; the reception at Athens of non-Attic *Greeks* is a frequent theme in tragedy. See Davies 1977–78, pp. 111–12.

[55] A. R. W. Harrison 1968, pp. 165, 193; Whitehead 1977, pp. 89–96. See also *OT* 411.

[56] Harpocration s.v. *aprostasiou*; Suda s.v. *pōlētai* 2.

daughter: if he should fail, then 'Sipylus, on the fringes of barbarism, where our generals' family had its origin, shall be a city, and Phthia shall deserve to bear no name' (952-4). He thus contrasts the Lydian town of Sipylus, the home of Tantalus, great-grandfather of the Atridae, with his own undoubtedly Greek ancestral home in Phthia. But the insult goes deeper than this. When Demosthenes wanted to cast Meidias in an unflattering light, he suggested that his opponent, although adopted, had inherited 'bad blood' from his real, barbarian mother, which explained the savagery and impiety in his temperament, *to tēs phuseōs barbaron . . . kai theois echthron* (Dem. *Meid*. 149-50):[57] in *IA* Achilles not only slights Agamemnon's lineage, but implies that his cruelty, derided in the foregoing trimeters, can be explained by his oriental ancestry. Thus when the tragedians wished to make a character insult a Tantalid, they could always resort to the argument from genealogy. Plato's Socrates might also have approved of the point raised by Teucer, though for a different reason: in an unusually liberal observation in *Theaetetus* (174e-75b) he says that the man who devotes his time to philosophy is not impressed by noble birth, since *every* man has countless thousands of ancestors, amongst whom have been rich and poor, kings and slaves, Greeks and barbarians. But it is fascinating to find in the rarified world of tragedy insults borrowed from the xenophobic discourse of the law courts, heroic figures discrediting a mythical Greek king by allusions to his barbarian ancestry, like Aeschines' repeated allegations that Demosthenes' own mother was Scythian (2. 78, 180; 3. 172).

The ambiguity of the boundary between Hellas and barbarism, as we have seen, is most apparent in the case of the communities on the northern periphery of Greece. Their ethnicity was questionable especially when their speech—Herodotus' second criterion of Hellenicity—was not intelligible to Greeks from further south. The pride the Greeks felt in their beautiful language is reflected in Philoctetes' emotional response to hearing it used on deserted Lemnos for the first time in years (Soph. *Phil*. 225, 234-5). They were sensitive to the differences between the dialects of Greek: the Athenians, predictably, imagined that their own Attic was the envy of the Hellenic world (Thuc. 7. 63), and the Messenians, it is observed by Thucydides' Demosthenes, would be dangerous to the Spartans since they spoke the same dialect

---

[57] See Dover's remarks (1974, pp. 85-6).

and were therefore indistinguishable (4. 3).[58] This is why the army encircling Thebes in *Septem* is described as 'heterophone' (*heterophōnos*, 170): it speaks Greek, but another dialect. Aeschylus wanted to suggest the deep psychological fear which alien speech can arouse, even if only an alternative dialect of the same language, and in this case could not call the aggressors 'barbarians' when they were well known to have been Greeks (see fr. adesp. 645. 3 where the armies around Thebes are called 'Panhellenic'). It has been argued that in the formulation of the drama as a struggle of the freedom and *sōphrosunē* of Thebes against the violence and hubris of her attackers there still lived on the spirit of the Persian wars, and that the enemies are recognizably portrayed as barbarians.[59] But Aeschylus did not intend to portray the invaders, however brutal, as speakers of a non-Greek language; he was suggesting, rather, that their behaviour was like that of barbarians, for the invention of the 'vocabulary of barbarism' had greatly enriched the language available to the poets in their portrayal of mythical Greeks (see below, chapter 5. 1). He may, moreover, have inherited the near-monstrous character of the Seven from the *Thebais*, whose moral framework presupposed sympathy toward the besieged:[60] this poem may in turn have owed their terrifying aspect to an origin as demons in an Assyrian ritual text.[61]

Tydeus perhaps represents a special case. Thucydides observed that the largest tribe in Aetolia spoke an 'incomprehensible' language (*agnōstotatoi de glōssan*, 3. 94) and Polybius did not wish to include the 'majority of the Aetolians' among the Greeks (18. 5. 7–8). It is interesting, therefore, that in Euripides' *Phoenissae* Tydeus the Aetolian is described as 'appearing strange in his arms, semi-barbarian' (*meixobarbaros*, 138); the last word is applied by Xenophon to the half-Hellenized tribes of Caria (*Hell*. 2. 1. 15).[62] But in *Phoenissae* the reference is surely not to Tydeus' language, but to his outlandish arms, the javelin and light shield (see 139–40), which Euripides is contrasting with the hoplite equipment of his own compatriots: Thucydides

[58] See Hutchinson 1985, p. 72.

[59] This view was originated by Snell (1928, pp. 78–81). See also *Septem* 463, where the muzzle-pipes on the frontlets of the horses of Eteoclus (one of the Seven) let forth a 'barbaric sound' (*barbaron bromon*).

[60] Reinhardt 1960, pp. 14–15.

[61] See Burkert 1981, pp. 41–2.

[62] See also the term *mixellēnes* ('half-Greeks') used by Hellanicus in his discussion of the Sintians of Lemnos (4 *FgrH* F 71a).

comments in similar vein on the light-armed troops of Aetolia (3. 98). There is therefore no reason to believe that all the lost tragedies about the Aetolian royal house, Althaea, Meleager, and the Caledonian boar hunt, portrayed these people as anything other than Greek.

The word *barbaros* originally referred solely to language, and simply meant 'unintelligible': that it could retain this sense in the fifth century is shown by the use of a cognate in the description of the clangour of birds (Soph. *Ant.* 1002, see Ar. *Av.* 199–200). Thus even a Greek dialect was occasionally described as 'barbarian' if it were thought sufficiently incomprehensible. When Prodicus called Pittacus' Lesbian brogue 'barbarian' in Plato's *Protagoras* (341c), he was not implying that the Lesbians did not speak Greek, but that it was difficult to understand them.[63] But it would never have been claimed that Mytilene was outside the boundaries of Hellas, whereas until Alexander had conquered half the world, the Macedonians, who lived in the 'grey area' between Hellas and Thrace, failed to convince everyone that they were not barbarians. Their speech was parodied by the fifth-century comic poet Strattis,[64] and is famously illustrated by a passage in Plutarch where Alexander slips into his native Macedonian (*Alex.* 51): 'he leapt up and shouted in Macedonian (*Makedonisti*), calling on his armour-bearers.' The question is whether this Macedonian speech was actually a non-Greek language, or a hybrid patois, Doric or Aeolic Greek overlaid with Thracian and Illyrian vocabulary. The consensus of modern opinion argues for the latter, but certain un-Greek vowel changes have never been accounted for, and the problem may never be solved.[65]

There had already long been controversy over the Macedonian royal family's claim to Hellenicity when Herodotus wrote his *Histories* (5. 22), and the earlier genealogists reflected the Macedonians' ambiguous ethnic status when they kept their eponymous ancestor Macedon out of the mainstream Hellenic stemmata. He was made only the son of a *sister* of Hellen (Hes. fr. 7), 'a declaration that the . . .

[63] Gorgias' Sicilian dialect may have been one factor behind the suggestion that he was a barbarian at Ar. *Av.* 1700–1.

[64] In a play entitled *Macedonians* or *Pausanias*. See Strattis fr. 28. 2 Kock, and above, ch. 1 n. 55.

[65] The studies of Stanley Casson (1926, pp. 157–9) and Dascalakis (1965, pp. 59–95) concluded that the Macedonians spoke a form of Doric Greek. But Hammond and Griffith argue that although their language contained a considerable amount of Thracian and Phrygian vocabulary, it was basically an Aeolic dialect like Thessalian (1979, pp. 46–54).

Macedonians . . . are not Hellenes, nor quite on a level with Hellenes, but akin to them'.[66] Pindar and Bacchylides both wrote encomia for Alexander I (Pind. frr. 120–1, Bacch. fr. 20B), which would presuppose that the royal family at least was to be regarded as Greek, but Thrasymachus the sophist strongly asserted the contrary (85 B 2 *DK*), and the debate assumed greater significance and acerbity during the fourth century (see, for example, Dem. 3. 24; 9. 31–2; 10. 34). But tragedy could be used to validate by genealogy the claims of a people to Hellenic origin even where it was not clear that they were Helleno-phone. Euripides' plays about the mythical forebears of the Macedon-ian king Archelaus, supposedly composed while the poet was enjoying the hospitality of his court, cannot have portrayed the Macedonians as anything other than Greek: indeed, he seems to have gone to some lengths to prove their Hellenicity. The mythical Archelaus, who spoke the prologue of the play which bore his name, produced a detailed genealogy tracing his line through the Argive stemma to Inachus (frr. 1, 2). Hyginus *Fab*. 219, which looks as if it recounts the plot of this play, indicates that it provided an aetiological myth explaining how the Greek hero came to oust the indigenous barbarian king Cisseus (probably the Trojan queen's father in *Hecuba*)[67] from Aegae, and to found the 'Hellenic' kingdom of Macedonia.[68] It is possible that Euripides even invented the mythical Archelaus in order to clear the name of his host, the historical Archelaus, who was illegitimate and had recently won his throne by intrigue and murder; if so, his plays were designed to verify the propagandist genealogy and show the historical king to be a fit monarch, the descendant of Argive heroes.[69]

Euripides may also have sought to prove the Hellenic origin of another race, the Molossians. Thucydides unequivocally includes these northern tribesmen among a list of barbarians (2. 80).[70] In Euripides'

[66] M. L. West 1985, p. 10. Hellanicus promoted Macedon to the status of *grandson* of Hellen (4 *FrgH* F 74).

[67] Euripides had altered Hecuba's ethnicity. In the *Iliad* she is the daughter of Dymas the Phrygian (16. 718), but the prologue of *Hecuba* states that her father was Cisseus (3), an epic Thracian (*Il*. 11. 222–3), apparently the original occupant of Macedonia who was ousted by Euripides' Archelaus. See Rose 1963, pp. 144–5 n. 4.

[68] On the genealogies of the Macedonian royal house and its foundation myths see Dascalakis 1965, pp. 97–105; Harder 1985, pp. 129–37.

[69] See Dascalakis 1965, pp. 105–10.

[70] Although see Hammond and Griffith 1979, p. 45. They argue that when in such contexts Thucydides referred to tribes in northern Greece as *barbaroi*, he was talking about a primitive level of civilization rather than any linguistic difference.

Andromache Menelaus is concerned that the son of the heroine, unnamed in the play but called 'Molottos' in the list of characters is, in view of Hermione's childlessness, likely to inherit the kingdom of Phthia, and become a barbarian ruler of Greeks (663–6). But Thetis explains *ex machina* that destiny has another fate in store for the boy: his mother is to marry Helenus in Molossia, where her son will beget a prosperous dynasty (1243–9). Molossus, the son of the Greek Neopto-lemus and the Phrygian Andromache, thus linked with Achilles, Neoptolemus' father, will rule the northern tribe named for him, classified as a 'barbarian people' by the historian Thucydides. It has been proposed that *Andromache* was composed as a compliment to the Molossian royal family, as the Macedonian plays were written for Archelaus, and that it was actually performed in Molossia.[71] The young Molossian king Tharyps was probably sent for an education at Athens: Plutarch writes that he was the first to 'Hellenize' and civilize his country (*Pyrrh.* 1). That he was actually granted Athenian citizenship is confirmed by epigraphic evidence.[72] While it is unnecessary to suppose that the play could only have been performed in Molossia,[73] the presence of Tharyps at Athens some time after 429 BC, and his earning of citizenship, both suggest that in *Andromache* Euripides was attempt-ing to pay him and the Molossians (however primitive) a compliment, by bestowing upon them a Greek ancestor descended through Achilles from Aeacus.[74]

4 THE COMMON LAWS OF HELLAS

The tragedians' preoccupation with the ethnicity of their mythical characters has been illuminated by the application of two of Herodotus' ethnological criteria, genealogy and language. His third was the religious bond which existed between all Greeks, but he made his Athenians formulate this not in terms of distinctive Hellenic gods, as Dionysius of Halicarnassus was later to do (*Ant. Rom.* 1. 89), but in

---

[71] Robertson 1923.

[72] Ibid., p. 59.

[73] Various venues have been suggested as a result of a scholion on line 445 stating that the play was not produced at Athens. Page, for example, argued that it was produced at Argos (1936, pp. 223–8).

[74] For a discussion of Euripides' influential version of the Molossian genealogy see Dakaris 1964, pp. 68–101.

terms of their shared temples and rituals, *thusiai*. Similarly, the poets only rarely exploited the possibility of attributing different gods to the barbarians, Aeschylus' Cotyto and Re being possible exceptions. They did not even support Herodotus' basing of a bond between all Greeks on their shared temples and rituals. The dearth of information about the scenery of the fifth-century theatre should perhaps preclude drawing conclusions about the representation of foreign buildings, but the Taurians' temple in *IT* seems to have been constructed on purely Doric lines (113–14).[75] Nor are there more than rare attempts to distinguish barbarian religious rituals from those of Greeks, exceptions here being human sacrifice and Thracian heliolatry. Why, when the playwrights represented foreigners, did they so rarely use the names of their gods, or attempt to suggest their practice of strange rituals? Aeschylus, however ignorant about Zoroastrianism, knew a good deal about Egypt: why do his references to the Egyptians' different gods in *Supplices* stop short at implication? Sophocles and Euripides both reveal the influence of Herodotus' *Histories*. Why, therefore, did they refrain from exploiting when they could the strange names and cult practices he had unearthed?

It might be argued that these questions are in themselves redundant, that there is absolutely no reason why the barbarians of the Greek tragic stage should not worship Greek gods, just as they speak Greek iambic trimeters; the tragedians, the argument might go, were simply not interested in differentiation in this sphere, any more than Shakespeare was concerned with comparative theological realism when in *Timon of Athens* his Greeks, like good Elizabethan Englishmen, say grace and swear by the cherubim and seraphim. Or it could be argued that the role of the Olympian gods was so fundamental to the epic poems from which the tragedians drew most of their plots that this was one aspect of their literary legacy with which they did not care to tamper. But three factors suggest that the matter cannot be left here. First, the small handful of instances in which barbarian gods or rituals *are* pointed out shows that the idea did cross the poets' minds, and that introducing foreign gods into the tragic theatre did not actually contravene a taboo. Secondly, the comic poets revelled in allusions to foreign religion: besides the Triballian god in Aristophanes' *Aves*, the plays and fragments are full of explicit references to Bendis, Sabazius,

---

[75] See Miller 1929, pp. 105–19; Bacon 1961, pp. 132–5.

Isis, Serapis, Horus, Egyptian animal worship, and Syrian abstinence from fish.[76] Thirdly, and perhaps most importantly, the tragic texts express a profound concern with defining the difference between Hellenes and barbarians in terms of language and politics: why not in terms of religion, an area which anthropologists agree is one of the most important determinants of ethnic identity? The problem can partially be solved, once more, with the help of Herodotus.

The historian's work on the gods of different countries is marked by two interdependent principles. He hardly ever disputes the existence of foreign gods, and he nearly always identifies a foreign god with a Greek name.[77] His cosmopolitan approach to religion, indeed, allowed him to find a Greek equivalent in his polytheistic system for all but the most 'barbarous' of foreign deities: the Apsinthians' Pleistorus (9. 119) whose cult included human sacrifice, Salmoxis, whose very godhead he for once calls into question (4. 94-6), and, surprisingly, the Lydians' version of the Mother goddess, whom he names 'Cybebe' (5. 102).[78] In all the numerous other instances (except local river deities) where he discusses foreign gods, he recognizes in them Greek gods under other names. Fifty-seven foreign gods are cited as identical with Greek gods, and the Greek name is given in every case, but the barbarian name is supplied in addition in only seventeen.[79] The Greek names are used even when he discerns striking differences in cult practices: Babylonia has hierodules, but in the temple of 'Aphrodite' (1. 199). Persians worship 'Zeus' but without statues, temples, and altars (1. 131). The Egyptians celebrate festivals of 'Dionysus', but, astonishingly to a Greek, do not dance at them (2. 48). When he follows his normal practice of using only the Greek name for a foreign god—Aphrodite for Astarte, Zeus for Ahuramazda, Pan for Mendes, or Dionysus for Osiris—he offers no explanation, because he assumed that the identification would seem natural to his audience, which therefore cannot have found them as startling as they sometimes appear to a modern eye.[80] 'Herodotus and his Greek readers instinctively believed that foreign gods were not different beings from the gods they knew under

---

[76] See Long's chapter on barbarian religion in Greek comedy (1986, pp. 20–48).

[77] On Herodotus' *interpretatio Graeca* see Linforth 1926; Burkert 1985b; Hartog 1988, pp. 241–8.

[78] On the reasons for this exception see Linforth 1926, p. 24; Hartog 1988, p. 75.

[79] Linforth 1926, p. 5.

[80] See e.g. the bald statement that 'Zeus and Dionysus are the only gods worshipped by the Ethiopians' (2. 29).

Greek names, but identical with them. It was indifferent whether the
Greek or foreign name was used, but it was altogether more natural to
use the familiar Greek name.'[81]

The apparently Hellenic gods of the barbarians of tragedy should
therefore be approached keeping in mind both the divine framework
of epic and this ethnographic principle of identification. It was natural
enough for the playwrights to attribute worship of Greek gods to the
barbarian cultures they represented, however incongruous the effect
may seem to a twentieth-century audience, conditioned to understand
religion in terms of messianic and monotheistic faiths which aim to
convert unbelievers or adherents to 'false' religions to the one true god.
The tragedians' choice of Greek names for their barbarians' gods also
reflects the ethos of the City Dionysia, a festival attended by Greeks
from numerous cities for the celebration of Panhellenic gods. This
does not necessarily mean, however, that the more travelled or
educated spectator at the Dionysia was not perfectly aware that the
'same' divinities went by different names abroad, for occasionally the
tragedians show themselves conscious of their own convention of
identifying Greek and foreign gods. The Egyptian Danaus seems to
refer to this very principle when he recognizes a statue of Hermes, but
explains that it represents the god 'in his Hellenic form' (Aesch. *Supp*.
220), and Euripides even allows Iphigeneia to question the practice in
making her openly reject the Taurians' identification of their savage
goddess with Artemis, her own Hellenic heavenly patroness (*IT* 389–
91).[82]

Despite the ancient principle of the identification of the gods
honoured by different peoples, it would still be surprising if the
tragedians had made no attempt to extend their exposure of the
inferiority of the barbarians to the religious sphere, and indeed there
was one aspect of the tragedians' differentiation of foreigners which
might be defined as religious, though it has little to do with specific
gods. Barbarians are denied access to the fundamental Greek code of
conduct, the body of 'socio-religious' tenets variously called the
'unwritten', the 'ancestral', or the 'common' laws. These constituted
simultaneously an expression of the most fundamental and ancient

[81] Linforth 1926, pp. 10–11.
[82] It may be relevant that Herodotus had not said that he agreed with the Taurians'
identification of their maiden goddess with Iphigeneia, but had merely recorded it without
comment (4. 103).

taboos, and a didactic charter of 'decent' behaviour which was invested at times with a sanctity far greater than the strict observance of ritual. The conception of the 'unwritten laws' so famously invoked in Sophocles' *Antigone* and *OT* (*Ant*. 454–5, *OT* 863–71) was probably an ancient rather than a fifth-century formulation; these laws seem to have enshrined such integral taboos as the killing of guest or host, family member or suppliant, incest, and failure to bury the dead. The 'common laws' were more usually presented as positive 'commandments': honour your parents, your gods, and your guests (for example, Xen. *Mem.* 4. 4. 19–20). Xenophon makes Socrates equate the unwritten laws and the popular 'commandments' (ibid.), but it is possible that the identification was not explicit in the fifth century;[83] it has been argued that there was a qualitative distinction between the transcendental divine laws in Sophocles and the 'homely and somewhat elementary rules of popular ethics' expressed in Xenophon's moral precepts.[84] But such conceptual bodies of taboo and imperative were surely fluid and variable, and any attempt to systematize the ancient evidence from different literary genres is probably doomed to failure. The one certainty is that the advent in the sixth century of comparative ethnography (which was probably the very catalyst which forced the invention of the philosophers' distinction between nature and *nomos*),[85] and the further development by the sophists of the relativism which had sprung from ethnography,[86] forever cast doubt on the universality of such laws. The question began to be asked whether non-Greek peoples also abided by and comprehended them, or whether they were to be understood as the laws common to the Hellenes but not to mankind, and therefore one of the most significant areas in which the Greeks' ethical and religious superiority was manifested.[87]

[83] On the 'unwritten laws' in the fifth century, and the claim that their origin was ancient and 'popular', see Ehrenberg 1954, pp. 22–50, 167–72. But *contra* see the sceptical view of Ostwald 1973; he is not convinced of the existence of a belief in such laws in the fifth century. The idea of a 'common Hellenic law' is particularly prevalent in Euripides' *Heraclidae*, *Supplices*, and *Orestes*.

[84] Ehrenberg 1954, p. 170.

[85] Heinimann 1945, p. 9.

[86] There are signs of ethnographic (and theological) relativism already in Xenophanes 21 B 16 *DK*: the Ethiopians say their gods have snub noses and dark hair; the Thracians that theirs have blue eyes and red hair.

[87] The 'common laws of Hellas' in tragedy and Thucydides are treated as a *sub-category* of the 'unwritten laws' by de Romilly 1971, pp. 40–3.

The most famous statement of the ethnographers' discovery of the cultural relativity of taboo is the anecdote in Herodotus which he opens with these trenchant remarks: 'everyone without exception believes that their own native customs are by far the best ... there is plenty of evidence that this is the universal human attitude' (3. 38). In illustration Herodotus tells the story of Darius' seminar on comparative theology. Indians eat their parents' corpses—an act of the greatest impiety by Greek standards—but the Greeks cremate their dead, which is correspondingly appalling to the Indians; 'custom rules everything' concludes Herodotus, paraphrasing Pindar (fr. 169a. 1). But it has been seen that the tragedians hardly availed themselves of the opportunity to portray specifically barbarian religious custom, or, for that matter, barbarian horror at Greek custom.

The philosopher, poet, and polymath Hippias was a great relativist, for he regarded many important laws of social behaviour, for example the taboo on incest, as culturally determined and not laid down by any ordinance of the gods (Xen. *Mem.* 4. 4. 20). But even he admitted that at least some unwritten laws must have been established by the gods for *all* mankind since 'men who could not all have come together, and do not speak the same language, could not have made them' (ibid. 4. 4. 19). Occasionally the tragedians, especially Euripides, seem to take a universalist line. In *Andromache* the heroine, in the interests of modesty, begs Hermione to be silent on the subject of Aphrodite. The Spartan princess chauvinistically responds 'we do not run our city according to barbarian laws' (243), but to Andromache 'shameful behaviour' is disgraceful *wherever* it is found, in Europe or Asia (244), implying that female forwardness is *universally* objectionable. Similarly, the Taurian Thoas is horrified to hear that Orestes killed his own mother: 'Apollo!' he declares, 'even a barbarian would not dare to do that' (1174), and indeed Xenophon's Hippias did include matricide among the few crimes he thought were universally forbidden by the laws of heaven. Demosthenes went a step further than Hippias, for he equates the unwritten laws precisely with the *anthrōpina ēthē*, those beliefs which *all* mankind holds in common (*de Cor.* 275).[88] But the playwrights, despite their neglect of foreign gods and ritual, delighted their Panhellenic audience by normally identifying the unwritten laws with what else but the common and ancestral laws of the Hellenes. It

---

[88] See Kranz 1951, p. 236.

is not that they implied that the barbarians had *other* divine rules for social conduct, but that they did not have any at all. Thus any contravention of religious taboo may invite reference to the culprit's barbarian blood, or if he or she is a Greek, a comparison with barbarian conduct. So many plots involved both barbarians, and the sacrilegious violation of divine law, that it would indeed have been surprising if this opportunity to celebrate the supposed unity and superiority of the Panhellenic ethico-religious consciousness had been passed by.

In chapter 3 it was shown that tragedy characterized barbarians as failing in three of the cardinal Hellenic virtues—intelligence, courage, and self-restraint. The fourth virtue, *dikaiosunē*, becomes relevant here. It is a difficult concept to define, but its implications can be seen from the range of vices with which it was thought to correspond. Sometimes its opposite is *adikia*. In Herodotus it is bound up with the virtues of the democratic polis, and distinguishes the citizen who respects the principles of equality and freedom of speech;[89] it is found in association with concern for *to nomimon*, observance of custom or law (Xen. *Cyr.* 8. 8. 2–13), and the next section will show how barbarians are *adikoi* in their disrespect for civic law and legal processes. But elsewhere, for example in Plato's *Euthyphro*, the opposite of *dikaiosunē* is impiety (*asebeia*), the flouting of the laws of heaven.[90]

One of the most important taboos was the violation of the ancient law which protected both guest and host. Herodotus may make his Xerxes aver that 'the laws of all mankind' dictate that it is wrong to kill the ambassadors of a foreign power (7. 136), but to Euripides the killing of a guest provided an opportunity for a character to castigate such behaviour not only as wrong, but as un-Greek: Agamemnon informs the Thracian Polymestor, who has murdered his guest for gold, that guest-friend murder (*xenoktonia*) 'is something *we* Greeks consider disgraceful' (*Hec.* 1247–8). No less shocking was the violation of the rights of the suppliant: the violent removal of suppliants from their place of sanctuary was an action integral to the plots of many tragedies.[91] In Aeschylus' *Supplices* the Egyptian herald's attempt to abduct the Danaids is referred directly to his barbarian provenance (914), and in Euripides' *Heraclidae*, where the 'common laws of Hellas'

---

[89] See Kunsemüller 1935, p. 23.
[90] Ibid., p. 9.
[91] See Gould 1973, pp. 85–90.

are repeatedly invoked,[92] even the Argive Copreus' contravention of
this most sacred of laws provokes the response from the Athenian
Demophon that although the culprit's clothes are Hellenic, his deed is
that 'of a barbarian hand' (131).

In the most flamboyant passage of anti-barbarian rhetoric in extant
tragedy Euripides' Hermione attributes to the entire barbarian *genos*
various crimes which constituted for the Greeks the breaking of
absolute taboos (*Andr*. 168–78):

You must understand what part of the world you are living in. There is no
Hector here, no golden Priam. But you are so uncivilized as to have the gall to
sleep with the son of the very man who murdered your husband, and bear
children to him. That's what all barbarians are like. Fathers have intercourse
with daughters, sons with mothers, sisters with brothers, close relatives
murder one another, and no law forbids such crimes. Don't import your
barbarian customs here! It's not *right* for one man to have two wives . . .

Murder within the family (175) was of course by Greek standards a
particularly shocking crime. There are, however, few enough family
murders committed by foreigners in comparison with the gallery of
matricides, parricides, and infanticides produced by the royal houses of
mythical Hellas: Orestes, Alcmaeon, Oedipus, and Althaea are a few
who spring to mind. Perhaps Euripides was contemplating this
paradox when he made his Taurian king wince at the news that
Orestes had murdered his own mother (*IT* 1174). A similar paradox is
explored in *Medea*, where Jason rhetorically claims that Medea's
murder of her children is something 'no Greek woman' would ever
have committed (1339–40), but the mythical paradigm of infanticidal
mothers adduced only minutes earlier was the Greek Ino (1282–9).[93]
Indeed, it was one of Euripides' favourite sources of irony to explore
the tension between the outrageous acts which were the very stuff of
Greek myth and the contemporary ideology which claimed that only
barbarians committed such deeds (see below, chapter 5. 2). But often
the superiority of Panhellenic religious law is left unquestioned. The
pollution caused by murder, for example, was felt at a deep psychological level,[94] and Eurystheus appeals to the *Greek* law which will

---

[92] See especially line 1010 and fr. ii. 3 Diggle. See also 219, 324, Eur. fr. 853, and Collard
1975, ii, pp. 440–1, where the comments printed are those of T. C. W. Stinton.

[93] Hyginus assembled many of the mythical parents who had killed their own children
in *Fab*. 238, 239.

[94] See Antiphon *Tetr*. 2. 1. 2; Lysias 12. 24; Parker 1983, pp. 124–30.

dictate that the man who kills him will necessarily incur pollution (*Heracl*. 1010); Tyndareus accuses Menelaus of having turned into a barbarian during his long period abroad when his son-in-law attempts to help the polluted matricide Orestes (*bebarbarōsai, chronios ōn en barbarois*, *Or*. 485).

The taboo on incest is nearly universal to mankind,[95] and yet Athenian law curiously permitted marriage between a half-brother and sister provided that they had different mothers.[96] Another of the crimes of which Hermione accuses 'the entire barbarian genus', however, is incest between the closest of blood relations, between father and daughter, son and mother, brother and sister (174–5). Once again, each variety of this supposedly barbarian practice was exemplified between Greek agents in myth,[97] indeed in well-known tragedies. Did not Thyestes sleep with his daughter Pelopia, and Oedipus with his mother Jocasta? In the *Aeolus*, a famous play by Euripides himself, Macareus impregnated his full sister Canace and persuaded their father to allow all his sons to marry their sisters.[98] Hippias claimed that incest was not outlawed by divine ordinance on the ground that some peoples allowed it, and his argument seems to have been echoed by a character in the *Aeolus*, for a fragment asserts the relativist view that an act is not shameful if those who perform it do not think it is (fr. 19).[99] Dionysus puts forward a similarly relativist position in *Bacchae*, for when Pentheus suggests that the barbarians' adherence to Dionysiac religion reveals their lower moral standards (483), he answers that in this respect they are actually superior, but that *their customs differ* (484). A Sophoclean fragment (937) advises that it is best to abide by 'the local laws'.

The tragic echoes of sophistic relativism in regard to ethnography, however, are surprisingly rare, and Hermione regards the practice of

[95] See la Barre 1970, pp. 69, 101, 559. For an anthropologist's view of incest taboos and exceptions to them see Arens 1986.   [96] A. R. W. Harrison 1968, p. 22.

[97] For a list of mythical figures who had committed incest see Hyginus *Fab*. 253, 'Quae contra fas concubuerunt'. On incest in Greek myth see Guépin 1968, pp. 273–6.

[98] See the hypothesis to the play (*Pap. Oxy*. 2457, edited and discussed by Turner 1962, pp. 70–3), and Lloyd-Jones 1963, p. 443. The issue of which sister was to marry which brother was decided by lot (fr. 39); Canace's lot did not fall to Macareus (hypothesis 30–3). The play earned considerable notoriety: see Ar. *Nub*. 1371–2 with the schol. ad loc.; *Ran*. 1081.

[99] This fragment probably came from one of Macareus' speeches in the famous debate with his father, on which see Jäkel 1979, pp. 103–9. On the relation of Hippias' thought to the *agōn* of *Aeolus* see Dodds 1973, p. 100.

incest in foreign lands as the reprehensible result of an *absence* of proper laws (*Andr.* 176) rather than a matter of differing convention. The fifth-century Greeks, indeed, defined their monogamous marital ideal by comparing it with the allegedly deviant forms of relationship to be found in foreign lands (see below, chapter 5. 1). Perhaps in composing Hermione's speech Euripides was thinking of the rumour that Cambyses had married two of his full sisters (see Hdt. 3. 31), though Herodotus asserts (ibid.) that this type of marriage had never been customary in Persia. Herodotus, however, was wrong. There is clear evidence that the Persian royal family, like the Egyptian,[100] encouraged its members to intermarry. Incestuous marriage (*xvaētvadaθa*) is advocated in the *Avesta*,[101] and Atossa married two of her brothers successively. Rather less reliable is Plutarch's report that the Artaxerxes who ascended the throne in 436 BC married his own daughters, exposing the Persian king to the charge of Hermione's first variety of incest (Plut. *Art.* 23. 4). The author of the sophistic *Dissoi Logoi* adduced exactly the same variations on the theme of incest, referring them specifically to Persia, in order to defend his radically relativist argument *against* the existence of absolute and universal moral laws (90. 2. 15 *DK*): normally this thinker derives his ethnographic examples ultimately from Herodotus, but in this instance he may be echoing Hermione (even though she appropriated the taboo on incest to 'civilized' Hellas) and thus demonstrating the interdependence of sophistic thought and tragic rhesis.

5 A RHETORIC FOR THE DEMOCRACY

The fourth criterion of Hellenic ethnicity which Herodotus put in the mouth of his Athenians was that of *ēthea homotropa*; all the Greeks shared a similar way of life and customs, everything which might be

[100] See Hopkins 1980, pp. 306–7.

[101] Next-of-kin marriage was recommended in the *Vištasp Yašt* (*SBE* xxiii, p. 332), *Yasna* 12, and *Visparat* 3 (*SBE* xxxi, pp. 250, 342). The subject was fully treated in the lost *Nask* 16. It is also mentioned in the Pahlavi texts which were translations of the *Avesta* (*SBE* xviii, pp. 232, 387). E. W. West discussed the whole question (*SBE* xviii, appendix 3), and concluded that marriages with relatives closer than first cousins are indeed likely to have received encouragement in the Achaemenid period, a view more recently endorsed by Boyce 1982, pp. 75–7. The practice has received considerable attention from comparative anthropologists: for a discussion and fuller bibliography see Duchesne-Guillemin 1970, pp. 206–10.

understood as components of the modern concept of 'culture'. Occasionally the tragic poets use this kind of ethnographic termino- logy. Medea complains that she finds herself bound by new customs and laws she did not learn at home (*Med*. 238–40); Hecuba asks if paying honour at a tomb is some Greek custom (*nomos ē ti/thesmion . . . Hellanōn*, *Tro*. 266–7). Helen in Egypt laments the gods' abandonment of her amongst 'barbarian customs' (*barbar' ēthē*, *Hel*. 273–4). But normally the tragedians preferred to focus on one of the components of *ēthē*—clothing and music, values and morals, or political practice. Ethnography, behaviour, and politics were all covered by 'ethics' according to the categories of the early Ionian thinkers, and the demarcation between them was not nearly so clear as it is today.[102] Xenophanes even used examples from comparative ethnography to illustrate 'an epistemological moral' (21 B 16 *DK*);[103] from Herodotus, Hippocrates, and the *Dissoi Logoi* through to Plato and Aristotle there is extensive cross-fertilization between ethnography and moral or political theory. That tragedy concentrated so often on these areas underlines its role as 'civic discourse', as a vehicle for political and ethical pronouncements.

The most significant 'cultural' difference the Athenians felt between themselves and others was in *politeia*, literally, 'the life of the polis'. The polis was believed to be a linear advancement on the scattered settlements inhabited by both the earlier Greeks and some contemporary barbarians (see Thuc. 1. 5), and was the institution on which the philosophy of Protagoras and other leading sophists was centred. To many of them it represented the highest rung on the ladder of human evolution, and Protagoras' anthropological enthus- iasm for tracing the technological inventions which had brought primitive man up to the level of civilization enjoyed by fifth-century Athenians is probably reflected in various tragic passages, especially Prometheus' speeches where he lists the skills he had disclosed to man (*PV* 447–68, 476–506), the 'many wonders' ode in *Antigone* (332–75), and the interest in the means of survival Philoctetes had managed to find on deserted Lemnos.[104] The Greek view of their own distant past

[102] Barnes 1987a, p. 12.

[103] Barnes 1982, p. 142; see above, n. 86. For Xenophanes' connections with the ethnographers see Heidel 1943, pp. 266–77.

[104] For tragedy's interest in 'culture heroes' such as Prometheus and Palamedes, and its reflection of 'Protagorean' ideas on the progress on humankind, see Edelstein 1967, pp. 43– 4; M. L. West 1979, p. 147.

had many points of contact with their perception of barbarians; Thucydides lists customs which the Greeks had given up but which barbarians still practised (1. 6). Thus although tragedy conventionally designates both Greek and barbarian communities as *poleis*, occasionally the question is even asked whether a particular barbarian settlement can be granted the title at all. In *Hecuba* Polymestor has a palace, but apparently no polis, and arrives at the Greek camp in the Chersonese 'from the Thracian mountains' (963), a suitable place for a barbarian characterized by bestial imagery; Achilles in *IA* doubts that Sipylus in Lydia deserves to be called a polis (952). But generally the distinction between Greek and foreign communities takes a more theoretical form.

The sophists may have debated which of the fundamental laws were universal and which culturally relative, but the Thucydidean Pericles implies that the 'unwritten laws' could flourish best in a democracy (2. 37), and it is in the contrast drawn between democracy and despotism that the most conscious and powerful contrasts between Hellene and barbarian are drawn in tragedy as elsewhere. The breathtaking anachronism of the democratic procedures imported into the heroic Greek cities of tragedy (the voting at the Argive assembly in Aeschylus' *Supplices*, Theseus' exposition of democratic theory in Euripides' play by the same name, the apparently kingless Athens of *Eumenides*, the process of debate and voting reported in Euripides' *Orestes*)[105] found its counterpart in denunciation of the tyrannical regimes of the barbarians. Epic provided the tragic poets with no embryonic theoretical political science, no excoriation of the monarchies of Priam or Rhesus or Sarpedon, no contrast of despotic Troy with Achaean rule of the *dēmos*. This is the most significant area in which the ancient stories were reformulated in the light of the fifth-century Greeks' perceptions of themselves and of foreign civilizations. The poet who made a character in a lost tragedy cry, 'O Tyranny, beloved of barbarian men' (fr. adesp. 359), was writing in the new tradition of political philosophy, whatever the myth he had chosen as the vehicle for such rhetoric.

The queen in *Persae* was surprised that Athens had no king (241–3): Hecuba queen of Troy is struck by the rights enjoyed even by slaves under Greek law (*Hec*. 291–2). The barbarian political psychology is

---

[105] See Easterling 1985, pp. 2–3, 9.

most fully developed in Aeschylus' *Supplices*. Pelasgus finds an opportunity to expatiate on the Greek (or rather, Athenian) democratic process during his altercation with the lawless Egyptian herald (942–9), but it is the Danaids who express blatantly anti-democratic sentiments, which must have been particularly loaded with meaning in 463 BC, when constitutional reform was a red-hot issue at Athens.[106] When Pelasgus insists that he can take no decision until he has consulted all his citizens, the Egyptian women respond with a panegyric for a barbarian tyrant: 'But *you* are the city and *you* are the people. You are a leader who need submit to no judgement. You rule the altar, the hearth of the land, by your own will and single vote, and yours is the single sceptre with which from your throne you direct all affairs' (370–5). The cultural importance of defining democracy by comparison with barbarian monarchy or tyranny is further demonstrated by the numerous occasions on which it occurs in tragic rhetoric, even in plays with no barbarians in sight. In *Heraclidae* the significantly-named Demophon, 'voice of the people', is concerned to find a way both to save the suppliants' lives and to avoid criticism from his citizens. To illustrate the nature of his relationship with the *dēmos* he naturally invokes its supposed opposite: 'I do not hold a tyranny like the barbarians, but by acting justly I win a just response' (423–4).

An important claim of the rhetoric with which the Athenians authorized their democracy was that it ensured freedom for all, instead of the slavery they believed other political constitutions inflicted on all but the ruling élite; it did not seem to concern them that their own democracy was itself a minority rule. When in the fourth century Demosthenes appealed for assistance to be given to the Rhodians in their attempt to liberate themselves from the Carian satrapy, he calls them 'slaves of barbarians, slaves of slaves' (15.15), for in the eyes of the democratic Athenians, all those living under a tyrant's sway were slaves themselves. A Sophoclean character declared that even free individuals turned into slaves if they attended upon a tyrant (fr. 873), and Helen, stranded in Egypt, finds her status as good as servile, since 'amongst barbarians all are slaves except a single man' (Eur. *Hel*. 276). Herodotus might have agreed with Helen about the political climate of Egypt, for despite his admiration for that country he admitted that it had been unable to survive for long without a monarchical form of government,

---

[106] In *Supplices* it is of course the Athenian democratic ideal which is applauded, and projected on to the Argives: see Grossmann 1970, p. 148.

the implication being that only politically mature communities could support the extension of freedom beyond a tiny minority (2. 147). But Helen was not talking exclusively about Egypt. Tragic rhesis provided a vehicle for popular generalization about the undemocratic regimes of the barbarians, in the darkest hours of the Peloponnesian war consonant with the struggle for the preservation of Athenian democracy.

Other phenomena associated with tyrannical or monarchical regimes were also illustrated from the barbarian world, even in purely Greek contexts. In Sophocles' *OT* Oedipus has jumped to the false conclusion that Creon wants to seize power and has bribed Teiresias into helping him. Wealth and *turannis*, he begins, are always marred by envy (380-2); the people of Thebes bestowed on him his kingship (*archē*), but now it is this kingship from which 'Creon the faithful (*ho pistos*), my friend from the beginning, longs to drive me out, covertly stalking me, and setting against me this wile-weaving *magos*, this treacherous charlatan . . .' (385-8). Two aspects of this passage deserve attention. First, its emphasis on subterfuge, for Pericles was proud of the openness of political behaviour under democracy (Thuc. 2. 37); the language is clearly intended to bring to mind the stories of the machinations and court intrigues of Persia of the kind familiar to us from Herodotus and Ctesias. Creon is ironically labelled *ho pistos*, 'the faithful one' (385), the title conferred on the Persian king's closest confidants, and Teiresias becomes as his lackey a scheming *magos*.[107] But it is also implied that a ruler on whom all the power in a state devolves cannot afford to have friends because none can be trusted, and an important component of the Greeks' own self-identity was the importance attributed to *philia*, the friendship which bound different individuals, families, and states together. The Athenians' theoretical explanation for the supposed absence of friendships in barbarian countries[108] was that their constitutions were not democratic: the harsh and uneducated tyrant was thought to find friendships almost impossible (Plato *Grg.* 510b-c), and in the *Symposium* Pausanias

[107] See Rigsby 1976. More than one authentic *magos* (*makuš*) in charge of sacrifices and libations has turned up in the Persepolis tablets: see Hallock 1969, no. 758. 4. But to the Greeks the word had pejorative overtones suggestive of a sham diviner or magician. See Heraclitus 22 B 14 *DK*, Eur. *Or.* 1497, Hippocrates *de Morbo sacro* 1. 10, 6. 354 (other references in M. L. West 1987, p. 282), and Bickerman and Tadmor 1978, p. 251.

[108] The Greeks' claim that ritualized friendship was an exclusively Greek institution was of course quite false. Herman 1987, pp. 12 and 51, fig. 4, produces Assyrian evidence from the ninth century BC.

supposes that homoerotic relationships and their concomitant activities,[109] philosophy and sport, are held to be disgraceful by barbarian leaders since it is not in their interest to encourage friendships between their subjects (182b–c). Several other passages in tragedy are informed by these ideas. Prometheus regards the tyrant's isolation and inability to trust his friends as inherent to his estate (*PV* 224–5); in *Hecuba* Odysseus says, 'you barbarians do not count your friends as friends' (328–9); Helen in Egypt muses on her friendlessness among barbarians (*Hel*. 274). One would certainly search in vain to find anywhere among the barbarians portrayed on the tragic stage an equivalent of the mythical paradigms of male friendship enjoyed by Achilles and Patroclus in Aeschylus' *Myrmidones*, and by Orestes and Pylades in numerous plays; their supreme loyalty to each other is markedly contrasted with the isolation of the barbarian Thoas in Euripides' *IT*.[110]

Closely related to the concept of barbarian tyranny was the idea that the Greeks' antipathy towards the rest of the world was irresoluble, a fact of nature (Dem. *Meid*. 49): '*cum alienigenis, cum barbaris aeternum omnibus Graecis bellum est eritque*', as Livy puts it (31. 29. 15). Hecuba denies the possibility of any manner of friendship between Greek and barbarian (*Hec*. 1199–1201), and Hector in *Rhesus* rebukes his Thracian ally: *as a barbarian* he has betrayed other barbarians to the Greeks by his procrastination in coming to the aid of Troy (404–5). The historical point at which the truceless war had begun was a matter of dispute: Herodotus opened his work with a discussion of the supposedly Persian theory that the perpetual enmity between Greece and Asia had begun with the abduction of Io and was consolidated by the Trojan war (1. 4). But the historian himself seems to blame the eternal hostility on the Lydian annexation of the Greek cities in Ionia, and later he dates the 'beginning of the troubles' much more recently, to the Athenians' sending of twenty ships to assist the Ionians in their revolt (5. 97).[111]

The Greeks believed that the barbarians looked with covetous eyes

---

[109] Formal friendship was definitely a male affair: male–female or female–female alliances were almost unheard of (Herman 1987, p. 34).

[110] All Hyginus' examples of mythical friendships are between Greek males: he adds Pirithous and Theseus, and Diomedes and Sthenelus (*Fab*. 257). For friendship under discussion in the tragedians, sophists, and Thucydides, see Fraisse 1974, pp. 72–106.

[111] See Wardman 1961.

upon Hellas, and some were never convinced that the Persians might
not invade again; the prayers which opened the Athenian assembly
seem to have included a curse on anyone who might betray Hellas to
the barbarians (see *Thesm*. 337, 365–6). In *Troades* Euripides therefore
makes Helen expand on the promises that the three goddesses had
respectively given to Paris on the day of his judgement between them.
To the pledges of the two who lost the contest the poet adds significant
detail not in the tradition.[112] Athena's gift of military prowess is
formulated as leadership in a war which will subdue Hellas (925–6),
and Hera's gift of a tyranny would apply not only to Asia but also to
Europe (927–8). Helen argues that by marrying Paris she had therefore
saved Hellas from enslavement. The sophistic defence with which
Euripides supplies Helen thus relies on the theory of the 'barbarian
peril'.[113] Similarly, Rhesus is made to boast like a latterday Xerxes that
he will lead an army against Greece and crush her (*Rhes*. 471–3). The
theory of natural and perpetual enmity between Greek and barbarian
was to find its most explicit formulation in Plato's *Republic* (5. 470a–
71b), but it was tragic drama which in the fifth century provided the
medium for its promulgation.

If the war between the two halves of humanity were perpetual, and
if it were intolerable that barbarians should have mastery over Greeks,
then Greeks must rule barbarians. This logical step was especially easy
to take since the Athenians at least acquired the vast majority of their
slaves from barbarian lands; most of the barbarians with whom
ordinary Athenians had contact on a daily basis were slaves.[114] They ran
a permanent debate on the morality of enslaving other *Greeks*,
whether the inhabitants of the islands who had seceded from the
empire and been reduced, the Spartan helots, or the Penests in
Thessaly.[115] But in the view eventually made explicit by Aristotle,
barbarian and slave were considered to be more or less identical (*Pol*.
1. 1252b 7–9). Tragedy was not immune to the equation of slave with
barbarian; in *Alcestis* Pheres objects to being reprimanded like a slave
from Lydia or Phrygia (675–6). It is therefore a mystery why so few

---

[112] Stinton 1965, p. 36 and n. 1.

[113] On which see Baslez 1981.

[114] See Baldry (discussion contribution) in *Grecs et barbares* 1962, p. 74; above ch. 3
n. 29. Pritchett 1956, pp. 280–1, estimates from the evidence of Attic grave stelai that at
least 70 per cent of all slaves were imported barbarians. A considerable number of the
remainder must have been bred from slaves in the house.

[115] See e.g. Morrow 1939, pp. 32–6; Vidal-Naquet 1986, pp. 168–88.

tragic servants of Greek characters, except those brought back to Troy for the service of Helen or Clytaemnestra, are explicitly envisaged as foreign (see chapter 5. 1). Cilissa, the nurse in *Choephoroe*, who is probably supposed to be a Cilician, is exceptional. But the tragedies of Euripides in particular frequently express the chauvinist imperative that Greeks must rule barbarians, not *vice versa*. A character in his early *Telephus* already vocalizes this view (fr. 127), and if Hermione remains childless, Menelaus demands to know in *Andromache* (664–6), are the Asiatic slave's barbarian sons to inherit Neoptolemus' kingdom and thus rule over Greeks? Again, one of the reasons Iphigeneia agrees to die is in order to prevent barbarians, who are *douloi*, from lording it over Greeks (*IA* 1400–1), the very words which Aristotle adduced to support his equation of slave and barbarian.[116]

This popular rhetorical topos perhaps echoes the sentiments typical of the formal patriotic orations to be heard in the fifth century at the Panhellenic festival at Olympia, and of the epitaphioi delivered at Athens: in his epitaphios, for example, Gorgias said that victories over barbarians called for hymns of praise, but those over Greeks for dirges (82 B 5b *DK*).[117] All through the Peloponnesian war the Athenians gathered annually at the city's burial ground to lay coffins in the earth for the dead of each tribe and listen to a speech in their praise (Thuc. 2. 34): though the custom may not have been inaugurated until the mid-460s,[118] it was felt, like tragedy, to represent an important component of the 'civic discourse' of Athens, and to be inseparable from the city's democratic constitution.[119] The two genres seem to have reached their acmes simultaneously and extensively to have cross-fertilized one another.[120] The speech was invested with quite as much significance as the interment itself; Thucydides' Pericles opens his by remarking that the institution of the formal epitaphios itself has often been praised by those who deliver it (2. 35). It is therefore

[116] For a fascinating discussion of Aristotle's theory of natural slavery and its influence, see Pagden 1982, ch. III.

[117] On Gorgias' choices of venue for encouraging Panhellenic consciousness see Sakellariou 1981, p. 129. On political rhetoric in the second half of the fifth century see von Wilamowitz-Moellendorff 1893, i, pp. 169–73.

[118] Jacoby 1944b, pp. 51–3.

[119] Loraux 1986, pp. 172–220.

[120] See especially Theseus' speech at Eur. *Supp.* 429–55. On the similarity of theme and expression in epitaphioi and tragedy see Schröder 1914; Loraux 1986, pp. 48, 65–9, 97, 107–8, etc.

intriguing to find Odysseus in *Hecuba* concluding his cynical exegesis of the reasons why Polyxena must be sacrificed with the explanation that men will not perform well in armies unless they see the dead honoured; 'you barbarians', he adds, 'neither count your friends as friends *nor admire your dead*' (328–30). He suggests that the policy can only assist Greece to the detriment of her enemies (330–1). His charge appears to have had little basis in historical fact, at least in the case of the Persians, who according to Herodotus honoured men who had distinguished themselves in war more than any other people he knows of (7. 238), but it appears all the same that Euripides is providing Odysseus with an argument drawn from patriotic pride in yet another of the institutions which supported the Athenians' democratic ideal.[121]

The concept of democracy was inseparable from the concept of the rule of law, and it was above all by their *dikaiosunē*, or respect for the mastery of law, that the Greeks sought to distinguish themselves from other peoples (see Hdt. 7. 104). It seems to have been Protagoras who first produced a theoretical analysis of the basis of democracy, arguing that it must be governed by *nomos*; the unidentified sophist known as Anonymus Iamblichi, who was probably working during the Peloponnesian war, propounded a pro-nomos position which claimed that tyranny emerges from *anomia* (89. 7. 12 *DK*). Even the worst possible men brought up within a society with lawcourts and laws are to be rated higher than lawless primitives (Plato *Prt.* 327c–e). The tragedians often presented the limits of justice as commensurate with the boundaries of Hellas, and in doing so invented as a corollary the rhetorical topos of the lawlessness of the barbarians. Medea, who has been transported to Greece from her native land, should be grateful, avers Jason, that he has allowed her to know justice, laws, and the ascendancy of law over strength (536–8). When Tyndareus criticizes Orestes it is not because he has contravened some ancient taboo by killing his own mother, but because by taking the matter into his own hands he failed to appeal to the *Hellenic* law of justice (*Or.* 494–5). In Euripides the most explicit statement of the superiority of Greek arbitration over barbarian brawling is Agamemnon's rebuke to Polymestor which precedes the most formal 'forensic' debate in extant tragedy;[122] he tells him to put barbarism (*to barbaron*) out of his heart and like an Athenian on trial deliver an apologia (*Hec.* 1129–30).

[121] See Plato *Menex.* 249b; Lycurgus *Leocr.* 46–51.
[122] Duchemin 1968, p. 161.

By far the most extensive examination of the lawlessness of barbarians occurs, however, in Aeschylus' *Supplices*. The Egyptian herald rejects absolutely the need to conform to Argive law while on Argive soil, and the suggestion that as a foreigner he requires an Argive *proxenos* to state his case (916–20).[123] When he threatens war on Pelasgus he is made to deride the use of courts and witnesses in settling disputes: in such matters, he says, 'the judge is Ares' (934–7). But the Egyptian women are as contemptuous of Greek law as their cousins. Aeschylus goes out of his way to make them dismiss the suggestion that they should prove *sub judice* that their cousins have no rights over them (387–91). The women respond to the voice of Greek *eunomia* that they will never be made subject to the power of men, the implication being 'even if they are legally within their rights' (392–3). Nor must it be forgotten that Aeschylus' audience, as Pelasgus hints (388–9), would have been in sympathy with the legal case of the sons of Aegyptus who, under Athenian law, would have had the legal *right* to marry their cousins, as *epiklēroi*, at least after Danaus' death.[124] The practical reason for this law, the retention of property within the family, is even advanced explicitly by Pelasgus (338).

Lastly, an essential component of both democratic politics and the judicial process was speech-making: Isocrates, the notable fourth-century Panhellenist, went so far as to argue that it was *logos*, though an Athenian speciality, which above all differentiated Greeks from barbarians: 'So far has our city distanced the rest of mankind in thought and in speech that her pupils have become teachers of the rest of the world, and she has brought it about that the name "Hellenes" no longer suggests a race but an intelligence' (*Paneg.* 50). The view that the Greeks were distinguished from other peoples by their superior intelligence had already been current in the fifth century (Hdt. 1. 60);[125] the close connection in the Greek mind between intelligible

---

[123] The *proxenoi* were the most privileged class of non-citizens resident in Athens, exempt from paying the metic tax (Whitehead 1977, pp. 13–14). In reality a stranger such as the Egyptian herald would have had to find a *proxenos* to represent him. There are other aspects of Athenian law prescribing the conditions under which foreigners might reside in the city which inform Aeschylus' interpretation of the Danaid myth: at 609 Danaus states that the Argives have accepted him and his daughters as metics. See also 963–4 and 994–5, with Whitehead 1977, p. 35. [124] See Thomson 1973, pp. 189–90, 289.

[125] Some have thought that this passage of Herodotus means the opposite (see Lloyd-Jones 1983b, p. 200 n. 45). But see Dodds' remarks, recorded in Lloyd-Jones' *addenda* (ibid., p. 236).

speech and reason 'made it easy to take the view that *barbaroi* who
lacked *logos* in one sense were also devoid of it in the other'.[126] And so
the tragedians assisted their audience to define themselves in terms of
their monopoly on *logos*. A few barbarians in tragedy are credited with
intellectual powers, for example Medea (285, 677, 741); but she effects
her trickery through deceit and with the drugs in which Hermione
believes all Asiatic women are skilled (*Andr*. 157–60), for subversive
barbarian guile is not the same as the Greek power of reasoned
persuasion through speech-making, *peithō*.[127] Jason, his wife bitterly
observes, persuaded her to leave Colchis with *words* (*Med*. 801–2).
Euripides fr. 139 implies the uselessness of talking rationally to a
barbarian; both the anonymous fragment which refers to a barbarian
'in *logos* and in manner' (346a), and Agamemnon's objection to
Teucer's supposedly barbarian speech at *Ajax* 1259–63,[128] play on the
ambiguity of the concept of barbarian *logos*. Both passages were
probably understood as referring as much to the content of the
barbarian's words, and to their passionate delivery, as to their mis-
management of the Greek tongue (see also fr. adesp. 696, *barbarostome*,
'barbarous-mouthed'). In a perfect marriage of medium and message
the Athenians' democratic rhetoric, so often directed against the
barbarians, had come to denigrate them for their supposed ignorance
of the art of speaking itself.

[126] Baldry 1965, p. 22.
[127] On barbarian deficiency in the art of persuasion see further Buxton 1982, pp. 58–9,
64, 161–3.
[128] 'Are you not aware that, as an alien, you must bring a free man here to represent your
case to us in your place? If you were to speak (*legontos*) it would be incomprehensible to me,
for I do not understand the language of barbarians (*tēn barbaron . . . glōssan*)'.

5

Epilogue: The Polarity Deconstructed

I BARBARIC GREEKS

THE last chapter's examination of the reflection in tragic rhesis of the cultural antinomies by which the Greeks demarcated their world from barbarism largely concentrated on aspects of civic life—politics, law, speech-making. But the polarity informed their apprehension equally of the domestic and familial life of the barbarian world: the 'civilized' Greek monogamous marital norm, and the ascendancy of the male, were defined by the fifth-century ethnographers in terms of deviations from them in other cultures, and this structural opposition likewise underpins the tragedians' manipulation of myth. Two such deviations, polygamy and incest, have already been discussed (see above chapters 3. 6 and 4. 4); the Greeks constantly thought they had found evidence in foreign cultures for these and others, including promiscuity. Herodotus discusses such barbarian practices no fewer than fourteen times.[1] He claims, for example, that all the Persians had a number of wives and even more concubines (1. 135). The historical veracity of this statement is questionable, for although no legal code survives from Achaemenid Persia, all the cuneiform texts from Sumerian times to the latest Babylonian period only attest to one word for 'wife', *dam*, which is quite distinct from all other terms for concubine or courtesan.[2] But the tragedians echoed the ethnographers' findings, and although polygamy was particularly associated with Thrace, Hermione implies that it was practised by *all* barbarians (Eur. *Andr*. 177–8).

Relations between the sexes which departed from the Greek norm of the ascendancy of the male were projected on to and discerned in other cultures, just as mythical cities controlled by slaves (another subordinate group whom Aristotle equates with women and identifies with barbarians) were sometimes located in the 'other', barbarian

---

[1] See Rosellini and Said 1978, especially section 6, 'Vierges libertines, hommes efféminés et femmes viriles'.

[2] Pembroke 1967, p. 4.

world.[3] Sophocles' Oedipus famously echoes Herodotus' classic exposition of the radical inversion of sex-roles he believed existed in Egypt, when he denounces his sons for sitting at home and doing 'women's work' while their sisters assume the external, 'masculine' responsibilities (*OC* 337–45, Hdt. 2. 35). But it was the total over-turning under matriarchy of the 'normal' male control of both the *oikos* and the polis where the association between powerful women and the non-Greek world, long validated by myth in the story of the Amazons,[4] was now rationalized and formalized by ethnography and consequently exploited by the tragic poets. Greek ethnographers constantly thought they saw evidence for matriarchal rule in the barbarian world, a reversal of the Hellenic norm,[5] although they were probably mistaken; the Amazons are now thought never to have existed,[6] the theory of universal primeval *Mutterrecht* formulated in the nineteenth century by Bachofen has been repudiated,[7] and even Herodotus' discernment of a matrilineal system of inheritance in Lycia (1. 173, a cornerstone of Bachofen's argument) may well have arisen out of a misunderstanding of Lycian epigraphic evidence.[8] The powerful barbarian women of the ethnographers and mythographers therefore have more bearing on the Greek male's own definition of himself by comparison with the outside world than on the actual social structures prevailing in Egypt or Asia or the Pontus at the time, but there can be no doubt either that the Greeks believed that women were dangerously powerful in barbarian lands, or that the belief deeply affected the tragedians' formulation of various characters and scenes in their plays.

When women in tragedy 'get out of hand' reference is frequently made, whether explicitly or implicitly, to barbarian mores. Sometimes 'transgressive' females are actually barbarians: in Aeschylus' *Supplices* the women who are refusing to submit to the institution of marriage

---

[3] Vidal-Naquet 1986, pp. 2–7.

[4] Zeitlin 1978, pp. 151–3; Tyrrell 1984.

[5] On the association of the inversion of sex roles with the *Aussenwelt*, see Kenner 1970, p. 134.

[6] See Devambez 1981, pp. 642–3; Tyrrell 1984, pp. 23–5; Lefkowitz 1986, pp. 17–27. Bamberger 1974 argues that the overthrow of matriarchies in myth, though ahistorical, is designed to justify in the form of a mythical 'social charter' the contemporary reality of patriarchy.

[7] Bachofen 1861.

[8] Pembroke 1965.

(and thus rejecting the only role for citizen women sanctioned in ancient Athenian society) are of course colourfully characterized as barbarians in speech, appearance, and behaviour. The myth of the masculine Heracles' enslavement to the Lydian Omphale, dramatized in satyric form by Ion and Achaeus but stressed in Sophocles' tragic *Trachiniae*, represents a radical inversion of the established Greek power structure; it provides an external mythical reference for the destruction of Heracles, whom no beast nor villain could subdue, by his wife Deianeira, 'Manslayer'. Euripides' Colchian Medea is the paradigmatic 'transgressive' woman, and her overbearing nature cannot fully be understood without reference to her barbarian provenance.[9] The woman who gets out of hand may, however, not necessarily be a barbarian herself; among the most powerful women in extant tragedy is undoubtedly Aeschylus' Clytaemnestra. But on close examination a brilliant device is shown to have been deployed in the presentation of this 'woman of manly counsel' (*Ag*. 11): the 'vocabulary of barbarism' has been transferred to illuminate the psychology and motivation of a *Greek*.

It has been observed occasionally in passing that outrageous behaviour even of Greeks in tragedy could invite a comparison with barbarian conduct: dragging a suppliant from sanctuary is described as the 'act of a barbarian hand' (*Heracl*. 131), and in Aeschylus' *Septem* the representation of the hubristic Greek army encircling Thebes drew on language suggestive of barbarism. But this device was exploited by the tragedians far more subtly in their portrayal of several Greek principals, and even of supernatural beings (the Erinyes). It was discovered that the 'vocabulary of barbarism', the symbols and actions and language outlined in chapters 2 and 3, which the poets had invented to define their non-Greeks, had the potential to enrich the language they used in evoking *any* character's excess, transgression, subversiveness, or departure from the Hellenic virtues. The origins of this development were almost certainly political: it was seen in chapter 2. 1 how in the 480s ostracized aristocrats with tyrannical or oligarchic leanings were caricatured in the public imagination as 'Medes'. But it

---

[9] Although Knox 1979, pp. 306–11, questions whether Medea is portrayed by Euripides as an oriental *witch*, Page 1938, pp. xviii–xxi, was certainly right to stress the importance of her foreignness to the play. Shaw 1975, pp. 258–64, argues that one of the most important themes of the play is her cultural isolation, and that it is in the subordination of her female instincts as a mother to her 'masculine' desire to dominate that she is most fully 'barbarian'.

was Pausanias and Themistocles, heroes of the war against Persia, who paradoxically provided the prototypes of the 'barbaric Greeks' of tragedy, seduced by luxury and power.[10] After his famous generalship at Plataea, Pausanias the Spartan allegedly began to become arrogant and tyrannical, and gave way to the temptation of colluding with Persia (Thuc. 1. 94–5). When his overtures from the Hellespont to the Persian king met with an encouraging response (Thuc. 1. 130),

> he thought even more of himself and was unable to live any more in the usual way, but used to depart from Byzantium dressed in Median clothing, accompanied by Median and Egyptian bodyguards, and held Persian-style banquets ... He made himself inaccessible and treated everyone so high-handedly that no one was able to go near him.

Themistocles learned the language and customs of the Persian court and retired to enjoy its hospitality (Thuc. 1. 138). But when the playwrights represent mythical Hellenes behaving like barbarians they are not necessarily referring to any historical individual, but to the abstract principle, of which Pausanias' career was a concrete illustration, indicated in Euripides' *Orestes* by the verb *barbaroō* (485): any behaviour suggesting that someone was breaking the 'laws of Hellas', transgressing their socially authorized role, or was in danger of committing hubris, could now be defined as 'not Greek'.

In the *Oresteia* Aeschylus used numerous items from the 'vocabulary of barbarism' to delineate the kind of anarchic society governed by passion and violence which the Athenians in *Eumenides* replace with the rule of law. Clytaemnestra of course represents the classic case of the dominant woman in tragedy. Winnington-Ingram in 1948 first drew attention to the importance of her masculinity to the motivation of the trilogy;[11] more recently Zeitlin's feminist analysis has interpreted it as portraying the struggle of the sexes within the conjugal relationship, leading to the eventual ratification of the superiority of the male. Aeschylus, she argues, suggestively adduces mythical parallels to the threat presented to the rule of men (embodied in Agamemnon, Orestes, and Apollo) by the insurgent Clytaemnestra and her Erinyes: the Lydian Omphale who dominated Heracles, and the murderesses Althaea, Scylla, and the Lemnian women (*Ag.* 1040–1, *Cho.* 602–38). But Zeitlin recognizes that the conflict resolved by the

---

[10] On Pausanias and Persia see e.g. Blamire 1970.
[11] Winnington-Ingram 1948b.

trilogy is not only sexual, for it 'places Olympian over chthonic on a divine level, Greek over barbarian on the cultural level, and male above female on the social level'.[12] It might be added that it places democracy over anarchy or tyranny on the political level (see especially *Eum*. 696–8). All of these polarities are interconnected, and thematically interact with one another throughout the trilogy.

The association, for example, of the chthonic and female Erinyes with barbarism is made explicit in one of Apollo's speeches in *Eumenides*, for when describing a place where he imagines they belong, he evokes a grim torture chamber where men 'impaled beneath the spine moan long and piteously' (189–90). The horror of persecution by the Erinyes is thus illustrated with an image from the 'vocabulary of barbarism', impalement, for they are the barbarians of the supernatural world, the savage executors of talionic justice in opposition to the rule of law. Other punishments Apollo associates with 'the place' where they belong include beheading, gouging out of eyes, castration, and mutilation (187–9), all forms of punishment which have been seen to be unequivocally associated with barbarian society: pitilessness is described as 'barbarousness of heart' at *Helen* 501. But it is the presentation of the antipathy between Greek and barbarian as an analogue to that between male and female which illuminates the important scene in *Agamemnon*, where the woman persuades the man who had previously been 'just as much at pains to emphasize the constitutional checks to his authority as . . . Pelasgus'[13] (see 844–6) to lapse into the conduct deemed appropriate only to an eastern despot, and walk over the purple fabrics to his death.

It is cumulatively suggested throughout the scene that not only is Clytaemnestra, the manly woman, comparable to a barbarian flatterer of monarchy, but that her weak-willed husband, in bowing to her wishes, is rejecting Greek values and resorting to the dangerous luxury which was thought to rot the core of barbarian, especially Persian, society. Agamemnon arrives on a chariot (see 906), which may have been one of the Aeschylean 'danger signals', and significant language implies that he has somehow become 'softened' during his period abroad.[14] From the moment Clytaemnestra enters attended by maids

[12] Zeitlin 1978, p. 149.
[13] Fraenkel 1950, ii, p. 388. He, however, defends Agamemnon against the charge of subsequently falling into barbarism.
[14] See Tyrrell 1984, p. 63.

carrying the purple cloth, it is apparent that the woman has assumed the 'male' role by taking the upper hand,[15] and this perversion of the 'natural' order can find its symbols and associations only in the other, un-Greek world. A passage of the queen's famous speech of flattery is in its hyperbolic adulation so unlike the normal Hellenic mode of panegyric discourse as to have prompted its wholesale excision by Dindorf (895–902):[16] she hails her husband as the dog which guards the fold, the mainstay of the ship, the pillar of the roof, only son to a father, land to men lost at sea, dawn after a storm, and a stream to a thirsty traveller. In the speech she delivers as he enters the palace, she adds that he is like the warmth which comes in winter-time, or the coolness of the home in summer (968–72). It was Wilamowitz who first observed that several of these specific comparisons find astonishingly close parallels in an Egyptian hymn of the Middle Kingdom to Khakaure Sesostris III discovered on a hieratic papyrus,[17] but Kranz *may* have overstated the case in assuming that Aeschylus was acquainted with specific Egyptian literature.[18] The important point is that he had a clear idea of the kind of anaphoric encomia rendered to barbarian monarchs by their subjects, and that his audience would have responded to the hubristic and un-Greek tone of Clytaemnestra's language,[19] especially if the first speech were accompanied by her proskynesis, the un-mistakably barbarian gesture of obeisance. The direction in which her conduct has pointed is certainly made explicit by Agamemnon's rebuke as he tries to resist his own impulse towards decadence: 'do not pamper me like a woman nor grovel before me like some barbarian with wide-mouthed acclaim, and do not bring down envy in my path by strewing it with fabrics' (918–22). Femaleness, barbarism, luxury, and hubris are thus ineluctably drawn into the same semantic complex, as interconnected aspects of all that Greek manhood should shun.

Has Clytaemnestra really prostrated herself during her speech of flattery or during Agamemnon's response? Nowhere else in extant tragedy is it suggested that a *Greek* resorts to prostration before a mere

[15] On Clytaemnestra as androgyne see Tyrrell 1984, pp. 93–112.

[16] Dindorf 1870, p. xcii.

[17] von Wilamowitz-Moellendorff 1927, pp. 287–8. The hymn appears in English translation in Lichtheim 1973–80, i, pp. 199–200.

[18] Kranz 1933, p. 102.

[19] And perhaps to its funereal overtones: see the discussion of this scene in Seaford 1984b. Compare the Danaids' heavily anaphoric encomium, discussed above, p. 193.

mortal (see chapter 2, n. 188); someone in a lost play (possibly not a tragedy) indignantly asked, 'am I to prostrate myself before *you*, a barbarian?' (fr. adesp. 118a). This is why it has been doubted that Clytaemnestra can have performed proskynesis,[20] and suggested that it was her maids who performed the gesture.[21] It is possible that Agamemnon's words are only a warning, or a rhetorical exaggeration of the extent of the queen's fawning behaviour. But her actual prostration would underline incomparably the shocking subversion of the state of Argos and the decadence of its rulers, the Greek queen tempting her husband to hubris, greeting him like a Persian menial grovelling before the king of kings, in a powerful visual signifier of despotism. The barbarian gesture is backed up by other ambiguous actions and language. The strewing of fabrics on the floor (as opposed to hanging them on the wall) remained in the fifth century a sign of oriental extravagance (see Xen. *Cyr.* 8. 8. 16); the carpet was not generally available until Alexander's day.[22] The purple colour of the material, though suggestive of civic ritual and of blood, also connotes eastern opulence;[23] in *Orestes* the purple cloth Helen is weaving for Clytaemnestra's tomb comes from the Phrygian spoils (1434–6). The image of the victorious leader trampling his enemies underfoot may have been familiar from oriental art and literature; a hymn to the Assyrian king Assurnasirpal calls him 'the mighty hero, who has trampled on the neck of his foes, who has trodden down all enemies'.[24] Perhaps Aeschylus is consciously alluding to this arrogant posture in making the queen describe her husband's *foot* as the 'plunderer of Ilium' (907) just before she instructs her attendants to strew his path with the purple cloth.[25]

The triumph of Clytaemnestra, the marking of the temporary

---

[20] Fraenkel 1950, ii, pp. 416–17.

[21] Thomson 1966, ii, p. 73.

[22] See Schroff 1932; Fraenkel 1950, ii, pp. 413, 417. On the significance of the carpet scene see also Dover 1977,

[23] See Goheen 1955, pp. 115–26.

[24] Luckenbill 1926, p. 169. See also the anaphoric Egyptian hymn in honour of Thutmose III translated in Lichtheim 1973–80, ii, pp. 36–7: 'I came to let you tread on Djahi's chiefs, I spread them under your feet throughout their lands . . . I came to let you tread on those in Asia . . .'

[25] See the remarks of Fraenkel 1950, ii, p. 412. It is also relevant to this scene that the Greeks believed that the Persian king was forbidden to touch the earth with his feet, which always had to be protected by a carpet or a footstool. See Dorothy Burr Thompson 1956, p. 288.

ascendancy in the trilogy of the female over the male, the distortion of the 'natural' order, thus find a wealth of images in the other distorted world of barbarian protocol. But concomitant on female strength is masculine weakness, a phenomenon which likewise draws its thematic references from the *Aussenwelt*. Medea, the barbarian woman, accuses her husband of *anandria* ('lack of *andreia*', *Med.* 466); courage, 'manliness', was one of the cardinal Hellenic virtues. Aegisthus is also accused of womanly weakness, for Clytaemnestra's paramour can never be her equal (*Ag.* 1625, *Cho.* 304).[26] The Greek mind could only 'conceive of two hierarchic alternatives; Rule by Men or Rule by Women'.[27] Agamemnon's downfall had been heralded by his yielding to the hubristic values embodied in his passage across the purple, but Aegisthus represents the subordinate male, the effete lover, a type who dwelt in the same realm of the Greek imagination as the dominant woman, and was with her associated with that abstract subversion of the 'natural' Greek order for which concrete parallels were drawn from the invented barbarian world, by an extraordinary interaction of ethnographic theory and the mythical abstraction of the tendency towards self-indulgence in the human psyche.

The relationship between Clytaemnestra and Aegisthus subverts both the sexual hierarchy and the political order, for in Greek eyes despotism was inextricably linked both with dominant women (Arist. *Pol.* 5. 1313b 32–5; 6. 1319b 27–9) and with uncontrolled or illicit sexual desires: 'the *despotēs* is prey to desire (*erōs*), both sexual desire and desire for power, illegitimate love and love of power'.[28] In Herodotus the transgressive desire denoted by the term *erōs* is attributed only to tyrants and kings:[29] Pausanias, the 'barbaric Greek' *par excellence*, had the desire (*erōs*) to become '*turannos* of all Greece' (Hdt. 5. 32). A Euripidean character defined the connection (fr. 850); 'tyranny is besieged from all sides by terrible desires' (*deinois erōsin*). Choral passages in *Agamemnon* suggest that the aim of the adulterous queen and her lover is the establishment of a formal tyranny (1354–5, 1364–5),[30] and in *Choephoroe* they have achieved their goal. The poet

[26] For the femininity of Aegisthus in Aeschylus and Sophocles see Vernant 1983, pp. 134–8.

[27] Zeitlin 1978, p. 153.

[28] Hartog 1988, p. 330.

[29] See Bernadete 1969, pp. 137–8 and n. 9.

[30] See Grossmann 1970, pp. 218–26. Aegisthus is given a bodyguard, a mark of the tyrant (see above ch. 3. 8), in the *Oresteia* and both *Electra* plays: see Knox 1957, p. 214 n. 20. For a

uses numerous themes from the 'vocabulary of barbarism' to stress the despotic and unconstitutional nature of their rule. Argos is run by a pair of murderous tyrants (*tēn diplēn turannida/patroktonous te*, 973–4) who luxuriate in and waste the material goods Agamemnon had *worked* to accumulate (*hoi d' huperkopōs/en toisi sois ponoisi chliousin mega*, 136–7; see also 942–3). But Agamemnon had razed Troy as Xerxes had destroyed the temples of the acropolis, and had arrived, like Xerxes, in a chariot; now he is persuaded to walk the purple just as Priam would have done (*Ag.* 935–6), the barbarian king of a city whose blood was 'tyrannical' (828). The behaviour of all these three Greek principals thus associates them with the barbarian world by the deployment of the semantic complex surrounding either the sexual transgressor or the tyrant, the Aeschylean 'danger signals' which prepare the audience for imminent catastrophe.[31]

Euripides and Sophocles both followed Aeschylus in their use of such significant vocabulary and themes when portraying decadent Greeks. The Theban Eteocles of *OC* is accused by his brother of being a tyrant, and luxuriating (*habrunetai*) in his palace (1338–9); the first words of the despotic Hermione in *Andromache* describe the delicate golden headdress (*kosmon . . . chruseas chlidēs*) and embroidered clothes she has brought with her from Sparta (147–8). In *Troades* Hecuba taunts the Spartan Helen by saying that Menelaus' palace could not provide the means by which she could indulge her indecent taste for luxury (*tais sais enkathubrizein truphais*, 997). Clytaemnestra's decline into violence and decadence in Euripides' *Electra* is materialized in the chariot in which she arrives to visit her daughter, and in the retinue of Phrygian slave women of whom she is so proud (998–1003). In *Orestes* Helen has brought back with her from Troy exquisite riches and a troop of Phrygian eunuchs in whose mutilation the idea of eastern effeminacy is grimly reified: the connection in the Greek imagination of luxurious and transgressive women with feminized men is demonstrated by Hellanicus' allegation that it was Atossa herself who had introduced eunuchs to the Persian court (4 *FgrH* F 178a, b). Helen's Greek husband Menelaus, the slave of Eros, has been seduced like his historical counterpart Pausanias into oriental softness. He has become

fuller discussion of his characterization as an aspiring tyrant in *Agamemnon*, see Podlecki 1986, pp. 94–5.

[31] On the means by which Aeschylus implies that Agamemnon has not been an ideal monarch, see also Podlecki 1986, pp. 87–94.

'barbarized', approaches 'in great *habrosunē*',[32] and wears his hair in golden curls down to his shoulders like the epicene Lydian Dionysus of *Bacchae* (*Or*. 485, 349, 1532; see *Bacch*. 235).[33]

The language the poets had invented for portraying their barbarians therefore greatly enriched their portrayal of mythical *Greek* wrong-doers. But this, it must be stressed, does not mean that every king and every reference to wealth or gold automatically represents one of the danger signals drawn from the symbolic complex constructed around *barbarian* monarchy.[34] Oedipus is a *turannos* but he is no 'barbaric Greek', and if every single description in tragedy of a palace as rich or golden was suggestive of barbarian excess there would be none left unimpugned. Terms such as *turannos* are in the fifth century semantically unstable,[35] that is, their connotations are unusually ambiguous and only ascertainable from the context, for thematic associations work cumulatively and in conjunction with one another. The poets chose to omit or use suggestive words and symbolic actions according to their presentation of the worth or reprehensibility of a particular character. The words *turannos*, *ploutos*, *chrusos*, and *basileus* can be almost benign, as can language suggestive of softness or luxury, at least in reference to women. But in conjunction with, for example, cruelty or Phrygian slaves their ambiguity is resolved into something more sinister. The presence of any one item in the poets' 'vocabulary of barbarism' is by no means always significant: cumulatively, however, the implications become unmistakable.

---

[32] M. L. West 1987, p. 207, wants to excise *Or*. 349–51, where the chorus remark on Menelaus' entrance: 'from his great elegance (*habrosunē*) it is plain to see that he is of the Tantalids' blood'. One of his reasons is that the sentence is 'silly (Menelaus' elegance, whether of gait or apparel, cannot be evidence of his descent)'. But gait *was* construed morally by the Greeks, and surely the other passages in the play where Menelaus' orientalization is stressed must protect this one: on the possible significance of emphasizing his Tantalid genealogy, see above, ch. 4. 3.

[33] It may be relevant that this effeminate barbarized Greek was played by the same actor who took the parts of Electra (a woman) and the Phrygian (a eunuch), both of which required virtuoso singing at a high pitch. See M. L. West 1987, p. 38.

[34] Alföldi 1955 argued that all tyrants in tragedy, even Greek ones like Oedipus, wore oriental clothes, and that all references to hubris, luxury, etc. immediately brought to mind 'barbarian' excess. See Bacon's refutation of this unsophisticated view (1961, pp. 29–30 n. 13).

[35] See above, ch. 3. 8.

2 NOBLE BARBARIANS

As the argument has progressed it has occasionally been observed that a poet subverts the polarity of Greek and barbarian by other means. Many of the crimes which in the fifth century had come to be associated with the barbarians—incest, intra-familial murder, human sacrifice—were the very stuff of Greek myth, and a rich source of tragic irony was provided by the tension between the 'past' and the 'elsewhere', between the deviant acts of the ancient heroes in the anarchic time before the polis, and the supposed mores of the contemporary barbarians. In *IT*, for example, Euripides uses imagery to link Agamemnon's sacrifice of his daughter with the human sacrifices practised by the Taurians, his choice of language quietly undercutting the superficially jingoistic tenor of the play, implicitly deconstructing the orthodox polarization of Hellene and barbarian. A thorough treatment of this phenomenon would require a longer study. But one corollary of the 'barbaric Greek' which must briefly be assessed is that of the 'noble barbarian'. Several characters of barbarian ethnicity in extant tragedy are invested with 'Hellenic' virtues such as courage and self-control, in which they equal or surpass their Greek counterparts. The integrity of the Trojan Cassandra in *Agamemnon* stands in stark contrast to the corruption of the Argive characters; Polyxena in *Hecuba*, the heroine of *Andromache*, and the long-suffering captives of *Troades* all cast the Greek characters with whom they interact into an unflattering light. Moreover, in several passages of Euripides the superiority of the Hellenic character is *explicitly* called into question. No study of the barbarian in this genre can lay claim to completeness without at least an attempt to define the reasons behind the poets' occasional inversion of the moral hierarchy.

In the cases of barbarian 'seers' such as Cassandra, Theonoe, and probably Aeschylus' Thracian Phineus (the blinded prophet who became the *victim* of barbarians, albeit supernatural ones, the ravenous Harpies),[36] their moral integrity can be explained by the Greeks'

---

[36] Deichgräber 1974, p. 16, thinks that Phineus wore the standard theatrical 'blind mask' of the prophet, as Teiresias did (Pollux 4. 141). At least two of the fragments of Aeschylus' *Phineus* refer to the harpies (frr. 258, 259a), and the priestess' speech describing the Erinyes which opens *Eumenides* exemplifies the vivid language the poet could use in the delineation of such monstrous beings. Indeed, he makes the priestess draw an explicit comparison

schizophrenic view of barbarian spirituality, discussed in chapter 3. 7.[37] This book has argued that the tragedians were surprisingly occupied with the ethnicity of their mythical characters, and has suggested some reasons why. Their characters' relationship with the gods, however, was not just one of a number of pervasive issues, but the fundamental question of the genre. The type of the priest or prophet best exemplified by Teiresias is therefore quite exceptional, for it is his or her inmost nature, as an intimate of the gods, to be a conspicuous example of 'Hellenic' virtue. Amphiaraus, the seer in *Septem*, is 'self-restrained, righteous, virtuous, and pious' (610);[38] Proteus, the Egyptian prophet, was 'the most *sōphrōn*' man in the world (*Hel*. 47). When the visionaries are, like Proteus, barbarians, their 'ancient wisdom', their knowledge of the deeper workings of the universe, and their mantic role simultaneously transcend and are underlined by their foreign provenance. But this still leaves all the other noble barbarians unexplained.

An obvious reason why some barbarians escape denunciation is simple dramatic expediency. An aim of tragedy was to inspire pity (Arist. *Poet*. 1452a 3): certain kinds of *pathos* must produce pity (for example, the execution of Cassandra or the sacrifice of Polyxena), and the emotional response of an audience is heightened in proportion with the moral worth of the victim. The sight of a *bad* person falling from prosperity to misery can arouse neither pity nor fear (ibid. 1453a 1–7). But this does not explain why the Greek characters in *Hecuba*, *Andromache*, and *Troades* appear to have been consciously portrayed as inferior to some of their barbarian victims; in a reversal of behavioural roles, it is implied that the Greeks are susceptible to 'barbarian' excess, cruelty, or despotism. Most of the noble barbarians of tragedy are Trojan: in them the heroic characterization inherited by the tragic poets from the homogeneous milieu of epic is not automatically replaced by the new fifth-century dramatic barbarian. A passing expression of Hecuba in *Troades* testifies to this tendency to exempt them from the classification 'barbarian'; she says that she bore the finest of sons 'such as no Trojan *nor Greek nor barbarian* woman could ever claim to have borne' (477–8). But Euripides frequently designates

between the Erinyes and a picture she has seen of the harpies 'taking Phineus' meal' (50–1), perhaps recalling his own *Phineus* of fourteen years previously.

[37] On Cassandra as a *mantis kora* in tragedy, see Mason 1959, pp. 84–93. She will have worn the ritual clothes of the prophetess (Pickard-Cambridge 1968, pp. 202–3).

[38] See Kunsemüller 1935, p. 37.

the Trojans as *barbaroi*. Hecuba's formulation underlines the ambiguity of the status of the Trojan royal family, inherited from archaic poetry. Unlike other foreigners, their barbarism is stressed or ignored simply according to the poet's purpose at the time: Sophocles' Priam, Euripides' Paris, or the outspoken Hector of *Rhesus* may indeed become barbarous Phrygians, but the poets apparently did not care to alienate sympathy from the widows of Troy, whose sufferings were recounted in the cyclic epics and were eternally popular themes in the visual arts. Their gender was a contributory factor; the male virtues in myth are physical and mental prowess, and the role of male non-Greeks is usually to be defeated. But women's worth was thought to lie in their commitment to home and family, a virtue which, far from being diminished when they are cast as bereaved wives and mothers, is positively enhanced. Something of the *Iliad*'s objective view of the equality of misery undergone by both sides in the Trojan war breaks through and negates the Hellene-barbarian antithesis in several Euripidean passages, for example the lovely ode in *Hecuba* where the Trojan captives not only lament their own plight, but also imagine Spartan women beside the Eurotas, lost in grief for husbands or sons (629–49, 650–6).

Another reason why a tragedian might seek to play down his critique of the barbarian world might be that his characters' invective was directed against another Greek state; in Euripides' *Andromache* the fervour of the attack on the Spartans, expressed in the pejorative portrayal of Menelaus and Hermione, forces the spectator into comparing these Greeks with the courageous Andromache, and pitying her, as the chorus does, 'even though she is Asiatic' (119–21). The Spartans' vituperative emphasis on her barbarian provenance (e.g. 261, 649–52) is ironically deflated in contrast with her manifest virtue and their own malevolence. It is significant that the plays where Greeks are shown in a poor light are always concerned not with Athenians but with their enemies in the Peloponnesian war, especially the family of the Atridae (increasingly associated not with Argos but with Sparta), or Thebans.[39] Even Sophocles' *Ajax* already ironically juxtaposes the Phrygian Tecmessa and half-caste Teucer, whose goal is to observe the

---

[39] Zeitlin 1986 argues that in tragedy Thebes 'provides the negative model to Athens' manifest image of itself with regard to its notions of the proper management of city, society, and self' (p. 102), a function analogous to that which this book has argued was performed by the barbarian world.

'unwritten law' that the dead must be buried, with the cynical Achaean Atridae; a passage in one of Teucer's speeches to Menelaus adumbrates later Athenian protests at the expansionist policies of Sparta (1097–108).

In *Andromache* Hermione is repeatedly called the 'Spartan' or 'Laconian' woman (e.g. 29, 194, 889), and the Asiatic heroine herself delivers a denunciation of the Spartan character which lies parallel to, and undercuts, the viciousness of Hermione's anti-barbarian rhetoric (see chapter 4. 4):

O Spartans, hated by the entire world more than any other people, you treacherous intriguers, masters of falsehood, weavers of wicked schemes! With your twisted and diseased minds, your circuitous thoughts, how unjustly you enjoy your prosperity in Hellas! What crimes are you *not* capable of? Is not murder your habit, sordid profit your goal? Is it not clear to everyone that you say one thing and think another? My curses on you! (445–53).

Peleus later returns to the same theme, criticizing the freedom enjoyed by the young women of Sparta who by custom practised athletics alongside the men (595–600).[40] In this play the Spartans have gravitated to the conceptual space elsewhere occupied by non-Greeks, for the vices imputed to them—treachery, cunning, duplicity, lust for power, lawlessness, self-aggrandizement, and female freedom—are familiar themes from rhetoric against the barbarians. Similar stress is laid on the treachery of the Spartans in *Troades* (see below): it is not to Hellas in general but to 'the Dorian land' that the Trojan women are enslaved (234). When the Peloponnesian or Theban characters turn into 'enemies', the logic of the tragic narrative dictates that the barbarians almost imperceptibly turn into 'friends', and assume the role of surrogate Athenians; *Andromache* and *Troades* fight the Peloponnesian war on a mediated poetic plane.[41] The conceptualization of the war between Athens and Sparta was heavily dependent on the archetypal narratives of the Athenian struggle with Persia. If tragic representation of the Trojan war was to turn the Spartans into 'barbarians' and assimilate them to the archetype of the arrogant Persians, then the 'Athenians' of this mythical world, however paradoxically, must be the Trojan victims of Spartan aggression. Similar patterns affect Herodo-

[40] On the freedom of the women of Sparta and the Athenians' fascination with it see Cartledge 1981; Powell 1988, pp. 243–6.

[41] See above, ch. 4, n. 14.

tus' portrayal of the Persians and Scythians. Normally, of course, the Persians are luxurious and tyrannical. When fighting the even more barbarous Scythians, however, they begin to behave like good Greek hoplites; the internal structure of the historian's narrative does not seem to be able to cope with more than a binary opposition. Even the Scythians, in their turn, can behave like surrogate 'Greeks' when they come into conflict with the most supremely 'other' of Herodotus' tribes, the Amazons.[42] For even barbarian men are not quite so strange as barbarian women.

The historical reasons behind Euripidean characters' attacks on Laconian mores or psychology are not difficult to define. In *Andromache* and *Troades*, however, the poet seems to have gone out of his way to make his audience confront the unsatisfactory basis of the assumption that the barbarian character was generically inferior, to an extent which cannot be fully explained even by the redirection of his characters' vitriol from the barbarian world to Sparta. It might be hoped that further illumination could be gained by examining the tragedians' reflection of some of the more radical views circulating in the contemporary Athenian intellectual milieu.[43] Illustration of the arguments used by the tragic poets in their exploration of the Hellene-barbarian antithesis has been adduced in this and the previous chapter from the fragmentary speeches of both Gorgias and Thrasymachus, and from many speeches and philosophical dialogues of the fourth century almost certainly reflecting arguments constructed by the sophists contemporary with the tragedians: most instances seem to have presupposed the superiority of Greeks over barbarians. The more 'liberal' views expressed by Socrates in Plato's *Theaetetus*, and by the Xenophontic Hippias, are exceptional (see above, chapter 4. 3 and 4). But a few Euripidean passages where the antithesis of Hellene and barbarian is explicitly questioned have indeed been thought to reflect the views of the more radical sophists of the second half of the fifth century.

Hippias was perhaps the foremost 'cosmopolitan' of the enlightenment. He was well-travelled, claimed to have read literature in foreign languages (86 B 6 *DK*), and wrote a treatise entitled *The Nomenclature of Peoples* which may suggest an interest in barbarian genealogies

---

[42] See Hartog 1988, pp. 258–9.
[43] On the nature and extent of the relationship between sophistic thought and tragic poetry see e.g. Bignone 1938, pp. 140–52; Pfeiffer 1976; J. H. Finley 1967, ch. 11.

(86 B 2 *DK*). In Plato's *Protagoras* (337c–d) his words are probably to be interpreted as advocating the removal of the *nomos* of barriers between different cities. He is known to have written tragedies himself (86 A 12 *DK*), which supports the suggestion that he might have influenced the major tragedians. In Xenophon's *Memorabilia* Hippias' view that some laws are universal, and therefore divinely ordained for all mankind, points to a less Hellenocentric view of the unwritten laws than that taken by others. On the other hand, his advocacy of relativism, and defence of incest in foreign countries on the ground that some social practices are culturally determined, and therefore variable, may have informed the *agōn* of Euripides' *Aeolus*.

Hippias' cosmopolitanism has been linked with a theme recurring in the fragments of Euripides, the anonymous tragic fragments, and in the comic poets, namely that all the world is home for a good man.[44] A typical example is Euripides fr. 1047: 'Every sky is open to the eagle's flight, every land is his fatherland to a noble man.' But how far-reaching are such statements? In asserting that a man's homeland is wherever he happens to find himself, can the poets be considered to be truly adumbrating the cosmopolitanism of the Cynics or Stoics, or bridging the gap *'vom nationalen Hellenentum zum weltbürgerlichen Hellenismus'*?[45] The chauvinist world-view of tragedy assumes that the boundaries of decency are commensurate with the borders of Hellas, and the opinion of Hellas the only opinion that matters. Orestes claims to have helped 'all Hellas' by killing his mother; Menelaus is known 'by all the Hellenes' to love his wife (*Or*. 565, 669). Furthermore, another variation on Hippias' theme was expressed by Heracles in a lost play, in answer to a question about his place of origin (fr. adesp. 392): 'I am Argive *or* Theban, for I do not claim to belong to any single place. Every Greek city is my fatherland.' Now although Heracles did traditionally have two birthplaces, the second part of this fragment must raise the suspicion that the unspoken assumption in the other fifth-century expressions of similar sentiments was that by 'every land' was really meant 'every *Greek* land'. It can be proven neither that such

[44] Instances of the theme are collected by Diggle 1970, pp. 130–1. It already occurs in a fragment attributed to Democritus (*andri sophōi pasa gē batē. psuchēs gar agathēs patris ho xumpas kosmos*, 68 B 247 *DK*). But see Diels' warning, quoted by Kranz *ad loc.*: 'Der Kosmopolitismus ist bereits bei Euripides ausgesprochen, aber die Form bei Dem. ist banal. Bedenken bleiben.'

[45] Nestle 1901, p. 367.

ideas truly called into question the orthodox assumption that barbarians were inferior to Greeks, nor that Hippias was the source of such sentiments.[46] Our information about this sophist's views on the non-Greek world stops tantalizingly short of any specific statement, and there is no reason to suppose, as some scholars have,[47] that Euripides was indebted to him in his 'Trojan plays' produced in 415 BC, *Alexander*, *Palamedes*, and *Troades*, which come closer than any other extant fifth-century Athenian source to subverting the antithesis on a moral level of Greek and barbarian.

Scodel argued that alongside the topics of slavery, nobility, and intelligence, the opposition of Hellene and barbarian was one of the thematic continuities which lent to the plays (not a trilogy in the strict sense) 'some trilogic unity'.[48] In the extant *Troades* the Greek Helen is seen as the bane of both sides in the war and the Trojans are therefore portrayed as the innocent victims of Greek immorality; moreover, 'there is a positive transfer of "barbarian" values to the Greeks'.[49] It is in Hecuba's speech during her *agōn* with Helen that the Trojans are most conspicuously orientalized (969–1032), and this, argues Scodel, is because Hecuba is caricaturing the Greek view of the barbarian world, a view implicitly controverted by the dignity and nobility of the Trojans in comparison with the baseness of their conquerors: 'the Greeks of this play do more than bring home a Helen who epitomizes Persian decadence. They are repeatedly characterized as stupid, cruel, impious, without self-control, cowardly, and servile. In fact, they are almost caricatures of barbarians.'[50] In contrast, the Phrygian Hector, as defender of his homeland from Spartan aggression, was pre-eminent in the 'Hellenic' virtues of intelligence and courage (674). The great climax to which this line of thought leads is the murder of the infant Astyanax, an act denounced by Andromache in a famous paradoxical apostrophe where the Greeks are at last explicitly credited with behaving like barbarians: 'O Greeks who have invented barbaric crimes' (*ō barbar' exeurontes Hellēnes kaka*, 764).

An important reason behind Euripides' radical inversion of the

---

[46] It would be pleasant to be able to believe Plutarch's anecdote in which *Socrates* claims to be a citizen neither of Athens nor of Hellas, but of the whole world (*de Exilio* 600f).

[47] Nestle 1901, p. 365; see also Untersteiner 1954, p. 252.

[48] Scodel 1980, pp. 105, 112–14.

[49] Ibid., p. 113.

[50] Ibid., p. 114.

moral hierarchy in this play, produced in the middle of the Peloponnesian war, is clearly his reinterpretation of the myth of Troy to the detriment of the 'Dorians', for during this bitter period of the conflict the Athenian stage could characterize the Trojans as victims of outrageous Spartan violence and sacrilege. But do his Andromache's iconoclastic words point to the theories of any recognizable thinkers? The first play of the trilogy, *Alexander*, included a debate in which the hero argued that he must be allowed to compete in an athletics contest, despite his upbringing as a slave. Fragment 52 asserts both that men of high and low birth are physically identical, and that intelligence is bestowed by the gods rather than by wealth. Scholars long drew a connection between this fragment and a passage of Antiphon's *On Truth*.[51] Antiphon the sophist is generally accepted to have been an Athenian, or working in Athens, in the second half of the fifth century, though the exact date of the treatise is not known;[52] other Antiphontic passages have also been connected with arguments raised in tragedy.[53] The possibility that Euripides' 'Trojan plays' owed something to *On Truth* was thought to be further supported by the presence in another fragment from *Alexander* (56. 2) of the rare word *aglōttia*, which also occurs in Antiphon's fragments (87 B 97 *DK*).[54]

The papyrus text from which *On Truth* was read is very mutilated, but recently a new papyrus, joining physically with the other, has greatly improved understanding of the important passage (87 B 44 fr. B col. ii *DK*) which was thought to have influenced Euripides' 'Trojan plays'.[55] Barnes has published a translation of a provisional version of the text of this passage, produced by the two papyri taken together, which reads as follows (for the sake of clarity I have substituted 'barbarians' when Barnes translates *barbaroi* as 'foreigners'):[56]

The laws of our neighbours we know and revere: the laws of those who live afar we neither know nor revere. Thus in this we have been made barbarians

---

[51] See e.g. Luria 1924 and 1929; Scodel 1980, p. 89.

[52] Agreement still has not been reached as to whether this sophist is to be identified with Antiphon the orator. *On Truth* is usually assigned to the decade 440–30 BC (J. H. Finley 1967, pp. 90–103).

[53] See Grenfell and Hunt 1915, pp. 94–5; Moulton 1972, pp. 350–7.

[54] See Luria 1924; Moulton 1972, pp. 351–2 n. 49.

[55] The new papyrus was first edited by Funghi 1984. For a discussion of its implications see Caizzi 1986.

[56] *Pap. Oxy.* 1364 fr. 2. ii + *Pap. Oxy.* 3647 frr. i–iii; Barnes 1987b, p. 5.

with regard to one another [*pros allēlous bebarbarōmetha*]. For *by nature* we are all in all respects similarly endowed to be barbarian or Greek. One may consider those natural facts which are necessary in all men and provided for all in virtue of the same faculties—and in these very matters none of us is separated off as a barbarian or as a Greek. For we all breathe into the air by way of our mouths and noses, we laugh when we are happy in our minds and we cry when we are in pain, we receive sounds by our hearing and we see with our eyes by light, we work with our hands and we walk on our feet...

Before the discovery of the new papyrus (*Pap. Oxy.* 3647), the opening words were traditionally supplemented to give the argument that in honouring *men of a noble house* above others we behave like barbarians, because all men, Greek or barbarian, are by nature exactly the same.[57] It was believed that Antiphon was an iconoclast who was questioning the validity of the distinctions both between high and low birth, and between Greek and barbarian. Although critics were divided as to which of these two distinctions was given priority in the lost argument preceding the fragment, they were unanimous that this passage of the treatise was extraordinarily radical.[58] But a salutary warning against basing interpretations of ancient texts on supplements has been presented by the contents of the new papyrus, for it renders impossible the reference to 'men of a noble house', and instead makes the reading 'the laws of those who live afar', contrasted with the laws 'of our neighbours', look virtually unavoidable.[59] This disproves once and for all the theory that Antiphon was attacking the distinction between high and low birth. Decades of publications on his egalitarianism in terms of social class therefore have to be discarded.[60] So does the view which brought this egalitarianism into association with the *agōn* of Euripides' *Alexander*. It can no longer even be hypothesized that Antiphon, any more than any other fifth-century intellectual, called into question the institution of slavery.[61] The first person to have

[57] [τούς ἐκ καλῶν πατέ]ρων ἐπ[αιδοῦ]μεθά τε κ[αὶ σεβόμεθα,] τούς δὲ [ἐκ μὴ κα]λοῦ οἴκ[ου ὄντας] οὔτε ἐπ[αιδούμε]θα οὔτε σεβόμ[εθα. The supplements were by Wilamowitz and Hunt.

[58] See, amongst many others, Havelock 1957, pp. 255–8; J. H. Finley 1967, p. 101; Guthrie 1971, p. 153; Kerferd 1981, pp. 157–9.

[59] Reading Funghi's τούς δὲ [τῶν τη]λοῦ οἰκ[ούν]των.

[60] See the remarks of Caizzi 1986, pp. 63–6; Barnes 1987b, p. 4.

[61] Nestle insisted that as a proponent of the claims of *phusis* rather than *nomos* Antiphon must have extended his argument to the questioning of slavery (1942, p. 377).

adopted this position may have been Alcidamas, Gorgias' pupil, well into the fourth century.[62]

The discovery of the new papyrus shows that in this section Antiphon was not concerned with the 'horizontal' stratifications of social class, but exclusively with the *physical* homogeneity of the human race. He was concerned to prove that it is not nature but *nomos* which divides Greeks from barbarians. Antiphon seems to be using a demonstration of the biological homogeneity of humankind to support his case that the laws of nature are prior to, and more important than, the laws of each discrete human community. Perhaps this pro-*phusis* notion formed part of a polemic against some democratically-minded sophists' belief in the beneficial effects of *nomos*; Protagoras, for example, argued that *nomos* was the *sine qua non* of civilized life for man.[63] Antiphon's demonstration that all men are by nature exactly alike, because we all breathe through our mouths and noses, laugh and cry, and work with our hands . . ., echoes the 'biological' approach to mankind, with its stress on the human race as a whole, inherent in Anaximander's map, and Anaxagoras' idea that while all animals have *nous*, only men have hands (59 A 102 *DK*).[64]

In *Troades*, however, Euripides is not addressing himself to a biological distinction, but to the idea that Greek *ethics* were superior to those of barbarians. Andromache's words at 764 assume that Greeks can behave like barbarians, and the demeanour of the Trojans throughout the play could be interpreted as an example of Trojans behaving like ideal Greeks.[65] It is known that Antiphon argued that it was different *nomoi* rather than different physiology which made different communities look upon others as barbarians (in respecting only the laws of our neighbours and not the laws of those who live far away 'we have been made barbarians with regard to one another'). But

[62] Σ Arist. *Rhet*. 1. 1373b; see also the sentiment expressed in a fragment of Philemon, a writer of New Comedy (fr. 95 Kock): 'Even if someone is a slave, he is made of the same flesh. For nobody was ever born a slave by nature.'

[63] See above ch. 4. 5. For the possibility that *On Truth* was written in response to Protagoras, see Funghi 1984, p. 4.

[64] See Baldry 1965, pp. 24–5, 44–5. Funghi 1984, p. 4, thinks that Antiphon's argument lies broadly in the same tradition as the cosmological and anthropological speculations of Anaxagoras and Democritus.

[65] This view can be pushed too far, however; the Trojan kingdom, although victimized, is certainly envisaged in this play as having been guilty of pride and excess. See above ch. 3. 8 with n. 185.

there is no evidence that he expressed an opinion on the relative virtues of Greek and barbarian *nomoi*, let alone suggested that Greeks could behave like barbarians or that barbarians could behave like Greeks. It is therefore as difficult to extrapolate an explicit questioning of the ethical distinction Greeks made between themselves and other peoples from the fragments of Antiphon's treatise as from the dim indications of Hippias' cosmopolitanism.

The question of Euripides' reasons for his reversal in some plays of the moral roles ascribed to his Greeks and barbarians must therefore be left open. No specific contemporary thinker can be proven to have been as radical as his Andromache, though it is difficult to believe that he was alone among his brilliantly argumentative contemporaries in exposing the weaknesses inherent in this particular cornerstone of orthodox opinion. But equally there can be no proof that he personally subscribed to any one view, for his plays are full of expressions of mutually exclusive and contradictory beliefs, and much critical attention has been wasted in attempting to reconcile the different arguments his characters adopt in support or refutation of different positions, and the examination in his plays of the relation between Hellene and barbarian is no exception. One scholar, for example, can speak confidently of Euripides' 'own belief in the superiority of Greek institutions',[66] while another concludes, on the other hand, that 'far from believing in a natural state of slavery in barbarians, Euripides takes pains to show that what matters are the qualities of a person and not one's social status'.[67] Passages can be adduced, of course, to refute either critic's verdict. Especially fruitless is the approach which tries to justify Euripides' contradictory statements about the barbarians by tracing his ideological development from liberalism early in his career to chauvinism in his plays from about 415 onwards. Apart from anything else it is simply not true that the plays until *Troades* were all 'sympathetic' to the barbarians, while the later ones were unanimously hostile, as one scholar argues;[68] Euripides' *Telephus* of 438 and *Erechtheus* of the 420s both seem to have taken a 'patriotic' line.

It seems always to need repeating that this tragedian cannot be made sense of biographically or chronologically but only as a poet of the

---

[66] Haarhoff 1948, p. 55.

[67] Synodinou 1977, p. 58.

[68] Fornara 1971, pp. 31–2. He thinks that Euripides suddenly conceived a dislike for barbarians after becoming acquainted with Herodotus' *Histories*!

sophistic enlightenment. In his dramas he expertly formulated in the mouths of his mythical characters arguments adopted by both sides on nearly every issue of contemporary interest. They defend women and criticize them, eulogize aristocracy and question its institution, praise the gods and query their existence. It is in this context, the current rage for 'two arguments', that the conflicting views on the barbarians expounded on the one hand in, say, *Telephus* and *Orestes*, and on the other in *Andromache* and *Troades*, should be appraised. A favourite claim of some of the sophists was that they could produce a case to defend any imaginable position, however untenable if judged by traditional or absolute criteria, and Euripides' own views on the barbarian character cannot therefore be ascertained any more than what he personally thought about women, aristocrats, or Dionysiac religion. He can argue a case from the barbarian's point of view if the dramatic occasion so demands (just as the rhetors Polycrates and Isocrates managed to defend Busiris) as competently as from the Greek's. This sophistic skill is succinctly defined by a character in his own lost *Antiope* (fr. 189): 'if one were good at speaking one could have a competition between two arguments in every case.'

Euripides' overturning of the orthodoxy in regard to the relative worth of Greek and barbarian is the paradigm of the rule-proving exception. His inversion in a few plays of the moral statuses normally attributed to Greeks and barbarians shows not that he or his contemporaries had disowned the usual belief in Hellenic superiority over other peoples (indeed, the assertions of it in the fourth century and beyond were to increase in vehemence and acerbity), but that it was so fundamental a dogma as to produce striking rhetorical effects on being inverted.[69] Just as the gynaecocratic Lemnians and Amazons of myth, and the powerful Clytaemnestras and Medeas of tragedy, were only conspicuous because Greek society was run by men, so the noble barbarians stood out in relief because their kind was normally denigrated. The barbaric Greeks and noble barbarians of Euripides therefore *presupposed* the invented ethnocentric world of tragedy

---

[69] Even on a simple terminological level the barbarian was attractive to the sophists, for *barbaros* and its cognates were eminently suited to the word play and alliteration enjoyed by the teachers of rhetoric. See Gorgias 82 B 11. 7 *DK* (*ho men epicheirēsas barbaros barbaron epicheirēma*); Eur. *IT*. 31; *Or*. 485; Plato *Resp*. 7. 533d 1 (*tōi onti en borborōi barbarikōi tini*). Several hundred years later someone was to write on a wall at Pompeii: '"barbara" barbaribus barbabant "barbara" barbis' (Buecheler 1930, p. 167, no. 351).

which it is hoped this book has illuminated. They embody an ironic and sophistic reversal of the accepted premise that Greeks are superior to the rest of the world, a canon so often underlined by the tragedians in their dramatic celebrations of the collective Hellenic identity of the Athenian empire, performed between the expulsion of Xerxes and the end of the Peloponnesian war.

Bibliography

ALEXANDERSON, B., 1967: 'Darius in the Persians', *Eranos*, lxv. 1–11.

ALEXIOU, M., 1974: *The Ritual Lament in Greek Tradition* (Cambridge).

ALFÖLDI, A., 1955: 'Gewaltherrscher und Theaterkönig', in *Late Classical and Medieval Studies in Honor of Albert Mathias Friend, Jr.*, 15–55 (Princeton).

ALLEN, W. S., 1947: 'The name of the Black Sea in Greek', CQ xli. 86–8.

AMANDRY, P., 1960: 'Sur les "épigrammes de Marathon"', in F. Eckstein (ed.), *ΘΕΩΡΙΑ* (Festschr. W. H. Schuchhardt), 1–8 (Baden-Baden).

ANDREWES, A., 1956: *The Greek Tyrants* (London).

ANTHES, R., 1961: 'Mythology in ancient Egypt', in Kramer (ed.), 15–92.

ANTI, C., 1952: 'Il vaso di Dario e i Persiani di Frinico', *Archaeologia Classica*, iv 23–45.

APTE, M. L., 1985: *Humor and Laughter: an Anthropological Approach* (Ithaca/London).

ARENS, W., 1979: *The Man-Eating Myth: Anthropology and Anthropophagy* (Oxford/New York/Toronto/Melbourne).

—— 1986: *The Original Sin: Incest and its Meaning* (New York/Oxford).

ARMAYOR, O. K., 1978a: 'Herodotus' catalogues of the Persian empire in the light of the monuments and the Greek literary tradition', *TAPA* cviii. 1–9.

—— 1978b: 'Herodotus' Persian vocabulary', *Ancient World*, i. 147–56.

ARTHUR, M., 1972: 'The choral odes of the Bacchae of Euripides', *YCS* xxii. 145–79.

BACHOFEN, J. J., 1861: *Das Mutterrecht: eine Untersuchung über die Gynaikokratie der alten Welt nach ihrer religiösen und rechtlichen Natur* (Stuttgart).

BACKHAUS, W., 1976: 'Der Hellenen-Barbaren-Gegensatz und die hippokratische Schrift περὶ ἀέρων ὑδάτων τόπων', *Historia*, xxv. 170–85.

BACON, H. H., 1961: *Barbarians in Greek Tragedy* (New Haven).

BADIAN, E., 1981: 'The deification of Alexander the Great', in H. J. Dell (ed.), *Ancient Macedonian Studies in Honor of Charles F. Edson*, 27–71 (Thessaloniki).

BALDRY, H. C., 1965: *The Unity of Mankind in Greek Thought* (Cambridge).

BALSDON, J. P. V. D., 1979: *Romans and Aliens* (London).

BAMBERGER, J., 1974: 'The myth of matriarchy: why men rule in primitive society', in M. Z. Rosaldo and L. Lamphere (eds.), *Woman, Culture and Society*, 263–80 (Stanford).

BANTON, M., 1977: *The Idea of Race* (London).

—— 1981: 'The direction and speed of ethnic change', in Keyes 1981a (ed.), 32–52.

BARNES, J., 1982: *The Presocratic Philosophers*[2] (London/Boston/Melbourne/ Henley).

—— 1987a (transl.): *Early Greek Philosophy* (Harmondsworth).

—— 1987b: 'New light on Antiphon', *Polis*, vii. 2–5.

BARRON, J. P. AND EASTERLING, P. E., 1985: 'The cyclic epics', *The Cambridge History of Ancient Literature*, i. 106–10 (Cambridge).

BARTH, F. (ed.), 1969: *Ethnic Groups and Boundaries* (Bergen/Oslo/London).

BASCHMAKOFF, A., 1939: 'Origine tauridienne du mythe d'Iphigénie', *Bulletin de l'Association Guillaume Budé*, lxiv. 3–21.

BASLEZ, M.-F., 1981: 'Le péril barbare, une invention des Grecs?' *L'Histoire*, xxxix, September. 36–44. Reprinted in C. Mossé (ed.), *La Grèce ancienne*, 284–99 (Paris 1986).

—— 1984: *L'Étranger dans la Grèce antique* (Paris).

BASSETT, S. E., 1931: 'The place and date of the first performance of the *Persians* of Timotheus', *CP* xxvi. 153–65.

—— 1933: 'Achilles' treatment of Hector's body', *TAPA* lxiv. 41–65.

BAUER, W. (ed.), 1980: *China und die Fremden* (Munich).

BAYFIELD, M. A., 1904: review of Sidgwick 1903, *CR* xviii. 161–3.

BEAZLEY, J. D., 1955: 'Hydria-fragments in Corinth', *Hesperia*, xxiv. 305–19.

BENEDICT, R., 1942: *Race and Racism* (London).

BENGSTON, H., 1954: 'Hellenen und Barbaren: Gedanken zum Problem des griechischen Nationalbewusstseins', in K. Rüdinger (ed.), *Unser Geschichtsbild*, 25–40 (Munich). Reprinted in *Kleine Schriften*, 158–73 (Munich 1974).

BENVENISTE, E., 1966: *Titres et noms propres en iranien ancien*[7] (Paris).

BERNADETE, S., 1969: *Herodotean Enquiries* (The Hague).

BERNAND, A., 1985: *La Carte du tragique; la géographie dans la tragédie grecque* (Paris).

BEST, J. G. P., 1969: *Thracian Peltasts and their Influence on Greek Warfare* (Groningen).

BETHE, E., 1914: *Ilias* (*Homer: Dichtung und Saga*, i. 1–2) (Leipzig/Berlin).

—— 1966: *Der troische Epenkreis* (Darmstadt). Reprint of *Homer: Dichtung und Saga*[2], ii. 2 (Leipzig/Berlin 1922).

BICKERMAN, E. J., 1952: 'Origines gentium', *CP* xlvii. 65–81.

—— and Tadmor, H., 1978: 'Darius I, pseudo-Smerdis, and the Magi', *Athenaeum*, lvi. 239–61.

BIELENSTEIN, H., 1980: *The Bureaucracy of Han Times* (Cambridge/London/ New York/New Rochelle/Melbourne/Sydney).

BIGNONE, E., 1938: *Studi sul pensiero antico* (Naples).

BLAIKLOCK, E. M., 1952: *The Male Characters of Euripides* (Wellington).

BLAMIRE, A., 1970: 'Pausanias and Persia', *GRBS* xi. 295–305.

BLEGEN, C. W., 1963: *Troy and the Trojans* (London).

BLOCH, H. (ed.), 1956: *Abhandlungen zur griechischen Geschichtschreibung von Felix Jacoby* (Leiden).

BLOMFIELD, C. J. (ed.), 1818: *Aeschyli Persae*² (Cambridge).

BOARDMAN, J., 1975: *Athenian Red Figure Vases: the Archaic Period* (London).

—— 1980: *The Greeks Overseas*² (London).

—— 1982: 'Herakles, Theseus, and Amazons', in D. Kurtz and B. Sparkes (eds.), *The Eye of Greece: Studies in the Art of Athens*, 1–28 (Cambridge/London/New York).

BODDE, D., 1961: 'Myths of ancient China', in Kramer (ed.), 367–408.

—— 1986: 'The state and empire of Ch'in', in Twitchett and Loewe (eds.), 21–102.

BOEDEKER, D. D., 1974: *Aphrodite's Entry into Greek Epic* (Leiden).

BOLOGNA, C., 1978: 'Il linguaggio del silenzio: l'alterità linguistica nelle religioni del mondo classico', *Studi Storico Religiosi*, ii. 305–42 (Rome).

BOLTON, J. D. P., 1962: *Aristeas of Proconnesus* (Oxford).

BOVON, A., 1963: 'La représentation des guerres perses et la notion de barbare dans la 1re moitié du Ve siècle', *BCH* lxxxvii. 579–602.

BOWRA, C. M., 1930: *Tradition and Design in the Iliad* (Oxford).

—— 1960: 'Homeric epithets for Troy', *JHS* lxxx. 16–23.

BOYCE, M., 1982: *A History of Zoroastrianism*, ii (Leiden/Cologne).

BRACCESI, L. (ed.), 1979: *I Tragici greci e l'occidente* (*Il Mondo antico*, ix) (Bologna).

BREMMER, J. (ed.), 1987a: *Interpretations of Greek Mythology* (London/Sydney).

—— 1987b: 'Oedipus and the Greek Oedipus complex', in Bremmer 1987a (ed.), 41–59.

BRIGHAM, J. C., 1971: 'Ethnic stereotypes', *Psychological Bulletin*, lxxvi. 15–38.

BROADHEAD, H. D. (ed.), 1960: *The Persae of Aeschylus* (Cambridge).

BRONEER, O., 1944: *The Tent of Xerxes and the Greek Theater* (University of California Publications in Classical Archaeology, i. 12. 305–12). (Berkeley).

BROWN, P., 1985: 'This thing of darkness I acknowledge mine: *The Tempest* and the discourse of colonialism', in J. Dollimore and A. Sinfield (eds.), *Political Shakespeare*, 48–71 (Manchester).

BROWN, W. N., 1961: 'Mythology of India', in Kramer (ed.), 277–330.

BRUNT, P. A., 1966: 'Athenian settlements abroad in the fifth century BC', in *Ancient Society and Institutions* (Studs. V. Ehrenberg), 71–92 (Oxford).

BUCHHOLZ, E., 1883: *Das Privatleben der Griechen im heroischen Zeitalter* (*Die homerischen Realien*, ii. 2) (Leipzig).

BUCK, C. D., 1955: *The Greek Dialects* (Chicago).

BUECHELER, F. (ed.), 1930: *Carmina epigraphica*² (*Anthologia Latina*, ii. 1) (Leipzig).

BURELLI, L., 1979: 'Euripide e l'occidente', in Braccesi (ed.), 129–67.

BURKERT, W., 1966: 'Greek tragedy and sacrificial ritual', *GRBS* vii. 87–121.

—— 1979: *Structure and History in Greek Mythology and Ritual* (Berkeley/Los Angeles/London).

—— 1981: 'Seven against Thebes: an oral tradition between Babylonian magic and Greek literature', in C. Brillante, M. Cantilena, and C. O. Pavese (eds.), *I Poemi epici rapsodici non omerici e la tradizione orale*, 29–51 (Padua).

—— 1983 (Engl. transl.): *Home Necans: the Anthropology of Ancient Greek Sacrificial Ritual and Myth* (Berkeley/Los Angeles/London).

—— 1984: *Die orientalisierende Epoche in der griechischen Religion und Literatur* (Sitzungsberichte der Heidelberger Akademie der Wissenschaften, philosophisch-historische Klasse, i) (Heidelberg).

—— 1985a (Engl. transl.): *Greek Religion, Archaic and Classical* (Oxford).

—— 1985b: 'Herodot über die Namen der Götter: Polytheismus als historisches Problem', *Mus. Helv.* xlii. 121–32.

—— 1987: 'Oriental and Greek mythology: the meeting of parallels', in Bremmer 1987a (ed.), 10–40.

BURN, A. R., 1984: *Persia and the Greeks*[2], with a postscript by D. M. Lewis (London).

BURNETT, A. P., 1971: *Catastrophe Survived: Euripides' Plays of Mixed Reversal* (Oxford).

—— 1977: '*Trojan Women* and the Ganymede ode', *YCS* xxv. 291–316.

BUTTS, H. R., 1942: *The Glorification of Athens in Greek Drama* (Iowa Studies in Classical Philology, xi) (Ann Arbor).

BUXTON, R. G. A., 1982: *Persuasion in Greek Tragedy: a Study of Peitho* (Cambridge).

CAIZZI, F. D., 1986: 'Il nuovo papiro di Antifonte', in F. Adorno et al. (eds.), *Protagora, Antifonte, Posidonio, Aristotele* (Studi dell' Accademia Toscana di scienze e lettere 'La Colombaria', lxxxiii), 61–9 (Florence).

CALDER, W. M., 1969: 'The date of Euripides' *Erechtheus*', *GRBS* x. 147–56.

CALMEYER, P., 1975: 'The subject of the Achaemenid tomb reliefs', *Proceedings of the Third Annual Symposium on Archaeological Research in Iran*, 233–42 (Tehran).

CAMERON, G. G., 1948: *Persepolis Treasury Tablets* (Chicago).

CARPENTER, T. H., 1986: *Dionysian Imagery in Archaic Greek Art* (Oxford).

CARTLEDGE, P. A., 1981: 'Spartan wives', *CQ* xxxi. 84–105.

—— and Harvey, F. D. (eds.), 1985: *Crux: Essays in Greek History presented to G. E. M. de Ste. Croix* (London).

CASSON, L., 1971: *Ships and Seamanship in the Ancient World* (Princeton).

CASSON, S., 1926: *Macedonia, Thrace, and Illyria* (Oxford).

CAZZANIGA, I., 1950: *La Saga di Itis* (Milan/Varese).

CHADWICK, J., 1976: *The Mycenaean World* (Cambridge).

CHAPOUTHIER, F., 1944: 'A propos d'un éventail de l'exotisme dans Euripide', *REA* xlvi. 209–16.

CHEW, S. C., 1937: *The Crescent and the Rose: Islam and England during the Renaissance* (New York).

CHIAPELLI, A., AND BENSON, M. J. B., AND FREDI, R. L. (eds.), 1976: *First Images of America: the Impact of the New World on the Old* (Berkeley).

CLIFTON, G., 1963: 'The mood of the *Persai* of Aeschylus', *G&R* x. 111–22.

COLLARD, C. (ed.), 1975: *Euripides' Supplices* (Groningen).

COMBELLACK, F. M., 1981: 'The wish without desire', *AJP* cii. 115–19.

CONACHER, D. J., 1974: 'Aeschylus' *Persae*: a literary commentary', *Serta Turyniana* (Studs. Alexander Turyn), 141–68 (Urbana/Chicago/London).

COOK, J. M., 1985: 'The rise of the Achaemenids and establishment of their empire', in Gershevitch (ed.), 200–91.

COUCH, H. N., 1932: 'The loathing of the Danaids', (abstract), *TAPA* lxiii. 54–5.

CUNLIFFE, B., 1988: *Greeks, Romans and Barbarians: Spheres of Interaction* (London).

DA RIOS, R. (ed.), 1954: *Aristoxeni elementa harmonica* (Rome).

DAKARIS, S. I., 1963: 'Das Taubenorakel von Dodona and das Totenorakel bei Ephyra', *Neue Ausgrabungen in Griechenland* (*AK* suppl. i), 35–54.

—— 1964: *Οἱ γενεαλογικοὶ μῦθοι τῶν Μολοσσῶν* (Athens).

DALE, A. M., 1968: *The Lyric Metres of Greek Drama* 2 (Cambridge).

DANDAMAEV, M. A., 1976 (Germ. transl.): *Persien unter den ersten Achämeniden* (Wiesbaden).

DASCALAKIS, A. P., 1965 (Engl. transl.): *The Hellenism of the Ancient Macedonians* (Thessaloniki).

DAUGE, Y. A., 1981: *La Barbare: recherches sur la conception romaine de la barbarie et de la civilisation* (Coll. *Latomus*, clxxvi) (Brussels).

DAUX, G., 1968: 'Chronique des fouilles et découvertes archéologiques en Grèce en 1967', *BCH* xcii. 711–1142.

DAVIES, J. K., 1977–78: 'Athenian citizenship: the descent group and the alternatives', *Classical Journal*, lxxiii. 105–21.

—— 1978: *Democracy and Classical Greece* (Glasgow).

—— 1984: 'The reliability of the oral tradition', in Foxhall and Davies (eds.), 87–110.

DE ROMILLY, JACQUELINE, 1971: *La Loi dans la pensée grecque des origines à Aristote* (Paris).

—— *et al.* (eds.), 1974: *Eschyle, les Perses* (Paris).

DE STE. CROIX, G. E. M., 1972: *The Origins of the Peloponnesian War* (London).

—— 1981: *The Class Struggle in the Ancient Greek World* (London).

DEICHGRÄBER, K., 1939: *Die Lykurgie des Aischylos* (Nachr. der Gesellschaft der Wissenschaften zu Göttingen, philosophisch-historische Klasse, n. f. i. 3) (Göttingen).

—— 1974: *Die Persertetralogie des Aischylos* (Akademie der Wissenschaften und der Literatur, Abhandlungen der geistes- und sozialwissenschaftlichen Klasse, iv) (Göttingen).

DELCOURT, M., 1934: 'Orient et occident chez Eschyle', *Mélanges Bidez* (Annuaire de l'Institut de philologie et d'histoire orientales, ii), 233–54 (Brussels).

—— 1958: *Hermaphrodite: mythes et rites de la bisexualité dans l'antiquité classique* (Paris).

DELEBECQUE, É., 1951: *Euripide et la guerre du Péloponnèse* (Études et Commentaires, x) (Paris).

DENNISTON, J. D., 1954: *The Greek Particles*² (Cambridge).

DETIENNE, M., 1979 (Engl. transl.): *Dionysos Slain* (Baltimore/London).

DEVAMBEZ, P., 1981: 'Amazones', *Lexicon iconographicum mythologiae classicae* i. 1. 586–653 (Zurich/Munich).

DIAKONOFF, I. M., 1985: 'Media', in Gershevitch (ed.), 36–148.

DIAMOND, S., 1974: *In Search of the Primitive: a Critique of Civilization* (New Brunswick/London).

DIGGLE, J. (ed.), 1970: *Euripides' Phaethon* (Cambridge).

—— 1987: 'The prophet of Bacchus: *Rhesus* 970–3', *Stud. Ital.* series 3. v. 167–72.

DIHLE, A., 1965: 'Zur Geschichte des Aethiopennamens', in *Umstrittene Daten: Untersuchungen zum Auftreten der Griechen am Roten Meer*, 65–79 (Cologne/Opladen).

DILLER, A., 1937: *Race Mixture among the Greeks before Alexander* (Illinois Studies in Language and Literature, xx) (Urbana). Reprinted Westport, Connecticut, 1971.

DILLER, H., 1962: 'Die Hellenen-Barbaren Antithese im Zeitalter der Perserkriege', in *Grecs et barbares*, 39–68.

DINDORF, W. (ed.), 1870: *Aeschyli tragoediae*⁵ (Leipzig).

DODDS, E. R., 1951: *The Greeks and the Irrational* (Berkeley/Los Angeles/London/Oxford).

—— (ed.), 1960: *Euripides Bacchae*² (Oxford).

—— 1973: 'The sophistic movement and the failure of Greek liberalism', in *The Ancient Concept of Progress*, 92–105 (London).

DORNSEIFF, F., 1935: 'Homerphilologie', *Hermes*, lxx. 241–4.

DÖRRIE, H., 1972: 'Die Wertung der Barbaren im Urteil der Griechen', in Stiehl and Lehmann (eds.), 146–75.

DOVER, K. J., 1963: 'Notes on Aristophanes' *Acharnians*', *Maia*, xv. 6–25. Reprinted in Dover 1987, 288–306.

—— 1974: *Greek Popular Morality in the Time of Plato and Aristotle* (Oxford).

—— 1977: 'I tessuti rossi dell' *Agamemnone*', *Dioniso*, xlviii. 55–69. Translated in Dover 1987, 151–60.

—— 1987: *Greek and the Greeks: Collected Papers*, i (Oxford).

DREWS, R., 1969: 'Aethiopian Memnon: African or Asiatic?' *Rh. Mus.* cxii. 191–2.

—— 1973: *The Greek Accounts of Eastern History* (Cambridge, Mass.).

—— 1976: 'The earliest Greek settlements on the Black Sea', *JHS* xcvi. 18–31.

DUCHEMIN, J., 1968: *L'ΑΓΩΝ dans la tragédie grecque*² (Paris).

DUCHESNE-GUILLEMIN, J., 1970: 'Reflections on "yaoždā" with a digression on "xvaētvadaθa",' in Puhvel (ed.), 203–10.

— 1979: 'La royauté iranienne et le xvarənah', in G. Gnoli and A. V. Rossi (eds.), *Iranica*, 375–86 (Naples).

DUMÉZIL, G., 1924: *Le Crime des Lemniennes: rites et légendes du monde Égéen* (Paris).

DUNBABIN, T. J., 1957: *The Greeks and their Eastern Neighbours*, ed. J. Boardman (Society for the promotion of Hellenic studies, suppl. viii) (London).

DUNKEL, H. B., 1937: 'Panhellenism in Greek tragedy' (diss., Chicago).

EASTERLING, P. E., 1984: 'Kings in Greek tragedy', *Estudios sobre los géneros literarios*, ii. 33–45 (Salamanca).

— 1985: 'Anachronism in Greek tragedy', *JHS* cv. 1–10.

EDELSTEIN, L., 1967: *The Idea of Progress in Classical Antiquity* (Baltimore).

EDWARDS, R. B., 1979: *Kadmos the Phoenician* (Amsterdam).

EHRENBERG, V., 1935: *Ost und West: Studien zur geschichtlichen Problematik der Antike* (Schriften der philosophischen Fakultät der deutschen Universität in Prag, xv) (Brünn/Prague/Leipzig/Vienna).

— 1954: *Sophocles and Pericles* (Oxford).

— 1973: *From Solon to Socrates*[2] (London).

EILERS, W., 1940: *Iranische Beamtennamen in der keilschriftlichen Überlieferung*, i (only volume published, Abhandlungen für die Kunde des Morgenlands, xxv. 5) (Leipzig).

EITREM, S., 1928: 'The necromancy in the Persai of Aischylos', *Symbolae Osloensis*, vi. 1–16.

ELIADE, M., 1955 (Engl. transl.): *The Myth of the Eternal Return* (London).

— 1982: *A History of Religious Ideas*, ii (Chicago/London).

ELSE, G. F., 1965: *The Origin and Early Form of Greek Tragedy* (Cambridge, Mass.).

— 1977: 'Ritual and drama in Aischyleian [*sic*] tragedy', *ICS* ii. 70–87.

EUBEN, J. P. (ed.), 1986: *Greek Tragedy and Political Theory* (Berkeley/Los Angeles/London).

FEAVER, D. D., 1960: 'The musical setting of Euripides' "Orestes"', *AJP* lxxxi. 1–15.

FENIK, B., 1968: *Typical Battle Scenes in the Iliad: Studies in the Narrative Technique of Homeric Battle Description* (*Historia* Einzelschr., xxi) (Wiesbaden).

FIEDLER, L. A., 1974: *The Stranger in Shakespeare* (St Albans).

FINLEY, J. H., 1967: *Three Essays on Thucydides* (Cambridge, Mass.).

— 1978: *Homer's* Odyssey (Cambridge, Mass./London).

FINLEY, M. I., 1962: 'The Black Sea and Danubian regions and the slave trade in antiquity', *Klio*, xl. 51–9.

— 1965: Review of *Grecs et barbares*, *JHS* lxxxv. 221.

— 1979: *The World of Odysseus*[2] (Harmondsworth).

FISHMAN, J. A., 1983: 'Language and ethnicity in bilingual education', in W. C. McReady (ed.), *Culture, Ethnicity, and Identity: Current Issues in Research*, 127–37 (New York/London/Paris).

FITTIPALDI, M. F., 1979: 'The Fall of the City of Troy and its Significance in Greek Poetry from Homer to Euripides' (diss., Yale).

FOLEY, H. P., 1985: *Ritual Irony: Poetry and Sacrifice in Euripides* (New York).

FORNARA, C. W., 1971: 'Evidence for the date of Herodotus' publication', *JHS* xci. 23–34.

FORSDYKE, J., 1956: *Greece before Homer* (London).

FOXHALL, L. AND DAVIES, J. K. (eds.), 1984: *The Trojan War: its Historicity and Context* (Bristol).

FRAENKEL, E. (ed.), 1950: *Aeschylus' Agamemnon* (Oxford).

FRAISSE, J.-C., 1974: *Philia: la notion d'amitié dans la philosophie antique* (Paris).

FRÄNKEL, H., 1975 (Engl transl.): *Early Greek Poetry and Philosophy* (Oxford).

FRANKFORT, H., 1948: *Ancient Egytian Religion* (New York).

FRIEDMAN, J. B., 1981: *The Monstrous Races in Medieval Art and Thought* (Cambridge, Mass./London).

FRIEDRICH, J., 1919: 'Das Attische im Munde von Ausländern bei Aristophanes', *Philologus*, lxxv. 274–303.

FROIDEFOND, C., 1971: *Le Mirage égyptien dans la littérature grecque d'Homère à Aristote* (Publications universitaires des lettres e sciences humaines d'Aix-en-Provence) (Aix-en-Provence).

FRYE, R. N., 1964: 'The charisma of kingship in ancient Iran', *Iran. Ant.* iv. 36–54.

— 1972: 'Gestures of deference to royalty in ancient Iran', *Iran. Ant.* ix. 102–7.

FUNGHI, M. S. (ed.), 1984: 'Antiphon, περὶ ἀληθείας', in H. M. Cockle (ed.), *The Oxyrhynchus Papyri*, lii. 1–5 (London).

GAGARIN, M., 1976: *Aeschylean Drama* (Berkeley/Los Angeles/London).

GARVIE, A. F., 1969: *Aeschylus' Supplices: Play and Trilogy* (Cambridge).

— (ed.), 1986: *Aeschylus' Choephori* (Oxford).

GASTALDI, E., 1979: 'Eschilo e l'occidente', in Braccesi (ed.), 19–89.

GEORGES, P., 1981: 'The Persians in the Greek Imagination 550–480 BC' (diss., Berkeley).

GERMAIN, G., 1954: *Genèse de l'Odyssée: le fantastique et le sacré* (Paris).

GERSHEVITCH, I. (ed.), 1985: *The Cambridge History of Iran*, ii (Cambridge).

GILBERT, P., 1949: 'Souvenirs de l'Égypte dans l'Hélène d'Euripide', *l'Ant. Class.* xviii. 79–84.

GOHEEN, R. F., 1955: 'Aspects of dramatic symbolism: three studies in the "Oresteia"', *AJP* lxxvi. 113–37.

GOLDHILL, S., 1987: 'The Great Dionysia and civic ideology', *JHS* cvii. 58–76.

— 1988: 'Battle narrative and politics in Aeschylus' *Persae*', *JHS* cviii. 189–93.

GOMME, A. W., 1954: *The Greek Attitude to Poetry and History* (Berkeley/Los Angeles).

GOOSSENS, R., 1935: 'L'Égypte dans l'Hélène d'Euripide', *Chron. d'Ég*. x. 243–53.

—— 1962: *Euripide et Athènes* (Brussels).

GOULD, J., 1973: 'Hiketeia', *JHS* xciii. 74–103.

GOW, A. S. F., 1928: 'Notes on the *Persae* of Aeschylus', *JHS* xlviii. 133–58.

Grecs et barbares 1962: (*Ent. Hardt*, viii) (Geneva).

GRENFELL, B. P. AND HUNT, A. S. (eds.), 1906: *The Hibeh Papyri*, i (London).

—— (eds.), 1915: *The Oxyrhynchus Papyri*, xi (London).

GRIFFIN, J., 1976: 'Homeric pathos and objectivity', *CQ* xxvi. 161–87.

—— 1977: 'The epic cycle and the uniqueness of Homer', *JHS* xcvii. 39–53.

—— 1980: *Homer on Life and Death* (Oxford).

GRIFFITH, M. (ed.), 1983: *Prometheus Bound* (Cambridge).

GROONEBOOM, P. (ed.), 1960: *Aischylos' Perser*, i (Göttingen).

GROSSMANN, G., 1970: *Promethie und Orestie* (Heidelberg).

GUEPIN, J.-P., 1968: *The Tragic Paradox* (Amsterdam).

GUTHRIE, W. K. C., 1971: *The Sophists* (Cambridge). First published as *A History of Greek Philosophy*, iii. 1 (Cambridge 1969).

GUYOT, P., 1980: *Eunuchen als Sklaven und Freigelassene in der griechisch-römischen Antike* (Stuttgart).

GWYN GRIFFITHS, J. (ed.), 1970: *Plutarch's de Iside et Osiride* (Cardiff).

HAARHOFF, T. J., 1948: *The Stranger at the Gate*[2] (Oxford).

HAARMANN, H., 1986: *Language in Ethnicity: a View of Basic Ecological Relations* (Berlin/New York/Amsterdam).

HAINSWORTH, J. B., 1969: *Homer* (*G&R* New Surveys in the Classics, iii) (Oxford).

HALDANE, J. A., 1965: 'Musical themes and imagery in Aeschylus', *JHS* lxxxv. 33–41.

HALL, E., 1987a: review of Long 1986, *CR* xxxvii. 199–200.

—— 1987b: 'The geography of Euripides' *Iphigeneia among the Taurians*', *AJP* cviii. 427–33.

—— 1988: 'When did the Trojans turn into Phrygians? Alcaeus 42. 15', *ZPE* lxxiii. 15–18.

—— 1989: 'The archer scene in Aristophanes' *Thesmophoriazusae*', *Philologus*, cxxxiii. 38–54.

—— forthcoming: 'Asia disarmed: the Persian spoils and Aeschylus' *Persae*'.

HALLIDAY, W. R., 1933: *Indo-European Folk-Tales and Greek Legend* (Cambridge).

HALLO, W. W., 1957: *Early Mesopotamian Royal Titles: a Philologic and Historical Analysis* (American Oriental Series, xliii) (New Haven).

HALLOCK, R. T., 1969: *Persepolis Fortification Tablets* (Oriental Institute Publications, xcii) (Chicago).

HAMMOND, N. G. L. AND GRIFFITH, G. T., 1979: *A History of Macedonia*, ii (Oxford).

— and Moon, W. G., 1978: 'Illustrations of early tragedy at Athens', *AJA* lxxxii. 371–83.

HAMPE, R., 1967: *Kult der Winde in Athen und Kreta* (Sitzungsberichte der Heidelberger Akademie der Wissenschaften, philosophisch-historische Klasse, i) (Heidelberg).

HANDLEY, E. W. AND REA, J. 1957: *The Telephus of Euripides (BICS* suppl. v) (London).

HARDER, A. (ed.), 1985: *Euripides' Kresphontes and Archelaos (Mnem.* suppl. lxxxvii) (Leiden).

HARRISON, A. R. W., 1968: *The Law of Athens*, i (Oxford).

HARRISON, F. E., 1960: 'Homer and the poetry of war', *G&R* vii. 9–19.

HARTOG, F., 1988 (Engl. transl.): *The Mirror of Herodotus: the Representation of the Other in the Writing of History* (Berkeley/Los Angeles/London).

HASLAM, M. W. (ed.), 1986: *The Oxyrhynchus Papyri*, liii (London).

HAVELOCK, E. A., 1957: *The Liberal Temper in Greek Politics* (London).

HEADLAM, W., 1898: 'Aeschylea', *CR* xii. 189–93.

— 1900: 'Upon Aeschylus I', *CR* xiv. 106–19.

— 1902: 'Ghost-raising, magic, and the underworld', *CR* xvi. 52–61.

HECHT, R., 1892: *Die Darstellung fremder Nationalitäten im Drama der Griechen* (diss., Königsberg).

HEIDEL, W. A., 1943: 'Hecataeus and Xenophanes', *AJP* lxiv. 257–77.

HEINIMANN, F., 1945: *Nomos und Physis* (Basle).

HELCK, W., 1964: 'Die Ägypter und die Fremden', *Saeculum*, xv. 103–14.

HEMBERG, B., 1950: *Die Kabiren* (Uppsala).

HENRICHS, A., 1969: 'Die Maenaden von Milet', *ZPE* iv. 223–41.

— 1976: 'Despoina Kybele: ein Beitrag zur religiösen Namenkunde', *HSCP* lxxx. 253–86.

— 1981: 'Human sacrifice in Greek religion: three case studies', in *Le Sacrifice dans l'antiquité (Ent. Hardt*, xxvii), 195–242 (Geneva).

— 1982: 'Changing Dionysiac identities', in B. F. Meyer and E. P. Sanders (eds.), *Self-definition in the Graeco-Roman World (Jewish and Christian Self-definition*, iii), 137–60 (London).

HERINGTON, J., 1985: *Poetry into Drama: Early Tragedy and the Greek Poetic Tradition* (Berkeley/Los Angeles/London).

HERMAN, G., 1987: *Ritualised Friendship and the Greek City* (Cambridge/London/New York/New Rochelle/Melbourne/Sydney).

HERMANN, A., 1937: 'Nysa', *RE* xvii. col. 1628–61.

HERZFELD, E., 1938: *Altpersische Inschriften* (Berlin).

HILTBRUNNER, O., 1950: *Wiederholungs- und Motivtechnik bei Aischylos* (Berne).

HIND, J. G. F., 1983–4: 'Greek and barbarian peoples on the shores of the Black Sea', *Archaeological Reports*, xxx. 71–97.

HIRSCH, S. W., 1985: *The Friendship of the Barbarians: Xenophon and the Persian Empire* (Hanover/London, New England).

HODDINOTT, R. F., 1981: *The Thracians* (London).

—— 1986: 'The Thracians and their religion', in A. Fol, B. Nikolov and R. F. Hoddinott (eds.), *The New Thracian Treasure from Rogozen, Bulgaria* (British Museum Publications), 21–33 (London).

HÖFER, O., 1916–24: 'Thamyras', in W. H. Roscher (ed.), *Ausführliches Lexikon der griechischen und römischen Mythologie*, v. 464–81 (Leipzig).

HOLZBERG, N., 1973: 'Zur Datierung der Gygestragödie P. Oxy. 2382', *Živa Antika*, xxiii. 273–86.

HOOKER, J. T., 1980: *The Ancient Spartans* (London/Toronto/Melbourne).

HOPKINS, M. K., 1963: 'Eunuchs in politics in the later Roman empire', *PCPS* clxxxix (n.s. ix). 61–80.

—— 1980: 'Brother–sister marriage in Roman Egypt', *Comparative Studies in Society and History*, xxii. 303–54.

HORST, J., 1932: *Proskynein* (Gütersloh).

HOWALD, E., 1937: *Der Mythos als Dichtung* (Zurich/Leipzig).

HUGILL, W. M., 1936: *Panhellenism in Aristophanes* (Chicago).

HULTZSCH, E., 1904: 'Zum Papyros 413 aus Oxyrhynchus', *Hermes*, xxxix. 307–11.

HUTCHINSON, G. O. (ed.), 1985: *Aeschylus' Septem contra Thebas* (Oxford).

HUXLEY, G. L., 1960: *Achaeans and Hittites* (Oxford).

—— 1969: *Greek Epic Poetry from Eumelos to Panyassis* (London).

IRWIN, E., 1974: *Colour Terms in Greek Poetry* (Toronto).

ISAACS, H. R., 1975: 'Basic group identity: the idols of the tribe', in N. Glazer and D. P. Moynihan (eds.), *Ethnicity: Theory and Experience*, 29–52 (Cambridge, Mass./London).

ISAJIW, W., 1974: 'Definitions of ethnicity', *Ethnicity*, i. 111–24.

JACOB, O., 1928: *Les Esclaves publics à Athènes* (Paris).

JACOBY, F., 1912: 'Hekataios von Milet', *RE* vii. 2. 2667–750.

—— 1944a: *ΓΕΝΕΣΙΑ*: a forgotten festival of the dead', *CQ* xxxviii. 65–75. Reprinted in Bloch 1956, 243–59.

—— 1944b: 'Patrios nomos: state burial in Athens and the public cemetery in the Kerameikos', *JHS* lxiv. 37–66. Reprinted in Bloch 1956, 260–315.

JÄKEL, S., 1979: 'The Aiolos of Euripides', *GB* viii. 101–18.

JANE, C., (transl.) 1960: *The Journal of Christopher Columbus* (London).

JANKO, R., 1982: *Homer, Hesiod and the Hymns: Diachronic Development in Epic Diction* (Cambridge).

JANSSEN, T. H. (ed.), 1984: *Timotheus' Persae* (Classical and Byzantine Monographs, vi) (Amsterdam).

JEANMAIRE, H., 1939: *Couroi et Courètes* (Lille).

JEREMIAS, A., 1900: *Hölle und Paradies bei den Babyloniern* (*Der alte Orient*, i. 3) (Leipzig).

JOHANSEN, H. F. AND WHITTLE, E. W. (eds.), 1980: *Aeschylus, the Suppliants* (Copenhagen).

JOUAN, F. 1966: *Euripide et les légendes des chants cypriens* (Paris).

JOUANNA, J., 1981: 'Les causes de la défaite des barbares chez Eschyle, Hérodote, et Hippocrate', *Ktema*, vi. 3–15.

JÜTHNER, J., 1923: *Hellenen und Barbaren: aus der Geschichte des National-bewusstseins (Das Erbe der Alten*, series 2. viii) (Leipzig).

—— 1939: 'Herkunft und Grundlagen der griechischen Nationalspiele', *Die Antike*, xv. 231–64.

KABBANI, R., 1986: *Europe's Myths of Orient: Devise and Rule* (Basingstoke/London).

KAHN, C. H., 1979: *The Art and Thought of Heraclitus* (Cambridge).

KAIMIO, M., 1977: *Characterization of Sound in Early Greek Literature* (Commentationes humanarum litterarum, liii) (Helsinki).

KADRIDIS, J. TH., 1971: 'ἀεὶ φιλέλλην ὁ ποιητής?', in *Homer Revisited*, 54–67 (Lund). Translated from *WS* lxix. 1956, 26–32.

—— 1975: 'Licht und Finsternis in dem Botenbericht der Perser des Aischylos', *GB* iv. 145–54.

KANNICHT, R. (ed.), 1969: *Euripides' Helena* (Heidelberg).

KARAGEORGHIS, V., 1982: *Cyprus: from the Stone Age to the Romans* (London).

KASSEL, R., 1966: 'Kritische und exegetische Kleinigkeiten II', *Rh. Mus.* cix. 1–12.

KAZAROW, G. I., 1954: 'Thrace', *The Cambridge Ancient History*, viii (corrected reprint of 1930 edition), 534–60 (Cambridge).

KEARNS, E., 1985: 'Religious structures after Cleisthenes', in Cartledge and Harvey (eds.), 189–207.

KEES, H., 1953: *Das Priestertum im ägyptischen Staat* (Leiden/Cologne).

KEIL, H. (ed.), 1874: *Scriptores artis metricae* (*Grammatici Latini*, vi) (Leipzig).

KEIPER, P., 1877: *Die Perser des Aischylos als Quelle für altpersische Altertumskunde* (diss., Erlangen).

KENNER, H., 1970: *Das Phänomen der verkehrten Welt in der griechisch-römischen Antike* (Klagenfurt).

KENT, R. G., 1953: *Old Persian*[2] (New Haven).

KERÉNYI, C., 1976 (Engl. transl.): *Dionysos* (Princeton/London).

KERFERD, G. B., 1981: *The Sophistic Movement* (Cambridge).

KEYES, C. F. (ed.), 1981a: *Ethnic Change* (Seattle/London).

—— 1981b: 'The dialectics of ethnic change', in Keyes 1981a, 3–30.

KIERDORF, W., 1966: *Erlebnis und Darstellung der Perserkriege* (*Hypomnemata*, xvi) (Göttingen).

KING, L. W. AND THOMPSON, R. C., 1907: *The Sculptures and Inscription of Darius the Great on the Rock of Behistun in Persia* (British Museum Publications) (London).

KIRK, G. S., 1964: 'Objective dating criteria in Homer', in G. S. Kirk (ed.), *The*

Language and Background of Homer, 175–90 (Cambridge). Reprinted from *Mus. Helv.* xvii. 1960, 189–205.

— 1985: *The Iliad: a Commentary*, i (Cambridge/London/New York/New Rochelle/Melbourne/Sydney).

KISO, A., 1984: *The Lost Sophocles* (New York/Washington/Atlanta/Los Angeles/Chicago).

KITTO, H. D. F., 1961: *Greek Tragedy: a Literary Study* [3] (London).

KLINGNER, F., 1940: 'Über die Dolonie', *Hermes*, lxxv. 337–68.

— (ed.), 1952: *Varia variorum* (Festschr. K. Reinhardt) (Münster/Cologne).

KNOX, B., 1957: *Oedipus at Thebes* (New Haven/Oxford).

— 1979: *Word and Action: Essays on the Ancient Theater* (Baltimore/London).

KORZENIEWSKI, D., 1968: *Griechische Metrik* (Darmstadt).

KRAMER, S. N. (ed.), 1940: *Lamentation over the Destruction of Ur* (Chicago).

— (ed.), 1961: *Mythologies of the Ancient World* (New York).

— 1963: *The Sumerians: their History, Culture, and Character* (Chicago/London).

KRANZ, W., 1933: *Stasimon: Untersuchungen zu Form und Gehalt der griechischen Tragödie* (Berlin).

— 1951: 'Das Gesetz des Herzens', *Rh. Mus.* n. f. xciv. 222–41.

KULLMANN, W., 1960: *Die Quellen der Ilias* (*Hermes* Einzelschr., xiv) (Wiesbaden).

KUNSEMÜLLER, O., 1935: *Die Herkunft der platonischen Kardinaltugenden* (diss., Erlangen). Reprinted New York 1979.

KYRIAKIDES, S. P., 1955: *The Northern Ethnological Boundaries of Hellenism* (Thessaloniki).

LA BARRE, W., 1970: *The Ghost Dance: Origins of Religion* (London).

LATTE, K., 1950: 'Ein antikes Gygesdrama', *Eranos*, xlviii. 136–41. Reprinted in *Kleine Schriften*, 585–9 (Munich 1968).

LATTIMORE, O., 1962: *Inner Asian Frontiers of China* [2] (Boston).

LATTIMORE, R., 1943: 'Aeschylus on the defeat of Xerxes', in *Classical Studies in Honor of William Abott Oldfather*, 82–93 (Urbana).

LAUROT, B., 1981: 'Idéaux grecs et barbarie chez Hérodote', *Ktema*, vi. 39–48.

LAWLER, L. B., 1964: *The Dance in Ancient Greece* (London).

LAWRENCE, A. W., 1951: 'The Acropolis and Persepolis', *JHS* lxxi. 111–19.

LAWSON, J. C., 1934: 'The evocation of Darius (Aesch. *Persae* 607–93)', *CQ* xxviii. 79–89.

LEAF, W. (ed.), 1902: *The Iliad* [2], ii (London/New York).

LEFKOWITZ, M. R., 1986: *Women in Greek Myth* (London).

LEMBKE, J. AND HERINGTON, C. J., 1981 (transl.): *Aeschylus' Persians* (New York/Oxford).

LESKY, A., 1951: 'Die Maske des Thamyris', *Anzeiger der österreichischen Akademie der Wissenschaften*, lxxx. 8. 101–10. Reprinted in *Gesammelte Schriften*, 169–75 (Berne/Munich 1966).

— 1959: 'Aithiopika', *Hermes*, lxxxvii. 27–38. Reprinted in *Gesammelte Schriften*, 410–21 (Berne/Munich 1966).

— 1977: 'Tragödien bei Herodot?', in K. H. Kinzl (ed.), *Greece and the Eastern Mediterranean* (Studs. F. Schachermeyr), 224–30 (Berlin/New York).

Lévy, E., 1981: 'Les origines du mirage scythe', *Ktema*, vi. 57–68.

Lewis, D. M., 1968: 'Dedications of phialai at Athens', *Hesperia*, xxxvii. 368–80.

— 1977: *Sparta and Persia* (Leiden).

— 1985: 'Persians in Herodotus', *The Greek Historians: Papers presented to A. E. Raubitschek*, 101–17 (Stanford).

Lichtheim, M., 1973–80 (transl.): *Ancient Egyptian Literature* (Berkeley/Los Angeles/London).

Light, I., 1981: 'Ethnic succession', in Keyes 1981a, 54–86.

Limet, H., 1972: 'L'étranger dans la société sumérienne', in D. O. Edzard (ed.), *Gesellschaftsklassen im alten Zweistromland und in den angrenzenden Gebieten* (Abhandlungen der bayerischen Akademie der Wissenschaften, philosophisch-historische Klasse, n. f. lxxv), 123–38.

Linforth, I. M., 1926: *Greek Gods and Foreign Gods in Herodotus* (University of California Publications in Classical Philology, ix. 1) (Berkeley).

— 1931: 'Two notes on the legend of Orpheus', *TAPA* lxii. 5–17.

Lippmann, W., 1922: *Public Opinion* (New York).

Lloyd-Jones, H., 1963: review of Turner 1962, *Gnomon*, xxxv. 433–55.

— 1966: 'Problems of early Greek tragedy: Pratinas, Phrynichus, the Gyges fragment', *Estudios sobre la tragedia Griega* (Cuadernos de la Fundación Pastor, xiii), 11–33.

— 1983a: 'Artemis and Iphigeneia', *JHS* ciii. 87–102.

— 1983b: *The Justice of Zeus*² (Berkeley/Los Angeles/London).

Lobel, E., 1949: 'A Greek historical drama', *Proceedings of the British Academy*, xxxv. 207–16.

Lochner von Hüttenbach, F., 1960: *Die Pelasger* (Vienna).

Loewe, M., 1986: 'Introduction', in Twitchett and Loewe (eds.), 1–19.

Long, T., 1986: *Barbarians in Greek Comedy* (Carbondale/Edwardsville).

Lonis, R., 1981: 'Les trois approches de l'Ethiopien par l'opinion gréco-romaine', *Ktema*, vi. 69–87.

Loraux, N., 1986 (Engl. transl.): *The Invention of Athens: the Funeral Oration in the Classical City* (Cambridge, Mass./London).

Lordkipanidze, O., 1985: *Das alte Kolchis und seine Beziehungen zur griechischen Welt vom 6. zum 4. Jh. v. Chr.* (Konstanz).

Lovejoy, A. O. and Boas, G., 1935: *Primitivism and Related Ideas in Antiquity* (Baltimore).

Luckenbill, D. D., 1926: *Ancient Records of Assyria and Babylonia*, i (Chicago).

Luria, S., 1924: '*ΑΓΛΩΤΤΙΑ*', *Aegyptus*, v. 326–30.

— 1929: 'Noch einmal über Antiphon in Euripides' Alexandros', *Hermes*, lxiv. 491–7.

MAAS, P., 1962 (Engl. transl.): *Greek Metre* (Oxford).

MARTIN, S. R., 1975: 'The Greek Tragedians and the Aethiopis' (diss., Cincinnati).

MASON, P. G., 1959: 'Kassandra', *JHS* lxxix. 80–93.

MATTHEWS, V. J. (ed.), 1974: *Panyassis of Halikarnassos* (*Mnem.* suppl. xxxiii) (Leiden).

McLEOD, W. E., 1966: 'The Bow in Ancient Greece, with Particular Reference to the Homeric Poems'. Summary of diss., Harvard 1966, *HSCP* lxxi. 329–31.

McNEAL, R. A., 1985: 'How did Pelasgians become Hellenes?', *ICS* x. 11–21.

MEIGGS, R., 1973: *The Athenian Empire* (corrected edition) (Oxford).

— and Lewis, D. M., 1969: *A Selection of Greek Historical Inscriptions to the End of the Fifth Century BC* (Oxford).

MELCHINGER, S., 1979: *Die Welt als Tragödie*, i (Munich).

MERKELBACH, R., 1968: 'Les papyrus d'Hésiode et la géographie mythologique de la Grèce', *Chron. d'Ég.* xliii. 133–55.

METTE, H.-J., 1963: *Der verlorene Aischylos* (Berlin).

MEULI, K., 1921: *Odyssee und Argonautika: Untersuchungen zur griechischen Sagengeschichte und zum Epos* (Berlin). Shortened version in *Gesammelte Schriften*, ii. 593–676 (Basle/Stuttgart 1975).

— 1935: 'Scythica', *Hermes*, lxx. 121–76. Reprinted in *Gesammelte Schriften*, ii. 817–79 (Basel/Stuttgart 1975).

MICHAELIDES, S., 1978: *The Music of Ancient Greece: an Encyclopaedia* (London).

MICHELINI, A. N., 1982: *Tradition and Dramatic Form in the Persians of Aeschylus* (Leiden).

MIKALSON, J. D., 1983: *Athenian Popular Religion* (Chapel Hill/London).

MILLER, W., 1929: *Daedalus and Thespis*, i (New York).

MOMIGLIANO, A., 1971: 'La libertà di parola nel mondo antico', *Rivista Storica Italiana*, lxxxiii. 499–524.

— 1975: *Alien Wisdom: the Limits of Hellenization* (Cambridge).

— 1979: 'Persian empire and Greek freedom', in A. Ryan (ed.), *The Idea of Freedom: Essays in Honour of Isaiah Berlin*, 139–51 (Oxford).

MORETTI, L., 1957: 'Olympionikai, i vincitori negli antichi agoni olimpici', *Atti della accademia nazionale dei Lincei*, series 8. viii. 55–198 (Rome).

MORROW, G., 1939: *Plato's Law of Slavery in its Relation to Greek Law* (Illinois Studies in Language and Literature, xxv. 3) (Urbana).

MOSLEY, D. J., 1971: 'Greeks, barbarians, language and contact', *Ancient Society*, ii. 1–6.

MOSS, P. E., 1979: 'Persian Ethnography in Aeschylus'. Summary of diss., North Carolina at Chapel Hill, *Dissertation Abstracts*, xl. 5A. 2648.

MOULTON, C., 1972: 'Antiphon the sophist, "On Truth"', *TAPA* ciii. 329–66.

MOUNTFORD, J. F., 1929: 'Greek music in the papyri and inscriptions', in J. U.

Powell and E. A. Barber (eds.), *New Chapters in the History of Greek Literature*, series 2, 146–83 (Oxford).

MOUTSOPOULOS, E. A., 1984: 'Musique grecque ou barbare (Eurip., Iph. Taur. 179–184)?', *Eirene*, xxi. 25–31.

MUHLY, J. D., 1970: 'Homer and the Phoenicians; the relations between Greece and the near east in the late bronze and early iron age', *Berytus*, xix. 19–64.

MÜLLER, C. C., 1980: 'Die Herausbildung der Gegensätze: Chinesen und Barbaren in der frühen Zeit', in Bauer (ed.), 43–76.

MÜLLER, K. E., 1972: *Geschichte der antiken Ethnographie und ethnologischen Theoriebildung*, i (Wiesbaden).

MÜLLER, R., 1980: 'Hellenen und "Barbaren" in der griechischen Philosophie', in *Menschenbild und Humanismus der Antike*, 111–34 (Leipzig).

MURRAY, G., 1934: *The Rise of the Greek Epic*[4] (Oxford/London).

—— 1939 (transl.): *Aeschylus: the Persians* (Oxford).

—— 1940: *Aeschylus: the Creator of Tragedy* (Oxford).

—— (ed.), 1947: *Aeschyli septem quae supersunt tragoediae*. Corrected reprint of 1938 edition (Oxford).

MURRAY, O., 1980: *Early Greece* (Glasgow).

NAGY, G., 1979: *The Best of the Achaeans: Concepts of the Hero in Archaic Greek Poetry* (Baltimore/London).

—— 1983: 'On the death of Sarpedon', in C. A. Rubino and C. W. Shelmerdine (eds.), *Approaches to Homer*, 189–217 (Austin).

NESTLE, W., 1901: *Euripides: der Dichter der griechischen Aufklärung* (Stuttgart).

—— 1942: *Vom Mythos zum Logos*[2] (Stuttgart).

NEWMAN, W. L. (ed.), 1887: *The Politics of Aristotle*, i (Oxford).

NIKOLAIDIS, A. G., 1986: 'Ἑλληνικὸς-βαρβαρικός', *WS* xx. 229–44.

NILSSON, M. P., 1911: 'Der Ursprung der Tragödie', *Neue Jahrbücher*, xiv. 609–42. Reprinted in *Opuscula Selecta*, i. 61–145 (Lund 1951).

NORTH, H., 1966: *Sophrosyne: Self-Knowledge and Self-Restraint in Greek Literature* (Cornell Studies in Classical Philology, xxxv) (New York).

NYLANDER, C., 1970: *Ionians in Pasargadae* (Uppsala).

O'CONNOR-VISSER, E. A. M. E., 1987: *Aspects of Human Sacrifice in the Tragedies of Euripides* (Amsterdam).

OLIVER, J. H., 1960: *Demokratia, the Gods, and the Free World* (Baltimore).

OLMSTEAD, A. T., 1948: *History of the Persian Empire* (Chicago).

O'NEILL, E., 1942: 'Notes on Phrynichus' *Phoenissae* and Aeschylus' *Persae*', *CP* xxxvii. 425–7.

OPPENHEIM, A. L., 1977: *Ancient Mesopotamia*[2] (Chicago/London).

OSTWALD, M., 1973: 'Was there a concept ἄγραφος νόμος in classical Greece?', in E. N. Lee, A. P. D. Mourelatos, and R. M. Rorty (eds.), *Exegesis and Argument* (Studs. G. Vlastos, *Phronesis*, suppl. i), 70–104 (Assen).

OTTO, W. F., 1955: *Die Musen und der göttliche Ursprung des Singens und Sagens* (Düsseldorf/Cologne).

— 1965 (Engl. transl.): *Dionysos: Myth and Cult* (Bloomington/London).

PADUANO, G., 1978: *Sui Persiani di Eschilo: problemi di focalizzazione drammatica* (Rome).

PAGDEN, A., 1982: *The Fall of Natural Man: the American Indian and the Origins of Comparative Ethnology* (Cambridge/London/New York/New Rochelle/Melbourne/Sydney).

PAGE, D. L., 1936: 'The elegiacs in Euripides' Andromache', in *Greek Poetry and Life* (Studs. G. Murray), 206–30 (Oxford).

— (ed.), 1938: *Euripides' Medea* (Oxford).

— (ed.), 1941: *Select Papyri*, iii (Loeb edition) (Cambridge, Mass./London).

— 1951: *A New Chapter in the History of Greek Tragedy* (Inaugural lecture) (Cambridge).

— 1955: *Sappho and Alcaeus* (Oxford).

— 1959: *History and the Homeric Iliad* (Berkeley/Los Angeles/London).

— 1962: 'An early tragedy on the fall of Croesus', *PCPS* n. s. viii. 47–9.

— 1973: *Folktales in Homer's Odyssey* (Cambridge, Mass.).

— (ed.), 1975: *Epigrammata Graeca* (Oxford).

PAPACHRISTODOULOU, I. CH., 1973: '῎Αγαλμα καὶ ναὸς Κυβέλης ἐν Μοσχάτῳ ᾿Αττικῆς', ᾿Αρχαιολογικὴ ᾿Εφημερίς, 189–217.

PARKE, H. W., 1967: *Greek Oracles* (London).

PARKER, R., 1983: *Miasma: Pollution and Purification in Early Greek Religion* (Oxford).

PARSONS, P. J. (ed.), 1974: *The Oxyrhynchus Papyri*, xlii (London).

PASQUALI, G., 1924: 'Amonre nelle *Supplici* di Eschilo', *Rivista di Filologia*, lii. 246–8.

PATTERSON, C., 1981: *Pericles' Citizenship Law of 451–50 BC* (New York).

PATZER, H., 1962: *Die Anfänge der griechischen Tragödie* (Wiesbaden).

PEARSON, A. C. (ed.), 1917: *The Fragments of Sophocles* (Cambridge).

PEARSON, L., 1939: *Early Ionian Historians* (Oxford).

PEMBROKE, S., 1965: 'Last of the matriarchs: a study in the inscriptions of Lycia', *Journal of the Economic and Social History of the Orient*, viii. 217–47.

— 1967: 'Women in charge: the function of alternatives in early Greek tradition and the ancient idea of matriarchy', *Journal of the Warburg and Courtauld Institutes*, xxx. 1–35.

PERADOTTO, J. AND SULLIVAN, J. P. (eds.), 1984: *Women in the Ancient World: the Arethusa Papers* (Albany).

PERLMAN, S., 1976: 'Panhellenism, the polis and imperialism', *Historia*, xxv. 1–30.

PERROTTA, G., 1931: *I Tragici Greci* (Bari).

PFEIFFER, R., 1976: 'Die Sophisten, ihre Zeitgenossen und Schüler', in C. J.

Classen (ed.), *Sophistik* (Wege der Forschung, clxxxvii), 170–214 (Darm-stadt).

PHILLIPS, E. D., 1955: 'The legend of Aristeas: fact and fancy in early Greek notions of East Russia, Siberia, and inner Asia', *Artibus Asiae*, xviii. 161–77.

PICKARD-CAMBRIDGE, A. W., 1968: *The Dramatic Festivals of Athens*², revised by J. Gould and D. M. Lewis (Oxford).

PINSENT, J., 1984: 'The Trojans in the Iliad', in Foxhall and Davies (eds.), 137–62.

PISANI, V., 1934: '*Διονυσιακά*', *Stud. Ital*. xi. 217–26.

PLASSART, A., 1913: 'Les archers d'Athènes', *Revue des études grecques*, xxvi. 151–213.

PODLECKI, A. J., 1966: *The Political Background of Aeschylean Tragedy* (Ann Arbor).

—— 1984: *The Early Greek Poets and their Times* (Vancouver).

—— 1986: '*Polis* and monarch in early Greek tragedy', in Euben (ed.), 76–100.

POHLENZ, M., 1954: *Die griechische Tragödie*², i (Göttingen).

POKORNY, J., 1959: *Indogermanisches etymologisches Wörterbuch*, i (Berne/Munich).

POWELL, A., 1988: *Athens and Sparta: Constructing Greek Political and Social History from 478 BC* (London).

PRAŠEK, J. V., 1904: 'Hekataios als Herodots Quelle zur Geschichte Vordera-siens', *Klio*, iv. 193–208.

PRICKARD, A. O. (ed.), 1879: *The Persae of Aeschylus* (London).

PRITCHARD, J. B., 1954: *The Ancient Near East in Pictures* (Princeton).

PRITCHETT, W. K., 1956: 'The Attic stelai II', *Hesperia*, xxv. 178–328.

PUHVEL, J. (ed.), 1970: *Myth and Law among the Indo-Europeans* (Berkeley/Los Angeles/London).

RABE, H., 1908: 'Euripideum', *Rh. Mus*. n. f. lxiii. 419–22.

RADET, G., 1893: *La Lydie et le monde grec au temps des Mermnades (687–546)* (Paris).

RAECK, W., 1981: *Zum Barbarenbild in der Kunst Athens im 6. und 5. Jahrhundert v. Chr.* (diss., Bonn).

RAMSAY, W. M., 1927: *Asianic Elements in Greek Civilization* (London).

RANKIN, H. D., 1987: *Celts and the Classical World* (London).

RASCH, J., 1913: *Sophocles quid debeat Herodoto in rebus ad fabulas exornandas adhibitis* (Commentationes philologicae Jenenses, x) (Leipzig).

RAU, P., 1967: *Paratragodia: Untersuchung einer komischen Form des Aristophanes* (*Zetemata*, xlv) (Munich).

RAUBITSCHEK, A. E., 1960: 'The covenant of Plataea', *TAPA* xci. 178–83.

REBUFFAT, R., 1972: 'Le sacrifice du fils de Creon dans les Phéniciennes d'Euripide', *REA* lxxiv. 14–31.

REDFIELD, J. M., 1975: *Nature and Culture in the* Iliad: *the Tragedy of Hector* (Chicago/London).

REINHARDT, K., 1960: *Tradition und Geist: gesammelte Essays zur Dichtung*, ed. C. Becker (Göttingen).

—— 1961: *Die Ilias und ihr Dichter*, ed. U. Hölscher (Göttingen).

RENFREW, C., 1988: 'The Minoan-Mycenaean origins of the Panhellenic games', in W. J. Raschke (ed.), *The Archaeology of the Olympics: the Olympics and Other Festivals in Antiquity*, 13-25. (Madison, Wisconsin).

REYNOLDS, V., FALGER, V., AND VINE, I. (eds.), 1987: *The Sociobiology of Ethnocentrism: Evolutionary Dimensions of Xenophobia, Discrimination, Racism, and Nationalism* (London/Sydney).

RIBBECK, O., 1882: *Alazon: ein Beitrag zur antiken Ethologie* (Leipzig).

RICHARDS, G. C., 1934: 'Proskynesis', *CR* xlviii. 168-70.

RIGSBY, K. J., 1976: 'Teiresias as magus in *Oedipus Rex*', *GRBS* xvii. 109-14.

ROBERTSON, D. S., 1923: 'Euripides and Tharyps', *CR* xxxvii. 58-60.

RODZINSKI, W., 1979: *A History of China*, i (Oxford/New York/Toronto).

ROGERS, J. D., 1903: 'On the νομίσματα πύργινα of Aeschylus, Pers. 859', *AJA* vii. 95-6.

RÓHEIM, G., 1947: 'Dream analysis and field work', *Psychoanalysis and the Social Sciences*, i. 87-130 (London).

ROISMAN, J., 1988: 'On Phrynichos' *Sack of Miletos* and *Phoinissai*', *Eranos*, lxxxvi. 15-23.

ROOT, M. C., 1985: 'The parthenon frieze and the Apadana reliefs at Persepolis', *AJA* lxxxv. 103-20.

ROSE, H. J., 1950: 'Ghost ritual in Aeschylus', *Harvard Theological Review*, xliii. 257-80.

—— 1957-8: *A Commentary on the Surviving Plays of Aeschylus* (Amsterdam).

—— (ed.), 1963: *Hygini fabulae* (Leiden).

ROSELLINI, M. AND SAID, S., 1978: 'Usages des femmes et autres nomoi chez les "sauvages" d'Hérodote', *Annali della Scuola normale superiore di Pisa*, series 3. viii. 3. 949-1005.

ROSTOVTZEFF, M., 1922: *Iranians and Greeks in South Russia* (Oxford).

—— 1930 (Engl. transl.): *The Orient and Greece*² (*A History of the Ancient World*², i) (Oxford).

RUBEL, M. M., 1978: *Savage and Barbarian: Historical Attitudes in the Criticism of Homer and Ossian in Britain, 1760-1800* (Amsterdam/Oxford/New York).

RUSCHENBUSCH, E., 1966: *ΣΟΛΩΝΟΣ ΝΟΜΟΙ: die Fragmente des solonischen Gesetzwerkes* (*Historia* Einzelschr., ix) (Wiesbaden).

SAID, E. W., 1978: *Orientalism* (London).

—— 1986: 'Orientalism reconsidered', in F. Barker et al. (eds.): *Literature, Politics, and Theory: Papers from the Essex Conference 1976-84*, 210-29 (London/New York).

SAID, S., 1981: 'Darius et Xerxes dans les *Perses* d'Eschyle', *Ktema*, vi. 17-38.

SAKALIS, D. TH., 1984: 'Αἰσχύλος ἐτυμολόγος', *Δωδώνη*, xiii. 54-85.

SAKELLARIOU, M. B., 1981: 'Panhellenism: from concept to policy', in M. B.

Hatzopoulos and L. Loukopoulos (eds.), *Philip of Macedon*, 128–45 (London).

SALMON, P., 1965: *La Politique égyptienne d'Athènes (VIe et Ve siècles avant J.-C.)* (Académie royale de Belgique, mémoires, classe des lettres et des sciences morales et politiques, lvii. 6) (Brussels).

SANCISI-WEERDENBURG, H., 1983: 'Exit Atossa: images of women in Greek historiography on Persia', in A. Cameron and A. Kuhrt (eds.), *Images of Women in Antiquity*, 20–33 (London/Sydney).

SAUNDERS, E. D., 1961: 'Japanese mythology', in Kramer (ed.), 409–42.

SCHADEWALDT, W., 1952: 'Einblick in die Erfindung der Ilias', in Klingner (ed.), 13–48.

SCHMITT, R., 1966: 'Die Hesychglosse σάτιλλα. Eine Nachprüfung'. *Glotta*, xliv. 148–51.

—— 1978: *Die Iranier-Namen bei Aischylos* (Abhandlungen der österreichischen Akademie der Wissenschaften, philosophisch-historische Klasse, cccvii. 6) (Vienna).

SCHNABEL, P., 1923–5: 'Die Begründung des hellenistischen Königskultes durch Alexander', *Klio*, xix. 113–27.

SCHRÖDER, O., 1914: *De Laudibus Athenarum a poetis tragicis et ab oratoribus epidicticis excultis* (diss., Göttingen).

SCHROFF, A., 1932: 'Tapes', *RE* series 2. iv. A. 2251–3.

SCHWABL, H., 1962: 'Das Bild der fremden Welt bei den frühen Griechen', in *Grecs et barbares*, 3–23.

SCODEL, R., 1980: *The Trojan Trilogy of Euripides* (Hypomnemata, lx) (Göttingen).

SCOTT, W. C., 1984: *Musical Design in Aeschylean Theater* (Hanover/London, New England).

SCULLY, S., 1981: 'The polis in Homer: a definition and interpretation', *Ramus*, x. 1–34.

SEAFORD, R., 1980: 'Black Zeus in Sophocles' *Inachus*', *CQ* xxx. 23–9.

—— (ed.), 1984a: *Euripides' Cyclops* (Oxford).

—— 1984b: 'The last bath of Agamemnon', *CQ* xxxiv. 247–59.

SEGAL, C., 1971: *The Theme of the Mutilation of the Corpse in the Iliad* (Mnem. suppl. xvii) (Leiden).

—— 1978: 'The menace of Dionysus: sex roles and reversals in Euripides' *Bacchae*', *Arethusa*, xi. 185–202. Reprinted in Peradotto and Sullivan 1984, 195–212.

SHAPIRO, H. A., 1983: 'Amazons, Thracians, and Scythians', *GRBS* xxiv. 105–15.

SHAW, M., 1975: 'The female intruder: women in fifth-century drama', *CP* lxx. 255–66.

SIDERAS, A., 1971: *Aeschylus Homericus* (Hypomnemata, xxxi) (Göttingen).

SIDGWICK, A. (ed.), 1903: *Aeschylus' Persae* (Oxford).

SIMON, E., 1967: 'Boreas und Oreithyia auf dem silbernen Rhyton in Triest', *Antike und Abendland*, xiii. 101–26.

SINKO, T., 1934: 'De causae Rhesi novissima defensione', *l'Ant. Class.* iii. 223-9, 411-29.

SITTL, C., 1890: *Die Gebärden der Griechen und Römer* (Leipzig).

SJÖQVIST, E., 1973: *Sicily and the Greeks: Studies in the Interrelationship between the Indigenous Populations and the Greek Colonists* (Ann Arbor).

SMITH, M., 1975: 'A note on burning babies', *Journal of the American Oriental Society*, xcv. 477-9.

SMITH, W. (ed.), 1870: *Dictionary of Greek and Roman Geography*, ii (London).

SNELL, B., 1928: *Aischylos und das Handeln im Drama* (*Philologus*, suppl. xx. 1) (Leipzig).

—— 1952: 'Homer und die Entstehung des geschichtlichen Bewusstseins bei den Griechen', in Klingner (ed.), 2-12.

SNODGRASS, A. M., 1971: *The Dark Age of Greece: an Archaeological Survey of the Eleventh to Eighth Centuries BC* (Edinburgh).

SNOWDEN, F. M., 1970: *Blacks in Antiquity: Ethiopians in the Greco-Roman Experience* (Cambridge, Mass./London).

—— 1983: *Before Color Prejudice* (Cambridge, Mass./London).

SOLE, G. F., 1946: 'Il *daimon* ne "I Persiani" di Eschilo', *Annali della facoltà di lettere, filosofia e magistero della università di Cagliari*, xiii. 23-49.

SPECHT, F., 1939: 'Sprachliches zur Urheimat der Indogermanen', *Zeitschrift für vergleichende Sprachforschung*, lxvi. 1-74.

STAGER, L. E., 1980: 'The rite of child sacrifice at Carthage', in J. G. Pedley (ed.), *New Light on Ancient Carthage*, 1-11 (Ann Arbor).

STANFORD, W. B. (ed.), 1983: *Aristophanes' Frogs*². Reprint of 1963 edition (Bristol).

STEPHANOPOULOS, T. K., 1980: *Umgestaltung des Mythos durch Euripides* (Athens).

STEVENS, P. T., 1945: 'Colloquial expressions in Aeschylus and Sophocles', *CQ* xxxix. 95-105.

—— (ed.), 1971: *Euripides' Andromache* (Oxford).

STIEHL, R. AND LEHMANN, G., 1972: *Antike und Universalgeschichte* (Festschr. H. E. Stier, *Fontes et commentationes*, suppl. 1) (Münster).

STIER, H. E., 1970: *Die geschichtliche Bedeutung des Hellenennamens* (Arbeitsgemeinschaft für Forschung des Landes Nordrhein-Westfalen, Geistesgewissenschaften, clix) (Cologne/Opladen).

STINTON, T. C. W., 1965: *Euripides and the Judgement of Paris* (Society for the Promotion of Hellenic Studies, suppl. xi) (London).

STRASBURGER, G., 1954: *Die kleinen Kämpfer der Ilias* (diss., Frankfurt).

SUMNER, W. G., 1906: *Folkways: a Study of the Sociological Importance of Usages, manners, Customs, Mores, and Morals* (Boston).

SUTTON, D. F., 1971: 'Aeschylus' *Edonians*', in *Fons Perennis* (Studs. V. d'Agostino), 387-411 (Turin).

SYNODINOU, K., 1977 (Engl. transl.): *On the Concept of Slavery in Euripides* (Ioannina).

TAPLIN, O., 1977: *The Stagecraft of Aeschylus* (Oxford).

TAYLOR, M. W., 1981: *The Tyrant Slayers: the Heroic Image in Fifth Century BC Athenian Art and Politics* (New York).

THALMANN, W. G., 1980: 'Xerxes' rags: some problems in Aeschylus' *Persians*', *AJP* ci. 260–82.

THOMAS, H., 1962: 'Lands and peoples in Homer', in A. J. B. Wace and F. H. Stubbings (eds.), *A Companion to Homer* 283–310 (London).

THOMPSON, D. B., 1956: 'The Persian spoils in Athens', in *The Aegean and the Near East* (Studs. H. Goldman), 281–91 (New York).

THOMPSON, H. A., 1937: 'Buildings on the west side of the agora', *Hesperia*, vi. 1–226.

THOMSEN, R., 1972: *The Origin of Ostracism* (*Humanitas*, iv) (Copenhagen).

THOMSON, G. (ed.), 1966: *The Oresteia of Aeschylus*[2] (Amsterdam).

—— 1973: *Aeschylus and Athens*[4] (London).

TICHELMANN, L., 1884: *De Versibus ionicis a minore apud poetas Graecos obviis* (diss., Albertina).

TRENDALL, A. D. AND WEBSTER, T. B. L., 1971: *Illustrations of Greek Drama* (London/New York).

TREU, M., 1968: *Von Homer zur Lyrik: Wandlungen des griechischen Weltbildes im Spiegel der Sprache* (*Zetemata*, xii) (Munich).

—— 1971: 'Der euripideische Erechtheus als Zeugnis seiner Zeit', *Chiron*, i. 115–31.

TUCKER, T. G. (ed.), 1889: *The Supplices of Aeschylus* (London).

TUPLIN, C., 1985: 'Imperial tyranny: some reflections on a classical Greek political metaphor', in Cartledge and Harvey (eds.), 348–75.

TURNER, E. G. ET AL. (eds.), 1962: *The Oxyrhynchus Papyri*, xxvii (London).

TWITCHETT, D. AND LOEWE, M. (eds.), 1986: *The Cambridge History of China*, i (Cambridge/London/New York/New Rochelle/Melbourne/Sydney).

TYRRELL, W. B., 1984: *Amazons: a Study in Athenian Mythmaking* (Baltimore).

UNTERSTEINER, M., 1954 (Engl. transl.): *The Sophists* (Oxford).

VAN DER VALK, M. H. A. L. H., 1953: 'Homer's nationalistic attitude', *l'Ant. Class*. xxii. 5–26.

—— 1963: *Researches on the Text and Scholia of the Iliad*, i (Leiden).

—— 1966: 'The formulaic character of Homeric poetry and the relation between the Iliad and the Odyssey', *l'Ant. Class*. xxxv. 5–70.

VANOTTI, G., 1979: 'Sofocle e l'occidente', in Braccesi (ed.), 93–125.

VELKOV, V. I., 1967: 'Thracian slaves in ancient Greek cities (6th–2nd centuries BC)', *Vestnik Drevnei Istorii*, ci. 70–80. In Russian with English summary.

VENTRIS, M. AND CHADWICK, J., 1973: *Documents in Mycenaean Greek*[2] (Cambridge).

VERDENIUS, W. J., 1962: '*ΑΒΡΟΣ*', *Mnem*. xv. 392–3.

VERMASEREN, M. J., 1977: *Cybele and Attis* (London).

VERNANT, J. P., 1983 (Engl. transl.): *Myth and Thought among the Greeks* (London/Boston/Melbourne/Henley).

VIAN, F., 1963: *Les Origines de Thebes: Cadmos et les Spartes* (Études et Commentaires, xlviii) (Paris).

VIDAL-NAQUET, P., 1986 (Engl. transl.): *The Black Hunter: Forms of Thought and Forms of Society in the Greek World* (Baltimore/London).

VOGT, J., 1972: 'Die Hellenisierung der Perser in der Tragödie des Aischylos: religiöse Dichtung und historisches Zeugnis', in Stiehl and Lehmann (eds.), 131–45.

VON KAMPTZ, H., 1982: *Homerische Personennamen* (Göttingen).

VON SALIS, A., 1913: 'Die Göttermutter des Agorakritos', *Jahrbuch des deutschen archäologischen Instituts*, xxviii. 1–26.

VON SCHELIHA, R., 1943: *Patroklos: Gedanken über Homers Dichtung und Gestalten* (Basle).

VON WILAMOWITZ-MOELLENDORFF, U., 1883: 'Die beiden Elektren', *Hermes*, xviii. 214–63. Reprinted in *Kleine Schriften*, vi. 161–208 (Berlin/Amsterdam 1972).

—— 1893: *Aristoteles und Athen* (Berlin).

—— (ed.), 1895: *Euripides' Herakles*[2] (Berlin).

—— (ed.), 1914a: *Aeschyli Tragoediae* (Berlin).

—— 1914b: *Aischylos: Interpretationen* (Berlin).

—— 1927: 'Lesefrüchte', *Hermes*, lxii. 276–98.

—— 1931–2: *Der Glaube der Hellenen* (Berlin).

VOS, M. F., 1963: *Scythian Archers in Archaic Attic Vase Painting* (Groningen).

VOURVERIS, K. J., 1938: Αἱ ἱστορικαὶ Γνώσεις τοῦ Πλάτωνος A, Βαρβαρικά (Athens).

WALBANK, F. W., 1951: 'The problem of Greek nationality', *Phoenix*, v. 41–60. Reprinted in *Selected Papers*, 1–19 (Cambridge 1985).

WALSER, G., 1984: *Hellas und Iran: Studien zu den griechisch-persischen Beziehungen vor Alexander* (Darmstadt).

WARDMAN, A. E., 1961: 'Herodotus on the cause of the Greco-Persian wars', *AJP* lxxxii. 133–50.

WATKINS, C., 1970: 'Language of gods and language of men: remarks on some Indo-European metalinguistic traditions', in Puhvel (ed.), 1–17.

WATSON, B., 1961 (transl.): *Records of the Grand Historian of China* (New York/London).

WEBER, C. W., 1981: *Sklaverei im Altertum* (Düsseldorf/Vienna).

WEBER, F., 1904: *Platons Stellung zu den Barbaren* (diss., Munich).

WEBSTER, T. B. L., 1967: *The Tragedies of Euripides* (London).

WEIDAUER, L., 1969: 'Poseidon und Eumolpus auf einer Pelike aus Policoro', *AK* xii. 91–3.

WEIDNER, E., 1913: 'Βάρβαρος', *Glotta*, iv. 303–4.

WEIL, S., 1957 (Engl. transl.): 'The "Iliad", poem of might', in *Intimations of Christianity among the Ancient Greeks*, 24–55 (London). Reprinted in S. Miles (ed.), *Simone Weil: an Anthology*, 182–215 (London 1986).

WEILER, I., 1968: 'The Greek and non-Greek world in the archaic period', *GRBS* ix. 21–9.

WEISSBACH, F. H., 1911: *Die Keilinschriften der Achämeniden* (Leipzig).

WERNER, J., 1986: 'Griechen und "Barbaren": zum Sprachbewusstsein und zum ethnischen Bewusstsein im frühgriechischen Epos', paper delivered at the 17th International *Eirene* Conference (Proceedings forthcoming).

WEST, M. L. (ed.), 1966: *Hesiod, Theogony* (Oxford).

— 1968: 'Two passages of Aristophanes', *CR* xviii. 5–8.

— 1971: *Early Greek Philosophy and the Orient* (Oxford).

— 1979: 'The Prometheus trilogy', *JHS* xcix. 130–48.

— 1982: *Greek Metre* (Oxford).

— 1983a: 'Tragica VI', item 12, 'Aeschylus' Lykourgeia', *BICS* xxx. 63–71.

— 1983b: *The Orphic Poems* (Oxford).

— 1985: *The Hesiodic Catalogue of Women* (Oxford).

— (ed.), 1987: *Euripides' Orestes* (Warminster).

WEST, S., 1984: 'Io and the dark stranger (Sophocles, *Inachus* F 269a)', *CQ* xxxiv. 292–302.

— 1988: 'A commentary on Homer's Odyssey books I–IV', in A. Heubeck, S. West, and J. B. Hainsworth, *A Commentary on Homer's Odyssey*, i. 49–245 (Oxford).

WHALLON, W., 1961: 'The Homeric epithets', *YCS* xvii. 97–142.

WHATMOUGH, J., 1952: 'On "Triballic" in Aristophanes (Birds 1615)', *CP* xlvii. 26.

WHITEHEAD, D., 1977: *The Ideology of the Athenian Metic* (*PCPS* suppl. iv) (Cambridge).

WIEDEMANN, T. E. J., 1986: 'Between men and beasts: barbarians in Ammianus Marcellinus', in I. S. Moxon, J. D. Smart, and A. J. Woodman (eds.), *Past Perspectives: Studies in Greek and Roman Historical Writing*, 189–201 (Cambridge/London/New York/New Rochelle/Melbourne/Sydney).

WIENCKE, M., 1954: 'An epic theme in Greek art', *AJA* series 2, lviii. 285–306.

WIESEHÖFER, J., 1980: 'Die "Freunde" und "Wohltäter" des Grosskönigs', *Studia Iranica*, ix. 7–21.

WILL, E., 1955: *Korinthiaka* (Paris).

— 1980: *Le Monde grec et l'Orient* ², i (Paris).

WILLCOCK, M., 1976: *A Companion to the Iliad* (Chicago/London).

WILLETTS, R. F., 1962: *Cretan Cults and Festivals* (London).

WILLINK, C. W. (ed.), 1986: *Euripides' Orestes* (Oxford).

WILSON, J. A., 1956: *The Culture of Ancient Egypt* (Chicago/London). Originally published as *The Burden of Egypt* (Chicago 1951).

WINNINGTON-INGRAM, R. P., 1948a: *Euripides and Dionysus* (Cambridge).

—— 1948b: 'Clytemnestra and the vote of Athena', *JHS* lxviii. 130–47. Revised version in *Studies in Aeschylus*, 101–31 (Cambridge 1983).

—— 1963: Review of Bacon 1961, *JHS* lxxxiii. 162.

—— 1969: 'Euripides: poiētēs sophos', *Arethusa*, ii. 127–42.

YARCHO, B. N., 1982: 'The Athenian attitude to Thrace and Macedonia in Greek Comedy', *Eirene*, xviii. 31–42. In Russian.

YON, M., 1981: 'Chypre entre la Grèce et les Perses', *Ktema*, vi. 69–87.

ZEITLIN, F., 1978: 'The dynamics of misogyny: myth and mythmaking in the Oresteia', *Arethusa*, xi. 149–84. Reprinted in Peradotto and Sullivan (eds.), 159–94.

—— 1980: 'The closet of masks: role-playing and myth-making in the *Orestes* of Euripides', *Ramus*, ix. 51–77.

—— 1986: 'Thebes: theater of self and society in Athenian drama', in Euben (ed.), 101–41.

Index of Principal Passages Cited

The index contains references to the passages cited from Homer and extant tragedy. Fragments from lost plays are not cited; references to substantial discussion of these will be found in the general index under the name of the work concerned.

General Index

abandonment *see akolasia*

Achaeans: characterization, 7, 14–15, 21–5 and n.64, 26, 28–30, and nn.83–4, 88, 31 and nn.91–3, 32–5 and n.103, 40–5 and n.125, 54, 125; numbers named as slain in battle, 30; *see also* Greece, Greeks

Achaemenid dynasty 86, 157 and n.188; *see also* Persia and under individual kings

Acharnenses, Aristophanes, 18, 117 n.54, 125 n.75

Achilles: characterization, 20, 26, 27–8 and n.89, 34, 40 n.125; centrality of theme of wrath of, 27, 29; geographical origins, 7; portrayal of Memnon as equal of, 34 and n.106; relationship with Briseis, 43 n.134; use of names, patronymics of Hector and, compared, 30 n.87

Acusilaus, 117

adikia, 121–2, 187

Adonis, 36, 47

Aegyptus, 36, 125 n.76

Aeneas, 14, 33 n.103

Aeolus, Euripides, 189 and n.199, 216

Aegisthus, 208–9 and nn.26, 30

Aeschines, 117

Aeschylus: approaches to intentions of, 70–3; concept of ethnic boundaries of Hellas, 166, 167, 168, 171–2; conjectured *Thamyris*, 135–6; differentiation of barbarians, Greeks, p. x, 18, 79–100, 118–19, 120–1, 135–6, 178, 204–9; evidence on: concept of *barbaros*, 10, and Persian religion, 86–93 and n.174; identification of Trojans with Phrygians, 39 and n.120; influence on Euripides, 116; interest in geography, 75–6 and nn.79, 84, 93–4, 114–15, 133; interpretation of Persian history, 57–8 and nn.3–5, 69–70 and nn.52–3, 70, 71 n.63; knowledge of Egyptian literature, 206; mythical

foreigners, 101–2; mythologizing of Persian wars, 69–73 and n.63; source for later versions of Orpheus story, 143–4 and n.125, 84, 95 n.183; sources, 32 and n.98, 34, 63–4 and n.30, 74 and nn.74–8, 75–6 and n.84; *see also* under individual works

Aethiopes, Sophocles, 142

Aethiopis, 32 n.99, 33, 34

Aetnaeae, Aeschylus, 163, 166

Aetolia, Aetolians, 7, 170–1, 178–9

Agamemnon: and Alexandra, cult of, 20 n.61; belief in historicity of, 64, 65–6; characterization, 26, 57 n.4, 96, 169–70, 176, 177; comparable status of Hector, Priam and, 14–15; dead, status of Darius and, compared, 90–1; relations with Clytaemnestra, 203, 204–10 and n.13

Agamemnon, Aeschylus, 96 and n.188, 208–9 n.30

aglottia, 218

agria and cognates 19, 126–7

Ahriman, 88–9; *see also* Zoroastrianism

Ahuramazda, 88–9, 183 and n.80; *see also* Zoroastrianism

Aias Lokros, Sophocles, 32 n.99

Aiguptioi, Phrynichus, 73 and n.72

ailinon, 146 and n.136

Aithiops, *Aithiopes*, 140–3 and n.115; *see also* Ethiopia

Ajax, Sophocles, 57 n.4, 120

akolasia, 121–2, 125, 128 n.82

alazoneia, *alazōn*, 124, 125 and n.75

Abii, 114 n.46

Alcaeus, 13–14, 18, 38–9 and nn.117–20

Alcmaeonid family, 58

Alcman, 45, 50

Alcidamas, 219–20 and n.62

Alexander I, 180

Alexander, Euripides, 217, 218

nn. 59, 61, 210 n. 32; importance in Thrace, 130; in characterization of barbarians, 129–32; not performed by characters of low social status, 119 and n. 61; use in scenes of mourning, 131–2

sophia see intelligence

sophists, 57, 161–2 and n. 6, 215–16 and n. 43, 222 n. 69

Sophocles: concept of ethnic boundaries of Hellas, 166–7, 168, 169–70 and n. 28; differentiation of barbarians, Hellenes, p. x, 48 n. 158, 103–4, 110, 120–1, 128, 146, 147–8, 166–7; portrayal of decadent Greeks, 209–10; sources, 32–3 and n. 99, 34, 75–6, 132–4 and n. 93

sōphrosunē, 121 and n. 68, 125, 126–9, 152–3

Sparta, Spartans: attitudes to Lydia, 12 and n. 39; contribution to deposition of Hippias, 58; cult of Agamemnon and Alexander in, 20 n. 61; ethnic boundaries in, 171; freedom of women of, 214 and n. 40; guest-friendship with Croesus, 12 n. 39; ritual dressing of hair, 41; royal funeral rites, 44 n. 138; subject of inter-state invective, 213–15; terms used for barbarians, 10

spears, 81, 85–6 and n. 133, 137 and n. 100

speech: foreign accents, 118; Greek, barbarian song contrasted with, 130–2; *see also* language and vocabulary, voice

speech-making, 199–200

Ssu-Ma Ch'ien, 61–2

stereotypes, 102–3; *see also* ethnic stereotypes

Stesichorus, 37–8 and nn. 115–16, 45 and n. 144; *see also* under individual works

Strabo, 10 n. 34, 8 n. 22, 39

stratēlatai, 119–20, 154

stupidity, 121–2, 122–3

Sumeria, Sumerians, 4 nn. 4–5, 5 n. 11

Sunthōkoi, Phrynichus, 64 n. 27

sun-worship *see* heliolatry

supernatural, the, 48–50, 51–3 and n. 173, 54, 68

supplication, 53, 187–8, 203

Supplices, Aeschylus: anachronistic report of democratic processes, 192; barbarization of Danaus in, 36–7; differentiation of barbarians, Hellenes, p. x, 18, 118–19

and n. 61, 120 and n. 62, 123, 126, 130, 139 n. 110, 143 n. 122, 156, 192–3 and n. 106, 199 and n. 123, 202–3; ethnography in, 136, 172–3; knowledge of barbarian gods, 144–6; significance of personal bodyguard of Danaus, 156

Susa, 74 n. 76, 93–4 and n. 174, 142

Syria, 182–3

taboos *see* under individual subjects

Tamburlaine the Great, Marlowe, 99–100 n. 198

Tantalus, Sophocles, 73 and n. 72, 168

Tasso, Torquato, 99 n. 198

Taurians: characterization, 112, 122, 124, 148; Doric character of temple, 182; distinction between Scythians and, 110–12; influence of Herodotus on concepts of, 112, 134

Tauropolos, 111

Tecmessa, 120, 148, 213–14

Teiresias, 96 n. 188, 194, 211 n. 36, 212

Telegonia, 35

Telephus, Euripides, 174–5 and nn. 45, 47, 176 and n. 54, 221

Tempest, The, 48 and n. 153

Teres, 104–5 and n. 9

Tereus, 103–4, 104–5 and nn. 8–11, 125–6, 136, 137

Tereus, Sophocles, 103–6 and n. 9, 125–6, 136, 143 and n. 125

Tertullian, 124

Teucer, 42, 57 n. 4, 176–7, 213–14

Thamyris, Thamyras, 107, 129–30, 135–6 and nn. 95, 97

Thamyris, conjectural work by Aeschylus, 135–6

Thamyras, Antiphanes, 135

Thamyris, Sophocles, 129–30 and n. 86, 134–5

Tharyps, Molossian king, 181

Theaetetus, Plato, 215

Thebais, 22, 178 and n. 59

Thebes, Thebans, 151 and n. 164, 172, 213 and n. 39

Themistocles, 63 n. 26, 64 and n. 27, 66, 67 and n. 43, 203–4

Themistocles, Moschion, 63 n. 26

Theoclymenus, 112, 113, 122, 126, 150

DATE DUE